PASCAL FOR THE HUMANITIES

PASCAL *for the* HUMANITIES

NANCY M. IDE

upp

UNIVERSITY OF PENNSYLVANIA PRESS Philadelphia

Printed in the United States of America

Library of Congress Cataloging-in-Publication Data

Ide, Nancy, M.
Pascal for the humanities.

Includes index.
1. PASCAL (Computer program language). I. Title.
QA76.73.P2I33 1987 005.13'3 87-5866
ISBN 0-8122-1242-8

To Matthew and Drew

Contents

Preface

This text is intended as a textbook for courses designed to teach programming to students with a background in the humanities, and especially to students of language, literature, and linguistics. It may be useful as well to the humanist who wants to learn programming on his or her own. The text teaches programming in a different way from most introductory programming texts: instead of focusing on the function and form of the constructs of a particular programming language, this book teaches the reader to write specific programs to perform specific tasks, and introduces details of the programming language only as needed for the program at hand. Furthermore, all of the programs in the text manipulate characters and textual data, and some of the later programs perform some quite sophisticated textual analyses. All of these features are intended to make it easier for the humanist to master programming and programming concepts.

The rationale for this text and the approach it uses grew out of my own efforts to both learn and teach computer programming. I came to computer programming as a humanist, with a humanist's skills and intellectual habits, and I was taught to program by computer scientists, who had the skills and intellectual habits typical of people who are trained in the sciences. The ensuing struggle demonstrated to me as no other experience has, what the true difference is between the two cultures. I realized some time after I finally mastered computer programming that it was not primarily my lack of ability to deal with "scientific" material, as I assumed at the time, but rather the way in which programming and computing concepts in general were presented that made it difficult for me to learn to program. In the years that followed, during which time I was first a programming consultant for liberal arts faculty and students and then a teacher of computer science in a small liberal arts college, I became increasingly convinced that people with what I can describe only as a humanistic perspective learn programming and computer use much more readily if their attention is focused on the task itself rather than on the details involved. But, of course, programming (and, for that matter, much of the material in the sciences) is typically taught by presenting the student with a mountain of detail and very little context for it. So I began to teach a special section of programming at Vassar College, billed as "Programming for Humanists," that introduced programming in the process of solving particular problems. So far, a number of students who would have no doubt steered clear of computing altogether have cheerfully mastered basic programming and fundamental computing concepts and, in some cases, gone on to more advanced computer science courses. I have never yet encountered a student in the class (although I have in my conventional introductory programming class) who simply could not come to understand programming to some degree.

One of the first questions that arises when the idea of a course on computer programming for the humanities is mentioned concerns whether or not humanists need to learn to program at all. My answer is both yes and no, again based on personal experience. No, humanists don't need to write their own programs for literary and/or linguistic analysis or for anything else, and so they don't need programming skills for that purpose. But experience with computer programming provides an understanding of fundamental computing concepts, familiarity with the principles of algorithmic thought, and a grasp of the ways in which information is stored, accessed, and manipulated—all of which is essential to understand, and certainly to engage in, the increasingly complex computing projects now undertaken in humanistic disciplines. More importantly, significant experience with computer programming is a means to understand and develop the perspective and approach fostered by quantitative methodology, which continues to influence the methodological mainstream of liberal arts disciplines. As this influence grows, I believe there is an increasing need for both faculty and students in liberal arts disciplines to understand the ways in which the computer is and can be used within their fields as well as the broader conceptual basis of computer *science*. So, yes, humanists need to learn how to program, not in order to write their own software, but to learn how to look at the materials within their disciplines in new ways and intelligently utilize (and perhaps develop) tools that help them do it.

With all these factors in mind, this text sets out to provide an introduction to programming that focuses on the principles of algorithmic design that underlie the programming process and to present the material in a manner suited to the humanist's habitual mode of thought. The material from the course described above is the substance of the text. It involves a series of increasingly complex programs, each of which is concerned with some text processing task. Each program builds on the one before it, so that the number of language features added from problem to problem is kept to a minimum. By the end of the text, a relatively complex program involving the use of sophisticated data structures and data manipulation techniques is developed that is built from modules written over the course of the text. Building such a program familiarizes the reader not only with programming itself, but also with principles of modular design and the development and organization of large systems. This, in turn, acquaints the reader with general principles underlying quantitative methodology that many introductory courses and texts fail to teach, and which are very important for the humanities student to understand.

Each chapter in the text (except the first, which introduces programming and computers) begins with a discussion of a new problem that grows out of the one from the previous chapter. Depending on the nature of the problem, the discussion considers the types of information the computer can extract from a text and/or ways of looking at this information to yield meaningful results. In earlier chapters, where the problems are necessarily simpler, the focus is on the means by which a text is stored and retrieved within a program and the conceptualization of a text in terms of its machine representation. Later chapters consider how the perspective on a text that arises from its representation as a series of characters or words arranged in a defined sequence leads to specific research questions, and how, in turn, computer-assisted methods can help to answer these questions.

Following the discussion of the problem, each chapter then focuses on developing an English-language algorithm to solve it, in order to separate the process of arriving at a detailed set of steps to solve the problem from the actual implementation of these steps in a computer program. After the algorithm is fully developed, the programming language features necessary to write the program that implements the algorithm are introduced. Then the reader is taken step by step through the process of constructing the program itself, using the language features just introduced and incorporating program segments and modules from earlier chapters. This section of each chapter is typically the longest and most detailed, in order to show the reader just how algorithm is translated into program, and how individual statements and pieces of a program are fitted together to mean more than the sum of the parts.

Two additional sections fill out each chapter. First, a "Niceties" section provides more information about the language features introduced earlier in the chapter and often shows the reader alternative or more elegant ways to accomplish certain tasks or how to use what he or she has learned to perform additional tasks. An "Applications and Considerations" section follows, in which the relevance of the program in the chapter to actual computer applications is discussed. Methods, advantages, and problems involved in using the computer for the particular task at hand are discussed as well. Both of these sections are intended to be integral parts of the chapters—not appendixes or footnotes to the construction of the program—and contain material that is important to the continuity of the text.

Each chapter concludes with a series of exercises that are intended to be assigned after the material in the chapter has been covered in class. The exercises ask for programs that are variations of the program in the chapter, ranging in difficulty from the relatively simple to those reserved "for the adventurous programmer." The idea is to provide the student with a range of programming projects from which to choose according to how comfortable the reader feels with the material, as well as to suggest some of the ways in which the techniques developed in the chapter can be exploited to perform different kinds of tasks.

Many choices had to be made in the process of designing this text, the most obvious of which is the programming language in which the programs in the text are implemented. Pascal was chosen for several reasons. First, Pascal is widely available on both mainframe and microcomputers and, at least at the present time, is used as the teaching language in most colleges and universities. Second, the structure of Pascal is such that task sequences are easily broken down into logical, modular steps, a process fundamental to the quantitative approach with which this text intends to familiarize the reader. A choice that is bound to be more controversial is the decision to use *standard* Pascal, despite its limited string-handling facilities, rather than to use one or more of the more sophisticated versions of the language. Three arguments underlie this choice. Utilizing standard Pascal ensures that all of the programs in this text will run under any implementation of Pascal. And, since the overall purpose here is to teach programming *principles* and familiarize the student with general text-analytic methods rather than to provide a "cookbook" of ready-written programs, the fact that elegant string-handling facilities are not available is irrelevant to the purpose of the text. The reader can see the processes of data storage and manipulation, and perhaps see them in a more detailed and coherent way, without the built-in capabilities of many versions of Pascal. Finally, trying to address the peculiarities of the many versions of Pascal in the process of outlining the programs would seem to create more confusion than anything else. The users of this text will hopefully be able to use the programs and general procedures given here as a basis for implementation under the particular version of Pascal available to them. If not, the programs can be used as they are (or with minor changes to some of the names) under any implementation.

Other choices were made in the interests of clarity and straightforwardness. Several important features of the Pascal language are not covered in the chapters of the text, because adapting them to the programs in the text would have complicated the presentation unnecessarily. However, these language features—enumerated types, sets, the FORWARD statement, and the GOTO statement and labels (for closet BASIC programmers)—are important enough that any Pascal user should be aware of them, and so they are covered in Appendix D. One important feature of the Pascal language that has been omitted entirely from the text is pointer variables, which are used to implement linked lists. Linked lists are covered and implemented using arrays in Chapters Twelve and Thirteen. Thus the conceptual material underlying the use of pointer variables is treated in the text, and discussing another implementation of linked lists would add very little to the reader's understanding of programming principles. For this reason, pointer variables are not included.

Another choice made for the sake of straightforwardness involves the form of Pascal statements themselves. In the examples throughout the text, the BEGIN-END pair is included in all control structures that use it, even when Pascal allows it to be omitted. Similarly, all program statements in the text terminate with a semicolon, even though the semicolon is optional in certain circumstances. In both of these cases, Pascal is inconsistent in its requirements, and for the novice programmer it is often easier to remember a single way of doing things than to remember the exceptions. Also, when BEGIN-END pairs or semicolons are left out, the potential for errors exists in the event that statements are later added to the program. Including BEGIN-END pairs in every situation often yields a longer piece of code than could be written without them, but the straightforward practice of always including them seems worth the price. Early in the text, the reader is shown the situations in which semicolons and BEGIN-END pairs can be omitted, and I hope those who would do without them can adapt the programs in the text to their preferences.

A programming text cannot be all things to all people, and even at this point, there are many changes and additions I would like to make. I am sure that in the course of using the text, many readers will have ideas, suggestions, and comments to make, and in the interest of providing as useful a text as possible for my fellow humanists, I would very much like to hear them. Please write to me at the Department of Computer Science, Vassar College, Poughkeepsie, New York 12601 if you have anything to say about the text. In the meantime, I hope that your computing experiences are happy ones.

Poughkeepsie, New York
June 1986

Acknowledgments

Many of the ideas that led to the formulation of this text originated with John B. Smith, Robert A. Ariew, and me, in connection with a course in computing for liberal arts students offered at The Pennsylvania State University. I would like to thank Michael Sperberg-McQueen, who carefully read and commented on the first draft of the manuscript, and express my appreciation to Ian Lancashire and Diana Patterson for their helpful comments. I also want to thank the students in my courses on computing for the humanities over the past two years, whose comments and corrections contributed immeasurably to the final version of the text. Finally, I would like to thank my husband, Matthew, whose continual faith in my ability to do just about anything kept me going throughout this project.

1

Understanding the Basics

Computer programming seems complex to people who are not familiar with it, and, in fact, it is complex. The complexity stems largely from the fact that every facet of computer programming involves many details and many intricate relationships among the details. The amount of information with which the novice is confronted when he or she sets out to learn to program a computer is quite often overwhelming and confusing initially. Some people take this confusion to mean that computers are simply too difficult to understand, and give up the endeavor to learn. But this is not the case. You should understand that when you first begin to learn about computers, you enter into a foreign realm, one which is not, on the surface, "humanistic" and may not share much common ground with your previous experience. It is as if someone plucked you from your comfortable chair and suddenly put you on a street corner in a city with whose language and culture you are completely unfamiliar. For awhile, you are confused and disoriented as you are bombarded with experiences for which you have little or no context, but eventually you begin to see the underlying structure of the language and culture and begin to feel more and more comfortable. After a time, you are familiar enough with the new culture that it is difficult to remember how things in the strange environment looked and felt at first. In fact, you may be hard-pressed to tell a newcomer the things you have learned in order to enable him or her to overcome difficulties with the strange environment. So it is with computer programming—in order to become familiar with it, you must often tolerate some initial confusion. The amount of time it takes to feel somewhat comfortable with computer programming depends on how "foreign" you are to it, but before long, and often without your realizing exactly when, familiarity and comfort inevitably come.

When you become comfortable with programming methodology, you will have broadened your experience and perspective *in general*. Even if, after completing some or all of the programs outlined in this book, you never write a computer program again, you will have acquired not only a set of skills but also an understanding of a new approach to problem solving—one that can be applied just as well in humanistic disciplines as in the sciences. You will, in fact, learn something about the application of what might be called the "quantitative approach" to literary and linguistic analyses that is discussed in the Applications and Considerations section at the end of each of the remaining chapters in this text. But the understanding you will have has broader applications than the ones you will read about. You will acquire a set of concepts that will enable you to better understand not only the ways computers are used in the world around you, but also the perspective of the computer scientist and the scientist in general. No endeavor is more central to humanistic study than the attempt to consider a variety of perspectives on issues and problems of human interest, and so in a variety of ways, your venture into the world of computing contributes directly to your training as a humanist.

In order to gain a good understanding of the quantitative approach to problem solving and acquaint you with computers, computer programming, and the applications of computers and computing techniques to problems in the humanities, this book takes you step by step through the construction of a series of computer programs. All of the programs manipulate *textual data*—that is, letters and words rather than numbers—and the later programs perform some relatively sophisticated operations in order to produce research tools such as word indexes, concordances, and frequency distribution graphs for a given word or words in a particular text. Most of the programs are directly relevant to the study of literature and language, but should be at least interesting to all humanists. By going through the process of constructing the programs, you should become increasingly familiar with problem solving techniques, programming concepts, and computers in general, and the Pascal programming language and your computer system in particular. The process is designed to minimize confusion wherever possible, and hopefully you will emerge from the murk of confusion in a very short time.

COMPUTERS IN GENERAL

Like the human brain, the computer works on many levels. When the human brain performs any process—say, adding 1 and 2—the event can be considered at the level of abstract cognition, at the gross physical level (which part of the brain is involved), at the neurological level, at the biochemical level, and even at the level of the electron. Similarly, when a computer adds 1 and 2, you can be concerned with the result of the operation or you can consider the many different levels of internal processes that enable the event to take place. Obviously, human beings do not deal with the underlying processes that support every psychological event—you couldn't, or it would be nearly impossible to function. You deal instead only with the highest levels of abstraction, oblivious to the physical and even many of the psychological details of the brain's operation. And the same is true of the computer—you cannot be concerned with the goings on at every level all of the time. But you need some sense of what the levels are and how they work in order to begin.

The Overview

You have no doubt heard about *hardware* and *software*. Computer hardware is the physical stuff of which computers are made—electronic switches and circuitry, as well as bulkier items like printers and disk drives—and software involves the *programs* or sets of instructions that a computer performs. The analogy with the human brain is again useful to help explain these terms: hardware is analogous to the physical brain, and software is analogous to those processes that the brain can perform. Hardware and software are very general terms which are often used very loosely, and each one will be treated separately before considering their relationship.

Hardware. You can talk about the brain's "hardware" in terms of its large components—the cortex, cerebellum, medulla, etc.—or in terms of neurons and synapses. Similarly, computer hardware can be thought of in broad or very specific terms.

Broadly speaking, the large hardware components of the computer are the following:

1. The Central Processing Unit (CPU), which does the "computing."
2. Main storage or memory, sometimes called random access memory (RAM), where data is stored while a program is operating.
3. An input device or devices, most often a keyboard.
4. An output device or devices, most often a video display screen (sometimes called a CRT); printers are another common output device.

There are many kinds of computers—you are no doubt familiar with personal computers or microcomputers, such as the IBM PC or Apple Macintosh, and you may be familiar with larger computers that can be used by many people simultaneously. In all cases, a computer consists of the components listed above, and no more or no less.

The center of any computer consists of the parts given in 1 and 2 above, the Central Processing Unit and the memory. In fact, the term "computer" really describes only these two parts of the machine. The CPU does exactly what its name implies—it does all of the processing. If you give the computer an instruction to add 1 and 2, it is the CPU that does the adding. The memory is used by the CPU as a storage space while it is doing its processing. Take again the example of adding 1 and 2. For a computer, the values 1 and 2 do not exist as an abstraction or concept; in order for the computer to add 1 and 2, the numbers 1 and 2 have to "exist" somewhere. This is where main memory comes in. When the CPU is told to add 1 and 2, it first goes to main memory to retrieve the number 1 and then goes back to retrieve the number 2. These values must be put in main memory explicitly before the CPU is told to perform the addition, and when the CPU is instructed to add the two numbers it must be told exactly where to go in main memory to get them. Now, the CPU does have some circuitry that does addition, and it passes the two values it retrieves from main memory through this circuitry in order to "add" them together. When the result is obtained, it, too, must be stored in main memory—otherwise the result would not be retained.

Obviously, the relationship between main memory and the CPU is intimate. The brain analogy is once again useful to help understand this relationship. You can almost imagine a part of your brain in which the concept of a 1 and the concept of a 2 is stored, and another part that calls up these concepts when you are asked to add these two numbers together. The part that does the retrieving and the adding is analogous to the CPU. When the two numbers have been added, the result is held in "memory" of sorts. Your mental process is more obvious if you consider adding 63 and 234, since adding these two numbers is not as automatic as adding 1 and 2—you can almost feel a part of your brain doing the adding, and the result is actively retained in your short-term memory once it is obtained. Humans are not used to scrutinizing their mental processes quite this thoroughly, but you sometimes have to think in these very detailed terms in order to envision the way a computer operates. Like your mental processes, you won't have to think about the computer's processes in this kind of detail once you become familiar with them.[1]

Another level on which to consider the CPU and memory is that of the circuitry. This takes you down a level to something roughly analogous to the neurological level in the brain. You might wonder how the number 2 is represented in memory. The fact is that data representation as well as computational processes that the CPU can perform (basically, arithmetic and comparison of two things for equality) all boil down to electronics. The main memory is nothing more than a series of electronic switches, each of which can either be on or off—that is, each switch can either have current flowing through it or not. Now, here is where the sleight of hand comes in. Internally, it could be arbitrarily decided that if the switch is on, then that "state" represents the number 1, and if it is off, it represents the number 0. To represent more numbers, you need more switches. If you have two switches, you can represent four different things—both switches on is one thing, both off is another, the first on and second off a third, and the first off and the second on is a fourth. Suppose that off-on represents 1, on-off represents 2, and on-on represents 3 (these configurations are chosen because they are the actual ones used in most computers). All you have to do to make this computer work correctly is to design the circuitry in the CPU that performs addition such that when given the configuration for the number 1

1. A note of interest: biopsychologists, computer scientists involved in artificial intelligence work, and philosophers have considered and disagreed about the degree to which computational processes and the processes of the human brain are similar. This issue is central to the field of cognitive science.

and the configuration for the number 2, it takes them in and gives back the configuration for a 3. The CPU does not really "know" how to add; it just takes what it is given, manipulates it in some consistent way, and yields another configuration. The meaning assigned to that configuration is up to the designer of the machine.

By the way, each of the switches inside the computer's main memory is called a "bit." Eight contiguous bits (which can be in any of 256 different configurations, and thus can represent 256 different things) are called a "byte."

So far, the fact that everything inside the computer is just some arbitrary configuration is fine, because there is not much chance that the human user of the computer will ever see the way a 1 is represented or how the circuitry to perform addition looks. The only way that humans know what is inside the computer is through the use of *input and output devices*—parts 3 and 4 of the computer given in the list above. Input and output devices (or I/O devices) are the means by which humans can get information into and out of the computer's main memory. The analogy here is not with the brain itself but with the eyes, ears, and mouth, since these are the main mechanisms by which information is transmitted into and out of the brain.

The most typical input device for a computer is a keyboard; the most typical output device is a video display screen. For the moment, these two devices will serve as examples of their kind. When a human wants to input something into the computer's memory from a keyboard, this is what happens: the human types some character on the keyboard. For example, suppose the number 1 is entered. What has actually happened is that the human has pressed a key marked 1, but of course, the key only *represents* a 1—it is taken to be a 1 because the symbol that represents a 1 is on the key. When the key is pressed, the following happens: some sequence of on-off pulses that represent a 1 are sent from the keyboard into the computer and stored in its memory. There may be a translation from what is sent from the keyboard into yet another configuration that is ultimately stored in the memory, but this fact is not of much concern at this point since you never see the internal configuration anyway. Now if the number 2 were also stored in main memory, and the two numbers were then added together, the resulting configuration would be stored in main memory as well. Again, it really does not matter what this configuration is, as long as when the computer sends the configuration back to the user—by displaying it on an output device like a video display screen—the configuration it sends is ultimately translated into an instruction to display the symbol '3' on the screen. This is what input and output and computer memory are all about: arbitrary representations and translations from one representational scheme to another. The idea of representing concepts with symbols or configurations and translating them from one system of representation to another should be very familiar to humanists—the only difference here is that the representations are sometimes electronic.

Every computer has one CPU[2] and one main memory. But it may have several input and output devices. For instance, almost all computers have, in addition to keyboard input and video display screen output, access to a disk or disks

2. There are some exceptions, but in general this statement is true.

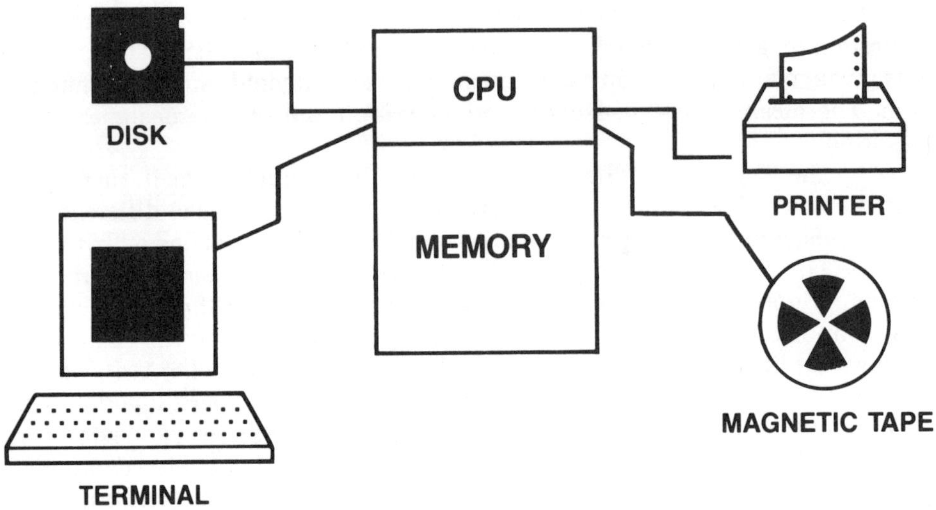

of one kind or another. Disks are interesting because they are both input and output devices—information can be taken from main memory and put on the disk, thus using the disk as an output device, but later the information can be taken from the disk and put back in main memory, in which case the disk functions as an input device. Printers, on the other hand, are output devices only—information can be taken from main memory and sent to the printer for display, but obviously information cannot be taken from the printer and put in main memory. Another common I/O device is the magnetic tape, which, like the disk, can be used as both an input device and an output device.

You should view the computer as a CPU/memory module connected to any of a variety of input and/or output devices, as shown in the figure. If you are using a microcomputer, you probably have a keyboard, a video display screen, a disk reader, and a printer. The main component of your system will be the CPU/memory module, which might be the physically smallest part of the machine. The I/O devices are connected to this module by wires, whether they are visible or not. Disk readers are usually enclosed in the same casing as the CPU/memory, and in some cases the video display screen is in the same casing as well. Nonetheless, the CPU/memory and the disk reader and video display screen are separate entities in terms of the operation of the system. If you are not using a microcomputer, you are no doubt using a computer that supports more than one user at a time, and if so, you probably sit in front of a computer *terminal* consisting of a keyboard and a video display screen. The CPU/memory unit of your computer is probably in another room or building, and you may never have seen it. Your I/O devices are probably a disk reader/writer (with a permanent or "fixed" disk in it) and a printer. Once again, you may never see either the disk or the printer. The wires connecting your keyboard and screen to the computer may be quite long indeed—you may even go across telephone lines to communicate with the computer. When this is the case, it is easier to see that the keyboard and video display screen are simply I/O devices wired into the CPU/memory unit.

The basic operation of a computer involves (1) bringing data from an input device into main memory, (2) manipulating the data and storing the results in main memory, and (3) sending the results to an output device. The information with which a computer works must be brought into main memory because in general, data *must* be in main memory in order for the computer to work with it. Outputting results is necessary or there is not much point to the operations performed on the data.

Before going on, you may find two additional facts about the computer's main memory interesting. First, although the examples discussed above use numbers, characters (such as letters, digits, and other symbols) can be stored in main memory just as easily. This will become important to know when you start writing the programs outlined in the later chapters of this text. Second, the amount of main memory a computer has available determines how much the computer can do—obviously, the more memory available, the more data the computer can work with. Since programs are also stored in main memory while they are running (see the next section), big programs require more main memory to run. Microcomputer users are familiar with terms like '64K' and '128K' to describe the size of their computer's memory—a '64K machine' has 64,000 bytes of main memory and a '128K machine' has 128,000 bytes of main memory. The bigger the number, the more your computer can do.

Software. Hardware is only half of the story of the computer. Software is the other half, and it consists of *programs* that run on the machine. Programs are sets of instructions that are performed by the CPU. As you will see in the next chapter, the CPU can perform only a limited number of instructions, and all programs must be cast in terms of those instructions.

Going back to the analogy with the human brain, software can be seen as roughly similar to the sequence of steps the brain goes through in performing a certain process. For instance, to get to a certain room from a particular location in a given building, you might perform a sequence of steps like (1) go down the hall, (2) turn left, (3) go to the third door on the right. In a sense, this is a "program" for getting to that room. Computers execute similarly detailed sequences of steps to perform the kinds of actions they are capable of performing (obviously, computers don't move from room to room, but they do things like arithmetic very well indeed).

There are two additional and important similarities that you should consider between the way the brain deals with a set of steps like those given above and the way a computer executes a series of instructions. First, when your brain executes the set of steps given above, each is actually broken down into sub-steps. Take, for instance, the instruction "go down the hall." This obviously involves a whole series of operations, including the sending of messages to the legs to move and the processing of messages that are sent back to the brain by the legs and eyes and so on. All of these operations occur at a level below that implied in the instruction set and are taken care of by other "programs" in the brain designed specifically for handling I/O with the central nervous system and other parts of the body. This sublevel of activity goes on inside a computer as well. When a program runs, other programs are called upon to perform operations essential to carrying out the set of instructions given. For instance, receiving data from input devices and sending data to output devices is handled by a program called the 'operating system.' As you begin in the next chapter to learn how to write computer programs, one of the first things you will have to do is determine the level at which instructions are given to a computer—that is, how detailed the instructions must be. Broadly, the programs you will write can be considered to be at the level of the instruction set given above to find a particular room—you can simply tell the computer to add and it does the task, and the details of the operation are taken care of for you by other programs that already exist on your computer and operate in concert with your program.

This brings us to the second similarity between the brain and the computer: both the brain and the computer are capable of "storing" a set of instructions for later use. Once you learn how to get to the room down the hall, you no longer have to get the set of instructions from outside (from another person, for example)—you can simply go to storage, pull out the program, and run it again. Computer programs are the same—once they are written (the learning process), they can be stored and retrieved again for later use. (Note that the analogy with the brain is very loose here and is intended only to give a very general idea of how programs are re-used.) Computer programs are typically stored on disks, not in main memory, and called upon to execute as needed. You can write your own programs, store them, and invoke them when you want to, or you can use "packaged" or "canned" programs that have been written by other people and invoke them when they are needed.

Whether you use your own programs or programs that someone else has written, the same thing happens when the program is called upon to execute: the program is brought from disk to main memory, and the instructions within it are then executed, one at a time and in the order they appear. The program may include instructions to get data from an input device and bring it into main memory, and/or copy data from main memory to an output device. If *while the program is executing* the program gets input from the keyboard (which is typed in while the program executes by the user of the program) and sends output to the video display screen of a terminal or microcomputer, then the program is said to be *interactive* because the user of the program "interacts" with it while it executes. Most computer programs are interactive.[3] A non-interactive program requires no active participation by the user, who may not even be around the computer while the program executes.

Writing and Running A Program

Given all of this information about computer hardware and software, you can get an overall idea of what you will be doing in the rest of this book. As mentioned above, you will be writing computer programs in one of the more easy-to-use programming languages available, called Pascal. Again, these programs consist of sets of instructions—your task will be to devise the set of instructions

3. One kind of interactive program with which most people are familiar is the automatic teller machine at a bank, which sends data to a video display screen consisting of characters that spell out a message to enter some response, and then get data from the specialized keyboard that the user enters.

which, when executed, will cause the computer to perform a certain task or tasks. In the next chapter you will see the kinds of instructions that you have available to work with in Pascal and similar programming languages, such as Basic, Fortran, C, and a variety of others you may have heard about.

After you determine the set of instructions your programs will include, you have to get the program "into" the computer. Typically, in order to do this you must execute another, pre-written program called a *text editor* or just an *editor*. This program takes as input data whatever you type at the keyboard, and when you signal that you are finished typing, it sends a copy of what you entered to disk. From the text editor's point of view, what you enter is just a sequence of characters—the instructions themselves have no meaning to the editor.

The text editor will store your program in what is called a *file* on disk. Files are simply areas of the disk that are given names so that what resides there can be retrieved easily. Your text editor program will ask you to provide a name for the file in which it will store your program when you type the program in; later, you can get access to your program by specifying the name of the file in which it is stored. You will also give the name of the file in which the program is stored when you want to execute the program.

Once you have entered all the instructions and the text editor has stored them on disk, you can give a command to the operating system program (the one that is always running when no other program is running) to go to the disk, get the program, bring it into main memory, and let it execute.[4] When it is executing, your program has complete control of the computer; when it is finished, some other program (usually, the operating system) will take over and *its* instructions will begin executing. It is helpful to realize that some program is always executing when a computer is running, whether it is the operating system, the text editor, or your Pascal program. And although at first glance these three programs seem like very different beasts, you should view them simply as different computer programs performing as all computer programs do. Your commands are input to the operating system program, which performs certain instructions depending on the command it reads, and its responses to you are the program's output. Similarly, your program as you are typing it is input to the text editor program, and its output is both the messages it gives you and the copy of your program that it sends to the disk. The programs you will write will take input from the keyboard or a file on disk, process the input, and send output to the video display screen.

SUMMING UP

This chapter contains a lot of information, and you may be overwhelmed at this point. Again, much of what you see here is intended to give you an overall idea of computing, and some confusion is normal. You don't necessarily have to

4. The sequence of steps described here is slightly different in some cases—for instance, it is different if you are using Turbo Pascal.

understand and master all of the information in this chapter now. You can use it as a first immersion into the deep waters of computers and computing and come back to it later. Your understanding of computers will be built up piece by piece—the overall picture, which this chapter tries to provide, probably will not be clearly visible until you learn more. On the other hand, you may be feeling quite comfortable at this point. In either case, enjoy the experience; computers are fascinating and frustrating and ultimately a great deal of fun.

2

Reading and Writing Characters

As mentioned in the previous chapter, in order for a computer program to work with data of any kind, that data must be brought, or *read*, into the computer's main memory. And in order for the user of the program to see the results of the program's operation, a copy of those results must be sent, or *written*, to some output device like a printer or video display screen at a computer terminal or on a microcomputer. So, as you might expect, the most basic and pervasive operations performed in any computer program are the reading, or *inputting*, of data into main memory and the writing, or *outputting*, of results to some output device. Your first programming task will deal with these operations: you'll simply read some data into the main memory and write it out again where you can see it displayed. Along the way you'll learn some of the most fundamental programming concepts, get an idea of what a program in Pascal looks like, and begin to get a feel for the nature of the operations a computer can perform.

Before actually beginning to write a program, you'll need a better sense of the things a computer can do and the way it does them. A computer program consists of a sequence of commands, written in one of the many computer languages that can be understood by the machine, which the computer reads in and performs or *executes*, one by one, and in the order they appear.[1] What kinds

1. You will see there are some important exceptions to this statement in the paragraphs to come, but the notion of linear sequence underlies the order of execution in all computer programs.

of things do these commands tell the computer to do? Actually, the list is rather short; the computer can be told to

1. Perform basic arithmetic, like adding, subtracting, dividing, multiplying, and so on, using numbers that are currently stored in main memory, and store the result in a specified location in main memory.
2. Compare two pieces of data (numbers or letters) currently in main memory and determine if they are equal or not equal, or if one is less than or greater than the other.
3. Read a piece of data (a number or letter, for instance) from an input device like a keyboard (for instance, the keyboard of a microcomputer or computer terminal) and store it in main memory.
4. Send a copy of some piece of data currently stored in main memory to be printed on an output device like a printer or the display screen of a microcomputer or computer terminal.

In a programming language like Pascal, each command typically tells the computer to perform one or two of these operations. Notice that almost everything the computer does involves some manipulation or consideration of the contents of its main memory. This is the essence of the computer's mode of operation: as mentioned in Chapter One, you can think of a computer simply as a central processing unit (CPU), which actually performs the tasks listed above, and a big scratch pad—the main memory—in which information and results are stored and from which they are retrieved when needed. Everything a computer program does revolves around the contents of memory, and it is helpful at first to cast your understanding of the function of particular programming statements in terms of their effect on the contents of main memory. The task discussed in this chapter—reading characters into main memory—is essential to any program, for it is the means by which the data with which the program is to work is made accessible to the program. Thus reading in data is more or less a preliminary step in any program in order to set up the circumstances for its operation.

In addition to commands that tell the computer to perform one of the basic operations listed above, the programming language Pascal also includes another group of commands which do not call for performing a particular task, but which instead enable the programmer to modify the *order* in which commands are executed. These commands may tell the computer to

1. Repeat the execution of a command or group of commands a given number of times, or until some comparison (see number 2, above) yields a specified result.
2. Execute a certain command or group of commands if some comparison yields a specified result, and execute a different command or set of commands otherwise.
3. Move to another group of commands at some other location in the sequence, execute them, and return to the original location in the program afterwards.

Commands that specify these kinds of actions are called *control structures*, because they alter the sequence, or "flow of control," among a group of programming statements.

That's it. This is basically all the computer can do. It may not seem like much, and in fact is not, but eventually it should become clear that because of the speed with which the computer executes these commands, and especially because of its ability to repeat operations over and over, a simple computer program can be used to perform tedious and routine tasks that would take years if done by hand.

Since any task a computer is to perform must be expressed in terms of these commands only, obviously the sequence of commands in a program is very detailed. Initially, you may find dealing at this level of detail a little frustrating, but once you are used to the process and familiar with the form of individual statements, you will find programming far less tedious. And actually, this type of detail is no more foreign or difficult than the kinds of instructions we give all the time; for instance, recall the sequence of steps for finding a certain room given in Chapter One: (1) go down the hall, (2) turn left, (3) go to the third door on the right. A group of instructions like this one, expressed in a "natural" language like English and outlining the steps required to accomplish a specific task is called an *algorithm*. Computer programmers find it useful and often necessary to express a task in terms of an algorithm before translating it into a particular computer programming language, and this practice will be adopted throughout this book. The use of algorithms is especially valuable for novice programmers, because it enables you to think first about the sequence of steps, and *then* about the way to express them in a computer language, rather than to try to deal with both the steps involved and the details of their translation into Pascal at the same time.

The first step in writing the program that is the focus of this chapter, then, will be to develop an algorithm that describes in something like English the sequence of steps that the program will have to go through to accomplish the desired end. This first program is to read a line of characters that the program's user—that is, the person who runs the program and for whom its results are intended—enters from the keyboard, and to write a copy of that line of characters back out at the video display screen.[2] Programs that read from the keyboard while they are running are called *interactive*, because they actually stop at the point when data is to be read from the keyboard and wait for the user to enter the data. Thus the user effectively "interacts" with the program while it is running.

It is probably relatively easy for you to put yourself in the role of the user of this program and to imagine what will happen when the program is run. After instructing the computer to run your program, you will type a sentence at the keyboard (which will, of course, appear on the display screen as you type it), and then you will see the same sentence printed on the screen again. The user's point of view is from outside the computer; in this role you see the computer as a box off in a corner somewhere into which data is fed and from which results subsequently spew forth. In this case the data you feed in is a sentence, and the results (which aren't very exciting, but this is the first lesson, remember) are to see the sentence typed again on the screen. The user's point of view is one that is

2. This text assumes that the default input device for Pascal programs is the microcomputer or terminal keyboard, and that the default output device is the microcomputer or terminal display screen.

very important, because, after all, programs are written solely for the benefit of their users. But in order to write a program, or develop an algorithm that describes its steps, you will have to learn to think about the program from another perspective—that of the computer itself. In fact, in order to program a computer, you have to be able to think like one. You will have to shift your point of view to the *inside* of the computer, and imagine the data coming *in* and the results going *out*, rather than the other way around. From this point of view the keyboard and screen are boxes off in a corner somewhere, and your world consists primarily of main memory. Most of what you do involves manipulating or changing the contents of main memory, by bringing data into it or performing calculations and storing their results in it.

This idea of a shift in perspective to that of the computer may seem a bit strange, but it is actually vital to the programming process. A great deal of the difficulty experienced by novice programmers results from the failure to adopt the "internal" point of view when they try to write algorithms and computer programs. If you were trying to provide directions to get to a room, like the ones given above, you would adopt the point of view of the person for whom the directions are intended in order to do so, since he or she will actually perform these instructions. The difference here, of course, is that you must limit yourself to the kinds of operations the computer is capable of performing, and, in some cases, your directions must be more explicit. For example, to tell a person to find the first occurrence of the letter 'e' in a word, you simply say, "find the first 'e' in this word." For the computer, you would have to say, "Compare the first letter in the word to the letter 'e.' If they are the same, stop. If not, compare the second letter to the letter 'e'," and so on. Probably, the human's method and the computer's method of finding the first 'e' are similar, if not identical. But the computer does not automatically possess the human's understanding of the concept "find," which implies a process like the explicit one laid out for the computer. Along with learning to adopt the computer's point of view, then, you have to learn to be very specific in your directions to it.

Given your knowledge from the list given earlier in the chapter of the kinds of things a computer can do, and trying to adopt the computer's point of view, you are ready to attempt to develop an algorithm to read and write a line of characters entered by the user. You might come up with something like the following:

1. Read the line and store it in main memory.
2. Write a copy of the line on the display screen.

If this is something like your first inclination, then you are off to a good start; but unfortunately, this algorithm is not explicit enough for the computer because the term "line" has no meaning to the computer. Without your programming it to do so, it does not inherently recognize a sequence of characters and blanks that appear contiguously as a unit of any kind. However, the computer does recognize and distinguish individual characters, which may be any letter, digit, or other character that can be entered from the keyboard, *including a blank*. More about this later; for the moment just consider the fact that the computer can be instructed to read a single character from the input and store it in memory. Armed with this information, the algorithm above can be made more explicit:

1. Read a character from the input and store it in the main memory.
2. Write a copy of the character on the display screen.
3. Read the next character from the input and store it in the main memory.
4. Write a copy of this character on the display screen.

.
.
.
etc.

This algorithm could be extended to provide for reading any number of letters, but obviously this would be more work than making a copy of the sentence by hand. However, recall that it is possible to tell the computer to repeat a group of commands. With this facility in mind, the algorithm can be rewritten as follows:

1. Repeat the following:
   a. Read a character from the input and store it in main memory.
   b. Write a copy of the character on the display screen.

Notice that in this version of the algorithm, only a few commands are used to process potentially thousands of characters; much of the computer's power is derived from this ability to repeatedly execute commands at incredible speeds.

The set of steps above will accomplish the task of reading and writing a line of input, but there is one last problem with the algorithm: if one were to follow it literally, the process of reading and writing would continue forever, since there is no provision for stopping the process of reading and writing characters. If a program were written based on this model, it would contain what is called in the trade an *infinite loop*. Obviously, to make the algorithm explicit and complete, some means to stop the reading and writing process must be provided.

When should the steps in the algorithm above stop—that is, under what conditions should the process of reading and writing be terminated? Well, the reading should stop when all of the characters that the user enters have been read and written. Step 1, then, needs to be modified to say something like, "While there are more characters to be read, repeat the following." The algorithm thus becomes

1. While there are more characters to be read, repeat the following:
   a. Read a character from the input and store it in main memory.
   b. Write a copy of the character on the display screen.

This algorithm is a good enough description of the steps required to read and write the user's sentence so that you can turn to translating the sequence into Pascal. Before doing so, however, you should consider a question that may have crossed your mind already: why, in the above algorithm, are characters read and written one at a time, rather than reading all of the characters first and then printing them? Part of the answer is that by reading and writing a character at a time, only enough storage for a single character is required at any given time in order for the program to run, whereas if all of the characters are read first, enough storage must be available for all of them since they will be in main memory at the same time. At this point you are in no danger of running out of storage space in main memory, but once you begin to work with large amounts of data the concern will crop up. In general, when a choice exists you should always opt for the most "economical" process (in terms of the amount of storage required) in a computer program.

A second reason for using the one-character-at-a-time scheme outlined above is more compelling, but you need to know more about storing data in main memory before going into it. We will return to this question later on. In the meantime, turn your attention to your first lesson in Pascal.

ELEMENTS OF PASCAL

In this section and in sections under the same heading in the chapters to come, the elements of the Pascal language that are required to accomplish the task at hand will be described, and in the subsequent sections you will see how they are combined to create the program that will perform the desired function. As with any new subject, you will be confronted with the greatest amount of unfamiliar information in the early stages of learning, and so the volume of new information that you see below will be substantially reduced in the chapters to come.

The Program Framework

All programs written in any programming language must follow specific rules of format, which are peculiar to the language being used. The basic outline of any Pascal program is

Program Heading
Declarations
Program Statements

Each of these sections of a Pascal program will be discussed separately.

Program Heading. Programs that are written in Pascal always begin with a statement like the following:

```
PROGRAM First(INPUT,OUTPUT);
```

The words that are written in capitals are called *keywords*—they are words that "belong" to Pascal and are recognized within a program as having a specific meaning. Note that they appear in capitals here to distinguish them from other types of words in the program, but you may type them in any case you desire.[3] Words that appear in lower case, such as the word 'First,' are *user-defined* words. These are words that the user chooses, and they can consist of any sequence of

3. Within a program, Pascal does not distinguish between upper and lower case; so a word typed in upper case is considered to represent the same thing as that word typed in lower case. You may want to vary the case in your programs for readability, or to distinguish keywords from other words as in the examples in this text, or for aesthetic reasons.

letters and digits, as long as the word begins with an alphabetic character and does not exceed a specified length.[4] So, the line above could have been written

```
PROGRAM Herelgo(INPUT,OUTPUT);
```

or

```
PROGRAM WillWork(INPUT,OUTPUT);
```

but none of the keywords can be changed.

Pascal keywords are reserved within a Pascal program—that is, you cannot define a name in the program that is the same as one of the Pascal keywords.

A complete list of all Pascal keywords appears in Appendix A.

As a whole, the statement above is referred to as the *Program Heading*. The meanings of its parts are as follows:

- The keyword PROGRAM indicates that this is the beginning of a Pascal program.
- The user-defined name of the program is a name provided to the computer system for the purposes of labelling your program.
- The keyword phrase (INPUT,OUTPUT) tells the computer system that the program will be reading and writing data to and from specific, pre-defined devices (usually, the keyboard and display screen); the meaning of this phrase will be discussed more fully in the next chapter, and for the moment can be simply taken at face value as a necessary part of the program heading.
- Note that the statement ends with a semicolon. The semicolon functions something like a period in English; it signals the end of a program command or statement, which, like an English sentence, is the minimal unit of meaning in the Pascal language. You will see that the semicolon appears pervasively throughout all Pascal programs.

Declarations. As mentioned earlier, in order for the computer to manipulate data in any way, the data must be stored in the computer's main memory. Before a piece of data can be stored in memory, however, a slot in main memory must be reserved for it within the Pascal program. Slots to hold the data the program will use are reserved in the *Declarations section* of the program. Each slot is characterized by two pieces of information—a user-defined *name*, so that the slot can be referred to from within the program, and a *type*, which indicates whether the slot will hold numbers or characters (or some other type of data, to be considered in later chapters). The general format of a statement to reserve a slot in main memory for a piece of data is

4. The maximum length varies depending on the version of Pascal that you use, but the smallest maximum is usually 8 characters. A common maximum is 32 characters.

```
VAR Name : <type>;
```

where Name is the user-defined name, and <type> is replaced by one of the Pascal keywords indicating one of the valid data types. The basic Pascal data types are INTEGER, REAL, CHAR, and BOOLEAN.

Recall that for the program in this chapter, a slot in main memory capable of holding a single character will be required. To create such a slot, the following declaration can be used:

```
VAR Letter : CHAR;
```

Consider the various parts of this declaration:

- The keyword VAR signals the beginning of the Declarations section of the program.

The keyword VAR will appear only once within the Declarations section of the program, even if the names and type specifications for several slots in main memory follow it.

- Letter, in this example, is the name given to the slot in memory that is being reserved or "declared." The rules governing the form of such names are the same as those listed above for program names—they can be composed of any sequence of letters and digits, but must begin with an alphabetic character, and their length is determined by the version of Pascal that you are using. While any name can be used, it is helpful to both the programmer and the reader of a program to assign names that have some meaning in terms of what is to be stored in the memory slot. In this example, the name Letter is used because a single letter is being stored in the memory slot.

Pascal keywords cannot be used to name slots in memory since their meaning is already established.

- The colon is used to separate the name from its type; the type in this example is CHAR, which indicates to the computer that the slot is capable of holding a single character.
- The semicolon signals the end of the statement.

Together, declared names and the specific slots in memory with which they are associated are called *variables*. The reason for this is that while a variable's name and its location in memory remain constant throughout a program, the *contents* of the memory location may change many times. Variable names provide a means to refer to particular memory locations within a program, without regard for their specific contents; thus, you can write a program to read and store a character in Letter and then write the contents of Letter out again, and each time the program is run a different character can be read in and stored in the Letter variable. Since within the program you refer to the variable's name and not to the specific character that was input, your program will run regardless of the character that is input by the user.

You can declare two or more slots to hold characters like this:

```
VAR Letter1 : CHAR;
    Letter2 : CHAR;
```

Since Letter1 and Letter2 are of the same type, this statement could be abbreviated as

```
VAR Letter1, Letter2 : CHAR;
```

However, keep in mind that the names Letter1 and Letter2 refer to entirely different locations in main memory. You can think of them like this:

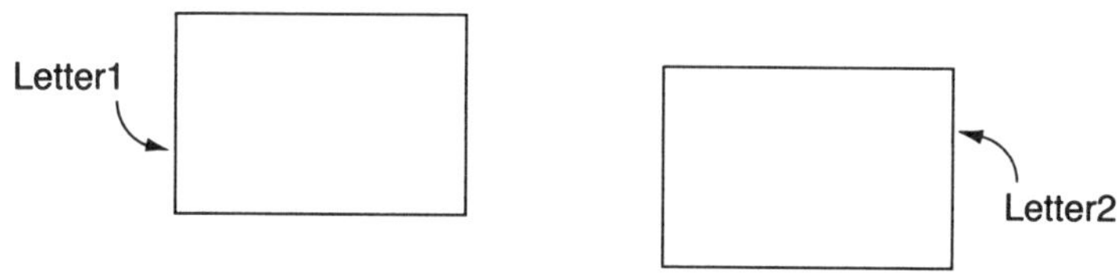

Both variables hold a single character, and may even hold copies of the same character, but they refer to entirely distinct memory locations. It is in fact useful to think of variable names as references to pointers to memory locations, as suggested by the picture. Internally, the computer actually translates the occurrence of a variable name to the address within main memory to which it refers; variable names are a convenience for programmers, so that locations can be referenced by names that make sense to them rather than by the numbers that actually address specific memory locations within the computer's main memory.

Certain uses of a variable name within a program simply refer to the contents of the variable without changing them, while other uses indicate that data is to be stored in the variable, thus destroying its previous contents. The differences will be clear when you learn about specific types of Pascal programming statements. You can think of the contents of a variable as you do the contents of a tape or cassette: the contents of the tape can be played back, or referenced, as often as you like without affecting them, but recording over the old contents destroys them entirely.

Program Statements. The Program Header and the Declarations are merely a prelude to the body of the Pascal program, which consists of the series of commands that will actually be executed to accomplish the intended task. Specific kinds of programming commands, or statements, will be introduced below and throughout the next several chapters; for now, simply note that these commands are always surrounded by the Pascal keywords BEGIN and END. The keyword END is followed by a period—this signals the end of the program to the computer system. So, the overall format of a simple Pascal program can be envisioned as

```
PROGRAM SomeName(INPUT,OUTPUT);
VAR Name1, Name2 : CHAR;
BEGIN
  <Program statements>
END.
```

All Pascal programs follow this basic format, although of course more or fewer variables, and with possibly different names and/or types, might be declared. Given the basic format, all that remains is to consider the form and function of specific programming statements. For this assignment, a statement to read and store data and a statement to write data to an output device are required.

Statements That Read Data

The Pascal command that, when executed, causes the computer to read a piece of data and store it in a designated memory slot is the READ statement. Its general form is

```
READ(<VariableName(s)>);
```

READ is the actual Pascal command that, when encountered by the computer, causes it to go to an input device, retrieve or read an item of data and store it. In the form above, the command indicates that the input data is to be read from a *default input* device—meaning that this is the device the computer reads from by default, unless it is told explicitly which input device it is to read from. In most cases, the default input device is the computer keyboard. So, when this statement is encountered the computer will stop and wait for the user to enter an item of data at the keyboard. This data will then be read and stored *in the variable or variables named in the READ statement*. After this is done the computer will go on to execute the next statement that appears in the program.

After reading an item of data, this item is effectively "consumed" from the input. This means that should another READ statement be subsequently executed, the computer will read the next item of input that the user has entered, or wait for another item of data to be typed if the user has not typed something already.

As an example of the READ statement, consider the following:

```
READ(Name);
```

Each of its parts is discussed below.

- READ itself is the Pascal keyword that signals that data is to be read from an input device and stored in some variable or variables in main memory.
- The parentheses are used to enclose the list of variables in which the data that is read will be stored. In most cases throughout this book, the list will consist of a single variable, as it does here, since it is both typical and advisable to read one item of data at a time.

- Name, in this example, is the name of the variable into which the data that is read is to be stored. As with all variables, the variable Name must be declared in the Declarations section of the program before it can appear in a program statement. The type of the variable that appears in the list associated with the READ statement dictates exactly what the "item of data" referred to above is considered to be, and therefore what is actually read and stored. If the variable has been declared with type CHAR, the computer will read a *single* character from the keyboard, regardless of how many characters may have been typed by the user. As mentioned above, a character is any character that can be entered from the computer keyboard—it can be 'f,' 'F' (these two are different!), '&,' '!,' or ' ' (blank). So, the action of the READ statement above is to retrieve the first character entered, whatever it may be, from the keyboard, and store it in the variable Name.

  As indicated above, more than one variable name can appear in the list within parentheses in a READ statement. When more than one variable is listed in a READ statement, items of data are read from the input until all of the variables listed are filled. A list of variables is specified by giving their names within the parentheses, separated by commas—so, for example, the statement READ(Letter1,Letter2); will read the first two characters the user enters and will store the first in the variable Letter1 and the second in Letter2.

  Note that if the variable Name contains data before the READ statement is executed, those contents are destroyed and replaced by the character that is subsequently read.

The READ statement is one of only two ways to alter the contents of a memory location from within a computer program.

  The other way to alter the contents of a memory location will be discussed in Chapter Four.

- As usual, the statement ends with a semicolon.

What is the action of the statement READ(Name); ? Well, assume that the user types the following line at the keyboard:

```
What is life?
↑
```

Before the READ statement is executed, you can imagine an input "pointer," represented by an arrow under the letter 'W' in the picture above, positioned at the character that is *about* to be read. When the READ statement is encountered, it will read one item of the proper type for each of the variables named in the associated list and store what it reads in that variable. In this example, only one variable, Name, appears in the list, and its type is CHAR, indicating that it is capable of holding a single character. Therefore, the READ statement goes to the input, gets a single character (in this case, the character 'W'), and stores it in the variable Name. After reading the character, it is consumed, thus moving the input pointer to the next input item—the character 'h,' in this case. This state of affairs can be envisioned like this:

```
What is life?
 ↑
```

What would happen if the following statements appeared in a program?

```
READ(Name);
READ(Name);
```

Because they appear one after another, the two statements will be executed one after another. If the user enters the sentence above, before the first statement is executed the input pointer will be under the 'W,' since nothing has been read yet. The first READ statement will read the 'W' and store it in **Name**, just as it was described above. At this point, the input pointer is under the letter 'h,' and the variable **Name** contains the character 'W.' You can envision the situation like this:

```
What is life?
 ↑
```

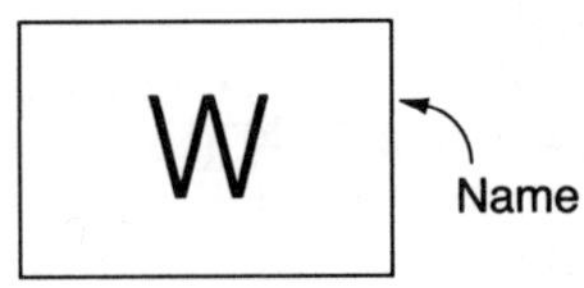

Now, when the second READ statement is executed, the following happens: the READ statement causes the computer to go to the input, get the next character—the character 'h'—and store it in the variable in the list, which is, of course, **Name**. This changes the situation depicted above in two ways: first, the input pointer advances to the next character, so that it points to the letter 'a.' Second, the character 'h' is stored in the variable **Name**, *obliterating the previous contents—the letter* 'W.' The new situation looks like this:

```
What is life?
  ↑
```

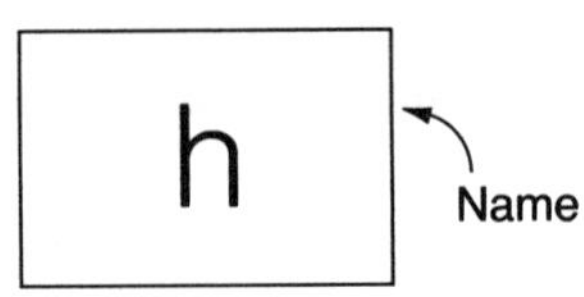

As a final example, consider the original input situation, with the input pointer under the letter 'W,' and then think about what would happen if the statement

```
READ(Letter1,Letter2);
```

were executed. The READ statement reads one item for each variable in its list, and since we will assume that both **Letter1** and **Letter2** have the type CHAR, this means that two characters will be read, and the first one read will be stored in **Letter1** and the second in **Letter2**. So, after this statement executes, the situation is

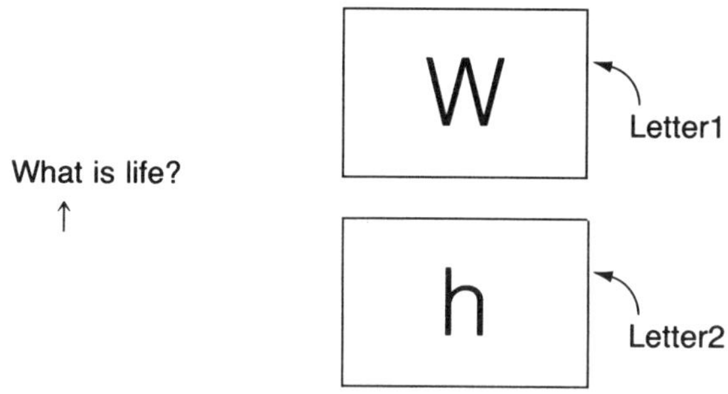

The next READ statement to be executed (if there is one) will read the letter 'a.'

This is a good opportunity to make an important point about variables. What are the contents of the variables Name, Letter1, and Letter2 before the READ statement puts something in them? Assuming that no other statements working with these variables appear in the program prior to the READ, they are empty—that is, no value has been stored in them. When a variable is declared in the Declarations section of the program, all that happens is that a location in memory is reserved for the variable, but nothing is actually put in that location. In fact, there may be old data from a previous use of that location still stored there, which is called "garbage" in the trade. Whatever is there, it is probably of no use to you, and so you should take careful note of the following:

Before a variable is given a value explicitly in a program, it has no value at all. Therefore, you should always give a variable a value before using it in any other way. Remember that the READ statement is one of only two ways to give a variable a value.

Statements That Write Data

As you might guess, the Pascal statement that causes a copy of the contents of some memory location to be written to an output device is

```
WRITE(Name);
```

Such a statement within a program constitutes a command to take a *copy* of whatever is stored in the variable Name and write it to an output device. If Name is a variable of type CHAR, the statement above will cause the single character stored in Name at the time this statement executes to be written on the default output device, which, again, is usually the display screen.

The WRITE statement does not affect the contents of a variable whose name appears within the statement; after the contents of the variable have been written out, the information stored in it remains intact and can be used again if desired.

As with READ, the parentheses in a WRITE statement can contain a list of variables to be printed, like this:

```
WRITE(Name1,Name2);
```

The variables are separated by commas. The variables are written out in the order in which they appear in the list. Unlike READ, it is quite usual to have a list of variables in a WRITE statement.

The WRITE statement above will cause the contents of the two variables Name1 **and** Name2 **to be written one after the other on the video display screen. The same would happen if two WRITE statements—for example,** WRITE(Name1); **and** WRITE(Name2); **were executed one after another.**

Pascal has another statement to write output called WRITELN (pronounced "write line," which is indicative of its function). WRITELN statements come in two forms. A WRITELN statement can appear alone, like this:

```
WRITELN;
```

in which case its action is to issue a "line eject," so that the next time a WRITE or WRITELN statement is encountered, what it writes will begin on a new line. WRITELN can also appear with an associated variable list, like WRITE:

```
WRITELN(Name);
```

in which case its action is

1. A copy of the contents of the variable (or variables) in its associated list is written to the video display screen.
2. A "line eject" is issued, so that the next time a WRITE or WRITELN statement is encountered, what it writes will begin on a new line.

The difference between the two forms of WRITELN given above is simply that when variables are included in the WRITELN statement, their contents must first be written out before the line eject is issued.

Some examples should make all of this a bit clearer. Suppose that two variables have been declared as follows:

```
VAR Letter1, Letter2 : CHAR;
```

and suppose that the variable Letter1 contains the character 'T' and Letter2 contains the character 'A.' Now what would be the effect of the following sequence of Pascal statements?

```
WRITE(Letter1);
WRITE(Letter2);
WRITELN;
WRITELN(Letter1,Letter2);
```

As a result of executing the first WRITE statement, a copy of the contents of the variable Letter1, the letter 'T' will be written to the screen. The second WRITE statement writes the contents of Letter2, the character 'A,' to the screen, upon which 'TA' is now printed. Finally, the WRITELN statement issues a line eject. The next statement causes the contents of the variables in its list, in the order they appear, to be written on the screen. So, 'TA' is once again displayed—but it appears on the line below the previous line that was written. As a result of executing the statements above, then, the following should appear at the display screen:

```
TA
TA
```

Note that after the second 'TA' is written, another line eject is issued, so that subsequent output will begin on the line below it.

Because a lone WRITELN statement does nothing more than issue a line eject, you can print several blank lines by issuing a series of WRITELN statements in a row.

For instance, these statements will generate a series of blank lines:

```
WRITELN;
WRITELN;
WRITELN;
WRITELN,
```

If a WRITE statement has printed something just prior to the appearance of this set of WRITELN statements, then the first WRITELN will go to a new line, and then three more line ejects will be issued, giving a total of three blank lines. If these statements are executed when you are positioned to write on a new line already, then four blank lines will be printed.

Printing Literals. In the examples above, the items in the lists associated with WRITE and WRITELN statements contained variables only. However, it is possible to write out not only the contents of a variable, but also any specified string of characters. This is done by enclosing the string in *single* quotation marks[5] and including it in the list of items to be written by a WRITE or WRITELN statement. For example, the statement

```
WRITELN('This is a literal string');
```

will cause the exact text of the string inside the single quotation marks to be printed. Literal strings behave the same way as any item in a list associated with

5. On most keyboards, the single quotation mark is on the same key as the double quotation mark.

a WRITE or WRITELN statement—they are printed according to the same rules and they can appear as a part of a list of items to be written, as follows:

```
WRITELN('Letter1 contains: ', Letter1);
```

This command would cause the string 'Letter1 contains: ' to be printed, followed by the contents of the variable **Letter1**, after which a line eject would be issued. If **Letter1** contains the letter 'T' the result will be

```
Letter1 contains: T
```

Constructing the Program

At this point you are ready to attempt to construct the program that will accomplish the assigned task: to read in and write out a line of characters entered by the user. However, recall the algorithm for the process:

1. While there are more characters to be read, repeat the following:
  a. Read a character from the input and store it in main memory.
  b. Write a copy of the character on the display screen.

You have seen statements in the preceding discussion of Pascal that will enable you to accomplish steps 1.a and 1.b. However, you have no way yet to deal with step 1, the part of the algorithm that specifies that steps 1.a and 1.b are to be repeated. For this, you'll need to become familiar with a programming construct called the loop.

In computer jargon, loops are simply groups of program statements that are executed repeatedly. Specific program commands indicate which portions of a program are to be repeated, and they also indicate under what conditions the loop is to continue executing. According to step 1, above, the loop should stop when there are no more characters to be read. It is easy to make the stipulation within the algorithm, but you may wonder whether or not the computer is able to know when the user is finished entering data at the keyboard. Happily, it can, because when the user enters a line of characters to be read by a Pascal READ statement, he or she must subsequently hit the carriage return key in order to "send" to the CPU.[6] The computer sees this carriage return as a special character, called the end-of-line character. So the program can specify that the process of reading and writing characters is to be repeated until this end-of-line character is encountered.

Before considering exactly how to do this in Pascal, you will need an idea of what a Pascal loop looks like and how it operates. The most common Pascal

6. In some implementations of Pascal (for instance, Macintosh Pascal) this is not the case; instead, characters are read as soon as they are typed. When this happens, if the user enters a carriage return at the end of the line it can still be used to signal the end of the input, and so the program outlined below will work. However, the output of the program will be considerably different, since each character will be *both* read and written as soon as it is typed. The user will see each letter in the line doubled as it is typed—for instance, if the user types "help," "hheellpp" will appear on the screen rather than two copies of the word "help."

looping command, and the one that you will need for this assignment, is called the WHILE loop. Its form is as follows:

```
WHILE <condition> DO BEGIN
   <statements>
END;
```

and its parts are described as follows:

- WHILE <*condition*> DO BEGIN is the loop's heading; it signals the beginning of the loop. Notice that although the header seems like an individual statement and therefore seems to need a semicolon at its end, the end of the WHILE statement really doesn't occur until the END, which is followed by a semicolon. Between the BEGIN and the END, any Pascal statement or statements can be included—so, in a WHILE loop you effectively imbed a statement or set of statements within a statement.
- <*condition*> is a generic symbol that will be replaced by an expression that tells the computer under what conditions the statements within the loop are to be executed. (Note that elbow brackets will be used throughout the text to distinguish generic program elements.) The condition is some assertion about a state of affairs—for instance, an assertion that a certain variable contains or *equals* a particular value. Such assertions are called *Boolean expressions,* named after the mathematician George Boole. A Boolean expression is simply one that makes an assertion that at any given time is either true or false. When a Boolean expression is used as condition in the heading of a WHILE loop, its truth or falsity determines whether or not the statement or statements within the loop will be executed.
- The statement or statements inside the loop can be any valid Pascal statements, and these are of course the statements that will be repeated as long as the condition on the loop holds true.
- The END statement signals that the end of the statements that are to be repeated has been reached.

When a loop like the one above is encountered, the following occurs: the condition in the header is checked, and if it is *true,* the statements between the header and the END statement are executed one after another until the END of the WHILE loop is encountered. Now, at this point, instead of continuing to execute statements sequentially and going on to the statement following the END of the loop as it would under normal circumstances, the computer *returns to the loop header,* and checks the condition again. If the condition is true at *this point,* the statements inside the loop are executed a second time. Then, the computer goes back to the loop's header at the top of the loop again, and checks the condition for truth or falsity—if the condition is *true,* the statements within the loop are executed once again. This process continues until, upon returning to the top of the loop and checking the condition in the header, the condition is found to be *false.* When this happens, the statements within the loop are *skipped,* and the sequential execution of statements is resumed with the statement *following* the END statement. It is all very methodical—almost excruciatingly so.

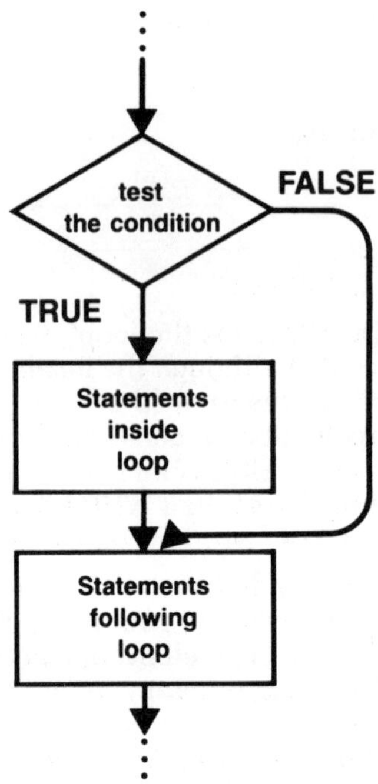

When the END of a WHILE loop is encountered after executing the statements within the loop, the computer always goes back to the top of the loop to check the condition again.

If the condition on a WHILE loop is false the first time the loop header is encountered, before the statements within the loop have been executed at all, the entire loop is skipped and the computer goes on to the statement following the loop's END. Therefore, it is possible that the statements inside a WHILE loop may never be executed at all.

The accompanying visual representation of the flow of events in a WHILE loop might help you to get the idea of how it operates. The arrows indicate the "flow of control" followed by the computer through the statements in the parts of the program depicted depending on the truth or falsity of the condition in the WHILE loop header.

The loop is one of the most fundamental of programming constructs. Probably every program you will ever write will contain at least one loop, if not more than one loop, and so it is worthwhile to spend a few minutes getting the hang of the way a loop operates if you don't have the idea already.

Armed with the WHILE loop, a much more specific outline of the program that you are to write can now be stated, using what you know about the general form of Pascal programs and expressing the steps in English-like, algorithmic language:

```
Program Heading
Declarations
  BEGIN
    WHILE not the end of the line DO BEGIN
      READ a character
      WRITE the character
    END;
    Issue a line eject
  END.
```

This program outline indicates that the statements within the WHILE loop—the READ and WRITE statements—are to be executed repeatedly as long as the end of the line has not been encountered—as indicated above, the computer knows that the end of the line has been encountered when the user enters a carriage return. Apart from rewording the condition under which the reading and writing process is to be continued, the set of statements above corresponds fairly closely to the algorithm outlined earlier. The WHILE loop header corresponds to step 1, and the READ and WRITE statements within the loop correspond to steps 1.a and 1.b. If the program is written according to this outline, the condition on the WHILE loop ("not the end of the line") will be checked before each repetition of the statements within the loop, and again, its truth or falsity will determine whether or not the statements inside the loop are to be executed another time or skipped. Thus the process of reading the next character from the input and writing it to the screen will be repeated as long as the end of the line is not detected. When the end of the line is detected, the statements in the loop will be skipped and the statements following the loop will be executed.

Notice that a statement to issue a line eject is included at the end of the program. The reason for this is that some computer systems do not print output written with a WRITE statement immediately, but rather hold the output (appending the output of successive WRITE statements to its "line" of output as it collects it) until a line eject is issued with a WRITELN statement. So, unless a WRITELN is issued, some systems will produce no output at all for the program above. It is a good idea to control your output in any case, by issuing a line eject when you intend for a line of output to be completed.

Notice that in the program outlined above, if for some reason the user enters *only* a carriage return character, the statements within the loop will never be executed; in this case the effect of the statement below the loop will be to write out nothing and issue a line eject.

One or two things need to be considered before translating this outline into a real Pascal program. First of all, you must determine exactly what to declare in the Declarations section of the program. Since the program reads single characters, obviously a variable of type CHAR will be needed. You might be wondering exactly how many slots in memory of this type will be needed; since potentially several characters will be read, you might be thinking that several slots will be needed. However, the algorithm calls for only one character to be read by the READ statement, and because that character is then written to the screen before another character is read, the space it occupied can be used to store the next character when it is finally read in. Therefore, only one variable of type CHAR need be declared. This is the more compelling reason alluded to earlier for reading and writing one character at a time—if all of the characters were to be read before they were written, room for each would have to be reserved. But how would you know how many characters would be read in and therefore how many slots to set up to hold them? You wouldn't, and the best you could do would be to reserve some arbitrary number of slots and hope the user does not enter more slots than you have room for. This is clearly sloppy, and in general, if you ever find yourself in a situation where your program is sloppy in this way, you should consider the likelihood that there is a better solution to be found.

In order to better understand the number and kinds of variables your program will need, consider exactly what the program will be doing and how the process of reading affects the contents of variables. When the WHILE loop is first encountered, its condition is evaluated to determine if it is true or false. If it is true (in this case, if the end of the line has not been encountered in the input) the loop will be entered and the statements that appear within it executed. The first time the loop in the outline above is entered, the READ statement will read the first character from the user's input and store it in the variable whose name appears in the list associated with the READ. The WRITE statement will then take a copy of the contents of the variable in its list, which should be the same as the one into which the READ statement stored what it read, and write it to the screen. The END statement will return control to the top of the loop, where the loop's condition is re-evaluated; if the end of the line has not been encountered, the loop will be entered again. Assuming this is the case, the READ statement will then execute a second time, reading the next character into the variable in its list. This is, of course, the same variable into which it read the first character, and so the original character will be erased and replaced by the character that is now read in. This is fine; the old character is not needed anymore. A copy of it has already been printed, and so there is no point in keeping it around. Therefore, you can re-use the same memory slot for each new character that is read in, since by destroying the old one you will have lost nothing.

The body of the program can now begin to take shape, based on the outline given above. First, the condition in the header of the WHILE loop must be expressed in Pascal. This condition should be some Pascal expression of the notion "WHILE the end of the line hasn't been encountered DO BEGIN." Actually, there is a very simple way to express just this in Pascal:

```
WHILE NOT EOLN DO BEGIN
```

"NOT EOLN" will be the condition under which the loop is to continue executing. Both NOT and EOLN are Pascal keywords, which should be obvious since they appear in capital letters. They often appear together, but are not part of a unit; you'll see other uses of NOT later.

EOLN, as you might have guessed, stands for "end-of-line." NOT EOLN basically means "not the end of the line." When the computer evaluates this condition, the following happens: the computer looks into the input at the character it is *about to read*—that is, the one to which the input pointer is currently pointing. If what it sees is the end-of-line carriage return character, the NOT

EOLN condition is determined to be false, which means, of course, that the loop will not continue to execute. If it sees any other character, NOT EOLN is true, and the loop is executed once again.

Next, the statement "READ a character" must be translated into Pascal. From the preceding section, you know that to read a character from the user's keyboard and store it in memory, you use the READ command, followed by the name of a variable in which the character is to be stored in parentheses. Assuming that you have declared a variable named 'Letter' with the CHAR type specification, the following statement can be used in the program in place of the algorithmic statement, "READ a character":

```
READ(Letter);
```

This will cause the first character the user enters to be read and stored in the variable 'Letter.'

The statement "WRITE the character" must also be translated into Pascal, and, like READ, its form is

```
WRITE(Letter);
```

This causes a copy of the character that was read and stored in the variable Letter by the preceding READ statement to be printed.

To complete the program, the statement "Issue a line eject" must be expressed in valid Pascal. To do so, the statement

```
WRITELN;
```

is all you need.

Now that all of the Pascal statements have been determined, you can put them together according to the algorithmic outline specified above. Assuming you are naming your program "First" and your variable "Letter," the program will look more or less like this:

```
PROGRAM First(INPUT,OUTPUT);
VAR Letter : CHAR;
BEGIN
  WHILE NOT EOLN DO BEGIN
    READ(Letter);
    WRITE(Letter);
  END;
  WRITELN;
END.
```

This is the basic form of this and most Pascal programs. However, for this program, one more thing needs to be considered, because if the program is written exactly like the one above, the following will happen when the program is finally submitted to the computer to be executed. The computer will proceed to interpret the program by executing each statement in the order it appears. The Program Heading will thus be encountered first. The Program Heading simply signals the beginning of the program, provides the program's name, and tells the computer that the program will be reading and writing to and from default input and output devices. Next, upon encountering the Declarations section, the computer will set aside the appropriate slots in main memory according to the specifications it sees there. The BEGIN statement signals that the commands that constitute the program follow. So far, everything that has been done is invisible to the user who is running the program. Then, when the computer sees the WHILE statement and its condition, it will go to the keyboard to look at the first character that the user has entered. But has the user entered anything? Well, it is possible, if he or she knew exactly how the program is supposed to work and could determine when to enter something. But chances are that nothing has been entered, and the computer's response is to simply sit and wait for something to appear. If the user does not figure out that he or she is supposed to enter something, you will have a classic stand-off situation, and you can be sure the computer will wait more patiently than the user.

The point of all this is that you should provide some signal to the person running the program that he or she is supposed to enter a line of input. It would be nice to print out something like

```
Enter a sentence, followed by a carriage return:
```

at the display screen before the program tries to read. This is easy, because, as you saw above, any literal string can be printed by simply enclosing it in single quotation marks and putting it in the list associated with a WRITE or WRITELN statement. Instructions issued by a program such as this one are called *prompts;* and you should adopt the practice of including a prompt in your program *anytime* the program is to read something from the user. The more general rule is always to consider how the program will behave in terms of what the user sees and to make the program as easy to use as possible. It should always be clear to the user what he or she is supposed to do. One way to ensure this is to write every program as if it will be used by people who do not know anything about computers and have very little idea of what the program does. Under this assumption, the first thing many programs do is to issue a 1 or 2 line explanation of what the program does. You may want to get yourself into this habit by providing for such an explanation in this first program; later, when your programs become more complex, you should definitely include such an introduction.

You will need to determine where in the program to put the statement that will cause the prompt to appear on the screen—does it go inside the loop? before the loop? after the loop? This is left as an exercise. If you have trouble figuring it out, try inserting it at various locations and then think through the steps that the program will perform as a result of each statement. Methodical, step by step analysis of a program's operations is a very good way both to determine when to do what in a program and to figure out why a program did something that you did not expect it to. Keep track of the contents of each variable and what has been printed so far as you go along.

You will also need to determine whether to use WRITE or WRITELN to issue the prompt. Again, this is left as an exercise; one way to figure it out is simply to experiment. Your choice between WRITE and WRITELN will determine whether or not the line the user enters will be typed on the same line as the prompt or on the following line.

SUMMING UP THE PROGRAM

You now have all the tools you need to write the first program. As mentioned earlier, to accomplish this first task you need to assimilate much more new information than will be required for later tasks. Consequently, this may well be the most difficult assignment for you, for you are getting used to not only the details of the Pascal programming language, but also the whole conceptual framework underlying the programming process.

Do not expect your program to run the first, or even the second, time. You will no doubt make at least a few typing errors the first time around, and you will rapidly discover that the computer does not tolerate even a single misplaced character. Read the Niceties section that follows this chapter on the details of program format and try to imitate the specified forms of the various statements exactly. But do not be afraid of errors—even the most experienced programmers spend hours "debugging" programs. The only difference between them and you is that they are familiar with the fact that error messages are simply a means to help find your mistakes.

It is important at this point to note that implementations of Pascal differ, especially in the ways in which they handle input and output. So-called "standard" versions of Pascal will perform the steps outlined in this chapter as they were described, but some popular versions of Pascal, such as Macintosh Pascal, will not produce a copy of the line the user enters, but rather will duplicate each letter immediately after it is typed (see footnote 6, above). In general, you should be aware that various differences in the many versions of Pascal exist and may change the way your program behaves.

Also remember that to a large extent, learning to program is a matter of learning to think about your task from a variety of perspectives. When you first start to think about writing a program, your perspective is that of the program's user, and so you envision the results that you will see, and the data that you will provide the program in order for it to produce those results. When you get around to thinking about the algorithm for the program, however, you have to start thinking from the computer's perspective, and think in terms of how main memory is affected by the commands that you execute. In the process of composing the program you may occasionally shift your perspective back to that of the user in order to envision the visible effects of what you (as the computer) are doing. Eventually, when the program is finally ready to be run, your perspective will once again be that of the user, but in order to debug the program you may have to switch back and forth between the computer's and the user's perspectives, in order to see how the program behaves, modify the program, see what the new behavior is, and so on. After awhile, this shifting of perspective will become second nature; it is so unconscious for most programmers that they forget to mention it to novice programmers.

The problem that is the focus of this chapter, getting information into and out of the machine, is absolutely fundamental to every program you will ever write. If you cannot get information into the machine, it is irrelevant; if you cannot get it out, the program is solipsistic. All of the programs you will write in subsequent chapters build on this one, so you should make an attempt to become familiar with the syntax and function of each of the statements in your program before going on.

NICETIES

Program Format

To write your program, you will probably use a text editor (which is itself a program, which takes what you type as its input data), which will enable you to type in the program in preparation for running it later, or submitting it to the computer to be executed. The writing phase is entirely separate from the running phase; while you are writing the program, what you type is not considered in terms of its meaning but is regarded simply as a group of isolated characters. When the program is run, its meaning is determined and the instructions in the program are executed by the computer.

You may have noticed in the examples in this chapter that the statements were laid out in certain patterns; specifically, statements were written one per line, the statements in the body of the program were all indented, and statements inside the WHILE loop were indented further. Also, upper and lower case were used wherever desired. Pascal allows its programmers what is called *free format* in writing a program—you can insert one or more blanks or even go to a new line anywhere, and you can use upper and lower case as you like. The only restrictions are that blanks cannot appear in the middle of keywords or variable names, since the computer uses the blank to determine where a word begins and ends, and you cannot use upper and lower case to distinguish two names. For example, you can't name one variable "LETTER" and another "letter" since before executing your program the computer translates program statements to upper case internally.

Given this freedom, you can make your program look as pretty as you want to. A well-laid-out program is considered a mark of good programming style, both because it looks nice and because it is easier to read, understand, and, as a result, to debug. For instance, indenting the statements in a loop clearly identifies them as a unit and shows at a glance where the loop begins and ends; in a short program like the one in this chapter that may not seem important, but later, when your programs are hundreds of lines long, it will make it far easier to locate specific portions of the program.

The following are a few suggestions for program layout that are consistent with the practice of most programmers. You should start now to develop good program formatting habits.

- Put each statement on a separate line. When a statement is too long to fit on one line, break it at a logical point and then indent the next line by 3 spaces.
- Insert at least one blank line between the sections of your program. Put a blank line (1) between the program heading and the declarations section, (2) between the declarations section and the BEGIN, (3) immediately fol-

lowing the BEGIN, to set off the statements in the body of the program, (4) after the last statement in the body of the program, just before the END.

- Indent all of the statements in the body of the program 3 spaces.
- Indent the statements inside a loop 3 spaces.
- Capitalize Pascal keywords and put variable and other user-defined names in lower case.

Comments

Pascal (and most programming languages) allow the user to insert messages in a program that are not properly part of the program, but which serve to explain what the program does—not to the computer, since it ignores comments, but to the reader of the program. Again, in large programs comments are absolutely vital. To insert a comment in a program, enclose it in curly brackets, like this:

```
{ This won't be considered part of the program }
```

or between the characters '(*' and '*)', like this:

```
(* This won't be considered part of the program *)
```

Comments can appear anywhere in a program.

The purpose of comments in a program is to make clear what the program is doing. Comments are used to explain individual statements as well as whole sections of the program whose function is not absolutely clear, so that the reader can see at a glance what the section does, rather than trying to interpret the individual statements. Comments are discarded when the program is run; they exist for the benefit of anyone who may read your program (including and especially the programmer himself), but do not in any way affect what the program does.

For the most part the program in this chapter is self-explanatory, so you probably won't need many comments. However, you should include in this and every program you ever write a "header" comment that gives the programmer's name, the date, and a brief explanation of the program's function. For example, you might include the following header comment in the program for this chapter:

```
PROGRAM FirstOne(INPUT,OUTPUT);
{  Your Full Name
   Today's Date
This program reads in a line entered by the user and prints it back out on the display
screen.  }
```

Notice that the comment can span several lines.

Although the program doesn't really need much commenting beyond this, you could put a comment just before the WHILE loop in the program that says something like "Read the line from the user" and one before the WRITELN at the end that says "Write the entire line to the display screen." What you do *not* want to do is to put a comment before the loop that says "Beginning of loop." Remember that the purpose of a comment is to elucidate what is not immediately obvious.

Three common mistakes occur when comments are used, mostly as a result of typing errors:

1. It is common to put short comments that refer to a particular statement on the same line as the statement and to its right, but beware of the following problem:

   ```
   READ(Letter);        { Read the
   WRITE(Letter);         next letter }
   ```

   The problem here is that the WRITE statement is considered to be part of the comment, and never gets executed. This program would run, but there would never be any output, and this is the kind of subtle error that people spend hours tracking down.
2. It is extremely easy to forget to close a comment with a right curly bracket, which makes the computer think that your whole program is a comment.
3. Similarly, it is common to put curly brackets inside a comment, and not realize that the computer thinks the comment has ended before it actually does. It then tries to interpret your comment as part of the program, and becomes entirely confused, often generating a whole stream of error messages.

More About WHILE

The form of the WHILE statement was given as

```
WHILE <condition> DO BEGIN
  <statements>
END;
```

When the loop contains only one statement, you can eliminate the BEGIN and END, like this:

```
WHILE <condition> DO <statement>;
```

However, the BEGIN and END do no harm even if the loop contains a single statement, and it is much easier to simply use them consistently. Also, if you leave them out and then decide to add a statement to the loop, it's very easy to forget to insert the BEGIN and END, which will then cause your program to behave very strangely. Throughout this text BEGIN and END will always be used with WHILE and in other constructs that follow the same pattern.

More About Semicolons

A similar situation exists for semicolons. In certain places, Pascal lets you leave them out, but if they appear they do no harm. Specifically, a semicolon can be omitted at the end of any statement that immediately precedes an END statement; so, the semicolon on the WRITE statement just before the END of the loop in the program for this chapter could be eliminated, as well as the one on the WRITELN just before the END that terminates the program. But again, if you leave a semicolon off the end of a statement that precedes an END, and then decide to insert a statement between that statement and the END, it is easy to forget to insert the semicolon—which of course would result in an error. The practice here will be to include them at the ends of all statements. (Note that semicolons are never used after the keyword BEGIN. Technically, statements in which the keyword BEGIN appears do not end until after the END with which BEGIN is matched. Thus the statements that appear between a BEGIN and END, each of which, of course, terminates with its own semicolon, are actually statements *within* another statement.)

APPLICATIONS AND CONSIDERATIONS

Obviously, the process of reading and writing characters is so basic that in one sense, there are no true "applications" of a program like the one described in this chapter. But in a very broad sense, there are many applications of a program that simply reads and writes characters, if you extend your concept of reading to include reading from any input device instead of the keyboard only (this will be discussed more in the next chapter). For instance; your computer system no doubt takes a command that causes the contents of a particular file on disk to be printed on the video display screen or, perhaps, on a printer. Recalling that the computer system is itself a program, you can easily imagine that when you enter a command that causes a file to be displayed or printed, a part of that program whose statements are very similar to those in the program described in this chapter is executed. You may think that some more elaborate method for printing is used in a program as sophisticated as a computer's operating system, but even though a more basic kind of programming language might be used to write the operating system program, the process of reading and writing characters you have seen here is very much the same.

EXERCISES

Modify the basic program in this chapter to do the following:

1. Have the program echo the user's input, as in the basic assignment, but add an additional comment of your choosing that is printed on the same line as the user's input. For instance, if the user enters "To be or not to be," the computer might respond:

```
To be or not to be      Is that all you have to say?
```

2. Print the user's sentence one letter per line.
3. Have the program print out an introductory comment explaining what it does.
4. (Somewhat tricky.) Instead of reading a sentence, ask the user to enter his or her

name. Then, have the program print "Hello, *name,*" (replacing *name* with the name read in), followed by any message of your choice.

5. (For the ambitious programmer.) Modify the program so that it will continue to read and print sentences until the user wants to stop. To signal that he or she no longer wants to continue entering sentences, the user should type a lone carriage return instead of a sentence.

3

Reading Data from Files

In the last chapter you saw how to read data from the user, store it in main memory, and then print it. For small amounts of input data, reading data from the keyboard is fine, but for large amounts of data it is inappropriate. The programs that you will write throughout the remainder of this text take as input a text which might be thousands of lines long. Obviously, it would be ridiculous to expect the user to enter even ten or twenty lines of text every time a program is run, let alone several hundred or thousand. So in this chapter you will modify the program you have already written to read its input data from an input device other than the keyboard.

It is possible to store data that will be read into a program permanently on one of several devices for data storage. Up until the mid-1970's or so, data that was to be kept permanently was often typed onto computer cards, and in some cases it still is. Nowadays, data is more often stored on magnetic disks or tapes. Each collection of data stored on the disk or tape is called a *file*, and disks and tapes can typically hold many files of data. Once the data is stored in a file on a disk or tape, it can be read by a computer program over and over again without modifying or destroying it.

It may be the case that the text you will use as input to your programs from now on has already been stored in a file. If not, you will need to enter and store a text in a file. The means by which the text is entered into the computer and stored on a disk or tape is dependent on the computer system you are using. In most cases, you will use the same text editor that you use to write your programs to enter the text and save it in a particular file on a disk. If so, it is interesting to note that your programs are also stored in files on a disk, and until you go about running these programs the files are seen simply as collected sequences of characters, just as the file containing the text is seen. The distinction between a program and data is made by the way in which the contents of the file are used.

The algorithm for the program to read data from a file rather than the keyboard is essentially the same as the one for the preceding program. Characters will be read and written one at a time, just as before, and a loop will be used to repeat the process of reading and writing until all the characters in the file have been read. A few additional language features will be needed to handle this kind of input, but their number is far fewer than in the previous chapter.

ELEMENTS OF PASCAL

Files

The word "file" was used above to indicate a collection of characters stored together on a disk or tape. In a Pascal program, the meaning of the word "file" is extended to include input from the keyboard as well, so that all characters entered from the keyboard during the course of a program's execution are seen as one continuous file of data, just as if they existed on a disk. Consequently, input from the keyboard and input from a disk or tape file are treated in exactly the same way, in terms of the way characters are read and with regard to concepts such as EOLN, which you saw in Chapter Two.

Like input from the keyboard, input from files stored on disk or tape cannot be accessed at random—that is, they must be read sequentially, from start to finish.

Within a Pascal program, each file is known by a programmer-specified name.[1] This name is used in the program to indicate which file the program is to read from in any given READ statement. Now, because this is the case, you may wonder why you never knew or used the file's name when you read from the keyboard, since it is treated the same way as any other file. First of all, although you were not aware of it, the file name for the keyboard was given in the Program

1. If the file exists on disk or tape, the name by which a file is known within the program may not be the same as the name that is associated with the file outside the program—that is, the name under which it is known on the disk or tape. The correspondence between the names for the file within and outside the program varies depending on the computer system you are using. On some systems the external name is assumed to be the same as the internal name, or some variant of the internal name (for example, the external name is sometimes assumed to be the internal name with a certain suffix attached to it). In some cases you may have to provide some indication within the program of the external name. In any case, if you don't know how the internal and external names correspond on your system, you will have to find out before running your program.

Heading—its name is INPUT, and if you recall, the heading on every Pascal program has the basic form

```
PROGRAM YouNameIt(INPUT,OUTPUT);
```

INPUT is a special file in Pascal, known as the *default input file*.[2] What this means is that anytime a READ or other command associated with an input file appears, if no file name is given, the command is assumed to refer to the file with the name INPUT. So when you say READ(Letter); the computer assumes you intend to read from the file associated with the name INPUT. If you want to read from another file, which you will for this chapter's problem, its file name must be given explicitly in the READ command, so that the computer knows to go elsewhere for its input.

You can read from both the keyboard and another input file—or many files for that matter—within the same program, by issuing the appropriate READ statements.

Before you can read from a file other than INPUT, some preliminaries must be taken care of. Because INPUT is a default input file, most of what needs to be done to establish and identify this file within a Pascal program is done automatically. But to establish a non-default file, several steps must be taken:

1. The name by which the file will be known within the program must be added to the list of files that appears in the Program Heading. If the name of the file is to be TextFile, the heading would look like this:

   ```
   PROGRAM ReadText(INPUT,OUTPUT,TextFile);
   ```

2. The file must be declared in the Declarations section, as follows:

   ```
   VAR TextFile : TEXT;
   ```

   TEXT is a keyword, and it is simply a type given to files that are treated the way we want our file to be treated—as a sequence of characters. Otherwise the declaration has the same form as any declaration: the name, followed by a colon, followed by the specification of the type of object the name represents.
3. Within the actual body of the program, a statement must be issued to ready the file for reading. If the name of the file is TextFile, the statement is

   ```
   RESET(TextFile);
   ```

2. OUTPUT, as you can guess, is also the name of a file, but it is a file to which output is written rather than one from which input is read. The name OUTPUT is the name for the display screen; it is the only output file you will be using in this text, and so here the discussion treats only files from which data is read. Writing to files other than OUTPUT is covered in the Niceties section at the end of this chapter. You can see here that the concept of a file is even broader than indicated above—in a Pascal program, a file is really any place from which input is read or to which output is sent.

This statement can appear anywhere before the first command that accesses the contents of the file appears. Its effect is to get the computer ready to read the first character in the file.

If you issue a second RESET command in a program after having read from the file, the next time the program is instructed to read from the file it will start at the beginning again,

---

Reading from Files Other Than INPUT

The Pascal statement for reading from files other than the default input file has the same form as does the command to read from INPUT, except that the name of the file from which the computer is to read appears as the first item in the variable list associated with the statement. Assuming a variable named Letter is declared with type CHAR, the following statement would indicate that a single character is to be read from a file named TextFile and stored in the variable Letter:

```
READ(TextFile,Letter);
```

The action of this READ statement is exactly the same for the file as it is when it reads from the keyboard; the only difference is where the input is taken from. As with input from the keyboard, you can imagine that an input pointer initially points to the first character in the file, and that a READ statement like the one above will go to the file, get a character, and store that character in the variable Letter. After this is done, the input pointer for this file moves along in the file by one character, just as it does when reading from INPUT. So, if the file called TextFile contains

```
What is life?
↑
```

and the input pointer is positioned as indicated, the action of the statement

```
READ(TextFile,Letter);
```

is to go to the file TextFile, read the 'W,' store it in the variable Letter, and move the input pointer along one character, so that the resulting situation is

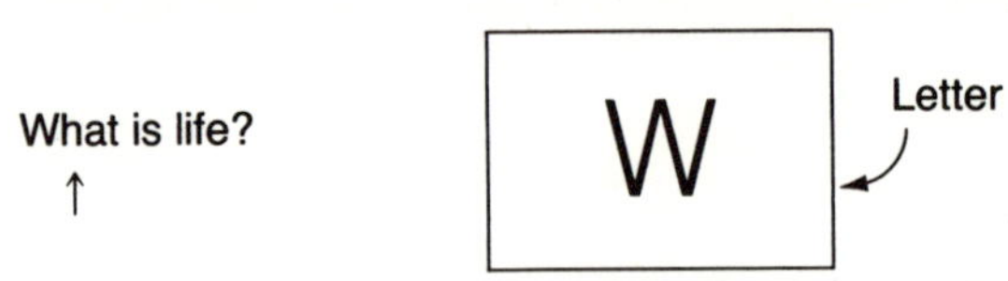

As you can see, the effect of the READ is exactly the same as it is when reading from the keyboard.

READLN

Just as the WRITE statement has a variant WRITELN, so does the Pascal READ statement have a READLN. Just like READ, the READLN statement can specify the name of the file from which it is to read, or no file name can be given and the reading will then be done from the default input file.

READLN's action is very similar to READ's, with one important difference. READLN works like this: when a READLN appears with an associated list (including the filename from which the computer is to read, if necessary), it will read and store in the same way as the READ statement. However, when it is finished reading, it will *discard all characters in the input up to and including the next end-of-line character,* thus causing the next statement that reads from the same file, if there is one, to read the first character on the next line. If READLN had been used instead of READ in last chapter's program, after the first character had been read from the input, the remainder of the line, including the carriage return character, would have been discarded—which would have defeated the purpose of the program.

Unlike READ, the READLN statement can appear *without* an associated list of variables. When READLN appears without an associated list (or with a list containing only the name of a file to which the READLN is to apply) nothing is read from the file. However, even though nothing is read from the file, everything up to and including the next carriage return character is discarded, as it is when any form of READLN statement is issued. So, if at some point in reading from a file named TextFile you decide that you want to start reading at the beginning of the next line, simply include the following command:

```
READLN(TextFile);
```

The next statement that reads from the file will pick up the first character on the line *following* the line that was being read before the READLN command was issued.

Suppose you are reading from a file named TextFile within your program, and the file contains the following three lines:

```
What is Life?<CR>
↑
Life is just<CR>
a bowl of cherries.<CR>
```

<CR> stands for the end-of-line (carriage return) character (you will hear more about carriage return characters in files below). The arrow, of course, indicates the point at which reading will begin. Think about what will happen if the following statement appears in your program:

```
READLN(TextFile,Letter);
```

Like READ, READLN will cause the computer to go to the input (in this case, because a file name is specified, it goes to the file TextFile), read the character

'W,' and store it in the variable **Letter**. The difference between READ and READLN is what happens next: *instead of moving along in the file by one character, the input pointer moves to the beginning of the* next *line in the input*. This means that after the READLN statement is executed, the situation is this:

```
What is Life?<CR>
Life is just<CR>
↑
a bowl of cherries.<CR>
```

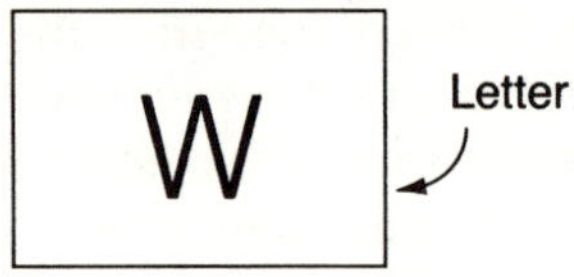

The input pointer moves to the *beginning of the next line in the input*, discarding the remainder of the line from which it read. Thus the action of READLN is to "read a line"—that is, to consume an entire line of the input. An entire line is consumed even if there are not enough variables in the list in the READLN statement to cause all of the data in the line to be read and stored, which is the case in the example above.

Another example: starting with the configuration given above,

```
What is Life?<CR>
↑
Life is just<CR>
a bowl of cherries.<CR>
```

consider the effect of the statement

```
READLN(TextFile);
```

Because there is no variable list in this statement, the process of going to the file, reading a character, and storing the character is not performed. So the only action of the statement is to re-position the input pointer in the file so that the situation becomes

```
What is Life?<CR>
Life is just<CR>
↑
a bowl of cherries.<CR>
```

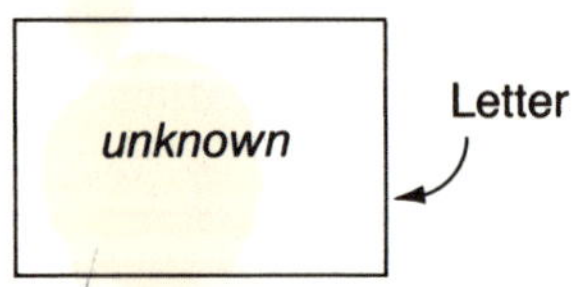

Now, it should be clear to you that reading from one file has absolutely no effect at all on any other file. To illustrate this, suppose that the file you are calling **TextFile** contains the familiar

```
What is Life?<CR>
↑
Life is just<CR>
a bowl of cherries.<CR>
```

and that the user at the keyboard has entered

```
Life is what you make it.<CR>
↑
```

reflecting a sentiment unlike that conveyed by the contents of the file **TextFile**. Now suppose that the following statements are executed:

```
READ(Letter1);
READ(TextFile,Letter2);
READLN;
READ(TextFile,Letter2);
READLN(TextFile);
```

What happens? Well, the first statement will go to the file INPUT, since no other specification is made in the READ statement, and read the letter 'L,' store it in the variable **Letter1**, and then move the input pointer along by one character so that it points to 'i.' **TextFile** is untouched; its input pointer is still under the letter 'W.' The second statement, however, affects **TextFile**, and so in this case, the 'W' is read, stored in **Letter2**, and the input pointer in **TextFile** is moved along so that it is under the letter 'h.' Here, INPUT (the keyboard) is unaffected. The third statement applies to the file INPUT since no file name is given, and its effect is to discard the remainder of the line and position the input pointer under the first character of the next line. Since (assuming the user has not entered more characters) there is no next line at this point, it is hard to describe what goes on in this situation—but you can assume that when and if another line of input is entered at the keyboard, the input pointer will be positioned under the first character. In the meantime, the perceivable effect of the third statement is to discard the remainder of the line "Life is what you make it." Again, this statement has no effect whatsoever on the file **TextFile**.

The fourth and fifth statements above do the following: the 'h' is read from **TextFile**, stored in **Letter2** (obliterating the letter 'W' that was stored there before), and the input pointer for that file is moved along under the 'a.' Input from the keyboard is unaffected. Then the READLN statement discards the remainder of the first line in the file **TextFile** and positions the input pointer at the beginning of the next line. So after executing the statements above, the final situation is:

```
What is Life?<CR>
Life is just<CR>
↑
a bowl of cherries.<CR>
```

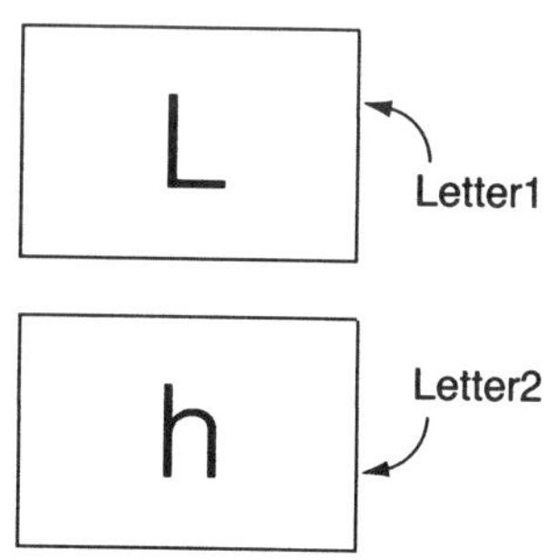

To summarize, the following lists the actions caused by the READ and READLN statements:

1. For each variable in the list associated with the READ or READLN statement, do the following:
   a. Go to the file named in the statement, or to the file INPUT if no file name is specified.

b. Get the next item in the input.
c. Store it in the variable.
d. Advance the input pointer by one character.

READLN includes these steps and adds a final step:

2. Move the input pointer to the beginning of the next input line.

Notice that if no variables are listed in a READLN statement, step 1 is skipped entirely.

EOLN

Carriage return characters can appear in any text file. When a text that is to be stored on a disk is initially typed into the computer, carriage return characters are typically entered at the end of each line. These characters can be detected by using EOLN, just as they were detected in the keyboard input for the previous program. As with the READ statement, when you use EOLN it assumes you are looking for the end-of-line character in the file INPUT unless otherwise specified; so the name of the file must be specified in order to ask the computer to examine the character it is about to read from a file other than INPUT in order to determine if it is the end-of-line character.

If the condition in the WHILE statement in the previous program were modified to apply to a file named 'TextFile,' it would look like this:

```
WHILE NOT EOLN(TextFile) DO BEGIN
```

This can be read roughly as, "while not end-of-line in the file TextFile, do . . ."

As with READ and READLN, the action taken when the condition NOT EOLN (TextFile) is encountered is the same, except that instead of looking into the input from the keyboard to see what is about to be read, the computer looks into the file named TextFile.

EOF

Since your program will be reading many lines from the file, the end-of-line character will not signal the end of the input, as it did in the previous program. (EOLN will still be used in the program, but for a different reason, explained below.) If not, how will the program know when all of the characters in the file have been read?

At the end of every file stored on disk or tape, a special end-of-file marker is inserted to indicate the place where the file ends.

Pascal has a feature called EOF, which is analogous to the EOLN feature, and which can be used to check if the character *about* to be read from a text file is the end-of-file character. It is used in the same way as EOLN; for instance, it could be used as follows to control the behavior of a WHILE loop:

```
WHILE NOT EOF(TextFile) DO ...
```

This statement tells the computer to check the character about to be read from the file TextFile, and if it is *not* the end-of-file character, the statements in the loop are to be executed. If it *is* the end-of-file character, the statements within the loop are to be skipped.

When you read from a file other than INPUT (assuming INPUT is the keyboard), you will always check for EOF before the first READ or READLN statement that reads from the file, and, in general, before any READ or READLN statement that reads from the file.

This check must be made because the end-of-file marker cannot be read, and the attempt to read it causes the system to issue a nasty message and halt your program unceremoniously. Therefore, you must be very circumspect when reading from a file—always look for the end-of-file marker before you leap into the file to read.

CONSTRUCTING THE PROGRAM

Since this program does the same thing as the program in the previous chapter, you do not need to write an entirely new program; instead, you can simply modify last chapter's program to direct the computer to read from a file rather than from the keyboard. So, the first thing to do is to change last chapter's program so that

1. The file name is included in the Program Heading.
2. The file name is declared in the Declarations section with type TEXT.
3. A RESET statement to ready the file for reading is inserted in the Program Statements section.
4. The condition on the WHILE loop reads NOT EOF (TextFile) instead of NOT EOLN.
5. The READ statement includes the name of the file in its list, so that the statement is now READ(TextFile,Letter);

Most of this is very straightforward, but one thing should be considered: the positioning of the RESET statement. RESET is a Pascal *statement* (not a declaration) and therefore must appear in the Program Statements section of the program. But where? Since the statement readies the file for reading, it is clear that it should be executed before the READ statement that reads from the file. But should it appear before the loop or just inside the loop? Well, the file needs to be readied only once. The RESET statement cannot appear within the WHILE NOT EOLN(TextFile) loop, because if it did, each time that loop executes the RESET statement would ready the file to be read *from the beginning*. So, the READ statement inside the loop would read the first character in the file over and over again, and the WRITE statement would print the character over and over again, infinitely. If it isn't clear to you why this is so, write out the program with the RESET statement just inside the WHILE NOT EOLN(TextFile) loop and trace through the program's action, keeping track of the next character to be read from the file at all times.

In general, a RESET statement is executed only once in a program and very often appears at the beginning of the program, since readying a file for reading is essentially a "housekeeping" step. As in life, housekeeping is usually taken care of early in order to get it out of the way.

Another consideration here is the prompt that was issued in the last program instructing the user to enter a line of characters. Obviously, the user will no longer be entering a line of characters—the text is read from the file instead. Therefore, the statement that issues this prompt should be deleted from the program. But if you included additional statements to print a statement of your program's purpose for the user in your original program, don't delete these; instead, modify them to describe the new program.

Looking at the program after these changes have been made, you might assume that the program should now run properly. Given what you know, this is a perfectly reasonable assumption, but unfortunately the program will not work, or at least will not work very well, if a few additional changes are not made. The reason why it will not work hinges on a somewhat strange but simple fact:

The end-of-line character, while perfectly distinguishable when EOLN is used to examine it, is read and stored by a READ or READLN statement as if it were a blank.

To understand why the program will not work with only the modifications mentioned above, trace through the behavior of the program as you have it so far—that is, with only the changes listed above that accommodate reading from a file on disk. Also assume that the file the program reads from contains the following text:

```
I was born in the year 1632, in the City of York,<CR>
of a good family, tho' not of that country, my <CR>
father being a foreigner of Bremen, who settled<CR>
first at Hull.<CR> <EOF>
```

Recall that <CR> stands for the end-of-line (carriage return) character; <EOF> stands for the end-of-file character.

The following happens when the program begins to execute. The Program Header is processed first, thus signalling the beginning of the program. Next the declarations are processed, and as a result a memory location is reserved in main memory that is capable of holding a single character and the name associated with the memory slot is Letter. The computer is also alerted to the fact that the TextFile is the name by which a file that contains characters will be known within the program.

Next the statements in the Program Statements section begin executing. The RESET statement will be the first statement in the program; it causes the file to be readied for reading, thus positioning the input pointer under the first character in the file. The next statement encountered is the WHILE statement, and when this statement is executed the character about to be read is examined. Since it is not the end-of-file character (it is the character 'I,' the first character in the file), the loop is entered. The first character is read from the file and then written to the screen. Control then returns to the top of the loop, and the next character is checked to determine if it is the end-of-file character, and so on.

Now consider what happens when the end of the first line has been reached—that is, just after the comma following the word 'York' has been read and printed. When control returns to the top of the loop, the next character, the end-of-line character, is examined to determine if it is the end-of-file character. Of course it is not, so the loop is entered and the end-of-line character is read in as a *blank* and stored in the variable Letter. This blank is then printed by the WRITE statement to the screen. Control returns once again to the top of the loop, and the next line of characters is read one by one and printed on the screen. Now if by some chance the input text is very short and contains fewer characters than can appear on a single line on the video display screen, the end-of-file character will be encountered before an entire line of output is written and the output will look exactly like the text in the file. But the chances are that the text contains more characters than a line's worth. If so, the output will likely be "wrapped around" onto a new line when the width of the screen is filled, or, on some systems, an error indicating that the output line is too long will be generated and the program will crash.

To solve this problem, all you have to do is to think about the program from the previous chapter in a slightly different way. That program is actually a program to read and write one line of text. This program is to be a program to read and write *several* lines of text—in other words, you need to *repeat* the process of reading a single line over and over again. You know how to make a program repeat something—you enclose the statements that should be repeated in a loop. So in this program, you need to add a loop that surrounds the entire body of the previous program (minus the prompt to enter a sentence, of course, which is not necessary here).

What should the condition on the outer loop (the one surrounding the WHILE NOT EOLN loop) be? Under what circumstances should the outer loop be stopped? The inner loop (the WHILE NOT EOLN loop) stops every time an end-of-line character is about to be read. You want to continue reading lines of text until there are no more lines in the text at all—in other words, you want to repeat the process of reading lines until the program is about to read the end-of-file character. So the condition on the outer loop should be that the loop is to continue as long as the character about to be read is *not* the end-of-file character.

The following algorithmic outline shows the general flow of the program:

1. Ready the file for reading.
2. While the character about to be read is not the end-of-file character, repeat the following:
   a. While the character about to be read is not the end-of-line character, repeat the following:
      (1) Read a character from the file.
      (2) Write the character.
   b. Issue a line eject.

This algorithm lacks only one thing. To discover what it is, and to get an idea of how the program will behave, consider what will happen if this sequence of steps is followed.

Step 1 readies the file for reading. After this, step 2 is encountered, and the first character in the file is examined. If it is not the end-of-file character, the program proceeds to execute steps 2.a through 2.b. In step 2.a, the *same* character (remember that nothing has been read from the file yet) is checked to see if it's the end-of-line character, and if not, the program performs steps 2.a.1 to 2.a.2. A character is then read and stored in main memory, the character is written to the screen, and the program returns to step 2.a. Clearly, steps 2.a.1 and 2.a.2 will be repeated several times, reading and writing the characters on the first line of the text, until the character examined at step 2.a is the end-of-line character. At this point, the first line of the text will have been printed, and the statements in the loop will be skipped, transferring control to step 2.b. Step 2.b causes a line eject to be issued, after which control returns to step 2.

Now consider what happens here. The last character read was the character immediately preceding the end-of-line character. When the end-of-line character was detected in step 2.a, steps 2.a.1 and 2.a.2 were skipped, and nothing was read subsequently. So the character that is about to be read is *still* the end-of-line character. This will cause problems. At step 2, the character is checked for end-of-file, and since it is not the end-of-file character the program will proceed to step 2.a. But at step 2.a, the end-of-line character is detected, causing steps 2.a.1 and 2.a.2 to be skipped. At step 2.b, a line eject is issued, producing a blank line. Control then returns to step 2 again, where the same end-of-line character is checked yet another time; and then the program proceeds to step 2.a, where once again the end-of-line character is detected and steps 2.a.1. and 2.a.2 are subsequently skipped. Another blank line is then written out, and the process repeats again and again, infinitely. Yes, this *is* an example of the proverbial infinite loop.

The solution to the problem is simple. All that really needs to be done is to throw out the end-of-line character and get ready to read the first character of the next line each time the inner loop (consisting of steps 2.a.1 and 2.a.2) ends. With this in mind, the final algorithm for the program can be stated:

1. Ready the file for reading.

2. While the character about to be read is not the end-of-file character, repeat the following:
  - **a.** While the character about to be read is not the end-of-line character, repeat the following:
    - **(1)** Read a character from the file.
    - **(2)** Write the character.
  - **b.** Issue a line eject.
  - **c.** Prepare to read from the beginning of the *next* line of input, by throwing away the carriage return that appears in the input file.

Only the Pascal implementations of steps 2 and 2.c remain to be considered.

Step 2 is the heading of a WHILE loop, the condition of which involves examining the character about to be read to see if it is the end-of-file character. If it is, the loop should not be executed. If it is not, the loop should be entered.

So, just as in the inner loop the condition is NOT EOLN, here the condition is, analogously, NOT EOF. Again, to indicate that a file other than INPUT is to be examined, the name of the file must be inserted following EOF. The heading on the loop will thus be

```
WHILE NOT EOF(TextFile) DO BEGIN
```

assuming that the name of the file with which you are dealing has been specified to be TextFile.

Step 2.c can be implemented by using the Pascal READLN statement, as described earlier in this chapter. As you recall, READLN causes any characters remaining on the current line of input to be discarded, and prepares for reading from the next input line. Here, as elsewhere, the name of the file to which the READLN operation is to be applied must be specified, if it is not to be applied to the default file, INPUT; so the form of the READLN statement that can be used here is

```
READLN(TextFile);
```

The READLN(TextFile); and WRITELN; statements that throw away the carriage return in the file and issue a line eject, respectively, must appear *between* the END of the WHILE NOT EOLN(TextFile) loop and the END of the WHILE NOT EOF(TextFile) loop. The basic outline of the loops' structure is therefore

```
WHILE NOT EOF(TextFile) DO BEGIN
  WHILE NOT EOLN(TextFile) DO BEGIN
                    .
                    .
                    .
  END;      { while not eoln }
      READLN(TextFile);
          WRITELN;
END;      { while not eof }
```

Note the use of comments in the statements above to indicate which BEGIN an END matches.

Mismatched BEGINs and ENDs are one of the most common sources of programming errors that are very difficult to track down. Indenting code and using comments to match BEGINs and ENDs will help to avoid this kind of error.

Many an hour has been spent searching for the missing or misplaced END of a BEGIN; Pascal has a way of blindly taking any END it sees to be the one that matches the last previous BEGIN, which, when an END has been forgotten, can cause some very strange behavior in a program.

Note that the order of the READLN(TextFile); and WRITELN; statements between the two ENDs in the program can be switched with no effect on the program's behavior. Why? Most of the time the sequence of statements within a program is crucial, but here we happen to have two statements whose actions do not interact in any way. The READLN(TextFile); statement affects the file TextFile, and the WRITELN; statement affects what is seen on the screen. It really makes no difference whether you issue a line eject to the screen first and then discard the carriage return in the input file or vice versa.

This completes the program, which in its final form is the following:

```
PROGRAM ReadFile(INPUT,OUTPUT,TextFile);
  { Prints the text contained in TextFile }
  { on the display screen }
VAR Letter : CHAR;
  TextFile : TEXT;
BEGIN
  RESET(TextFile);
  WHILE NOT EOF(TextFile) DO BEGIN
    WHILE NOT EOLN(TextFile) DO BEGIN
      READ(TextFile,Letter);
      WRITE(Letter);
    END;     { while }
    READLN(TextFile);
    WRITELN;
  END;     { while }
END.     { ReadFile }
```

Write it, run it, and if it does not run the first time you try it, trace through the program's behavior step by step as we did above. This is a good way to find the source of errors and learn the computing process at the same time.

SUMMING UP THE PROGRAM

While you are running the program for this chapter in order to debug it, you should use a short text, perhaps consisting of only a few lines. This way you avoid processing thousands of lines of text just to see if your program runs. Once the program is running properly, you can, if you want to, run it using a larger text. Changing the file that your program reads from may involve changing the file name within your program, or you may be able to insert an additional statement in your program to indicate the file that is to be called by the Pascal file name that appears in the Program Heading. In the latter case, only that statement would be changed. The means to associate a particular file with a Pascal file name within a program may vary depending on the computer system you are using, and you should be aware of how this is done before attempting to write this program.

CAUTION! It is easy to forget to insert the name of the file in a READ or READLN statement or after an EOF or EOLN. Since omitting the file name in a READ or READLN statement causes Pascal to assume that you are referring to the file INPUT, your program will simply apply the command to input from the terminal rather than to the file you intend.

Since the program for this chapter demands no input from the keyboard, if you forget the file name in a READ or READLN statement or after an EOF or EOLN, the program will stop and wait for the user to enter something at the terminal. Of course, the user has no way of knowing what is going on and the program will seem to "hang." So if your program seems to sit and do nothing for a long time (or runs only after you hit carriage return), check all of the places where the file name should appear to be sure it does.

NICETIES

A Word About Loops

When a loop is contained inside another loop, it is said to be *nested* inside that loop. A loop that contains another loop is called the *outer loop*, and, of course, the one inside the other is called an *inner loop*. You can nest loops to any degree you like—you can put a loop inside another loop that is inside another loop, and so on.

Nested loops are used often in computer programs, and so if you are unsure of the way they work, it is worth spending some time getting used to them. One way to think about how they work in an abstract way is to think of the inner loop's action as that of the second hand on a clock, and the action of the outer loop as that of the minute hand. For every time the minute hand goes around the clock, the second hand goes around many times. So it is with nested loops. For each time the statements in the outer loop (one of which is the inner loop, of course) are executed, the statements in the inner loop are executed many times. Thus the inner loop can be thought of as going around faster than the outer loop, whose movement is slow and cumbersome by comparison.

Comments

You should now begin to include comments within the text of your programs to explain the function of particular groups of statements. In this program a comment before each loop should be included which explains what the purpose of the loop is. Make sure that your comments do not clutter up the program and make it difficult to read—if necessary, insert blank lines before and after a comment to set it off from the program statements themselves. For example, the main body of your program could look something like this:

```
RESET(TextFile);        { Ready file for reading }
{ Process the entire file }
WHILE NOT EOF(TextFile) DO ...
  { Process a single line }
  WHILE NOT EOLN(TextFile) DO ...
                    .
                    .
                    .
```

You might also want to include comments that explain individual statements, such as the READLN(TextFile); statement that appears below the WHILE NOT EOLN(TextFile) loop, since the reason it is included in the program is not obvious from its form. A comment next to or above this statement saying something like "Throw away the carriage return at the end of the line" would be appropriate.

Writing to Files Other Than OUTPUT

The process of specifying that WRITE or WRITELN statements act upon a file other than the default output file named OUTPUT is almost identical to that for reading from files other than INPUT. The same preliminary steps must be taken:

1. The file name must appear in the Program Header.
2. The file name must be declared in the Declarations section of the program, with the type TEXT.
3. A statement must be inserted to ready the file for writing.

To give an example, suppose that you want to write to a file on disk. Within your program, that file will go by the name 'OutFile.'[3] Your Program Heading would be

```
PROGRAM WriteFile(INPUT,OUTPUT,OutFile);
```

or, if you are also reading from a file named TextFile within the same program,

```
PROGRAM WriteFile(INPUT,OUTPUT,TextFile,OutFile);
```

You can read and write to and from as many files as you want to in a Pascal program, as long as their names appear in the Program Heading and are declared in the Declarations section of the program.

Note that even if you do not use the files INPUT and OUTPUT in your program, it does not hurt to include their names in the Program Heading. Many programmers always include INPUT and OUTPUT in their Program Headings out of habit and because most programs use at least one of these files. However, note that in the basic program for this chapter, INPUT could be eliminated from the Program Heading because no input is read from the keyboard.

Next, OutFile must be declared in the Declarations section of the program with type TEXT, and this is done exactly as the declaration for TextFile was done. Once OutFile is declared, the only remaining preliminary step is to ready the file for writing; this is done not with a RESET statement, but with a REWRITE statement, as follows:

```
REWRITE(OutFile);
```

3. As with input files, your computer system may call your file by a different name from the name you give it within your program. If so, an extra step may be needed to associate the name 'OutFile' (or whatever name you choose) with the file's system name.

This statement appears in the Program Statements section, before the writing of the file is to begin. Like RESET, it typically appears at the beginning of the program since it is fundamentally a "housekeeping" step and because it is usually executed only once, before the real work of the program is done.

Writing to the file is analogous to reading from a file: the name of the file is given as the first item in a list associated with a WRITE or WRITELN statement. So you will have statements like

```
WRITE(OutFile,Letter);
```

or

```
WRITELN(OutFile,Letter);
```

or

```
WRITELN(OutFile);
```

or

```
WRITELN(Outfile,'The Name is ',Name);
```

Any form of WRITE or WRITELN statement is valid with files other than OUTPUT—to your program, all files look the same. You are the only one who knows that the output goes to a disk file rather than a screen.

APPLICATIONS AND CONSIDERATIONS

The applications of reading from a file and writing to the screen or a printer were discussed for the most part at the end of Chapter Two. However, having seen how to write to a file in the Niceties section of the chapter, you can probably understand another simple system function that involves a program like the ones you have seen so far: the copy operation. Most systems include a command that causes the computer system to copy one file to another, which is accomplished simply by reading the characters from one file and copying them into another. Your text editor program probably works along similar lines—it copies the characters you have typed into a file when you are finished entering them. If you use a text formatting program—one which takes as input a text you have typed that includes commands indicating how the text should appear when it is output—you are probably beginning to have an inkling of how that program works as well, since it reads in and writes out your text. The only difference here is that a text formatting program strips out your commands and prints the text according to the specifications in those commands.

EXERCISES

1. Write the program outlined in this chapter.

2. Modify the program outlined in this chapter to write a double spaced version of the text to the display screen—in other words, a blank line should appear after every line in the text.

3. (Slightly more difficult.) Modify the program so that its output goes to a file other than OUTPUT—say, to a file on disk, thus making a copy of the file in another file. The means to write to a file other than OUTPUT are outlined in the Niceties section of the chapter.

4. (For the adventurous programmer.) Modify the program so that before printing the text for the first time, it asks the user if he or she wants to see the printed copy. The user should be instructed to enter any letter followed by a carriage return if he or she wants to see the text, and a carriage return otherwise. After the text is printed, the program should ask if the user wants to see the text a second time, again instructing him or her to enter any character followed by a carriage return to signal yes, and a carriage return to signal no. The program should continue to prompt the user after every printing of the text, stopping only when the user finally enters a carriage return. This is trickier than it looks at first glance, so be careful. Hint: you will have to prompt the user and read his or her response at two places in the program.

4

Counting Letters, Lines, and Sentences

As you recall, anything with which a computer program is to work—whether it is numbers or characters—must be in main memory, and so now that you know how to bring the characters from a text file into main memory, you are ready to write programs that do something more with them. That is, instead of just loading a character into main memory and printing it out, you will write a program that examines the characters that are read in from the file in order to gather information about its components.

The basic problem for this chapter is to write a program that counts the number of letters, the number of lines, and the number of sentences in the text. This information in itself is only marginally interesting, but by extending the program only slightly it can provide important linguistic and stylistic information about the text. For instance, once you know the number of letters and sentences in a text, it is a trivial matter (even for a novice programmer) to divide the number of sentences into the number of letters and find out how many letters, on the average, appear in the sentences in the text. Statistics like this have been used as indications of an author's style; the average length of one author's sentences is often compared to the average length of sentences in a work of dubious authorship, and, based on the assumption that the average should be roughly the same for both texts if both were written by the same person, used to support or refute claims of common authorship. The program could also be extended to provide linguistic information, such as the proportion of vowels to consonants, the percentage of the text composed of particular letters (the letter 'e,' for instance), or, with a little extra effort, the number of words that contain or begin or end with a certain letter or string of letters (a prefix or suffix, for example). The exercises at the end of this chapter suggest even more possibilities. The Applications and Considerations section discusses the ways in which this kind of information has been used in actual literary and linguistic projects.

Before considering the language features that will be needed to count the letters, lines, and sentences in the text, you should get some idea of the steps that will comprise the program. This means that an algorithm must be composed. As will be the case throughout this text, the algorithm for this problem builds on what has been done in previous chapters, so a good place to start is with the algorithm for reading and printing a text.

If you recall, the guts of both the first and second programs involve reading a character, storing it in main memory, and writing it out again. In this program you won't need to write out the characters in the text, since the problem does not call for printing any of the characters of the text. But you will have to read the characters, since in order to examine them they must be brought into main memory. The characters will need to be examined to count how many of them are letters, if the program is to determine the number of letters in the text, and to count the number of lines and sentences as well. So the basis of this algorithm will be a loop to read all of the characters in the text into main memory, one by one, as before.

The rest of the algorithm is easy if you think very carefully about what you would do if someone told you to count all of the letters in a text. Although you might not explain your method quite this explicitly, what you would do is look at each 'item' (letter, digit, blank, etc.) in the text, most likely starting with the first and proceeding to the last, and ask yourself if it is a letter of the alphabet. If so, you would add one to a running total of the letters you had counted so far. If not, you would go on to the next item, and repeat the process. How would you count sentences at the same time? Your method would be similar: if you determined that an item was not a letter, then you would ask if it were one of the punctuation marks that signals the end of a sentence—a period, question mark, or exclamation point. If so, you would add one to a running total of sentences you had counted so far. To count lines, you would add one to a running total every time you encountered the end of a line.

This sequence of steps describes fairly accurately the steps the computer must take to accomplish this task. "Looking at" an item must be translated into the computer's terms, and this will be dealt with in the section of this chapter on Elements of Pascal. For now you should concentrate on the English language algorithm. The algorithm is an elaboration of the one for the previous two programs:

1. Ready the file for reading.
2. While the character about to be read is not the end-of-file character, do the following:
   a. While the character about to be read is not the end-of-line character, do the following:
      (1) Read a character and store it in main memory.

(2) If the character stored in main memory is a letter, add 1 to a running total of the number of letters in the text.
(3) Otherwise, if the character is a period, exclamation point, or question mark, add 1 to a running total of the number of sentences in the text.

b. Prepare to read from the beginning of the next line of input, by throwing away the carriage return that appears in the input file.

This algorithm is very similar to the one used in Chapters Two and Three. The main difference is that after each character is stored in main memory where it can be examined and manipulated by the computer, the algorithm provides for looking at the character to determine whether or not it is something we are interested in. Notice, however, that this algorithm provides only for counting letters and sentences, not for counting lines. The reason for this is that counting lines can't be accomplished by using the same strategy used to count letters and sentences. Your first reaction to this statement might be to say that it can, since there is a recognizable carriage return character—the one that is detected when EOLN is used. Why not just add a step 2.a.4 that says, "otherwise, if the character is a carriage return, add one to a running total of the number of lines in the text"? The answer hinges on the familiar fact that the carriage return character is read and stored as a blank. EOLN, you recall, looks at the character *about* to be read, and when it does, a carriage return is perfectly distinguishable from other characters. If, however, when the input pointer is pointing to a carriage return character, a READ or READLN is issued that contains a CHAR-type variable in its associated list, the carriage return character will be consumed from the input, but a *blank* will be stored in the CHAR-type variable. And you can't add a step to the algorithm that says, "if the character is a blank, add one to a running total of the number of lines in the text," because there is no way of knowing whether a real blank or a carriage return was read. Some other way of knowing when the end of a line has been encountered must be determined.

It probably won't take you long to realize (if you haven't already) that this algorithm already knows when the end of a line has been reached. Specifically, each time the whole of step 2.a is completed, you know that an end-of-line character has been detected because it is only when end-of-line is encountered that the repetition of steps 2.a.1, 2.a.2, and 2.a.3 stops. Just after the loop finishes, then, you know that you have just seen a line in the text, and therefore the algorithm can be modified to provide for adding one to a running total of lines in the text at this point. So, the algorithm is now

1. Ready the file for reading.
2. While the character about to be read is not the end-of-file character, do the following:
   a. While the character about to be read is not the end-of-line character, do the following:
      (1) Read a character and store it in main memory.
      (2) If the character stored in main memory is a letter, add 1 to a running total of the number of letters in the text.
      (3) Otherwise, if the character is a period, exclamation point, or question mark, add 1 to a running total of the number of sentences in the text.
   b. Prepare to read from the beginning of the next line of input, by throwing away the carriage return that appears in the input file.
   c. Add one to a running total of the number of lines.

Notice that step 2.c is taken every time the loop implicit in step 2.a finishes executing, whereas steps 2.a.2 and 2.a.3 are only taken under certain circumstances. This is because we *know* that the end-of-line character has been encountered at this point in the algorithm.

Notice that aside from the addition of steps to deal with counting letters, sentences, and lines, the only difference between this algorithm and the one for the last chapter's program is that here the characters are not written after they are read. That is because this chapter's program does not call for generating a copy of the text. However, the program should generate some kind of output—after all, it would be senseless to go to all the trouble of counting up the number of sentences, letters, and lines in the text without then printing this information so that the user can see it. So, a step needs to be added to the algorithm to provide for displaying these values.

Where should the step that writes the number of lines, letters, and sentences in the text be inserted in the algorithm? Clearly, you must wait until the entire file has been processed before you can write out the total number of lines, letters, and sentences in the text, since these values are not known until each character in the text has been read and examined. Step 2 and all of its sub-steps are the part of the algorithm that processes the file, from beginning to end—after the whole of step 2 is completed, the number of letters, lines, and sentences has been tabulated and can be printed. Therefore you should add step 3 to the algorithm above:

3. Print the number of letters, lines, and sentences.

Now you are ready to look at the elements of the Pascal language necessary to complete the program

ELEMENTS OF PASCAL

Numeric Variables

In order to keep a running total of the number of letters, lines, and sentences in your text, you will have to set up locations in memory designated to hold numbers instead of characters. Up until now you have declared only slots to hold characters. It is possible to store a character that happens to be a digit in a variable of type CHAR, but Pascal will not allow you to perform any arithmetic on in it—for instance, you can read the character '3' into a variable with type CHAR, but you cannot add to it, as you will need to do for this problem.

In Pascal, characters are characters and numbers are numbers, and if you want to treat something like a number, you have to store it in a slot designed to hold numbers.

There are two types of memory slots that hold numbers. One holds an *integer*, or whole number, and one holds a *real* or decimal number, which has digits to the right of the decimal point (even if those digits are zeros). They are declared like this:

```
VAR WholeNumber      : INTEGER;
    FractionalNumber : REAL;
```

The variable WholeNumber can hold any integer, such as 0, −35, 456, −192837, or 2, and FractionalNumber can hold numbers like 0.00, 1.5, −2.567, and so on. To decide when to use which kind of variable, simply consider what it is you'll be doing with it—if you are using it to count letters, for instance, declare the variable with type INTEGER, since you do not need or want digits to the right of the decimal point (obviously, there will be a whole number of letters in the text!). If you are dividing the number of sentences into the number of letters in the text and storing the result in the variable, and if you want to see the result to more than whole number precision, declare the variable in which the result will be stored with type REAL. The result of the division will yield a number with digits to the right of the decimal point, and by storing the result in a REAL variable, those digits will be retained and can be printed for your inspection.

Assignment Statements

The only means you have seen so far for storing something in a variable is the READ statement. The READ statement is used to bring in values from 'outside' (from the computer's point of view, of course). There is one other way to store values, which does not go outside but rather gets a value from within the program, called the *assignment statement*. Assignment statements have the following form:

```
ThisOne := <expression>;
```

- ThisOne is the name of the memory location in which the value is to be stored.
- ':=' is called the *assignment operator*. It indicates to the computer that what you are doing is assigning a value to the variable named on the left side of the assignment operator. *Note: the colon and equal sign are an entity; be sure not to put a blank between them.*
- *<expression>* can be any of several things, depending on the type of the variable on the left of the assignment operator; the simplest case is the one in which *<expression>* is a specific value. For example,

  ```
  ThisOne := 0;
  ```

  causes the value 0 (zero) to be stored in the variable ThisOne, replacing any value that was previously stored there. But note that the value 0 can be stored in ThisOne *only* if ThisOne has been declared with type INTEGER, since 0 is an integer value; that is:

The value that is stored in any variable must be of the same type as that with which the variable is declared.

- *<expression>* can be replaced by several other things, some of which will be shown below in the section on arithmetic expressions, and some of which will be discussed in the Niceties section at the end of the chapter.

The READ statement and the assignment statement are the only means by which values can be stored in main memory from within a computer program. Other statements access the values that are stored in memory; only READ and assignment statements can change them.

As a result of this, when a variable name appears on the left side of an assignment operator or in the list associated with a READ statement, the variable name refers to a particular *memory slot* where a value is to be stored. In all other contexts, a variable name effectively stands for or is replaced by the *value* that is stored in the memory slot with which the name is associated.

Arithmetic Operations

When the computer performs an arithmetic operation, the result is most often stored in a REAL or INTEGER variable. So arithmetic operations typically appear in assignment statements, where the variable on the left of the assignment operator is, as always, the slot in main memory where the result is to be stored, and the right side indicates the operation or operations to be performed. For example, if you want to add two and two and store the result in the type INTEGER variable ThatOne, use the statement

```
ThatOne := 2 + 2;
```

If you want to subtract one from the contents of the INTEGER variable ThisOne, and store the result in ThatOne, use

```
ThatOne := ThisOne - 1;
```

Notice that in this statement, any previous contents of the variable ThatOne are replaced by the results of the operation; the variable ThisOne, however, remains unchanged. The value of ThisOne is *used* in the operation, but it is not affected by it. Only the variable on the left side of the assignment operator is changed.

Considering this, what do you think the effect of the following statement would be?

```
ThisOne := ThisOne + 1;
```

This statement causes the computer to take the value currently stored in the variable ThisOne, add one to it, and store the result back into the variable ThisOne, which erases the previous contents. This is simply a way to add one to a value stored in memory.

Statements in the same form as the one above that adds 1 to ThisOne are used often in computer programs, because it is very common to use INTEGER-type variables as counters of one thing or another. Therefore, you should be sure to understand thoroughly how and why a statement like this works.

The sign for multiplication is an asterisk (*). So, a statement to multiply the value stored in ThisOne by the value stored in ThatOne, and store the result in the variable AnotherOne would be

```
AnotherOne := ThisOne * ThatOne;
```

For division, Pascal has an unusual convention. A distinction is made between two types of division: one which yields a REAL result, which includes numbers to the right of the decimal point; and one which yields an integer result, calculating only how many times one value goes into another and throwing any remainder away. For this problem, and probably for most cases where you want division in a computer program, REAL division is preferable, because in most cases it is necessary or at least desirable to see the digits to the right of the decimal point in the result of the division. INTEGER division will be covered in the Niceties section at the end of the chapter.

REAL division looks familiar:

```
YetAnotherOne := ThatOne / 3;
```

This statement divides the value stored in the variable ThatOne by 3, and stores the result (including digits to the right of the decimal point) in the variable YetAnotherOne.[1] It is important to note here that the variable YetAnotherOne *must* be a type REAL variable. If YetAnotherOne is an INTEGER variable, the computer will attempt to put a REAL result in an INTEGER slot, which, of course, won't work. Note also that in this example, the dividend (the variable ThatOne) and the divisor (3) are both of type INTEGER.

The dividend and the divisor in an expression involving REAL division can be of type REAL or type INTEGER. It is valid to have a dividend of type REAL and a divisor of type INTEGER, and vice versa.

More complex arithmetic operations can be performed, involving longer and more involved expressions and more sophisticated operations like square root and cosine. A list of Pascal functions for complex arithmetic operations is given in Appendix B.

1. This is a good place to note that the computer will store real values in a REAL-type variable with several digits to the right of the decimal point. Except for highly technical work, the user typically wants to see only one or two digits to the right of the decimal point. As you will see below, although the computer will always store many digits to the right of the decimal point, when it comes time to print the value you can request as many or as few decimal places as you want to see.

Printing Numbers

When the contents of a variable of type INTEGER or REAL are printed out with a WRITE or WRITELN statement, the computer inserts extra blanks at the left of the number unless you tell it to do otherwise. For instance, if you declare a variable ThisOne with type INTEGER and subsequently say

```
WRITELN(ThisOne);
```

the following will be printed if ThisOne contains the value 23:

```
|        23
```

where '|' represents the left side of the page. There are eight blank spaces between the left margin and the number 23. (This example assumes, of course, that no previous WRITE statements produced output that would appear previously on the same line.) Pascal always uses ten spaces when it prints integers, filling the spaces that are not taken up by the number itself with blanks. So if you print the value 4569, six spaces will appear to its left, and if you print 2, nine spaces will appear to its left.

Most of the time you will not want those extra spaces to appear, and, fortunately, Pascal gives you a way to control how many spaces appear to the right of a number when it is printed. In the WRITE or WRITELN statement, following the variable's name in the list, you can insert a colon followed by a number indicating the number of spaces to use when the number is printed; for example,

```
WRITE(ThisOne:4);
```

Now four spaces will be used for the number, and as before, extra spaces not used by the number are printed as blanks. If ThisOne contains the value 23, this WRITE statement will cause two blanks followed by the number 23 to be printed.

What if the number takes up more spaces than indicated in the width specification in the WRITE statement? Not to worry; Pascal expands the number of spaces just enough so that the number fits. This is an extremely important point that holds the key to the method most Pascal programmers use for printing numbers. Since you do not necessarily know how many spaces the value stored in some variable will take up, there is no sense in trying to specify a width to accommodate it exactly. And most of the time, you will not want to see any blanks to the left of the number. The solution is to specify a width of one; Pascal will then always stretch the width just enough to accommodate the number. For example, if ThisOne contains the value 423, the statement

```
WRITELN('The number is ',ThisOne:1);
```

will print

```
The number is 423
```

stretching the specified field width of 1 just wide enough to accommodate the number 423. Notice that the literal string 'The number is ' includes a blank at its right-most side, so that the blank will separate the phrase from the value itself. So, once again,

---

When you write a number, the field width specification will almost always be 1, because this is the only way to be sure that blanks are not printed to the left of the number.

Pascal's treatment of real values is even more peculiar. If no width is specified by the user in the manner shown above, 12 spaces are used, and the number is printed out in what is called *scientific notation* or *floating-point form*. It looks something like this:

```
|    -3.27064E+02
```

This actually represents the number −327.064. But fortunately, real numbers can be printed in a more readable format.

As with integer variables, real variables can be followed in a list associated with a WRITE or WRITELN statement by a colon and a number indicating how many spaces should be used when the number is printed. Again, a width that is too small to accommodate the number will cause Pascal to expand the field enough so that the number will fit. In addition, a second colon and a second number can appear that indicate how many digits to the right of the decimal point are to be printed. This is a signal to Pascal to abandon scientific notation and print the number in a more usual format. For example, the statement

```
WRITELN(Average:1:2);
```

will cause the following to be printed if Average contains the value 327.068:

```
327.06
```

The first number after the variable name, 1, indicates the total number of spaces to be used to print the *entire* number, including the digits to the right of the decimal point. Since one space is obviously inadequate, the width is expanded enough to accommodate the number. The second number, 2, indicates how many digits should appear to the right of the decimal point.

Unlike the first number in the field width specification for a real number, Pascal takes the second one literally and prints only the number of digits indicated to the right of the decimal point. Any digits to the right of the decimal point that do not fit are simply not printed.

Notice that an '8' was lost at the end of the number above, also that the 8 was simply chopped off, and the remaining value was not rounded to reflect this loss.

More information about formatting is included in the Niceties section at the end of this chapter.

IF-THEN and IF-THEN-ELSE Statements

For this chapter's problem, you will need a means to tell the computer to add one to a running total only under certain conditions—that is, when the character just read is a letter or punctuation mark indicative of the end of a sentence. This can be accomplished with the Pascal IF-THEN statement.

Like the WHILE statement, the IF-THEN statement instructs the computer to check a condition (for example, NOT EOF or NOT EOLN, which you used in your last program) and, on the basis of the results, proceed to one of two possible locations in the program. In the case of WHILE, as you recall, if the condition is true the program will execute the first statement inside the loop next; if the condition is false, the first statement *following* the loop is executed next. The IF-THEN statement works in a similar way: a condition is checked, and if it is true the statement "inside" the IF-THEN statement is executed next; otherwise, the next statement executed is the one immediately following the IF-THEN statement. A look at the general form of the statement may make this clearer. Its form is

```
IF <condition> THEN BEGIN
  <statement or statements>
END;
```

If the condition is true, the statement or statements inside the BEGIN-END are executed, after which the program continues on to the statement following the END.

The IF-THEN statement is not a loop like WHILE—it does not provide for the repetition of statements as the WHILE loop does. The IF-THEN statement says, in essence, "if the condition is true, execute these statements once and continue on; otherwise, skip these statements."

After the END of a WHILE loop is reached, control returns to the top of the loop and the condition on the WHILE statement is re-evaluated; then the statement in the loop may be repeated. But after the END of an IF-THEN statement is reached, the statement following the END is executed and there is no return to the beginning of the IF-THEN statement. So statements within an IF-THEN statement are not repeated *unless the IF-THEN statement is itself inside a loop.*

There is a variation on the IF-THEN statement which provides a slightly different way to govern which statements are executed and which are skipped. This is the IF-THEN-ELSE statement. Its form is

```
IF <condition> THEN BEGIN
  <statement or statements>
END
ELSE BEGIN
  <statement or statements>
END;
```

It works like this: if the condition is *true*, the statements between THEN BEGIN and the first END are executed. If the condition is *false*, the statements between the ELSE BEGIN and the second END are executed. In either case, the computer then continues on to the statement following the whole IF-THEN-ELSE statement (that is, the statement after the second END) once it has finished.

Whereas with IF-THEN the statements involved were simply either executed or skipped, with IF-THEN-ELSE one or the other of the sets of statements is always executed.

Note also that

The statements that appear between THEN BEGIN and END or ELSE BEGIN and END can be any of the valid Pascal statements, including IF-THEN and IF-THEN-ELSE statements, WHILE statements, and so on.

You should note that there is no semicolon following the first END in an IF-THEN-ELSE statement, whereas the END in the corresponding location in the IF-THEN statement has one. This is because the IF-THEN statement ends after the first END, whereas the IF-THEN-ELSE statement does not end until the second END appears.

If you accidentally insert a semicolon following the first END in an IF-THEN-ELSE statement, your program will generate an error because the computer will think that you are using IF-THEN instead of IF-THEN-ELSE, and it will wonder what the keyword ELSE is doing at the beginning of a separate statement.

Be careful! This is a common error.

The accompanying pictorial representation of the flow of events in IF-THEN and IF-THEN-ELSE statements might be helpful to understand how these statements work.

Together with the loop, IF-THEN and IF-THEN-ELSE are the most pervasive constructs in any program. The ability to repeat statements and the ability to choose between statements are the basis of the computer's power. You will use these constructs extensively, since there are actually no others.[2] So you should begin to think in terms of these statements whenever you attempt to translate some problem into an algorithm.

2. You will see in later chapters that the Pascal language includes other statements that provide variations on the basic processes of repetition and choice. For instance, another form of the loop checks the condition at the end of the loop rather than the beginning, and there is also a statement to allow for a choice among several alternative sets of statements instead of just two, as with IF-THEN-ELSE. But underlying all of these variations are the fundamental processes of repetition and choice.

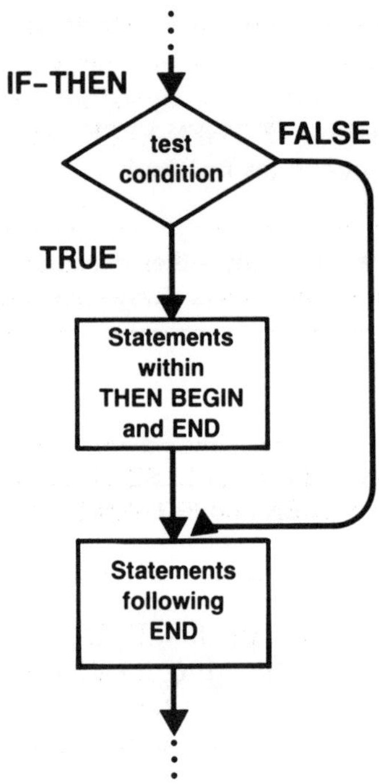

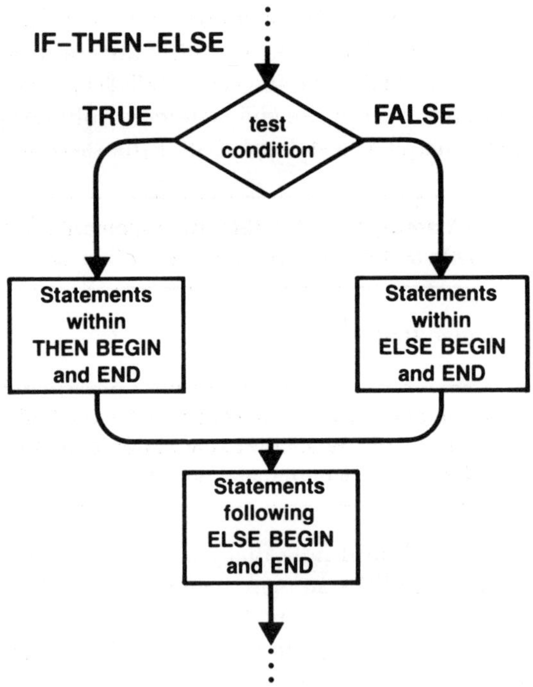

The Boolean Operator IN

Recall that one of the steps in the algorithm outlined at the beginning of the chapter is "if the character just read is a letter, add one to a running total of the number of letters seen so far." Given the discussion above of IF-THEN-ELSE, you should have at least an inkling that this is what you'll use to express this step in Pascal. You can re-cast the wording of the step in terms of the IF-THEN statement:

```
IF the character is a letter THEN BEGIN
  add one to a running total of letters
END;
```

Now you will have to learn how to express the condition in Pascal.

As in most computer languages, typical conditions in Pascal are expressed in terms of concepts like equality, inequality, less than, greater than, and so on.[3] So you will often see conditions like 'A = B' and 'A < B' (where 'A' and 'B' are variables and '<' stands for "less than"). Given this, it would be easy for you to establish a condition like

```
Letter = 'a'
```

where Letter is a variable of type CHAR and 'a' is a way to identify the character 'a' in a Pascal program. So, this condition can be read as, "the contents of the

3. See the Niceties section at the end of this chapter for a discussion of valid conditions in Pascal.

variable Letter are equal to the character 'a.'" (Recall that conditions are assertions of some fact, which is then judged to be either true or false.)

You cannot specify a *range* of values—like 'A through Z'—on one side of the equal sign in a condition like the one above, so it is impossible to specify a condition like, "Letter is equal to any letter of the alphabet." Fortunately, Pascal provides a way to deal with this situation with a minimum of hassle. A condition can be expressed as

```
Letter IN ['a'..'z','A'..'Z']
```

This can be read as, "Letter is IN the group of items consisting of the following: the letters 'a' through 'z' and the letters 'A' through 'Z.'"

There are several things to consider in order to understand and use this kind of statement:

- You must use square brackets (not curly brackets—they indicate a comment) to enclose the list following the keyword IN.
- The double dots (no space between) are a way of specifying a range of values that are sequential. So 'a'..'z' represents all of the letters from 'a' to 'z.' It may surprise you to know that the computer knows the alphabet—that is, that it recognizes that 'a' comes before 'b,' and so on. It does, but only because human beings arranged for it to do so. Since the computer deals only in numbers internally, all characters are represented by a numeric value. The numeric values associated with the alphabetic characters were deliberately assigned sequentially, so that 'a' is represented by a number that is one less than the number for 'b,' and so on. Different numbers are assigned to the lower and upper case letters so that the computer sees them as distinct, but within each set the numbers are sequential. This is why you must specify both the range of values between 'a' and 'z' and 'A' and 'Z.'

  The internal representation of characters is discussed more fully in Chapter Seven.
- Note that the single quotation mark is used around the letters. As in WRITE and WRITELN statements, Pascal regards anything surrounded by single quotation marks as *literal*—that is, indicative of the character or characters that appear. If the single quotation marks were not used here, Pascal would interpret the letters as variable names.
- The double dots are an entity and therefore must not be separated by a blank.
- Each of the two ranges 'a'..'z' and 'A'..'Z' is actually a member of a list of items that are considered to be in the group under consideration. That is why they are separated by a comma. The items in the list can be either individual characters or ranges, as in the example.[4] For example, if you want to specify the condition that Letter is a vowel, you could say

```
Letter IN ['a','e','i','o','u','A','E','I','O','U']
```

4. See the Niceties section for an explanation of how IN can be used with a variable of type INTEGER and a list of integer values.

Or, to assert that Letter is a punctuation mark, say

```
Letter IN ['.',',',';',':','?','!']
```

Note that *only literal values* (or constants—see Chapter Five) can appear in such a list; variables cannot be used in this context.

CONSTRUCTING THE PROGRAM

You now have all the tools necessary to solve this chapter's problem, and you can turn to implementing the steps required to solve the problem to count letters, lines, and sentences in Pascal. To start, recall the algorithm for the problem:

1. Ready the file for reading.
2. While the character about to be read is not the end-of-file character, do the following:
   - **a.** While the character about to be read is not the end-of-line character, do the following:
     - **(1)** Read a character and store it in main memory.
     - **(2)** If the character stored in main memory is a letter, add 1 to a running total of the number of letters in the text.
     - **(3)** Otherwise, if the character is a period, exclamation point, or question mark, add 1 to a running total of the number of sentences in the text.
   - **b.** Prepare to read from the beginning of the next line of input, by throwing away the carriage return that appears in the input file.
   - **c.** Add one to a running total of the number of lines.
3. Print the number of letters, lines, and sentences.

Before modifying the program from last chapter to implement the new parts of the algorithm in Pascal, some attention must be given to basic housekeeping that must be done in order to implement the algorithm. First, you should ask yourself if any new variables will be needed in this program. To determine this, you can look at the algorithm itself. Consider the steps in the algorithm that say to add one to a running total. You will need to declare a separate variable to hold each of your running totals—there are three for this problem, so you will need to declare three INTEGER-type variables in the Declarations section of the program. To make your program as readable as possible, give them names that help the reader of your program understand what the variables do—for instance, you might name the variable that is used to count sentences "SentenceCounter," the variable used to count letters "LetterCounter," and the variable used to count lines "LineCounter." Each of these variables should be given the type INTEGER. So you should add a declaration like the following to the end of the Declarations section of your program:

```
SentenceCounter,LetterCounter,LineCounter : INTEGER;
```

This line should be *added* to the end of the Declarations section of your program—the declarations of the variable Letter and the file TextFile must stay in the program because this program will read each of the characters from the file TextFile into Letter just as the previous one did. SentenceCounter, Letter-

Counter, and LineCounter are the only new variables that are needed in this program.

Another bit of housekeeping needs to be taken care of, but this will affect the Program Statements section of the program. Recall that the RESET statement in the previous program was said to be a housekeeping step because it prepared the scene for the actual work of the program by setting up the file. As you will soon see, it is often necessary to set up *variables* at the beginning of a program as well, to ready them for use by the central parts of the program. To see why, you will need to step back momentarily and think some more about INTEGER-type variables and their declarations.

When INTEGER-type variables are declared as in the example above, a memory slot is reserved for each one that is capable of holding an integer value. Each of the slots is also associated with one of the names in the list, and this name will be used to refer to the memory slot throughout the remainder of the program. Just after a variable is declared, what are the contents of the memory slot? You guessed it—*nothing*, except perhaps some junk left over from the last time the slot was used.[5]

A variable that has been declared but to which no value has yet been assigned within the program is called an undefined variable.

Now, within the body of the program you are in the process of constructing, you will need a statement like the following to add one to your running totals:

```
SentenceCounter := SentenceCounter + 1;
```

This statement takes the current contents of the variable SentenceCounter, adds one to it, and stores the result back in the variable SentenceCounter. The question you should next ask yourself is, what happens when I attempt to add one to the current contents of SentenceCounter the first time, if nothing has yet been stored in it? Three possibilities exist. Most likely, you'll get an error message saying that the variable is undefined and that it is therefore impossible to add one to it. A less friendly computer system will just add one to whatever happens to be left in the memory slot from its previous use—and you can be sure it will be some ridiculous number—and go merrily on its way. If this is the case, your program will run, but when you print out your final values the numbers will undoubtedly be absurd. A third possibility is that everything will work perfectly, because your version of Pascal very accommodatingly assigns the value 0 to any variable declared with type INTEGER as soon as it is declared. If so you are lucky, but it is very bad practice to rely on the good nature of your computer system for such things. The moral is that you should and in most cases must give each of the variables that is used as a counter an appropriate starting value, so that when 1 is added to it, there will be something stored in the variable to add 1 to. What starting value should you give to your counter variables? Zero, of

5. Some computer systems will automatically store the value 0 in an INTEGER-type variable at the time it is declared. More will be said about this below.

course, since initially that is the number of items you have counted. To give a variable to the value 0, use an assignment statement; for example, the assignment statement

```
SentenceCounter := 0;
```

gives the variable SentenceCounter the value 0. If this statement appears before SentenceCounter has been given any other value within a program, then this statement is said to *initialize* the variable.

One way to determine whether or not a variable needs to be initialized is to look at the first statement in the Program Statements section of the program that uses the variable. If the variable appears on the left side of an assignment operator (:=) only (not on both the left and right sides) or in a READ or READLN statement, then it does not need to be initialized, because by assignment or reading a value is being given to the variable. In any other case, an initial value should be assigned.

For instance, the variable Letter does not need to be initialized because its first appearance in the program is in a READ statement, which gives the variable a value. Giving Letter an initial value would be superfluous, since the READ operation obliterates its previous contents.

Like the RESET statement, initializing statements are fundamentally housekeeping steps that are taken care of first in the program, because they are executed only once and need to be executed before the main action of the program is underway. So, the first statements in the Program Statements section of this chapter's program will be the RESET statement and the statements that initialize the counters SentenceCounter, LetterCounter, and LineCounter, like this:

```
RESET(TextFile);     { ready the file }
  { initialize counters }
SentenceCounter := 0;
LetterCounter := 0;
LineCounter := 0;
              .
              .
              .
```

The order within the set of statements above is unimportant, since the action of none of the four statements affects the same variable or file.

Housekeeping taken care of, you can now turn your attention to step 2 of the algorithm and all of its sub-steps. Most of these steps have been implemented in Pascal already—you need to deal only with steps 2.a.2, 2.a.3, and 2.c (along with step 3) to complete the program. Steps 2.a.2 and 2.a.3 will be considered together.

Steps 2.a.2 and 2.a.3 say

2.a.2 If the character is a letter, add one to a running total of the number of letters in the text.

2.a.3 *Otherwise,* if the character is a period, question mark, or exclamation point, add one to a running total of the number of sentences in the text.

To translate this into Pascal, you might envision two IF-THEN statements, each handling one of the steps above. This will work, but consider this: if two IF-THEN statements appear, one after the other, the following will occur: the condition in the first IF-THEN statement will be checked. If true, 1 will be added to the counter for letters; if false, the statement to add 1 to the counter for letters will be skipped. In either case, the next statement executed will be the following IF-THEN statement, since it is next in the sequential flow of the program. So the character will be checked again, this time to see if it is a terminating punctuation mark. This is fine if the character is not a letter, but if the character *is* a letter, checking it again to see if it is a punctuation mark is superfluous, even though it will not do any harm.

It would be nice to avoid this superfluous action, if possible. What you want to say is something like this: if the character is a letter (the condition is *true*), add one to the letter counter; if it is not a letter (the condition is *false*), check if it is a terminating punctuation mark; if it is, add one to the sentence counter. Looking at the beginning of this paraphrase, what you have is a situation where you have two alternatives, and you want to take one or the other of them—either add one to the letter counter or go on to check if the character is a punctuation mark. And as you no doubt recall, the IF-THEN-ELSE statement is designed specifically for this situation. So you can construct a statement along the following lines:

```
IF the character is a letter THEN BEGIN
  Add one to the letter counter
END
ELSE BEGIN
  If the character is a terminating punctuation mark, add one to the sentence
  counter
END;
```

Translating the statement following the ELSE BEGIN into something even more like Pascal, you have

```
IF the character is a letter THEN BEGIN
  Add one to the letter counter
END
ELSE BEGIN
  IF the character is a terminating punctuation mark THEN BEGIN
    Add one to the sentence counter
  END;
END;
```

(Remember, any statement can appear in an IF-THEN or IF-THEN-ELSE statement, including another IF-THEN or IF-THEN-ELSE.) With this statement the character is checked to see if it is a terminating punctuation mark only if it is found not to be a letter, since the statements that are associated with the ELSE part of the IF-THEN-ELSE statement are executed only when the condition is false. Think through this statement carefully to be sure you understand how it works.

You should use IF-THEN-ELSE instead of two IF-THEN statements whenever you can, to avoid needless checking and increase your program's efficiency.

One or two other things about the IF-THEN-ELSE statement above deserve mention. First, notice where the semicolons appear. Since the IF-THEN statement within the ELSE BEGIN is a separate statement, it is followed by a semicolon. You can think of this IF-THEN statement as "nested" inside the other, encompassing IF-THEN-ELSE statement, just as loops can be nested within one another. Semicolons will also appear at the ends of the statements that add to the counters. Second, notice the indentation. The parts of the statement are clearly identifiable, and it is easy to tell where the THEN and ELSE parts begin and end. Indentation like this makes your program easier to read *and* easier to debug, since you can see what goes with what, and you can see that your ENDs are matched with BEGINs, etc. You can vary this format to your liking—some people like to put the THEN on the same line as the IF, for example—the point is that you should be able to identify what goes with the THEN and what goes with the ELSE.

How should the conditions on the IF-THEN-ELSE and IF-THEN statements above be implemented in Pascal? Look first at the IF-THEN-ELSE statement. The condition specified in algorithmic language is "the character is a letter." Now, assume that each character as it is read from the input file is stored in the variable Letter. To assert that the character stored in the variable Letter is a letter of the alphabet, you can say

```
Letter IN ['a'..'z','A'..'Z']
```

Similarly, the assertion that the character stored in the variable Letter is a period, question mark, or exclamation point can be expressed as

```
Letter IN ['.','?','!']
```

Putting these two assertions into the IF-THEN-ELSE statement yields

```
IF Letter IN ['a'..'z','A'..'Z'] THEN BEGIN
   Add one to the letter counter
END
ELSE BEGIN
   IF Letter IN ['.','?','!'] THEN BEGIN
      Add one to the sentence counter
   END;
END;
```

The last part of step 2 that needs to be dealt with is counting the number of lines in the text—step 2.c in the algorithm. All that is needed is to insert a statement to add one to the counter keeping track of the number of lines in the appropriate place in the program—as indicated in the algorithm, the appropriate place is just after the END of the inner WHILE NOT EOLN(TextFile) loop and just before the END of the outer WHILE NOT EOF(TextFile) loop. So the overall structure of the statements corresponding to step 2 in the algorithm is

```
WHILE NOT EOF(TextFile) DO BEGIN
  WHILE NOT EOLN(TextFile) DO BEGIN
    READ(TextFile,Letter);
    IF Letter IN ['a'..'z','A'..'Z'] THEN BEGIN
      Add one to the letter counter
    END { then begin }
    ELSE BEGIN
      IF Letter IN ['.','?','!'] THEN BEGIN
        Add one to the sentence counter
      END;     { then begin }
    END;     { else begin }
  END;     { while not eoln }
  Add one to the line counter
  READLN(TextFile);
END;     { while not eof }
```

Remember that you don't need to include a WRITE statement inside the WHILE NOT EOLN(TextFile) loop, since each character in the text will need to be read—but not written—in this program

The steps that add 1 to the letter, sentence, and line counters in the outline above will be implemented as simple assignment statements of the form given earlier. Thus to complete the Pascal implementation of this part of the algorithm, you must insert the statements

```
LetterCounter := LetterCounter + 1;
```

and

```
SentenceCounter := SentenceCounter + 1;
```

and

```
LineCounter := LineCounter + 1;
```

in the appropriate places within the framework above.

Finally, you have to implement step 3, the part of the algorithm that prints the final tally of the number of letters, lines, and sentences in the text. The statement or statements that do this (you can do it in either one or several statements), of course, appear *following* the set of statements that implement step 2—that is, after the END of the *outer* WHILE loop—since it is not until the WHILE NOT EOF(TextFile) loop completes executing that the entire file has been processed. Obviously, WRITE and/or WRITELN statements will be used here, and the exact statements to use are left to you to decide. In doing so you should give a lot of thought to the appearance of your program's output. Since the text itself is not being printed, the only information that will appear on the screen is the number of letters, the number of lines, and the number of sentences in the text. Now if your program simply prints three numbers, you may know what they represent, but you should write your programs for a user other than yourself—one who is not intimately familiar with its internal workings. Therefore, it is imperative that you provide a message along with each of the numbers that indicates what it represents. For instance, the output might look like this:

```
The number of letters in the text is 3948.
The number of sentences in the text is 76.
The number of lines in the text is 185.
```

To do this, you can simply include three items in the list associated with the WRITELN statement to print each of these lines out: the literal string that describes the number, the variable whose contents are to be printed out, and the literal string that follows the number—that is, the period. The statement to print the first line above would look like this:

```
WRITELN('The number of letters in the text is ',LetterCounter:1,'.');
```

Recall that specifying a field width of 1 for the variable LetterCounter causes Pascal to widen the space just enough to fit the number. Notice also that a blank appears within and at the end of the literal string preceding LetterCounter. Without that blank the line would look like this:

```
The number of letters in the text is3948.
```

By the way, the same output could be printed with the following three statements:

```
WRITE('The number of letters in the text is ');
WRITE(LetterCounter);
WRITELN('.');
```

The final program will look like this:

```
PROGRAM Count(INPUT,OUTPUT,TextFile);
  { Prints the number of letters, lines, and sentences }
  { in TextFile }
  VAR Letter : CHAR;
    LetterCounter, SentenceCounter, LineCounter : INTEGER;
    TextFile : TEXT;
BEGIN
  RESET(TextFile);
  WHILE NOT EOF(TextFile) DO BEGIN
    WHILE NOT EOLN(TextFile) DO BEGIN
      READ(TextFile,Letter);
      IF Letter IN ['a'..'z','A'..'Z'] THEN BEGIN
        LetterCounter := LetterCounter + 1;
      END     { then begin }
```

```
        ELSE BEGIN
          IF Letter IN ['.','?','!'] THEN BEGIN
            SentenceCounter := SentenceCounter + 1;
          END;     { then begin }
        END;     { else begin }
      END;     { while not eoln }
      LineCounter := LineCounter + 1;
      READLN(TextFile);
    END;     { while not eof }
              .
              .
              .
    Statements to write the results
              .
              .
              .
  END.     { Count }
```

SUMMING UP THE PROGRAM

Now that you have added IF-THEN and IF-THEN-ELSE statements, assignment statements, and arithmetic operations to your programming repertoire, the variety of problems you are capable of solving has increased dramatically. From now on, the programs that you write will be bigger and much more sophisticated, but the number of new language features you will learn will be relatively few. The problems you will solve in the remaining chapters will be more challenging and provide the means to accomplish genuinely useful tasks, tasks which can contribute significantly to the exploration of the linguistic, stylistic, syntactic, and semantic attributes of a text.

NICETIES

More About IF-THEN and IF-THEN-ELSE

Like WHILE, IF-THEN and IF-THEN-ELSE statements use the BEGIN-END construct, but if only one statement follows the BEGIN associated with the THEN or ELSE part of the statement, the BEGIN and END can be omitted. So, you can say

```
IF <condition>
  THEN <statement>;
```

or

```
IF <condition>
  THEN <statement>
  ELSE <statement>;
```

or

```
IF <condition>
  THEN <statement>
  ELSE BEGIN
    <statements>
  END;
```

or

```
IF <condition>
  THEN BEGIN
    <statements>
  END
  ELSE <statement>;
```

Although they can be omitted in these cases, BEGIN and END are always used in the examples throughout this book because, as explained earlier in connection with the WHILE statement, they do no harm if they appear with only one statement, and it is easier to remember one way of doing things than two. Also, it is easy to forget to insert the BEGIN and END if you add a statement to the THEN or ELSE part of your IF-THEN or IF-THEN-ELSE statement. However, none of the IF-THEN and IF-THEN-ELSE statements involved in this problem have more than one statement in any of their parts, and so you may find it more convenient to omit the BEGIN-END pairs.

More About IN

Earlier in the chapter you saw how to use IN in association with a character variable and a list of character values. IN can be used with a variable of type INTEGER and a list of integer values as well; for example,

```
ThisOne IN [1,2,5,7,9]
```

asserts that the value stored in the variable ThisOne is one of the values 1, 2, 5, 7, or 9. A range can be specified as well:

```
ThisOne IN [0..9]
```

asserts that the value stored in the variable ThisOne is included in the range of values from 0 to 9.

The Pascal CASE Statement

Suppose that you wanted to modify the program in this chapter to count up, separately, the number of times each of the vowels, ‘a,’ ‘e,’ ‘i,’ ‘o,’ and ‘u’ appear in the text. How would you go about it? You could set up a whole series of IF-THEN statements, each one of which would check for one of the vowels and provide for adding one to the appropriate counter if it is identified. However, Pascal, which was designed to be reasonably kind to programmers, provides an easier way to do this, with what is called the CASE statement.

The CASE statement looks like this:

```
CASE Letter OF
  'a','A'  :  BEGIN
                CounterA := CounterA + 1;
              END;
  'e','E'  :  BEGIN
                CounterE := CounterE + 1;
              END;
  'i','I'  :  BEGIN
                CounterI := CounterI + 1;
              END;
  'o','O'  :  BEGIN
                CounterO := CounterO + 1;
              END;
  'u','U'  :  BEGIN
                CounterU := CounterU + 1;
              END;     { case }
END;
```

Its parts are as follows:

- The heading, CASE Letter OF, tells the computer to look at the value currently stored in the variable Letter.
- 'a','A' is a *list* of values. If the value stored in Letter is one of these values, *the statement or statements following the colon is executed, and the rest are skipped.*

That describes, basically, how the CASE statement works. The value of whatever appears in the heading (between CASE and OF) is checked against the values specified in the various lists within the CASE statement. If it matches one of them, the statement or statements associated with that value are executed. Now for the bad news: if it doesn't match one of them, you might get an error, depending on the version of Pascal you are using. To solve this, you can enclose your entire CASE statement in an IF-THEN statement so that the CASE statement is executed only if you know that the value you are testing is among those within the CASE statement. For example, the CASE statement above could be modified in this way to be

```
IF Letter IN ['a','A','e','E','i','I','o','O','u','U']
  THEN BEGIN
    CASE Letter OF
      'a','A'  : BEGIN
                   CounterA := CounterA + 1;
                 END;
      'e','E'  : BEGIN
                   CounterE := CounterE + 1;
                 END;
      'i','I'  : BEGIN
                   CounterI := CounterI + 1;
                 END;
      'o','O'  : BEGIN
                   CounterO := CounterO + 1;
                 END;
      'u','U'  : BEGIN
                   CounterU := CounterU + 1;
                 END;
  END;     { case }
END;     { then begin }
```

The condition on the IF-THEN-ELSE statement ensures that the CASE statement is only executed if Letter contains a value that appears within the CASE statement.[6]

Notice that CASE works slightly differently from the way IF-THEN and IF-THEN-ELSE statements work. The item in the heading is not a condition; it is simply a value. There is an implicit condition in the CASE statement governing whether or not a statement or group of statements is executed, which is that *the item in the header has the same value as one of the values in the list preceding*

6. Many versions of Pascal allow an OTHERWISE clause to appear just before the END of the CASE statement to take care of cases where no match is found. This clause allows you to specify what should be done if none of the values listed in the CASE statement matches the one you have. Note that the OTHERWISE clause is not part of standard Pascal.

the statement or group of statements. So you could paraphrase the action of the CASE statement above in terms resembling an IF-THEN statement by saying, "if Letter equals 'a' or 'A', then execute these statements; else if Letter equals 'e' or 'E', execute these statements," and so on. The implication of this is that CASE is useful only when you are checking if some variable *equals* one of several values or small sets of values. You cannot check if it is less than or greater than a particular value, as you can in conditions in IF-THEN and IF-THEN-ELSE statements (see below, under *More About Conditions*); and you cannot specify a range of values with the '..' notation, as you can in conditions using IN—all of the values must be listed explicitly. So in the program outlined in this chapter CASE would not really be that helpful; you would have to list the entire alphabet, in both upper and lower case, in one of the lists within the CASE statement. Obviously, it is a lot easier to use IF-THEN or IF-THEN-ELSE with IN in this situation. However, there are some exercises listed at the end of this chapter for which the CASE statement would be very useful and much easier to manage than if the problem were handled by using IF-THEN and IF-THEN-ELSE statements.

Note the following facts about the CASE statement:

- The CASE statement has an END at its end, but no corresponding BEGIN.

The END that terminates a CASE statement represents the only instance within the Pascal language where an END appears without matching a corresponding BEGIN. Be careful!

- The item in the header whose value is checked can also be (1) a variable of type INTEGER, or (2) an arithmetic expression yielding a result of type INTEGER (not REAL!).[7] In this case, of course, the values listed would be integer values (whole numbers) instead of character values as in the examples above. So, you could have a CASE statement such as

```
IF ThisOne IN [0..9] THEN BEGIN
  CASE ThisOne OF
    1,2,3 : BEGIN
              WRITELN('Low');
            END;
    4,5,6 : BEGIN
              WRITELN('Medium');
            END;
    7,8,9 : BEGIN
              WRITELN('High');
            END;
  END;     { case }
END      { then begin }
ELSE BEGIN
  WRITELN('Out of range');
END;     { else begin }
```

7. The item can also be a variable of type BOOLEAN, which will be discussed in Chapter Seven. However, as you will see, Boolean variables can take on only one of two values, and so there can never be more than two alternatives associated with them. So it is just as easy to use IF-THEN-ELSE with Boolean variables.

or, assuming both ThisOne and ThatOne are variables of type INTEGER, the heading could be any of the following:

```
CASE ThisOne - ThatOne OF
CASE ThisOne + ThatOne OF
CASE ThisOne * ThatOne OF
```

but not

```
CASE ThisOne / ThatOne OF
```

since this yields a result of type REAL.

- All of the examples show a list of values in the CASE statement, but of course a single value may be associated with a statement or group of statements as well; for example,

  ```
  'A' : BEGIN ...
  ```

  is a valid list of values.
- As in most cases, when only one statement appears in a group associated with a list of values in a CASE statement, the BEGIN-END pair can be eliminated. Thus, the BEGIN-END pairs could be eliminated in all of the examples above.

More About Arithmetic Expressions

Arithmetic expressions that appear on the right side of an assignment operator can be more complicated than the ones shown earlier in the chapter. For instance, you can have expressions like

```
ThisOne := 3 + 5 / 2 - 4 * 2;
```

or any other combination you'd like. However, it is crucial that you realize that Pascal has its own way of evaluating this expression and others like it: the expression is scanned from left to right, and divisions and multiplications are performed at this time in the order they appear. Then the expression is scanned from left to right again, and addition and subtractions are performed in the order they appear. In this statement, 5 would be divided by 2 first, then 4 would be multiplied by 2; then 3 would be added to the result of the division of 5 by 2. The result of the multiplication of 4 by 2 would then be subtracted from this result.

This might yield a result very different from the one intended. Therefore, it is advisable to use parentheses to group the items you want to be taken together, as follows:

```
RealVariable := ((3 + 5) / 2) - (4 * 2);
```

Pascal honors the parentheses and performs the operations indicated for the grouped items in the way indicated. So here 3 is added to 5, the result is divided by 2, yielding the value 4; 4 is multiplied by 2 and this result is subtracted from 4. If you always use the parentheses, you won't have to worry about the way Pascal evaluates the expression by default.

Because this expression involves real division (indicated by the '/'), the variable in which the result is stored must be declared with type REAL since the result of the entire computation will be real (even though the answer could be expressed as a whole number). For division involving integers, and for which an integer result is desired, Pascal uses a different division operator.

If you want only an integer result—one with no digits to the right of the decimal point—and both the divisor and the dividend are of type INTEGER, the sign for division is the keyword DIV. So, to divide the value stored in ThisOne by 3 and store the result in ThatOne, you would use the statement

```
ThatOne := ThisOne DIV 3;
```

Note that the variable on the left of the assignment operator must be of type INTEGER. Now, it may be that 3 does not divide evenly into the value stored in ThisOne, leaving a remainder; but no matter, this is the point of distinguishing DIV from division yielding a real number result—with DIV, the remainder is thrown away, so the result is a whole, integer number.

The MOD Operator

Pascal includes one additional operator that is useful—the MOD operator. Like DIV and most other arithmetic operators, it is inserted between two numbers or numeric variables. When a MOD operation is performed on two numbers, it does the following: the number on the right of the MOD operator is divided into the number on the left of the MOD operator, as in division. But the result is not the number of times the number on the right goes into the number on the left; instead, the result of the MOD operation is the *remainder* that results when the number on the right is divided into the number on the left—the whole result of the division is thrown away, just as the remainder is thrown away when DIV is used. In fact, MOD does the exact opposite of what DIV does.

Examples: if ThisOne contains the value 10, ThatOne will contain the value 1 after this statement executes:

```
ThatOne := ThisOne MOD 3;
```

Ten divided by 3 is 3 with a remainder of 1; the whole result is thrown away and the remainder is the result. In this example,

```
ThatOne := 42 MOD ThisOne;
```

2 is the result, because 10 goes into 42 four times with a remainder of 2. The result of the following is 0:

```
ThatOne := ThisOne MOD 10;
```

because 10 goes into 10 one time with a remainder of 0.

In Chapter Eleven, you will see an interesting use of the MOD operator.

Arithmetic Expressions in WRITE and WRITELN Statements

Arithmetic expressions can appear in WRITE and WRITELN statements, and when they do, the result is printed. For example,

```
WRITELN('The average is ',ThisOne/ThatOne:1:3);
```

will cause the literal string 'The average is ' to be printed, followed by the result of the division of ThisOne by ThatOne. Note that the width specification is tacked onto the expression just as it would be to a variable.

More About Conditions

As mentioned earlier in the chapter, there are several standard kinds of conditions in programming that were not treated in the context of the program for this chapter. Conditions, of course, involve assertions which are then checked to see if they are true or false. The most common kinds of assertions in Pascal and similar languages involve assertions about equality and inequality, and about one value being less than, greater than, less than or equal to, and greater than or equal to, another value. Some examples will make this clearer.

First, look over this list of what are called *relational operators:*

```
=     (equal to)
<>    (not equal to)
<     (less than)
>     (greater than)
<=    (less than or equal to)
>=    (greater than or equal to)
```

Note that when a relational operator consists of two characters, no blank appears between them.

Now consider the following assertions and their meanings:

Letter = 'G'	(the value stored in the variable Letter is equal to 'G')
ThisOne <> 5	(the value stored in the variable ThisOne is not equal to 5)
ThisOne < ThatOne	(the value stored in the variable ThisOne is less than the value stored in the variable ThatOne)
ThatOne > 10	(the value stored in the variable ThatOne is greater than 10)
Letter1 <= Letter2	(the value stored in the variable Letter1 is less than or equal to the value stored in the variable Letter2)
ThisOne >= ThatOne	(the value stored in the variable ThisOne is greater than or equal to the value stored in the variable ThatOne)

When assertions like these appear in IF-THEN, IF-THEN-ELSE, and WHILE statements, as usual they are checked to see if they are true or false. Then, of course, the appropriate statements are executed.

Assertions like these can also be strung together with what are called *Boolean Operators*. The Boolean operators are AND, OR, and NOT. You have already seen NOT, which negates whatever follows it—for example, EOLN asserts that it is the end of the line; NOT EOLN asserts that it is not the end of the line. Here are some examples of AND and OR at work:

```
(Letter >= 'A') AND (Letter <= 'Z')
```

This asserts that Letter is greater than or equal to 'A' and Letter is less than or equal to 'Z'—in order for this entire assertion to be judged to be true, *both* the assertion that Letter is greater than or equal to 'A' and the assertion that Letter is less than or equal to 'Z' must be true. If it is true, you know that Letter is a capital letter.

```
(ThisOne = ThatOne) OR (ThisOne > 25)
```

This asserts that *either* ThisOne equals ThatOne, *or* ThisOne is greater than 25. The whole assertion is true if one or the other of the sub-assertions is true. It is also true if both are true. So if the variable ThatOne currently contains the value 0, this assertion is true if ThisOne contains 0 or any number over 25.

Note that the sub-assertions are enclosed in parentheses.

More complex assertions can be built up, but in most cases assertions are relatively simple, like the ones you've seen so far. If you find yourself creating a huge assertion with more than two Boolean operators, you are probably creating a monster that need not be created at all. Re-consider what you are doing if this happens, or consider using a CASE statement (see above).

Reading Numbers as Numbers

The READ and READLN statements you have used so far read characters from the keyboard or a file. If numbers appeared in the input, each digit was read individually as a separate character and stored in a variable of type CHAR. Arithmetic cannot be done on variables of type CHAR, so these digits were not usable within the program as numbers in the true sense of the word. However, you can read numbers as *numbers* from the keyboard or a file declared with type TEXT, by including a variable of type INTEGER or REAL in a READ or READLN statement. But things work differently when this is done, so read carefully.

For simplicity, the examples below will deal only with input from the keyboard. Any of them can be changed to apply to a file of type TEXT by inserting the file name within the parenthesis.

Suppose that ThisOne is a variable of type INTEGER. The statement

```
READ(ThisOne);
```

will go to the file INPUT (the keyboard) for its input and read a number and store it in the variable ThisOne as an integer value. For example, if the user enters '234<CR>', the number 234 will be stored in ThisOne when the READ statement above is executed.

When reading numbers, Pascal will read more than a single character if the number contains more than one digit.

If the variable into which the statement is reading is of type INTEGER, it will read the next sequence of contiguous numeric digits in the file (up to a large maximum) as a single number. These digits can be preceded by a plus or minus sign. So input such as '+234' and '−234' is perfectly valid. Once the computer starts reading a number, any non-numeric symbol that it encounters signals the end of the number.

In the example above, the carriage return character signals the end of the number, because it is a non-numeric character. So Pascal will read only the three digits '234' as the number.

Given the READ statement above, suppose the user enters 'A234<CR>' instead of simply '234<CR>'. What will happen? The program will crash because it is trying to read a non-numeric item into a numeric value.

Although you can read digits and any other character for that matter into a CHAR variable, only numbers can be read into INTEGER variables. If, when a READ or READLN statement is reading into an INTEGER variable it encounters a non-numeric character (except a blank—see below), an error will result.

If the user enters ' 234<CR>' (the number 234 preceded by a blank), there will be no error and the number 234 will be read just as if the blank did not appear before it:

Blanks preceding a number in the input are skipped over until a non-blank is encountered. At that point the reading process proceeds as outlined above.

One repercussion of this fact is that if ThatOne is also a variable with type INTEGER, and if the user enters '234 567<CR>', then the statement

```
READ(ThisOne,ThatOne);
```

stores the value 234 in ThisOne and the value 567 in ThatOne. Another repercussion is that if Letter is a variable of type CHAR and the user enters '234 567', then the statement

```
READ(ThisOne,Letter);
```

stores 234 in ThisOne and a *blank* in Letter. This happens because after reading

234, the input pointer is positioned at the blank that follows the number in the input. When reading characters, the next character in the input is read, no matter what it is. Seeing that **Letter** is a variable of type CHAR, the computer will read the next character as it always does when dealing with variables of this type.

Another consequence of the way numbers are read in Pascal programs—and one that has led to many an hour spent at a computer terminal trying to debug a program—is that if the user enters '234<CR>' and the statement

```
READ(ThisOne);
```

is executed, 234 will be stored in **ThisOne**, of course. Now if the next READ statement executed is

```
READ(Letter);
```

(note that any number of statements could appear between these two READ statements in the program—the only stipulation here is that none of them read from the keyboard) a blank will be stored in **Letter**. Why? The familiar song—the carriage return is read and stored as a blank, and since after 234 is read the input pointer is positioned under the carriage return, that is what is read when the next READ statement is executed.

Real numbers are read in the same way as integers, except that they are, of course, read into variables with type REAL, and that the characters '.' and 'e' or 'E' can be part of the number. That is, the numbers '234.56', '−987.023', '234e3', and '234E−2' are all valid input and will be read as entities.

If you think reading numbers is complicated, you are right. For that reason, you may want to heed the following bits of advice:

1. When reading numbers from the user at the terminal, use a READLN statement rather than a READ. This ensures that if the user enters a carriage return following the number (which on many systems she or he must do), it is thrown away and will not inadvertently be read by subsequent READ or READLN statements.
2. If you need to read more than one number, use a separate prompt and READLN for each one. For instance, if you need three numbers from the user, use statements like this:

```
WRITE('Enter the first number: ');
READLN(FirstNumber);
WRITE('Enter the second number: ');
READLN(SecondNumber);
WRITE('Enter the third number: ');
READLN (ThirdNumber);
```

where **FirstNumber**, **SecondNumber**, and **ThirdNumber** are variables of type INTEGER or REAL. It is much easier for the user to enter correct input if he or she only enters one thing at a time and does not need to be concerned about spaces between numbers and so on.

APPLICATIONS AND CONSIDERATIONS

With the program for this chapter, you have started to collect valuable information about your text. The number of letters, lines, and sentences in a text, together with similar statistics like the number of words and paragraphs in the text, can be of interest to writers. In fact, much of the latest software designed as "writing aids" and even some simple word processors will provide information of this kind about the text the user is working on if the user requests it. This obviously gives the user an idea of the length of the text he or she is writing. Usually the user can also request statistics such as the average number of letters per word, the average number of words per sentence, and the average number of sentences per paragraph. Average word length and average sentence length (and sometimes average paragraph length) are often used to determine the *readability* of a text. For example, a text with an average word length of no more than 2 and an average sentence length of no more than 10 might be considered to be grade school level; if the average word length is no more than 3 and the average sentence length is under 20, the text might be appropriate up through high school. Statistics above these levels could be regarded as suitable for a college-level audience. Readability indexes of this kind are actually used to determine if a text is suitable for use in schools at a certain grade level, and the index has become a sort of standard for evaluation of any text, so that, for instance, newspaper articles are often tested to ensure they are appropriate for people with, say, a high school education.

Another application of statistics of this kind is in the area of *stylistics*—that is, in studies of an author or authors' style. Style is very difficult to define in quantitative terms, but clearly, a text containing primarily long sentences and words differs stylistically from one with shorter words and sentences. For instance, everyone would agree that Hemingway's short and terse style is very different from Faulkner's, which is characterized by long, descriptive sentences and words. Because style affects the way the reader encounters the information contained in the words and sentences in the text, it ultimately contributes to the text's overall meaning—long sentences containing several clauses involve words in more complex syntactic relationships and thus provide the reader with more and different information about relationships among these words than short sentences do. The length of an author's words and sentences also sets a tone and mood that plays a role in determining the effect of the text on the reader.

Statistics of this kind have been used in a variety of ways by literary analysts. Perhaps the most well known application of quantitative stylistics is in authorship studies, where style in a work of unknown or doubtful authorship is compared to that of known authors to determine similarities or differences and, ultimately, to help determine the true author. The earliest use of this method was long before the age of computers at the turn of the twentieth century, when T. C. Mendenhall calculated, by hand, average word length for Shakespeare and several other authors—Bacon, Marlowe, and Jonson, for example—in order to determine authorship of Shakespeare's works. Obviously, his results were inconclusive, but he did generate some interesting statistics—for instance, he determined that the average word length for almost all of his authors is 3, whereas for Shakespeare and Marlowe it is 4. Later in this century and with the help of a computer, Mosteller and Wallace solved a very famous case of disputed authorship in *The Federalist Papers*. The authorship of 12 of the 88 existing papers was disputed, although it was known the author was either Alexander Hamilton or James Madison. Each of these men was known to have written several other of the *Papers*, and so a stylistic comparison of the disputed papers was made with those whose author was known. The situation was ideal for such a comparison because there would be no stylistic variations in the papers due to differences in genre or topic. Interestingly, the average sentence length in the known papers of Hamilton and Madison was almost identical—34.55 for Hamilton and 34.59 for Madison—and so this measure was thrown out as a possible indicator of difference in style between the two men. Eventually, Mosteller and Wallace looked at the vocabulary of the two authors and determined that the evidence favored Madison as the author of the disputed papers. In this as in most cases, statistics such as average word and sentence length provided few or no clues to the authorship of disputed works, although authorship attribution is one of the best known applications of this kind of statistic.

Statistics such as average word and sentence length can be used more successfully to show variations in an author's style between or within her or his own works. If, for instance, an author writes two novels and the average word and/or sentence length of one is significantly shorter[8] than the other, then this is interesting—it may be of interest to consider the differences in the subject matter and viewpoint of the two texts to determine the reason behind the variation in style. It is even more interesting to look within a text to see if words or sentences are significantly shorter in one part of the text than another.[9] For instance, shorter words and sentences in one portion of a text could indicate a more naive or restricted viewpoint or a quickening of action. In all cases, these statistics are not conclusive but provide information about a text that might not otherwise be apparent, and which can be used as a basis for further study of a text or texts.

You will be hearing more about ways to use these and other measures of style in later chapters.

EXERCISES

1. Modify the program outlined in this chapter to calculate and print the average number of letters per sentence and the average number of lines per sentence, as well as the number of letters, lines, and sentences.

You may want to run your program on two different texts by two different authors, to see if any differences exist between the two.

2. Modify the program so that it counts the number of times *each* of the letters 'E' (or 'e') and 'T' (or 't') occurs in the text, and prints these values along with the percentage of the letters in the text that these values represent.

8. Various statistical measures exist for determining whether or not differences are "significant."

9. In Chapter Eleven you will write a program that enables you to get information about different parts of a text.

A variation on this exercise would be to write a program which counts letters that occur more often in English than other languages that use the same alphabet, such as 'K' and 'W.' To see how great the differences between languages are, run the program on two different texts, each in a different language.

3. Modify the program to count the number of times each vowel, or, if you are more ambitious, each letter of the alphabet, occurs in the text, and print out these values along with the percentage of the total number of letters in the text these values represent. (Hint: use the CASE statement described in the Niceties section.)

4. Modify the program so that in addition to counting letters, lines, and sentences, it counts paragraphs as well. The program should assume a new paragraph is encountered when any line begins with a blank.

This program can be enhanced to compute the average number of letters and lines per sentence along with the average number of sentences per paragraph.

5. (More difficult.) Modify the program so that in addition to computing the number of letters, lines, and sentences in the text, it also counts the number of words (and, if you also compute the average number of letters and lines per sentence, computes the number of words per sentence and the number of letters per word as well). The program can assume that a word has been encountered when it encounters a blank (or carriage return). Note that you can't simply count blanks to accomplish this task, since two or more blanks may appear together in the file.

6. (For the adventurous programmer.) Modify the program so that instead of counting letters, lines, and sentences, it counts the number of words in the text ending in 'ED' or 'ed.' What you will be looking for is the letter 'E' or 'e', followed by the letter 'D' or 'd', followed by a blank (or the end-of-line character) or a punctuation mark. To be sure your program covers all possibilities, test it on a file that contains the word 'freed' and has as the last letter in the file the letter 'e'.

5 Identifying Words

So far you have been dealing with the text on a letter-by-letter basis, but most of the more interesting kinds of text analyses involve consideration of the words in the text. You can learn a lot about an author's style, for instance, by looking at his or her use of particular words; you can study the linguistic attributes of a text in greater detail by considering the features of the words that make it up; and you can analyze the content of the text—for instance, detect the presence of certain themes or topics—by identifying and locating words in the text with particular meanings.

The basic problem in this chapter will be to identify each word in the text, store it in main memory, and print it out on a separate line. You do not have to store a word in order to print it, since it can be printed letter-by-letter as in the programs for Chapters Two and Three—the idea behind this problem is to learn how to store whole words instead of individual characters in main memory, which in standard versions of Pascal means learning several new language features. Many non-standard versions of Pascal provide facilities that eliminate a lot of the details required to read, store, and manipulate strings of characters; but learning the details provided in this chapter will both enable you to write Pascal programs using *any* version of Pascal and give you a greater understanding of the way information is stored and handled within the computer. The features that must be learned are not overly complicated, and they are applicable to other very common programming situations, as you will see in Chapter Seven.

Turning to the problem, then: how is a computer program to go about identifying individual words within a text? To answer this, you will have to consider exactly what a word is. The dictionary defines a word as

1. a sound or a combination of sounds, or its written or printed representation, used in any language as the sign of a conception.
2. an element which can stand alone as an utterance, not divisable into two or more parts similarly characterized; thus *boy* and *boyish*, but not *-ish* or *boy scout*, the former being less than a word, the latter more.

This definition is not very useful computationally, primarily because the definition of a word as "the sign of a conception" cannot be translated into terms the computer can deal with. The computer does not have or know about conceptions, and it takes a vast amount of programming to create the illusion that it does to any noticeable degree. This definition is cast in human terms; all humans have and recognize conceptions, but computers clearly do not.

As you know from your experience with the computer so far, the computer deals with nothing but character after character after character. The characters have no meaning to the computer; the only thing that the computer can do is to distinguish one character from another. Given this, what is needed here is a graphic definition of a word, one that depends on the way the word looks, on the configurations of characters that distinguish a word, not how it sounds or what it stands for. In these terms, a word can be defined as any sequence of alphabetic characters preceded and followed by one or more blanks. This definition would make a program to identify individual words easy to write. But is this definition sufficient? In particular, does it suffice for things like "don't," Fred's," "it's," or "ex-marine" and "well-to-do?" "Don't" and "it's" are contractions standing for two words; should "don't" and "it's" be regarded as two words or one? If so, you could tell the computer that anything preceded or followed by one or more blanks *or an apostrophe* is a word. That would make "t" and "s" words, which might be alright since they really stand for the words "not" and "is," but the "s" at the end of "Fred's" might be a little more difficult to regard as a word by itself. And what about "well-to-do"—this is really three words strung together, but should it be regarded as three words or only one? Regardless of your decisions, one thing is obvious: the distinction between what is and is not a word is not clear-cut.

Other sequences of non-blank characters cause problems, too—such as numerals and digits (475, 10:45, MCMLXXXIV) and abbreviations (U.S.A.). The problem does not have a straightforward solution; the distinction between what is a word and what is not a word must be determined by the individual who is writing or using the computer to conform as closely as possible to his or her purposes. For the purposes of this problem, a word will be regarded in the simplest terms possible—as a sequence of one or more *characters* (non-blanks) preceded and followed by one or more blanks.

This definition has its own consequences. For instance, punctuation that is part of the text will be regarded as part of the word. In this chapter this problem will be ignored and punctuation will be included with a word, although one of the exercises asks you to print the words without punctuation. In Chapter Eight you will see how to get rid of the punctuation altogether.

On to the algorithm. Because this program will, as usual, read all of the characters in a file, you can use the framework of earlier algorithms for reading characters from a file as a basis for this one. The programs in Chapters Three and Four were built around the following framework: That algorithm is

1. Ready the file for reading.
2. While the character about to be read is not the end-of-file character, repeat the following:
   a. While the character about to be read is not the end-of-line character, repeat the following:
      (1) Read a character from the file.

      .
      .
      .
   c. Prepare to read from the beginning of the *next* line of input, by throwing away the carriage return that appears in the input file.

This chapter's program will be doing the following: when it finds the beginning of a word in the text (don't worry about how it does this yet), it will start storing characters and continue on until it finds the end of the word, and then it will print the word on a new line. So the output of the program is a vertical listing of the words in the text, not a copy of the text as in Chapter Three. Because of this, a fair amount of the algorithm above can be thrown out—specifically, the parts that are concerned with the end-of-line in the input. Why? Because here there is no reason to be concerned about the end-of-line at all. In Chapter Three's program, the end-of-line had to be found in order to provide for generating a line eject in the output every time a carriage return was detected in the input. In Chapter Four, end-of-line had to be detected in order to determine the number of lines in the text. But in this chapter's program, you need only know where a word ends—not where a line ends. In fact, the program will work best if it sees the carriage return characters in the file as blanks (word separators), which of course it will if no special provisions are made. So, this program will regard the text file as a continuous stream of characters, spread out in ticker-tape fashion, with no "lines" *per se* in it at all. In fact, this view of the text will be taken in all of the programs in the remainder of this book, although exercises at the end of several chapters will require detecting end-of-line.

Given this new view of the text, the algorithm above can be stripped down to be

1. Ready the file for reading.
2. While the character about to be read is not the end-of-file character, repeat the following:

   .
   .
   .

   Read a character from the file.

This version of the algorithm eliminates the inner WHILE loop that executes once for each line in the text and the statement below that loop that throws away the carriage return at the end of each line. Now characters are read continuously, one after another, without pausing at the end of each line as before. Carriage returns are read blindly as blanks.

The sketchy algorithm above will serve as the structural outline of the program for this chapter, and it needs to be filled in to provide for identifying and printing each of the words in the text as it reads the characters in the file. So some set of statements will fall under step 2, as usual, to do what needs to be done during the reading process in order to accomplish this.

What are the steps that this program will perform repeatedly until the end of the file is reached? Well, in order to print a listing of the words in a file, those words must first be read into the computer's main memory. Thus the general process to be repeated is

1. Read a word.
2. Print the word.

If these two steps are repeated until the end-of-file is encountered, the job will be done. These steps need some expansion in order to be implemented in Pascal, since in standard Pascal only individual characters (and not whole words) can be read.

Above, a word was defined for the purposes of this program as a string of characters surrounded by blanks. If this is true, then the process of reading a word will involve finding a non-blank character and then reading and storing characters until another blank is encountered. So the algorithm above can be expanded to be

1. Read characters until a non-blank is encountered.
2. Read and store characters until a blank is encountered.
3. Print the string of characters just stored on a new line.

This is closer to the set of steps that needs to be followed, but steps 1 and 2 are still not quite explicit enough to be translated directly into Pascal statements. In order to accomplish these steps, your program will have to read each character and look at it to see if it satisfies the criteria at hand for the step it is currently executing. So step 1 should be expanded to be

a. Read a character.
b. If the character is a blank, repeat step a.

You can probably see by looking at these steps that a loop is going to be involved, but notice that this is a funny sort of loop—the condition for continuing is not checked until *after* the step that is to be repeated (the statement that should therefore be inside the loop) is executed. And in fact the condition that the character just read is a blank *can't* be checked until after the first step executes, because it is hardly possible to check the character you just read until you have read it. Pascal will come to the rescue here with a new kind of loop, but let us return to the algorithm first.

Step 1, of course, effectively skips over blanks in the input and stops when it reads the first character in the word. Note that if the first character read from the file is a non-blank (meaning that there are no blanks at the beginning of the file and therefore no blanks to be skipped), the algorithm works just as well.

Step 2 can be expanded to be

d. Store the character just read as part of the word.
e. Read a character.
f. If the character is *not* a blank, repeat steps d and e.

Step d assumes that the first character of the word is read before this piece of the algorithm is encountered, which is, of course, the case since the blank-skipping process does not stop until a non-blank character has been read. This non-blank must be stored before going on to read additional characters in the word, if any exist. After that character is stored, another is read, and before storing it the character is checked to see if it is a non-blank too. If so, it is added to the word, and another character is read. If not, the process of storing and reading stops altogether.

Note that the same structure of repetition exists here as in the previous fragment—a condition is checked *after* the action of the loop has been performed, rather than before.

Step 3, print the word, does not require expansion because Pascal provides a means to print characters stored contiguously as words, as you will see below. (Yes, it is sometimes hard to know what an algorithm should be without knowing all that Pascal can and cannot do.)

If you put together the steps for reading, storing, and printing a word, you have the following:

a. Read a character.
b. If the character is a blank, repeat step a.
d. Store the character just read as part of the word.
e. Read a character.
f. If the character is *not* a blank, repeat steps a and b.
g. Print the word just stored on a new line.

This set of statements will process a single word. Now, how can this fit into the general algorithmic outline given initially? You want to repeat the step that processes a single word until there are no more words in the file to process—that is, until the end of the file is encountered. Therefore, you can simply insert steps a through g above wholesale into the outline given earlier as a sub-step of step 2, the part of the algorithm that repeats until the end of the file is reached. By doing this you are simply providing for repetition of the process of reading and printing a *word* until the end of the file is reached, rather than repetition of the process of reading a *line* as before. The final algorithm is therefore

1. Ready the file for reading.

2. While the character about to be read is not the end-of-file character, repeat the following:
a. Read a character.
b. If the character is a blank, repeat step a.
d. Store the character just read as part of the word.
e. Read a character.
f. If the character is *not* a blank, repeat steps d and e.
g. Print the word just stored on a new line.

Before implementing this algorithm, turn your attention to some new features of the Pascal language.

ELEMENTS OF PASCAL

Packed Arrays and Pascal's TYPE Statement

Pascal does not include among its basic types of variables a type in which a contiguous sequence of characters—called a *string* in computer jargon—can be stored. Only variables of type CHAR hold characters, and each variable of this type can hold only one character. However, there is a way in Pascal to declare space that can hold a string of characters.

Since a string of characters is nothing more than a sequence of individual characters, a memory space that can hold character strings can consist of a contiguous group of variables of type CHAR. You can picture it like this:

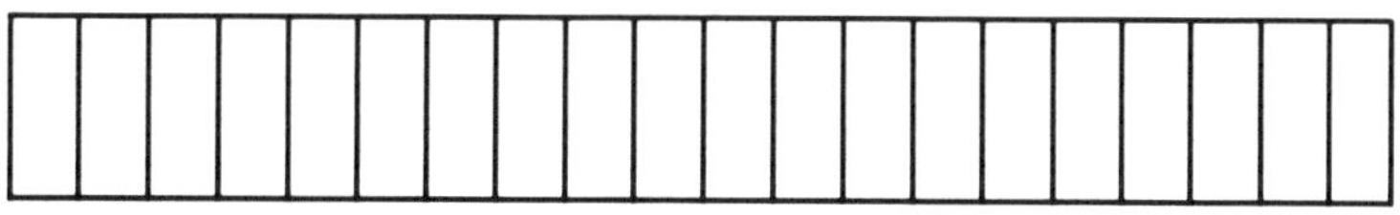

Each of the little boxes is an individual CHAR-type variable. To get Pascal to set up such a group of contiguous CHAR variables, you need to declare what is called a *packed array*.

An *array* in general is a sequence of variables that are all of the same type—any type. Arrays provide a means to declare and access groups of variables of the same type easily. Almost all computer languages have arrays; Pascal is alone in calling variables that hold strings of characters 'packed arrays.' You may have heard about arrays and you will hear more about them in Chapter Seven; much of what is said here about packed arrays applies to arrays in general, as you will see.

The packed array differs from the general array only in the way in which the computer stores it internally.[1] You do not have to be concerned with the differences, since they are invisible to you, but you will find that there are one or two things you can do with a packed array that you cannot do with an array because of this difference. These are described below.

You can think of the packed array exactly as the picture above shows it. It is really very simple. The difference between a packed array and the variables with which you are already familiar is this: the packed array, which, again, consists of a group of individual variables, is given a single name, as if it were a single variable; but the packed array actually consists of several *component* variables, all of which have the same type. The individual component variables are numbered, and you refer to them by giving the packed array name followed by the appropriate number in square brackets. For example, if the packed array is named "Word," you would refer to the individual slots within the array as Word[1], Word[2], Word[3], and so on. If you have stored a string of characters in

1. More specifically, the difference is that internally the variables of which the packed array is composed are stored one right next to the other. The component variables of an array, while you think of them and work with them as if they were stored contiguously, might not actually be stored that way.

the packed array, the first character is in **Word[1]**, the second character in the word is in **Word[2]**, etc.

How do you declare a packed array of CHAR variables? Usually, to declare any variable you specify the name of its type (e.g., CHAR, INTEGER, REAL) following the variable name in the Declarations section of the program. However, Pascal does not have a pre-defined name for a type consisting of a packed array of variables of type CHAR.[2] But Pascal does allow you to define and name new types, which can then be used as the type specification following the name of a variable or several variables in the Declarations section. These types are defined in the *Type Declarations section* of the program, which, when it appears, appears just before the Declarations section of the program (which, to distinguish itself from the Type Declarations section is often called the *Variable* or *VAR Declarations section* of the program). So, the general outline of a Pascal program now becomes

```
Program Heading
Type Declarations
Variable Declarations
BEGIN
  Program statements
END.
```

The type declaration for a packed array consisting of twenty variables of type CHAR would look like this:

```
TYPE <name> = PACKED ARRAY[1..20] OF CHAR;
```

where

- TYPE is the keyword signalling the beginning of the Type Declarations section, just as VAR signals the beginning of the Variable Declarations section.
- <*name*> is any user-defined name, which will later be used in the Variable Declarations section to define the type of a variable name that will be the name of the packed array.
- PACKED ARRAY . . . OF CHAR says that the type being defined here is a packed array, consisting of slots of type CHAR.
- [1..20] indicates that the packed array is to consist of slots numbered 1 through to 20; these numbers are the numbers used to identify the individual slots, as shown above. Any two integers can be used here, as long as the first is less than the second; almost all arrays consist of slots numbered starting at one, and you will probably never define an array any other way. The second number is the one that dictates the number of slots.

The name given to the type will appear as the type assigned to some variable name declared in the VAR Declarations section of the program. To give you an example, suppose that a type is declared as follows:

2. Note that CHAR, INTEGER, and REAL are the names of types of variables.

```
TYPE String = PACKED ARRAY[1..20] OF CHAR;
```

To declare a variable name with this type, you would say

```
VAR Word : String;
```

This gives the variable Word the type *String*, and so Word is now the name of a packed array consisting of 20 contiguously stored CHAR variables. Each of these individual CHAR variables is referred to by giving the name of the array followed by the number corresponding to its position in the array—in this case, Word[1], Word[2], Word[3], . . . ,Word[20]. Note that these numbers or "slot indicators" are called *subscripts;* if Word[1] appears in a program, it is said to have the subscript one.

You can picture the packed array Word like this:

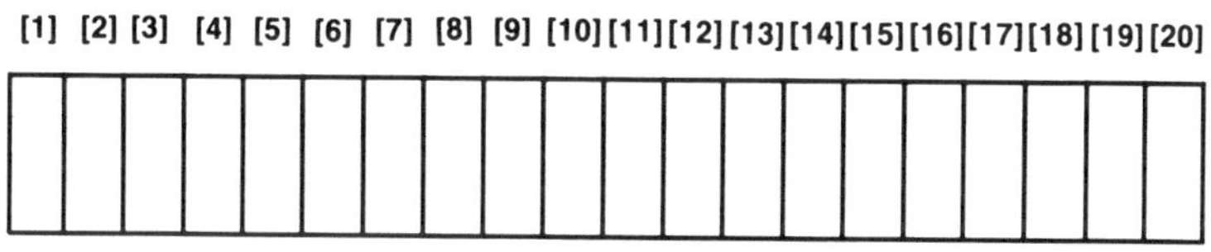

Note: "String" is a conventional name for packed arrays of type CHAR.[3]

Most of the time you will refer in your programs to individual slots (which can be thought of as individual characters) within the packed array. In fact, there are very few contexts in which Pascal allows referring to a packed array as a whole, by giving its name alone without a subscript.

The following list indicates those contexts in which a packed array can be referred to as a whole:

- You can write out the whole array by simply giving the array name in a WRITE or WRITELN statement. For example,

  ```
  WRITELN(Word);
  ```

  would write out the entire contents of the packed array named Word, from slots 1 to 20.

- You can assign a whole string of characters to the packed array as if it were a single entity, instead of assigning values to the slots one-by-one. For example,

  ```
  Word := 'orangutan           ';
  ```

3. If your version of Pascal provides string-handling capabilities, as discussed in the beginning of this chapter, it may have a "built-in" type named *String* that is very like the one defined above. In this case you can declare variables of type *String* without first defining the type. If the type *String* is built into your version of Pascal, you may in fact get an error if you attempt to use the type declaration for *String* shown above. In this case you should use another name for the type, and substitute it in every place where *String* is used here.

will store the letter 'o' in Word[1], the letter 'r' in Word[2], and so on. As usual, single quotation marks are used to delineate the literal string.

The string assigned to a packed array of type CHAR variables must be of the same length as the packed array itself—that is, the number of characters in the string to be assigned must be the same as the number of slots in the packed array.

This is the reason why eleven blanks are included following the word "orangutan" within the single quotation marks—the blanks make the string on the right side of the assignment operator the same length as the packed array on the left side of the assignment operator.

If another variable exists that has the same type as Word (type *String* in this case), a copy of its contents can be stored in Word as well since they are of the same length. For example, if a variable named Name had been declared with type *String*, the statement

```
Word := Name;
```

would be valid, and would cause each slot in Word to be given the same value as the corresponding slot in Name.

- You can compare the contents of one packed array of type CHAR variables with another in a condition. For instance, if you declare two variables of type *String* (as defined above) named Word1 and Word2, the following are legal conditions in an IF-THEN, IF-THEN-ELSE, or WHILE statement:

```
Word1 = Word2
Word1 <> Word2
Word1 < Word2
Word1 > Word2
Word1 <= Word2
Word1 >= Word2
```

Word1 and Word2 are considered *equal* if the contents of each slot in Word1 contain the same character as the corresponding slot in Word2. They are considered *not equal* if the contents of any slot in Word1 differ from the contents of the corresponding slot in Word2. To decide if Word1 is 'less than' Word2, Pascal turns to the numeric codes assigned to each character that are mentioned in Chapter Four.[4]

Recall that each letter is given a numeric code (and note that the codes for the upper case letters are different from the codes for lower case letters).[5] In fact, all characters, not just the alphabetic ones, have codes associated with them, and these codes are used to determine if the contents of Word1 are less than the

4. These numeric codes are used to determine equality and inequality of strings as well.

5. It is important to note that *whether the codes for the lower case letters are less than or greater than the codes for the upper case letters is dependent upon your computer system*. There are two standard codes used in computers: the ASCII (American Standard Code for Information Interchange) code, and the EBCDIC (Extended Binary Coded Decimal Interchange Code) code. Your computer probably uses one of these. Find out which, and then consult Appendix C to see a chart indicating the numeric codes representing each character on the keyboard.

contents of Word2. The process goes like this: the contents of the first slot in Word1 is compared to the contents of the first slot in Word2. If the numeric code for the character stored in Word1[1] is less in value than the code for the character in Word2[1], then the whole of Word1 is judged to be less than Word2—the condition Word1 < Word2 is true. If the code for the character stored in Word1[1] is *greater* than the code for the character in Word2[1], then Word1 is judged not to be less than Word2—the condition Word1 < Word2 is false. But if the contents of Word1[1] and Word2[1] are equal, no judgment is made. Instead, the comparison process is repeated with the next slot in each of the two packed arrays. If Word1[2] is less than Word2[2], the whole of Word1 is judged to be less than Word2. If Word1[2] is greater than Word2[2], then Word1 is determined to be greater than Word2. If they are equal, the next slot is examined, and the process is repeated for the next letter in each word. If the comparison process continues through the entire twenty slots and all are found to be equal, then Word1 is not less than Word2.

This all boils down to the fact that the computer uses alphabetical order, just as we would, to determine if whole words are "less than" (preceding in alphabetical sequence) or "greater than" (following in alphabetical sequence) one another. Try the comparison process above with two words like "orangutan" and "orange" to convince yourself, if you need to. You do not need to know the numeric codes—just remember that 'a' is less than 'b' is less than 'c,' and so on.

Individual slots in the array can be assigned values one at a time, by using statements like the following:

```
Word[1] := 'a';
```

which stores the letter 'a' in the first slot of Word, and

```
Word[7] := Letter;
```

which assigns the contents of the variable Letter, which must be declared with type CHAR, to the seventh slot in Word.

The variable on the left side of the assignment operator must have the same type as whatever is being assigned to it. Each slot in the packed array Word **has type CHAR, and so any single literal character, or any variable of type CHAR, may be assigned to it.**

REPEAT-UNTIL Loops

Pascal has another kind of loop that is an upside-down version of the WHILE loop. Like any good loop it causes the statements that appear within it to be repeated, and like the WHILE loop it uses a condition to decide whether or not to continue the repetition.

Unlike WHILE, the condition on a REPEAT-UNTIL loop is checked not at the beginning of the loop, but at the bottom, after the statement or group of statements in it have been executed.

The REPEAT-UNTIL loop looks like this:

```
REPEAT
  <statement or statements>
UNTIL <condition>;
```

<condition>, of course, is replaced by a Pascal condition of the sort you have seen already.

The REPEAT-UNTIL loop works like this: when the REPEAT part of the statement is encountered, the loop is entered immediately, without checking a condition. The statement or statements within the loop are executed. Then, at the bottom of the loop, the condition is checked; if the condition is *false*, control returns to the top of the loop (determined by the location of the keyword REPEAT) and the statement or statements in it are repeated. If the statement is *true*, the loop stops. There are two things to note here:

REPEAT-UNTIL loops continue when their conditions are false, and stop when their conditions are true; WHILE loops continue when their conditions are true, and stop when their conditions are false.

The statements within the REPEAT-UNTIL loop will always be executed at least once, whereas it is possible that a WHILE loop is never entered at all, if its condition is false when the loop is first encountered.

REPEAT-UNTIL loops, then, are useful when you cannot check the condition that is to govern the loop until the statements in the loop have executed at least once. This situation exists in this chapter's problem. A loop is to provide for continually reading characters until a non-blank is read; but how can you check if a non-blank has been read by the statement in the loop before the loop has executed for the first time? In languages that provide only WHILE-type loops, an extra, preliminary READ would have to be inserted just before the WHILE loop, to enable the condition to be checked at the beginning of the loop. Pascal's REPEAT-UNTIL was designed to avoid this slightly awkward practice.

A final note about REPEAT-UNTIL:

The REPEAT-UNTIL has no BEGIN-END pair associated with it, as do the other control structures in the Pascal language (IF-THEN and IF-THEN-ELSE and WHILE loops).

CONSTRUCTING THE PROGRAM

The algorithm outlined at the beginning of the chapter can now be implemented. If you have not read *More about Conditions* in the Niceties section of Chapter Four, you should do so before continuing.

Recall the algorithm:

1. Ready the file for reading.
2. While the character about to be read is not the end-of-file character, repeat the following:
   a. Read a character.
   b. If the character is a blank, repeat step a.
   d. Store the character just read as part of the word.
   e. Read a character.
   f. If the character is *not* a blank, repeat steps d and e.
   g. Print the word just stored on a new line.

Step 1 and the head of step 2 have been implemented in previous programs with a RESET statement and a WHILE NOT EOF(TextFile) statement. So you need to focus your attention on implementing steps 2.a through 2.g. It should be clear that steps 2.a and 2.b will be implemented as one loop, and steps 2.d, 2.e, and 2.f as another. Since in both cases a character must be read before we can check it to decide whether or not to continue the loop, both loops will be REPEAT-UNTIL loops.

Constructing the first loop is easy. All that needs to be done inside the loop is to read a character. The condition on the loop will then check the character; if it is *not* a blank, the loop is to stop. So, the statement inside the loop, the READ statement, is to be executed repeatedly *until* the character that was just read is *not equal* to a blank. This throws away blanks that may precede the next word in the text.

The character read within this loop is not stored in the packed array as it is read, because the program must first ascertain whether or not the character it read is a blank. If so, the character is not stored in the packed array at all; if not, it will be stored in the packed array in step 2.d. Thus the character can be initially read into a variable of type CHAR, as has been done in previous programs. A variable like Letter in previous examples can be declared for this purpose, and the lone statement within the REPEAT-UNTIL loop will then be

```
READ(TextFile,Letter);
```

The condition on the loop will check the contents of the variable Letter just after it is read; if it is a blank, the loop should continue, and if not, the loop should stop. Since a REPEAT-UNTIL loop stops when its condition is *true*, the condition on this loop should assert that "Letter is not equal to a blank." Recalling that the operator for "not equal to" is

```
<>
```

(see the Niceties section of the previous chapter), you can write this in Pascal as

```
Letter <> ' '
```

where ' ' is a blank space enclosed in single quotation marks. To type this, simply type a single quotation mark, then hit the space bar, and then type another single quotation mark. Remember that to the computer, the blank is just another character on the keyboard. Like all other characters, it has a numeric code associated with it, and so it can be compared to and distinguished from other characters by the same methods used for alphabetic and other characters.

There is one other condition under which this REPEAT-UNTIL loop should stop reading—if the character about to be read is the end-of-file character. As you know, computer systems take a dim view of attempting to read the end-of-file character. In any file that is not empty, the end-of-file character is always immediately preceded by an end-of-line character; the end-of-line character, as you recall, is stored as a blank when it is read. So when this loop reads the "blank" that precedes the end-of-file character, it will go on to check the condition that Letter is not equal to a blank; and because that condition is *false* the loop will execute another time—at which point the READ statement will be executed again and it will attempt to read the end-of-file character. The condition on the loop must be extended to prevent this. What needs to be said is, "continue repeating this loop *until* the character just read is not a blank or the character about to be read is the end-of-file character." Given the fact that NOT EOF(<*filename*>) asserts that the next character in the file whose name is substituted for <*filename*> is *not* the end-of-file character, it should make sense that EOF(<*filename*>) asserts that it is. So the condition on the loop should be modified to read

```
(Letter <> ' ') OR (EOF(TextFile))
```

Note the parentheses around each of the individual conditions—these ensure that Pascal sees each as an entity.[6] Remember that joining two assertions with OR will cause the whole condition to be true if one or the other or both assertions in the condition are true (refer to the Niceties section of Chapter Four for the full discussion of conditions like the one above). So the condition causes the loop to stop if the character read isn't a blank, or if the next character in the file is the end-of-file character, or if the character isn't a blank *and* the next character is the end-of-file character.[7]

Putting this all together, the loop looks like this:

```
REPEAT
  READ(TextFile,Letter);
UNTIL (Letter <> ' ') OR (EOF(TextFile));
```

After this REPEAT-UNTIL loop has stopped, the program should go on to read a word—a series of non-blank characters—from the file. The next step, then, is to set up another loop to read the next sequence of non-blank characters

6. If the parentheses around each condition were not included in this statement, you would get an error, because the computer, not knowing what goes with what in the statement, would first attempt to deal with the part that reads ' ' OR EOF(TextFile). Since this does not make sense, an error would result.

7. Since the end-of-file character is preceded by the end-of-line character, which is read as a blank, in this particular instance both assertions will never be true at the same time.

in the file, one by one, as specified in steps 2.d through 2.f of the algorithm. However, there is one set of circumstances under which the program should *not* go on to read characters: if the previous REPEAT-UNTIL loop, the one outlined above, stopped because the next character in the file is the end-of-file character, rather than because it encountered a non-blank. Here you have the classic IF-THEN situation: if, after completing the REPEAT-UNTIL loop that skips blanks, the character that is next to be read from the file is *not* the end-of-file character, then the next loop should be executed; otherwise, the loop should be skipped. The IF-THEN statement was designed specifically for situations such as this one. So the general form of the next section of the program will be

```
IF NOT EOF(<filename>) THEN BEGIN
   Statements to read and store characters constituting a word
END;
```

With this, the program goes on to try to read a word *only* if it will not run into the end-of-file character when it attempts to read the first character. Otherwise, the statements are skipped.

The REPEAT-UNTIL loop corresponding to steps 2.d through 2.f of the algorithm is something like the one above—it contains a READ statement, and the condition on the loop checks the character in order to decide whether or not the loop is to continue. This time, however, the loop is to stop not if the character *is not* a blank, but if it *is*. This loop has other work to do as well, since the characters must be stored in the packed array if they are not blank.

The first step here is to store the character read last by the previous character (the one that made the loop stop because it wasn't a blank, which is the first character in the word) in the packed array. The basic outline of the loop to read a word is

```
REPEAT
   Store the character just read in the next available slot in the packed array
   Read a character
UNTIL the character just read is a blank
```

The loop continues only if the character read is not a blank, so no non-blank characters are stored in the packed array. The character can be read into a variable like **Letter** and then transferred into the packed array after checking that it is not a blank.

What statement is needed to store the character in the packed array? Each character is to be stored in an individual slot in the array, and of course the characters should be stored in sequential slots, starting with the first. Since **Letter** contains the first character of the word when the statement to store it in the packed array is encountered, and since it is to be stored in the first slot, a statement like this could be used to store that first character, if the packed array has the name **Word**:

```
Word[1] := Letter;
```

Letter is a variable of type CHAR, and each slot in the packed array is of type CHAR, so this is a perfectly valid assignment. The only trouble with this statement is that it is to appear within the loop, which means that it may be executed several times—once for each character in the word. If the statement above is used, each character will be stored in the first slot in **Word**, overwriting whatever was there before. The remaining slots will remain empty. Therefore, this statement must be modified so that each time through the loop the *next* available slot in the packed array is referenced, instead of referencing slot 1 over and over again.

This can be done easily, because Pascal allows variables as well as numbers to reference the slots in an array. This means that some variable name can appear within the brackets, and whenever the statement is encountered, the contents of that variable will be substituted for its name within the statement and used to reference a particular slot in the packed array. The value of this variable can be changed every time the loop executes so that the next slot in the array is referenced on each pass through the loop. Since the slots in the array are referenced by integer values, the variable that is used in this context should be declared with type INTEGER.

Suppose that a variable named **Counter** is declared with type INTEGER. This variable can be given the value 1 before the first character is stored in the **Word** array. Then, within the REPEAT-UNTIL loop, the statement to store the contents of the variable **Letter** into a slot in **Word** can be modified to read

```
Word[Counter] := Letter;
```

The first time through the loop, **Counter** will have the value 1, and so whatever is stored in the variable **Letter** at this point will be copied into **Word[1]**. Then, within the loop, 1 can be added to the value stored in **Counter**, so that the next time through the loop, **Counter** will have the value 2. This will cause the statement above to store whatever is in **Letter** in the second slot in **Word**. As long as the statement to add 1 to **Counter** appears within the loop, you can be sure that each time the statement above is executed, the next slot in **Word** will be referenced. This statement would be

```
Counter := Counter + 1;
```

This process of using one variable as a subscript for an array variable is another that is fundamental to the programming process.

Almost without fail, whenever an array is involved you will use a loop to access the slots in the array successively, and use a variable like Counter, **above, as a subscript, and add one to it each time through the loop.**

As soon as you find yourself in a situation where you are dealing with an array, a loop and a counter variable should come to mind immediately.

The statements to read and store characters, then, can be set up as follows:

```
Counter := 0;
IF NOT EOF(TextFile) THEN BEGIN
  REPEAT
    Counter := Counter + 1;
    Word[Counter] := Letter;
    READ(TextFile,Letter);
  UNTIL Letter = ' ';
END;      { then begin }
```

You may wonder why Counter is set to 0 instead of 1 at the outset, and there is really no reason at this point why it could not be set to 1 initially as long as the statement to add 1 to Counter appeared below the statement to assign the value of Letter to Word[Counter] instead of above it. However, Counter may later be used to indicate the length of the word stored in the Word variable, and if the end-of-file is encountered in the initial REPEAT-UNTIL loop and nothing is ever stored in Word, the value of Counter will indicate that the word has a length of 0, which is entirely appropriate in such a situation. The plan to give Counter the value 0 when no word is read also explains why the statement that assigns Counter its initial value appears outside, rather than inside, the IF-THEN statement: if it appeared within the IF-THEN statement, Counter would not be set to 0 in the situation where the end-of-file was encountered.

A few minor modifications to the statements above need to be made before they are complete, but for now, consider the way the statements work. Suppose that the file that is being read by the program contains the following:

```
Mary Mary Quite Contrary
```

The first REPEAT loop in the program will read the 'M,' and as a result the loop will stop (since the condition Letter<>' ' is true). Next, the INTEGER variable Counter is set to 0, and then the condition on the IF-THEN statement checks that the next character to be read ('a') is not the end-of-file character. Since it is not, the statements within the BEGIN-END pair associated with the IF-THEN statement are executed. The second REPEAT-UNTIL loop (the one that reads the word) is now entered for the first time. One is added to the value stored in the variable Counter, which is currently 0, giving Counter a new value of 1. Since Counter has the value 1, when the next statement is encountered it will be interpreted as if the reference were to Word[1]; and the current contents of Letter (the character 'M') will be stored in Word[1]. Then the next character in the input—the character 'a'—will be read and stored in Letter. The bottom of the loop is reached at this point, where the assertion that Letter contains the character ' ' is checked for truth or falsity, and found to be false. Therefore the statements in the loop are executed again. Again, 1 is added to the current contents of Counter (the value 1), and the resulting value, 2, is stored in Counter, erasing the old contents. Now the current contents of Letter—the letter 'a'—are copied into Word[2], since the reference to Word[Counter] is interpreted as Word[2], based on the new contents of Counter. The packed array Word now contains the characters 'M' and 'a.'

You should continue the trace of the program's action to the point where the entire first word has been copied into the Word packed array. Pay particular attention to the way the variable Counter is used to reference the array—once again, this method of accessing an array is a staple of computer programming technique.

Two things need to be added to the statements above to make the program work properly. The condition on the second REPEAT-UNTIL loop must be extended, but this time there is no need to check for the end-of-file character. That is because, as you recall, the end-of-file character is always preceded by an end-of-line character. The end-of-line character is read as a blank, and this will stop the loop just before the end-of-file character is encountered. Before the program tries to read again, control will return to the top of the WHILE NOT EOF(TextFile) loop where end-of-file will be detected and the WHILE loop will terminate. However, you must make sure in the condition on the second REPEAT-UNTIL loop that the program does not try to store into a non-existent slot in the array. This could happen if the packed array contains, say, 20 slots, and for some reason a word exists in the input that is more than 20 characters long. In the examples, 20 slots were set up for the Word array because 20 seems like a good length as very few words in the English language even approach this number of characters, let alone exceed it. You are free to make your packed array bigger, but, recalling that space is a valuable commodity in the realm of computer programming, you should not make it any longer than you feel is necessary to accommodate the words your program will read in. In any case, as there is always a chance that some aberration will occur and a word will in fact be longer than the number of characters accommodated in your packed array, it is wise to add a condition on the loop that says it should stop if the character just read is a blank or if the slot the program will next attempt to store in does not exist. If the packed array is set up with 20 slots, this problem will arise when and if the program attempts to store in slot 21. If, for whatever reason, 21 or more contiguous characters appear in the text, this problem could very well occur, causing what is probably one of the most common errors in programming: going outside the *bounds* of an array. Your computer may indicate this error in a variety of ways; for instance, this kind of error is sometimes called an *access violation*, since your program is attempting to access parts of memory that do not necessarily belong to it (that is, the part of memory just beyond the end of the array). In any case, this is a common problem, and one worth guarding against.

Whenever you work with arrays and loops, always consider the possibilities for exceeding the array's boundaries and provide a condition on the loop to be sure you do not do it.

Here, the problem of exceeding the boundaries of your array can be handled by keeping an eye on the value of Counter. If ever the loop's bottom is reached and Counter contains the value 20, the loop should be stopped. If it is not, the next time through the loop the program will add one to Counter and, as a result, then attempt to store into Word[21], a non-existent slot. So the loop should stop if the character just read is a blank, or if Counter is equal to 20 (or the number of slots in your packed array, if different). The entire condition, then, can be expressed as

```
(Letter = ' ') OR (Counter = 20)
```

Once again, note the use of the parentheses to group the assertions properly.

The second modification to the statements above involves the Word variable. Most words, as mentioned already, will not take up the entire twenty slots in the array. Eventually, the packed array will be printed out, and if all twenty slots have not been filled, what will happen? The computer will try to print all 20 slots, but if nothing has been stored in one of them, what is there is probably what was left over from the previous use of the memory space. Your version of Pascal may simply print whatever it finds there, thus yielding what is called "garbage" in the computing world:

```
Mary$%&/!?p(*%)+*/?!
```

Or, your version of Pascal may be kind enough to print blanks; but once again, it is not at all wise to rely on this kindness.

To solve this problem, a statement can be inserted in the program at a point *before* any characters are stored in Word, that stores a blank in each of the 20 slots in the packed array. As you recall, this can be done in a single statement:

```
Word := '                    ';
```

Where should this statement be inserted? Not inside the REPEAT-UNTIL loop, or Word would be blanked out after each character is stored in it. Instead, the statement should appear just above the IF-THEN statement, before or after Counter is set to 0 (the order of the two statements is unimportant since they do not affect one another). Thus, if the end-of-file is the next character and nothing is ever stored in Word, the packed array will contain blanks, which is appropriate; otherwise, setting Word to blanks ensures a clean slate before storing the new word. As each letter is subsequently stored in the packed array, the blanks will be replaced, one by one.

Blanking out Word becomes even more imperative when you consider the grander plan of this program. The statements outlined so far, which skip spaces (if they exist) and then read a contiguous series of non-blank characters and store them in a packed array, provide for reading only one word. This entire set of statements goes inside the WHILE loop and is therefore repeated over and over for each word in the text. Thus, instead of garbage left over in Word, the last word read may instead be there. If it is longer than the next word read, what you may see printed is the new word together with the end of the previous one. This makes blanking Word out before each word is stored even more necessary.

Because the condition on the WHILE loop checks for the end-of-file, you can be sure, first, that the program does not attempt to read from an empty file (one that contains only the end-of-file character), and, second, that the first

REPEAT-UNTIL loop, which reads before doing any checking, does not attempt to read the end-of-file character at any time during the course of the program.

The last thing that needs to be done to make this program complete is to implement step 2.g by including a statement to write the word out. The statement that performs this function is left to you to determine as an exercise. Remember that the entire contents of a packed array can be written by including the name of the packed array, with no subscript, in a WRITE or WRITELN statement.

The whole program will look like this:

```
PROGRAM Words(INPUT,OUTPUT,TextFile);
  { Isolates and then prints each of the words }
  { in TextFile on a separate line }
  TYPE String = PACKED ARRAY[1..20] OF CHAR;
  VAR Letter : CHAR;
    Word : String;
    Counter : INTEGER;
    TextFile : TEXT;
BEGIN
  RESET(TextFile);
  WHILE NOT EOF(TextFile) DO BEGIN
    REPEAT
      READ(TextFile,Letter);
    UNTIL (Letter <> ' ') OR (EOF(TextFile));
    Counter := 0;
    IF NOT EOF(TextFile) THEN BEGIN
      REPEAT
        Counter := Counter + 1;
        Word[Counter] := Letter;
        READ(TextFile,Letter);
      UNTIL (Letter = ' ') OR (Counter = 20);
    END;      { then begin }
    Statement to print the word
  END;      { while not eof }
END.      { Words }
```

SUMMING UP THE PROGRAM

The structure of this program differs from that of the previous two programs because in this program no consideration of the end-of-line character is made. There is no need here to note when the end of a line appears in a text, as there was in the previous two programs, since this program is concerned only with the individual words in the text and not printing line-by-line or counting lines. Since the end-of-line character is read as a blank, it is simply seen as a separator of words.

The logic of this program is also more complex than that in previous programs, and more complexity means that there is more potential for the program to run, but run improperly. That is, while your program may be *syntactically* correct and you get no errors before the program executes indicating that a semicolon is missing or a variable name is undefined, when it actually starts to execute things go wrong. In this program there are two very obvious possibilities for errors: (1) the program attempts to read the end-of-file character, and (2) the program attempts to store something in a non-existent slot in the packed array. To avoid the first problem you should be sure that your program always checks for end-of-file each time it is about to read (except in the case where the previous character read is always a non-blank, as in the second REPEAT-UNTIL loop). You should also check to be sure that your program will run if for some reason the file from which you are reading is empty (that is, it contains only the end-of-file marker).

The second problem—trying to store in a non-existent slot in an array—is a very common one and deserves some attention. In general, you should understand the very intimate relationship between arrays (both packed arrays and ordinary arrays, which you'll see in Chapter Seven), loops, and "counter variables" like the one named Counter in the program. The situation in this program is typical of what you will see when you deal with arrays of any kind; that is, when it comes time to deal with the array within the program, four things occur:

1. An INTEGER-type variable is assigned a starting value (usually, 0 or 1) *before* the start of a loop.
2. Inside the loop, the counter is used as a subscript into the array.
3. Also inside the loop, one is added to the counter.
4. The condition on the loop includes a check that the value of the counter does not exceed the length of the array (20, in the examples in this chapter).

This scenario obviously enables access to each successive element of the array by using a counter variable as a subscript into the array and a loop that repeats once for each array element, adding 1 to the counter in each iteration. Notice also item 4 in the list: the check within the condition on the loop to ensure the counter does not become greater than the length of the array. This is the only way to ensure that the program does not attempt to access a non-existent element of the array—in the examples, that would be slot number 21. In general, when you get an error message that your program has attempted to access "outside the bounds of the array," the value of the counter variable is usually 0 (in which case for some reason it was not incremented before being used as a subscript) or one greater than the length of the array. If the source of your error is not clear, then the best way to find it is to construct a short sample text and run through the program's actions by hand, keeping track of the contents of each variable at each step and the character that will next be read from the input.

Since accessing the successive elements of an array is one of the most common manipulations of an array, you are going to see the four items outlined above in your programs again and again. Be sure that you understand how these things work together to get at the contents of an array.

One last word about loops—you should always be sure that the conditions on your loops are appropriate for the situation. In general,

---

The condition on a WHILE or REPEAT-UNTIL loop always involves variables whose values are changed within the loop, and/or a check for EOF or EOLN if a READ or READLN statement appears in the loop.

So if a variable appears on the left of an assignment operator within a loop, chances are that the condition on that loop should check its value. If a variable appears in a READ or READLN statement in a loop, its value may be checked in the condition as well, and there will almost always be a check for EOF or EOLN in the condition on the loop. There is no point in checking the value of a variable that does not change its value each time the loop executes, so be sure your condition does not bother with variables that remain unchanged by the loop's action.

NICETIES

Constants

Pascal provides a facility whereby the programmer can set up what are called *constants* within a program. In one respect, constants are like variables—they are named memory slots in which particular values are stored—but the difference is that the value stored in a constant *cannot be changed during the course of a program.* Instead, a value is assigned at the time the constant is declared, and that value is then substituted for the constant's name wherever it appears in the program. Because the value of a constant cannot be changed within the program, the name of a constant will never appear on the left-hand side of an assignment operator or in the list associated with a READ statement.

Constants are declared in a special area of the program just after the Program Heading, and before the type declarations (or variable declarations, if no type declarations exist). Thus the overall structure of a Pascal program can be extended to be

```
Program Heading
Constant Declarations
Type Declarations
Variable Declarations
BEGIN
  Program Statements
END.
```

The Constant Declarations section of the program begins with the keyword CONST, in the same way as the Type Declarations section begins with TYPE and the Variable Declarations section begins with VAR. After that, the constants are declared and at the same time, values are associated with them. These are the values that the constants will have throughout the program.

Suppose, for example, you want to set up a constant that will have the value 5. The constant declaration will look like this:

```
CONST Five = 5;
```

This declares a constant with the name Five, and stores the value 5 in the memory slot associated with that name. Now, within the program you can say

```
ThisOne := Five;
```

As long as ThisOne is an INTEGER variable, this is a legal assignment, and the result is that the value 5 is stored in the variable ThisOne. Note that although no type information is provided in the constant declaration, Pascal can determine the type of the constant by looking at the value assigned to it. Thus if an integer value is assigned, the type of the constant is assumed to be INTEGER; if a character is assigned, the type is assumed to be CHAR. For example, the constant declaration

```
CONST Alpha = 'A';
```

sets up a constant of type CHAR, that contains the letter 'A.' The assignment

```
Letter := Alpha;
```

assigns the value 'A' to the variable Letter, which must be a type CHAR variable.

Constants can be declared which contain a string of characters as well, as follows:

```
CONST Alphabet = 'ABCDEFGHIJKLMNOPQRSTUVWXYZ';
```

The value stored in this constant could be assigned or compared to any variable declared as a packed array with 26 slots.

You might wonder why constants are useful in a program, since their values are always known and thus could be given explicitly instead of specifying the constant name. The next few suggestions for using constants in the program for this chapter should answer this question.

In the program for this chapter the size of the packed array is used at two points within the program: in the declaration of the *String* type itself, and in the condition on the REPEAT-UNTIL loop that stores characters in the packed array. In a bigger program, the size of the array may be referenced many times, since the size of the array limits the number of times any loop which accesses individual slots in the array can execute.

Suppose that you set up your packed array to have 20 slots. Later, you decide to change the size to 30 slots. You will now have to go through the program and be sure to change every reference to the size of the packed array from 20 to 30. As careful as you might be, in a large program the chances are fairly good that you will miss one or two references, and as a result, later your program will not run at all, or will not run as it should.

Now suppose instead that you declare a constant at the beginning of the program as follows:

```
CONST StringLength = 20;
```

Now, when you declare your *String* type, you specify

```
TYPE String = PACKED ARRAY[1..StringLength] OF CHAR;
```

You can use a constant to indicate either or both of the upper and lower bounds of an array in a type declaration. However, Pascal does not allow the use of variables to specify the bounds of an array.

In the condition on the REPEAT-UNTIL loop that reads characters in the packed array, you can use StringLength instead of the value 20:

```
(Letter = ' ') OR (Counter = StringLength)
```

Now, when you want to change the size of your packed array, the only thing in the program that must be changed is the constant declaration. Again, in a longer program this could save a lot of time and avoid the possibility of missing a reference. Thus, the first and most important reason for using constants is to make a program easy to modify.

The second reason for using constants is to make your program easier to read and type. This is evident in the condition on the REPEAT-UNTIL loop that appears above: saying Counter = StringLength makes it immediately obvious what the purpose of the condition is, much more readily than saying Counter = 20. The readability of the program can also be enhanced by using constants for the blank (' ') and string of blanks ('   ') that are used in the program. The constants can be set up like this:

```
CONST Blank = ' ';
      Blanks = '                    ';
```

Then, within the program you can say

```
Word = Blanks;
```

and on the conditions in the REPEAT-UNTIL loops you can specify

```
Letter <> Blank
```

and

```
Letter = Blank
```

This will not help you much in terms of making changes to the program, since it is unlikely that you will change the blank or string of blanks later on, but the use of the constant names instead of the literal value within the program enhances both its readability and its neatness. Obviously, readability is enhanced only if your constant names are chosen to reflect the values stored in them, so choose your names appropriately.

Do not go overboard using constants. The blank is a good candidate for a constant because it appears more than once in a program, is likely to be used even more in later programs, looks messy in its literal form, and is awkward to type and therefore prone to errors. This does not apply to a value like 1, which is assigned to Counter within the program; it is obvious what the value is, and even if the value is used several times in the program, you save nothing by giving it a name. In fact, you are probably more likely to mis-type a name than the value 1 itself.

The Pascal FOR Loop

Pascal has one other kind of loop in addition to the WHILE and REPEAT-UNTIL loops. Both WHILE and REPEAT-UNTIL loops provide for what is called *indefinite iteration*—that is, the repetition of a process an indefinite number of times. This means that these loops may execute any number of times, depending upon the condition that governs the loop. The FOR loop is different in that it provides for what is called *definite iteration*. A FOR loop executes a fixed number of times; there is never any variation. Consequently, a FOR loop has no condition associated with it. Instead, the programmer specifies the number of times the loop is to execute.

The FOR loop has the following form:

```
FOR <variable> := 1 TO 10 DO BEGIN
   <statement or statements>
END;
```

The numbers 1 and 10 in this example are arbitrary; they are simply used here for illustration's sake. If *<variable>* is some variable of type INTEGER, any two integer values can be used here.

The FOR loop works like this: When the loop is first encountered, the variable named in the loop heading (called the *loop control variable*) is assigned the value specified just after the assignment operator—in this case, 1. The loop is entered and the statements are executed. When the loop ends, control returns to the top of the loop; *at this point 1 is added to the value currently stored in the loop control variable*. This value is then compared to the second value specified—10, in this example—and if it is not greater than this value (that is, if it falls within the range "1 TO 10"), the loop is entered again. Thus this loop will execute exactly 10 times, and as it does, the loop control variable will take on successively the values in the range specified in the loop's heading.

The loop control variable can be used within the loop: For example,

```
For Counter := 1 TO 20 DO BEGIN
   WRITELN(Counter);
END;
```

The action of this loop helps demonstrate the values the loop control variable takes on as the loop executes; this loop will print out the values 1 through 20, one per line. If you understand why this happens then you understand how the loop operates.

The loop control variable's value cannot be changed within a FOR loop. That is, the loop control variable cannot appear on the left side of an assignment operator or in a READ or READLN statement inside the loop. However, as shown above, the variable can be used in any context that merely accesses the value stored in it.

FOR loops are very often used with arrays and packed arrays to access each slot in the array. This is because it is very convenient to simply use the variable in the loop heading as a subscript for the array. For instance, if you want to print, on separate lines, the contents of each slot in a packed array named Word, and StringLength is a constant indicating the number of slots in the packed array, you can use the following loop:

```
FOR Counter := 1 TO StringLength DO BEGIN
  WRITELN(Word[Counter]);
END;
```

Pay particular attention to the way the variable Counter is used in this example to access each element of the array; this is a common programming construct, and one with which you should be very familiar.

Notice also that in the example above, the INTEGER-type constant StringLength is used to indicate the value at which the loop is to stop; in general,

---

Variables and constants can be used to indicate the starting and stopping values in a FOR loop heading, provided their type matches the type of the loop control variable.

If Counter, ThisOne, and ThatOne are all type INTEGER variables, then the following loop is valid:

```
FOR Counter := ThisOne TO ThatOne DO BEGIN
  WRITELN(Counter);
END;
```

The values that Counter takes on during the course of this loop depend on the values of the variables ThisOne and ThatOne at the time the loop is first encountered. If ThisOne has the value 5 when this loop starts to execute, and ThatOne has the value 45, then Counter will take on the values from 5 to 45 and the loop will thus execute 41 times. The result of executing this loop will be to print out the numbers 5 through 45, on successive lines.

It is not good programming practice (and it rarely makes sense) to change the values of variables used to indicate the starting and stopping values in a FOR loop within the loop itself. Even if you do, it is their values at the time the loop is first encountered that are used to determine the values at which the loop starts and stops.

FOR loops can be made to go backwards, if the heading reads like this:

```
FOR Counter := 10 DOWNTO 1 DO BEGIN
```

Here, Counter will start with the value 10, and one will be *subtracted* from its value each time through the loop, until it has taken on each of the values from 10 down to 1.

Character values can also be used to govern FOR loops:

```
FOR Letter := 'a' TO 'z' DO BEGIN
  WRITELN(Letter);
END;
```

This loop will write out the alphabetic characters 'a' through 'z.' Letter must be a variable of type CHAR in this case.

Subranges

Pascal allows you to declare a variable with a type that consists of a set of values that is a *subrange* of either the CHAR or INTEGER types.[8] Subranges of the type INTEGER are very handy when dealing with arrays, as you will see.

For example, Pascal allows you to declare a type in the Type Declarations section of the program like this:

```
TYPE StringBounds : 0..20;
```

and then to give that type to a variable in the VAR Declarations section of the program, like this:

```
VAR Counter : StringBounds;
```

This set of statements accomplishes the following: the declaration of the type, StringBounds, sets up a new type that consists of a set of values that are a subgroup of the set of INTEGER values. When a variable is declared with this type, *it can take on only the range of INTEGER values specified in the type declaration for* StringBounds. So, in this case, Counter can take on values between 0 and 20 only. If, during the course of the program, Counter is given any other value, an error will result.[9] This is one way of catching situations where a counter variable's value will cause the program to try to access a non-existent slot in the array *before* it happens. You are trading one error for another, of course, but this error is much easier to locate and fix. Instead of having to trace the value of

8. Subranges of *enumerated types*, which are described in Appendix D, are allowed in Pascal as well.

9. On some systems no error is generated if a variable declared with a sub-range of INTEGER type is given a value outside the specified range. In these cases the variable behaves just like any other INTEGER variable.

the counter and look through the program to see where its value went out of the range of valid subscript for the array, you know right away where it happened.

When a variable is given a type that is a subrange of INTEGER values, it can be treated like an INTEGER variable in terms of its use. That is, you can add to it, subtract from it, assign its value to a variable declared with type INTEGER, or assign to it the value stored in an INTEGER-type variable (as long as that value is within the appropriate range).

Subrange types can be used in the program for this and subsequent chapters to define the values of variables that are used as subscripts in the packed array Word. The subrange type can be defined like this:

```
StringBounds = 0..StringLength;
```

assuming StringLength is a constant indicating the length of the packed array. Counter, the variable that serves as a subscript of the packed array, can be declared with this type, thus limiting the range of valid values for this variable to 0 through the value of StringLength. Notice that although the range of valid subscript values for the array is actually 1 through 20, in order to accommodate the initialization of Counter to 0 before the loop in the main program, the subrange type must include the value 0 as well. You could, of course, change things around so that the initial value of Counter is 1, but then the subrange would have to extend to 21 since within the loop, Counter could be set to 21 quite legally (the condition on the loop would then check that the value of Counter is not *greater than*, rather than *equal to*, 20).

When you use a subrange type for a variable used as a subscript of an array within a WHILE or REPEAT-UNTIL loop, the range will typically be either 0 through the length of the array or 1 through one greater than the size of the array, depending upon the initial value given to the counter variable before the loop.

Throughout this text, the convention will be to initialize counter variables to 0 before a loop, so that subrange types for variables that index arrays will range from 0 to the size of the array.

You can use subranges to define variables that hold characters, too. For instance, if you say

```
TYPE  CapitalLetter = 'A'..'Z';
      SmallLetter = 'a'..'z';
VAR   Letter1 : CapitalLetter;
      Letter2 : SmallLetter;
```

Then Letter1 can hold *only* a capital letter and Letter2 can hold *only* a small letter. An attempt to store any other characters in these variables will cause an error.

In general, subrange types are good for trapping potential errors. Programs often crash or run incorrectly because a variable has a value that it should not have ever had at all. As your programs get bigger, it becomes more and more difficult to find the place where the incorrect value was given to the variable. So

---

Use subrange types whenever you can, especially for counter variables that are used as subscripts for arrays.

More About Type Declarations

This is a convenient place to make a point about type declarations. Without doubt, some experienced Pascal programmer will look at one of the programs you are writing and tell you that instead of going through all of that business declaring StringBounds as a type, you can simply declare Counter as follows:

```
VAR Counter : 0..StringLength
```

This is true. You could, in fact, declare Word like this:

```
VAR Word : PACKED ARRAY[1..StringLength] OF CHAR;
```

eliminating the type declaration of *String*. While this works, it has serious drawbacks because of the way Pascal decides whether or not two things are of the same type. In Pascal, variables are considered to be of the same type only if the *name* of their type is the same. This means that if you declare Word as shown above, and then declare Word2 like this:

```
Word2 : PACKED ARRAY[1..20] OF CHAR;
```

the two variables do not have the same type, since their types do not have the same name (because the types on these variables have no names, Pascal makes one up for each). The only way to give a type a name is to assign it one in the Type Declarations section of the program. To avoid both confusion and the possibility that two things that should be the same are not,

---

Always give your variables types that are either built-in (CHAR, INTEGER, REAL, or BOOLEAN) or declared in the Type Declarations section of the program. In other words, do not define new types in the VAR Declarations section of the program.

The "Snapshot" Approach to Debugging

Chances are you have already encountered the situation where your program does not run the way it should, but no matter how much you look at it, the program seems to be correct. As mentioned several times in the preceding chapters, a good way to check a program's behavior is to trace through the steps the program takes by hand, but even this may not help at times. What you can do in these situations is to let the computer help you trace the program's steps by printing out the values of appropriate variables as each step of the program is performed. This way, you can see exactly what is going on at each point in the program.

To do this, all you have to do is insert WRITELN statements at points in your program where you would like to see the values of certain variables. Quite often these statements are inserted within loops to enable you to see what is happening at each step along the way. Obviously, these statements should be taken out once you get the program to run properly.

An example will illustrate this best. Suppose that you forgot to add the condition on your second REPEAT-UNTIL loop that checks to see if the value stored in Counter is equal to the number of slots in the packed array. Your program runs fine for the first several words in the text, printing them out one per line as it should, but then generates an error when it attempts to read the word "narrator-commentator," (note that the comma is part of the word). You do not see the problem, and so you use the snapshot method to lead you to the source of the error.

The error message will probably indicate that something is wrong when you try to execute the statement

```
Word[Counter] := Letter;
```

It would be helpful to "watch" as the program executes this statement, and you can do that in a way by printing out the contents of each of the variables involved in the statement just before each execution of the statement. To do so, you can insert a statement like the following immediately before the statement above:

```
WRITELN('Letter= ',Letter,'Counter= ',Counter:1,'Word = ',Word);
```

Now every time the statement is executed you will see the contents of the variables involved in the problematic statement. This is called a "snapshot" because it has the effect of freezing the program's action for a split second, so that you can examine the contents of certain variables. Note that the WRITELN statement provides for printing labels for each variable's value so that you can easily identify the output.

When the program gets to the point just before the error occurs, you will see that the value of Counter is 21. This should tip you off to the cause of the problem; snapshots do not solve problems, but they provide information that can lead to a solution. After you have added the appropriate condition to the REPEAT-UNTIL loop to prevent the loop from executing if Counter is greater than 20, you can delete the WRITELN statement and run the program as usual.

APPLICATIONS AND CONSIDERATIONS

Determining where each word in the text begins and ends is a task that text formatting programs are faced with. Text formatters typically take as input a text the user has written. Often, the user imbeds commands within the text indicating that a new paragraph should be begun, a line is to be skipped, or that a certain line should be centered, etc. But since the user can type the text in any form he or she likes—one word per input line, if that is what the user wants to do—the bulk of the formatter's work is to read words and add them to the end of the current output line if there is room. If not, a new line is begun. So if the user's input is

```
But since the user can type the
text in any form he or she
likes---one word per input line,
if that's what the user wants to
do---the
bulk of the formatter's work
is to read words and add them
to the end
of the current output line if there is room.
If not, a new line is begun.
```

the output is

```
But since the user can type the text in any form he or she likes---one word per input
line, if that's what the user wants to do---the bulk of the formatter's work is to read
words and add them to the end of the current output line if there is room. If not, a
new line is begun.
```

The text formatter must read the whole word before it can decide whether or not to put it on the same line; if characters are printed one by one as they are read in, the formatter might discover that it had reached the end of the line in the middle of a word.

The output of such a text formatter has a ragged right edge and does not include hyphenation of any words. Justification of the right edge is a complex task and demands inserting blanks at intervals in the output line to yield a line of the desired length. Hyphenation is yet another problem—in order to hyphenate, a text formatter must "know" where it is legal to split a word. Some rules can be programmed into a text formatter for this purpose—for instance, when two consonants appear between vowels, the word can usually be split between the two consonants, but this is not always true (for example, consider the word "telephone"). Certain suffixes or prefixes can also be recognized by the text formatter, before or after which it is legal to break the word. But there are so many exceptions that typically, hyphenation requires that the text formatter have access to a dictionary that includes the hyphenation points for words that don't follow the rules. The text formatter will get a word, look it up in the dictionary (which usually contains only exception words), and if it is not there, it will apply the basic rules for hyphenation in order to determine the break point. Some text formatters allow you to add your own words and the rules for hyphenating them to the dictionary.

Having access to entire words also enables many more kinds of analysis to be performed. In particular, since whole words can be examined at once, rather than only one letter at a time, you can look at the words to see if they contain certain prefixes or suffixes or configurations of any kind. If they do, the words can be printed out, thus providing the user with a list of words that fit some description. Several of the exercises deal with this application.

EXERCISES

1. Modify the program in this chapter so that it counts and prints the number of words in the text.

2. Modify the program in this chapter so that in addition to identifying the words in the text, it counts the words *and* counts the number of letters and sentences in the text, as in the program for Chapter Four. Instead of printing the words in the text, the program should print the number of words, the number of letters, and the number of sentences in the text, along with the average length of the words in the text (average number of letters per word) and the average sentence length (average number of words per sentence).

3. Modify the program in this chapter to print out all of the words in the text without punctuation. To do this, you will have to use a loop to write out each character in the packed array one at a time. But before printing each character, check to see if it is a letter; if so, print it, but if not, do not. (Hint: use the FOR loop described in the Niceties section for this problem.)

4. Modify the program to print each word out backwards. If the input to the program is

```
Mary Mary Quite Contrary
```

the program should print

```
yraM
yraM
etiuQ
yrartnoC
```

Again, use the FOR loop described in the Niceties section for this problem.

5. Without adding any statements *outside* the WHILE loop that surrounds the body of the program, modify the program so that after all the words are printed, the program skips a line and prints, "End of the text."

6. Modify the program so that it stores only letters in the packed array—that is, no punctuation is stored in the packed array. You may, if you want, store hyphens and apostrophes if you'd like to consider them part of a word when they appear. (Of course, this will cause a problem if your text contains a word enclosed in single quotation marks (apostrophes), since these will be stored with the word.)

7. (Slightly more difficult.) Finding words in a text with certain prefixes and suffixes can be of linguistic interest in analyzing a text. Modify the program so that it prints out only words that end in "ing" or "ed". The output should be labelled with comment indicating the nature of the output. After all of the words are printed, print a message stating the number of such words that appear in the text. (This exercise can be modified to deal with any prefix or suffix you like.)

8. (Slightly more difficult.) Modify the program so that it prints out only words which contain some sequence of characters *anywhere* within the word. For instance, you might want to print out words which contain a particular root word, like "divi," such as "undivided," "divide," "indivisible," and so on. Or, to make things slightly more complicated, you may want to print words with either of the roots "scrip" or "scrib," so that words like "indescribable," "script," "ascribed," "inscriptive," "conscription," and so on would appear in the list. To decide which root words might be of interest, look over a portion of your text.

9. (A bit more difficult.) Do exercise 7 or 8, but prompt the user to enter the suffix, prefix, or root that will be searched for.

10. (A bit more difficult.) Instead of reading in words that are part of a text, read in a list of singular nouns from a file. The output of the program should consist of each of the words in the original list coupled with its plural form.

Your program probably will not be able to properly pluralize "mouse" (unless it fails on "house"), but it should be able to deal with differences in the plural forms of words like "kiss" and "bus" (assuming the plural is "busses") and perhaps even "fungus" and "memorandum."

11. (Very difficult.) Write a program that formats a text, as described in the Applications and Considerations section of this chapter. The input should consist of a text in any form, as shown in the example, and output lines that are a maximum of 80 characters in their width.

12. (For the adventurous programmer.) Do exercise 11, but let the user imbed commands in the input text that cause the program to start a new paragraph in the output text. Specifically, when the command '.pa' appears in the input, a new paragraph will be begun with the text that follows. The command should appear on a line by itself, with no other text. So, if the user enters

```
This is the first paragraph
of a sample text containing two paragraphs.
.pa
This is the second paragraph of the text,
and it should be indented
five spaces and start a new line.
```

the output is

```
   This is the first paragraph of a sample text containing two paragraphs.
   This is the second paragraph of the text, and it should be indented five spaces
and start a new line.
```

You can elaborate on this exercise to include other commands as well—for example, commands to leave blank lines or (if you are *very* ambitious) commands to center a line.

6 Using Procedures

The problem for this chapter is slightly different from the problems in the previous and subsequent chapters. Instead of writing a program to solve a new problem, you will write a program to do exactly the same thing as in the preceding chapter; however, the program's organization will be modified so that it uses what are called *procedures* in Pascal. Procedures are extremely important constructs in programming and they also take some getting used to, and that is why an entire chapter is devoted to familiarizing you with their use.

A procedure is a means by which a group of statements within a program can be set apart from the body of the program, at a special location just following the declaration of the program's variables. Unlike statements that appear in the body of the program, these statements are not executed when they are encountered in the program text. Instead, the group of statements is given a name, and at any point in the program where the statements are to be executed, this name is inserted. This causes the statements to be executed at that point in the program without their actually appearing there. The group of statements is called a *procedure*, and the name associated with the statements is the procedure's name.

That is the general idea behind procedures. You might wonder why anyone would want to do such a thing, and there are several reasons. First, if the statements need to be executed at more than one location in the program, instead of repeating them, only the name needs to be repeated. This can save a great deal of typing and shorten the program considerably. Second, by isolating a group of statements in this way, they can be easily tested independently of the rest of the program. When programs become large, it is often difficult to locate exactly where the source of an error occurs. If pieces of the program are tested separately, it is much easier to pinpoint where a problem arises. Third, by breaking a program down into groups of statements with specific functions, it is easy to see the overall structure and flow of events in the program. It is also easy to then extract a particular procedure, which performs a particular function, to use in another program if desired.

The most important reason to use procedures, though, is that they make programming, which is a relatively complex task involving a great deal of detail, much easier by breaking a problem down into several smaller problems that are more easily solved and managed. For example, recall that in the process of developing the algorithm in Chapter Five, the following outline of the overall process was given:

1. Read characters until a non-blank is encountered.
2. Read and store characters until a blank is encountered.
3. Print the string of characters just stored on a new line.

Steps 1 and 2, you will recall, required several sub-steps to implement. But by thinking of them in broad terms first, as in the algorithm above, and later working out the details for each step *individually*, the sequence of steps required to solve the problem was much easier to discover. If you had attempted to work out the detailed algorithm at the outset, with steps 1 and 2 fully expanded, you most likely would have had more difficulty managing the problem. This process of designing an algorithm in general terms and then breaking steps down into their sub-steps is called *top-down analysis*. The use of procedures makes designing programs from the top down simple, because the steps required for each "subtask" or general step are put in a separate procedure, which is isolated physically from the rest of the program. When you write the procedure, you can concentrate on the particular step it is to implement, thus freeing yourself for the time from consideration of the remaining steps in the program. This makes the programming process easier, because instead of writing complicated programs that require the management of a great deal of detail, you instead write small and very manageable procedures that are later put together in a single program.

A procedure can be regarded as a little program within itself, designed to perform a particular task. In Pascal procedures have a format very similar to a program's, even enabling the declaration of variables, constants, and types within them. Thus a procedure is a separate and self-contained *module*, and functions very much like a "program within a program." Dealing with these smaller modules simplifies programming considerably. Once you learn to use procedures, you will probably never have to manage a portion of a program larger than the program for the previous chapter.

Another advantage of procedures that should be mentioned is that once you have written a procedure to perform a specific task, it can be used in any program that needs it. This means that once you write a procedure to read a word, you can use this same procedure in any other program you later write that also needs to read a word. In fact, this is exactly what you will do as you write successive programs in the chapters in the remainder of this text—you will use procedures that you have already written whenever the sub-task they perform is part of the task at hand. Procedures save work and prevent errors by enabling you to use a set of statements that are known to work properly instead of re-writing and debugging a new piece of code.

By the way, the body of the program you will write in this chapter will look very much like the outline of the algorithm above. This is possible because the statements to perform steps 1 and 2 will be tucked away in procedures. When they need to be executed, only the name of the procedure will appear, not the statements themselves. Thus within the body of the program you will see only a few statements, and the flow of events in the program will be readily obvious to anyone who reads the program.

ELEMENTS OF PASCAL

The Procedure

A group of statements that is to be regarded as a procedure is included at the beginning of the program, just after the Variable Declarations section of the program and before the BEGIN statement that signals the beginning of the body of the program. This section of the program is referred to as the *Procedure Declarations section* of the program, and within this section any number of individual procedures may be declared. To reflect this, the overall structure of a Pascal program needs to be expanded as follows:

```
Program Heading
Constant Declarations
Type Declarations
Variable Declarations
Procedure Declarations
BEGIN
  Program Statements
END.
```

A procedure declaration has the general form:

```
Procedure Heading
BEGIN
  <Statements>
END;
```

You can declare as many procedures as you like in the Procedure Declarations section of a program. Each of the declarations has the form above, and all of the procedures that you declare are simply listed in this format, one after another.

If you get the idea that a procedure is something like a program, you are right. As you will see in a moment, a procedure is in fact very much like a miniature program, which can have its own variables, constants, types, and even its own procedures.

The Procedure heading has the following general format:

```
PROCEDURE <name>;
```

where PROCEDURE is a Pascal keyword indicating that this is the beginning of a procedure declaration, and <*name*> is any user-defined name that follows the rules governing the form of variable names.

The statements that constitute the body of the procedure appear within a BEGIN-END pair, as in a program. Note, however, that the END on a procedure is followed by a semicolon rather than a period. Any valid Pascal statement can appear within a procedure. The following is a valid procedure declaration:

```
PROCEDURE WriteHello;
BEGIN
  WRITELN;
  WRITELN('Hello');
  WRITELN;
END;     { WriteHello }
```

To give you an example of the way in which a procedure declaration is included in a program, the following shows how a procedure like WriteHello is included in a program:

```
PROGRAM Demonstrate(INPUT,OUTPUT);
  VAR SampleVariable : INTEGER;
  PROCEDURE WriteHello;
  BEGIN
    WRITELN;
    WRITELN ('Hello');
    WRITELN;
  END;     { WriteHello }
BEGIN
    .
    .
    .
END.     { Demonstrate }
```

From now on, the declarations and body of a program will be referred to as the *main program*, to distinguish it from the procedures that may be contained within it. Within the main program, any time you want the statements that are contained in a procedure to be executed, all you have to do is include the procedure's name as a separate statement. For example, suppose that you declare a procedure named WriteHello, as in the example above. To cause the statements within the procedure to be executed at any point in the main program, simply include the statement

```
WriteHello;
```

in the main program at the point where you want the statements within the procedure to be executed. When the statements within the program have been executed and the END of the procedure has been reached, control returns to the main program at the statement *following* the one that invoked the procedure. So it is as if the statements within the procedure were inserted in the main program at the point where its name appears. Or you can think of the situation as if a detour is taken from the main program through the procedure, after which the main program continues as usual.

For example, suppose that in the main program the following statements appear:

```
          .
          .
          .
WRITELN('This is written before the procedure executes');
WriteHello;
WRITELN('This is written after the procedure executes');
          .
          .
          .
```

After the first WRITELN statement executes and the line "This is written before the procedure executes" is printed on the screen, the program takes a detour to the procedure WriteHello and *the statements within WriteHello are executed in the order in which they appear there.* After the last statement in WriteHello executes and the END of the procedure is encountered, the program will return to execute the WRITELN statement below the statement that calls on WriteHello, and then it will continue on to execute the statements in the remainder of the program as usual. So the output of the statements above would be

```
This is written before the procedure executes
Hello
This is written after the procedure executes
```

The declaration of a procedure in the Procedure Declarations section is just that—a definition of what the procedure is, with no action taken at the time of declaration. The statements within the procedure are executed only when the name of the procedure appears within the body of the program.

Variables Within Procedures

Any variable or constant that is declared in the Variable Declarations section of the main program can be used in a procedure that is declared in the program. However, it is often the case that a variable is used only within the procedure, and not within the main program at all. In such a case, it is possible to declare the variable (or variables, if there is more than one) *within* the procedure. When this is done, the main program has no knowledge of the variable, and if a reference to the variable were made in the main program, an error would result indicating that the variable had not been declared. Variables that are declared within a procedure effectively "belong" to that procedure and are not accessible by the main program or, in most cases, by other procedures declared in the same program.[1]

To declare variables within a procedure, you use the same format as you do to declare variables within the main program. As in the main program, the Variable Declarations section in a procedure comes just before the BEGIN that signals the beginning of the body of the procedure. For example, suppose you want to declare a variable named Letter with type CHAR in a procedure named ReadWord. The declaration would look like this:

```
PROCEDURE ReadWord;
VAR Letter : CHAR;
BEGIN
  Procedure Statements
END;
```

This establishes a variable named Letter with type CHAR that is known only within the procedure. The main program cannot access its contents, store in it, or even refer to it; the variable belongs to the procedure alone. In fact, the variable actually "comes into existence" when the procedure begins to execute, and vanishes completely as soon as the procedure has finished executing.

If the procedure is executed more than once, any variable declared in the procedure is set up anew each time the procedure executes, just as if the declaration had been encountered for the first time. The variable does not retain its value from a previous execution of the statements within the procedure.

In general, each time the statements within a procedure are executed, it is as if a new "mini-program" were being executed from scratch.

The general rule of thumb for declaring variables within procedures, then, is this:

Whenever a variable name is used only within a particular procedure, and not in the main program or any other procedure, the variable should be declared within that procedure. This is simply good programming practice.

What would happen if a variable named Letter were declared in *both* the main program and in a procedure? Would an error result? As a matter of fact, no; what would happen is that *two* variables with the name Letter would be established, one for the main program, and one that would come into being when the procedure begins to execute and vanish when the procedure finishes executing. Any mention of the variable name Letter *within the procedure* would refer to

1. The exception to this rule involves procedures that are declared inside other procedures, which are described below.

the variable declared within the procedure and would not affect the other variable named Letter, the one belonging to the main program, at all.

Any reference to a variable always applies to the "most local" declaration of that variable.

Mention of Letter in the main program obviously refers to the variable with that name declared in the main program and cannot affect the variable Letter declared in the procedure, since at any time a statement in the main program is executing, the variables declared in any procedure do not exist.

VAR Parameters

Many of the variables that are used in a procedure appear only in the procedure, and so they can be declared within the procedure. However, in almost all cases some variable or variables that are used in the main program are used in the procedure as well. It was mentioned above that variables declared in the main program are known by and accessible to any procedure declared within the program, and so there should be no problem when variables are shared in this way. However, suppose that you write a procedure which includes statements that read a word from an input file. The word is stored in a variable named Word. Now suppose that you would like to execute the same procedure a second time within the program, but you would like the word the procedure reads to be stored in a different variable—say, AnotherWord. Unfortunately, the only thing you can do is to write another set of statements identical to those in the procedure, except that references to the variable Word must be replaced by references to the variable AnotherWord. This is clearly redundant, and it is this sort of redundancy that procedures were designed to avoid.

Pascal and most programming languages like Pascal solve this problem by enabling the programmer to establish "pseudonyms" within a procedure for variables that are declared in the main program. Each time the procedure is invoked, the programmer specifies which variable from the main program is to be associated with the pseudonym during the course of this particular incarnation of the procedure. Then, while the procedure is executing, *the main program variable is referenced by the pseudonym rather than by the name it has within the main program* (that is, the name given to the variable in the Declarations section of the main program). However, the association between the main program variable and the pseudonym becomes void after the procedure finishes executing. The next time the procedure is executed, the main program variable which is to be associated with the pseudonym must again be specified. This can be the same variable, or an entirely different one, and so the procedure can work with a different main program variable each time it is executed, if necessary.

In terms of the situation described above, where a procedure is to store characters in a main program variable named Word during its first execution and in a variable named AnotherWord in the second, this would mean that when the procedure is first executed, by giving its name as a statement within the main program, Word is specified as the variable associated with whatever pseudonym is set up within the procedure. If that pseudonym is NextWord, then during the first execution of the procedure, every reference to NextWord within the procedure is the same as a reference to Word. So if the procedure includes a statement like

```
NextWord[Counter] := Letter;
```

during the first execution of the procedure this is the same as saying

```
Word[Counter] := Letter;
```

Once the procedure has finished executing for the first time, the association between Word and NextWord is abolished. When the procedure is executed a second time, AnotherWord is specified as the variable that is to be associated with NextWord; so, the statement

```
NextWord[Counter] := Letter;
```

is now the same as saying

```
AnotherWord[Counter] := Letter;
```

Again, the association between AnotherWord and NextWord is abolished after the second execution of the procedure.

Let's look at how the association of main program variables and pseudonyms is accomplished. Continuing the example above, suppose that in the main procedure the variable Word is declared with type *String*, which is defined as a packed array of type CHAR with 20 slots. The function of the procedure is to read a sequence of characters into a *String*-type variable; in other words, to read a word. The first thing you want to do is to invoke the procedure in the main program, and have it store characters in the main program variable named Word. This will involve associating Word with the pseudonym when the procedure is called for the first time.

The pseudonyms in a procedure are established in the Procedure Heading, in parentheses following the procedure's name. To establish a pseudonym for a *String*-type variable, you would modify the Procedure Heading to look like this:

```
PROCEDURE ReadWord(VAR NextWord : String);
```

This says that within the procedure named ReadWord, NextWord is to be a pseudonym for some variable of type *String*.

Each pseudonym established within a procedure is associated with a specific type, just as a variable is in a declaration.

Setting up a pseudonym variable in a Procedure Heading does not have the same effect as a variable declaration; that is, in the example above, the declaration of NextWord **does not set up a slot in main memory that is referred to by the name** NextWord. **Instead,** NextWord **is simply another name by which the variable** Word **is known during the course of the procedure's execution.**

Now, when the procedure is invoked in the main program, the main program variable that is to be known by the pseudonym NextWord during this invocation of the procedure is provided in the statement that invokes the procedure, as follows:

```
ReadWord(Word);
```

Note that no type is specified here, as it is for the pseudonyms in the Procedure Heading; Word's type is already known from its declaration in the main program. But Word's type *must* be *String* in this case:

In order to be associated with a particular pseudonym, a variable in the main program must have the same type as the type of the pseudonym specified in the Procedure Heading.

As a result of the statement above, the procedure ReadWord is invoked, and at the outset it is established that NextWord will be a pseudonym for the main program variable Word *during the course of this invocation of the procedure*. One way to think of this is to see the name NextWord as referring to the same location in memory as the variable Word, like this:

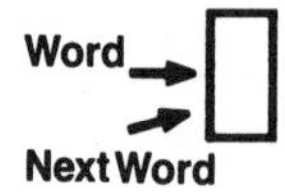

This, in fact, is exactly what is going on. Both the name Word and the name NextWord actually refer to the same memory slot while the procedure is executing. So anything that you do to the variable NextWord in the procedure will be effectively done to the main program variable Word; if within the procedure you store characters in the memory slot that goes by the name NextWord, they will be stored in the memory location that goes by the name Word, since these two locations are one and the same. After the procedure finishes executing, the pseudonym NextWord will disappear, but the memory location with which NextWord was associated will not; that memory location still goes by the name Word in the main program, and it will retain the effects of anything done to it during the course of the procedure. All that is changing is the names by which you can refer to the memory location, but the memory location itself functions as it always has.

If for some reason you make reference to a variable that is declared in the main program within a procedure in which it is also known by a pseudonym, you will affect the variable in the usual way. In effect, a variable with a pseudonym has two names within a procedure. However, it makes no sense at all to refer to the variable by its original name within the procedure; only the pseudonym should be used.

To see how all of this works, imagine the following scenario. Within the main program, the variable Word has been declared but given no value, and so the variable is empty. ReadWord is then invoked, and within the procedure NextWord is established as a pseudonym for Word. The procedure reads characters and stores a series of non-blank characters in the variable it calls NextWord, so that just before the procedure ends, the memory location associated with NextWord contains the characters 'Armadillo   '. When the procedure ends, the name NextWord disappears altogether, but remember that the memory location still remains and still goes by the name Word within the main program. Back in the main program, a WRITELN statement is next executed to print the contents of the variable Word. What is printed? Why, the string 'Armadillo   ', of course, since the memory location referred to by Word is the same as the one that had been known as NextWord while the procedure was executing.

The beauty of this setup is that later on in the program, the procedure ReadWord can be called again, this time with the statement

```
ReadWord(AnotherWord);
```

where AnotherWord is a variable of type *String*. When this statement is executed, the procedure ReadWord is invoked, but this time the pseudonym NextWord is set to correspond to the variable AnotherWord—that is, NextWord now points to the memory location associated with the variable AnotherWord. When characters are stored in NextWord within the procedure, they are actually being stored in AnotherWord, just as they were stored in Word when ReadWord was invoked earlier. The procedure is truly independent of the main program; the names it uses belong to it alone, and the procedure can be used in any situation, to read a word into a variable declared to be a packed array of type CHAR with 20 slots, regardless of the variable's name in the calling procedure. This independence makes the procedure suitable to be used in other programs, which might declare *String*-type variables with entirely different names. For this and other reasons that will be more obvious as your programs become increasingly complex, remember:

It is good programming practice to make procedures as independent of the programs that use them as possible.

Suppose that your procedure needs to share more than one variable with the main program? Easy enough; a list of pseudonyms can appear in the procedure heading, and a list of variables can appear in the statement that invokes the procedure. How does the computer know which corresponds with which? *By the order in which they appear.* The first variable in the list associated with the statement that invokes the procedure corresponds with the first pseudonym in the list in the Procedure Heading, the second variable corresponds to the second pseudonym, and so on. To use an example that will apply to the program for this chapter, suppose that in addition to using the Word variable that appears in the main program, the ReadWord procedure also uses the input file name that is declared in the main program. To establish a pseudonym for a file in the procedure in addition to the variable of type *String*, you can say

```
PROCEDURE ReadWord(VAR NextWord : String; VAR InputFile : TEXT);
```

Look at this statement closely. The two pseudonyms and their types are separated by a semicolon, as are variable declarations in the VAR Declarations section of a program or procedure. Note, however, that *the keyword VAR appears before each pseudonym.* As you will see later (in the Niceties section of this chapter), not all names declared in a Procedure Heading are pseudonyms. Here the keyword VAR indicates that the name *is* to be used as a pseudonym, and so it is imperative that it appear before the declaration of every name in a Procedure Heading that is to be treated as a pseudonym.

Given this Procedure Heading, the procedure ReadWord can be invoked from the main program as follows:

```
ReadWord(Word,TextFile);
```

where TextFile is declared in the Variable Declarations section of the main program with type TEXT. The statement indicates that Word is to be associated with the pseudonym NextWord, and TextFile is to be associated with the pseudonym InputFile during this invocation of the procedure. So within the procedure, any reference to the file from which characters are being read will use the name InputFile instead of TextFile; for example, within ReadWord, the READ statement will be

```
READ(InputFile,Letter);
```

Once again, this makes the procedures very general: it can be used to read from any file, or from two or more different files within the same program.

Any number of pseudonyms can be established in a Procedure Heading. Simply be sure that when the procedure is invoked, the variables in the invoking statement correspond by position with the pseudonyms. And remember, the types of the variables and their pseudonyms must match, or an error will result.

The variables that are listed when a procedure is called and their pseudonyms that appear in the Procedure Heading are called *parameters.* Each variable for which a pseudonym is established is said to be passed as a parameter to the procedure.

Since procedures should be written to be completely independent of the programs that invoke them, the following rule should always be followed when constructing a procedure:

All variables that are referenced in any way within a procedure should either be declared in the Variable Declarations section of the procedure, or should appear in the list in the Procedure Heading.

As mentioned above, a very common error when using parameters of the type described above is to forget to specify VAR before each name in the list in the Procedure Heading. Be careful; this will not cause an error message to be generated, but instead will cause the computer to treat the names differently than you expect it to (see the Niceties section for a description of other parameter types).

Procedures Within Procedures

It was pointed out above that a procedure is in many ways like a miniature program; it has a heading just as a program does, a Variable Declarations section, and a main body consisting of the statements that make up the procedure. The correspondence between a procedure's format and that of a program extends even farther, since the procedure may also contain a Constant Declarations section, a Type Declarations section, and even a Procedure Declarations section. Each of these sections appears in a location corresponding to the location at which they appear in a program: the Constant Declarations section, if it exists, appears just after the Procedure Heading; the Type Declarations section follows the Constant Declarations section, and the Procedure Declarations follow the Variable Declarations and precede the BEGIN statement that signals the beginning of the main body of the procedure.

If a constant is used *only* within a procedure and nowhere else in the main program or another procedure, it can be declared in the Constant Declarations section of that procedure. Similarly, a type that is used only for variables declared within a procedure can be declared within that procedure. And if a procedure is invoked from within a procedure and nowhere else in the program, this procedure can be declared within the procedure that invokes it.

Thus, any procedure can contain the declaration of another procedure. This means that it is possible that a procedure is contained within a procedure that is contained within a procedure that is contained within a procedure . . . *ad infinitum*, but in practice, as you might expect, procedures are usually declared at only one or two "levels" below that of the main program—that is, you might have a procedure declared in the main program that contains a procedure, but generally things don't go much farther than that. The relationship between procedures, whether they are declared side-by-side or one within the other, is governed by several rules and conventions, and these deserve some attention at this point.

Procedures can invoke, or *call*, one another only under certain circumstances:

- If two or more procedures are declared, one after the other, in the main program or in a procedure, any of these procedures can call a procedure that is declared before it in the sequence. So, if you have the following general setup,

```
PROGRAM WhoKnowsWho(INPUT,OUTPUT);
    .
    .
    .
  PROCEDURE One;
  BEGIN
    .
    .
    .
  END;     { One }
  PROCEDURE Two;
  BEGIN
    .
    .
    .
  END;     { Two }
  PROCEDURE Three;
  BEGIN
    .
    .
    .
  END;     { Three }
BEGIN
  .
  .
  .
END.     { WhoKnowsWho }
```

  Procedure Two can call procedure One, procedure Three can call procedures One and Two, but procedure One cannot call any other procedure.

- Any procedure can call a procedure that is declared immediately within it. So, if you have the setup

```
PROGRAM WhoKnowsWho2(INPUT,OUTPUT);
    .
    .
    .
PROCEDURE One;
  PROCEDURE Two;
  BEGIN
    .
    .
    .
  END;     { Two }
BEGIN
  .
  .
  .
END;     { One }
```

```
BEGIN
   .
   .
   .
END.     { WhoKnowsWho2 }
```

Procedure One can call procedure Two. But note that the main program cannot call procedure Two—that is, you cannot "skip a level." This is because procedure Two belongs to procedure One and in essence, comes into existence only when procedure One begins to execute.

What about knowledge of variables? Earlier, you saw that a procedure declared within the main program has access to variables declared within the main program. But does a procedure declared within another procedure, like procedure Two in the example setup just given above, have access to the variables declared in the main program? Yes. Access to variables propagates "downward" through levels of declaration, but not "upwards" back to an enclosing procedure or the main program. If you think of procedure One in the example above as the "child" of the main program and think of procedure Two as the child of procedure One, then you can describe access to variables as *inherited* by successive generations of procedures. But a parent does not have access to variables that originate with its children. Neither is there lateral inheritance; in the original scenario, where procedures One, Two, and Three were effectively siblings, none of the procedures has access to the variables declared within any of the others.

The area of a program over which a variable is known or accessible is called its *scope*. In the first setup above, the scope of variables declared in the main program is the main program plus all of procedures One, Two, and Three. The scope of variables declared in procedure One is procedure One only, the scope of variables declared in procedure Two is procedure Two only, and the scope of variables declared in procedure Three is procedure Three only. In the second scenario, the scope of variables declared in the main program is the main program plus procedures One and Two; the scope of variables declared in procedure One is procedures One and Two; and the scope of the variables declared in procedure Two is procedure Two only (assuming no additional procedures are declared within procedure Two).

If all of this seems a bit confusing, you should not worry, because procedures and parameter passing are notoriously difficult to understand when they are first encountered. You will master the details probably not by reading about them so much as by using them, where you can understand the rules and conventions in terms of specific examples and situations. It is also true that you will be working with the simplest situations ninety percent of the time, even when you are an old hand at programming. Therefore, you will probably do best to try to get a feel for the way things work here, but use the discussions of the situations in this and the following chapters to see how these concepts apply in particular cases. Once you have actually used procedures and parameters a few times, the concepts involved will no doubt seem relatively simple.

CONSTRUCTING THE PROGRAM

The task for this chapter is to take the program from last chapter and modify it so that it accomplishes the same thing but uses procedures. To do this the general flow of events in the program must be analyzed to determine the sub-tasks of the overall task, and the sub-tasks of the sub-tasks, if they exist, so that each sub-task can then be implemented as a separate procedure. As mentioned earlier, the process of taking a task and successively breaking it down into more and more specific sub-tasks is called *top-down analysis*. You will see how the process of top-down analysis proceeds as the main program is constructed below, followed by each of the procedures required for the program.

The Main Program

A top-down analysis of the task of writing each of the words in a text file proceeds in the same way as the analysis that led to the development of the algorithm for last chapter's program. You will recall that we started by focusing on the overall process that is repeated until the end of the file is encountered, which was at first broken down into the following two general steps:

a. Read a word.
b. Print the word.

Recall that step a was broken down several more times before the algorithmic description of this step was suitable to be implemented in Pascal. Here, however, the algorithm above will be used to describe the main program; rather than being expanded into several steps, assume that step a will be implemented as a procedure. Therefore, within the main program step a can be replaced by a call to a procedure that will contain the detailed set of statements required to read a word. If this procedure is given a descriptive name like ReadWord, the statements in the main program will provide a very understandable outline of the program's major steps.

Step b requires only a single Pascal statement to implement, and therefore it is senseless to construct a procedure for this step. So, a single WRITELN statement will be included in the main program to write out the word.

In the previous chapter the two steps above were integrated into the overall program outline, yielding the following general algorithm to describe the program's action:

1. Ready the file for reading.
2. While the character about to be read is not the end-of-file character, repeat the following:
  a. Read a word.
  b. Print the word.

This algorithm is specific enough to serve as a model for the main program, since step 2.a will be replaced by a single statement that calls on a procedure to perform the sub-task of reading a word. So the statements in the main program are

```
BEGIN
  RESET(TextFile);
  WHILE NOT EOF(TextFile) DO BEGIN
    ReadWord(<parameters>);
    WRITELN(Word);
  END;     { while not eof }
END.     { main program }
```

where <*parameters*> will be replaced by the parameters that are to be passed to the ReadWord procedure, Word is the *String*-type variable where the word will be stored, and TextFile is the name of the input text file. Let us leave the parameters to ReadWord unspecified for the moment; they can be filled in after the ReadWord procedure has been put together.

Notice how nicely the statements in the main program reflect the flow of events in the program. Instead of the bulky list of statements from last chapter's program within the WHILE NOT EOF(TextFile) loop, you have a clear outline of what is happening there. Furthermore, you can write the main program without thinking about what must be done to actually implement the steps that read a word until later. Having done this, you can then focus your attention to the statements that will go inside the procedure ReadWord without giving another thought to the overall program outline.

The ReadWord Procedure

Having constructed the main program, you can now concern yourself with the steps required to accomplish step 2.a in the algorithm, which will describe the statements that will ultimately appear in the ReadWord procedure. In Chapter Five, the step to "Read a word" was first broken down like this:

1. Read characters until a non-blank is encountered.
2. Read and store characters until a blank is encountered.

This version of the algorithm reflects the fact that the task of reading a word can be broken down into two parts, the first of which reads characters from an input file until a non-blank is encountered, and the second of which did the actual reading of the word by reading and storing characters until a blank is encountered. Actually, the first step, reading until a blank is encountered, is a sub-task or preliminary step in the process of reading a word. Thus it would make sense to organize the ReadWord procedure as follows: the main body of the procedure will consist of the statements which actually read and store the characters in a word. The statements to perform the preliminary step, which boils down to skipping blanks, can be put in a separate procedure and called from within the ReadWord procedure. This means that to develop the full algorithm to describe the ReadWord procedure, only step 2.b needs to be expanded. Recalling the final version of step 2.b from the previous chapter, the following set of algorithmic steps can serve as the basis for the Pascal statements in ReadWord:

1. Read characters until a non-blank is encountered.
2. Store the character just read as part of the word.

3. Read a character.
4. If the character is *not* a blank, repeat steps 2 and 3.

The Pascal implementation of step 1 will be a call to the procedure that performs this step. If this procedure is given the name SkipBlanks, the statement will be

```
SkipBlanks(<parameters>);
```

where <*parameters*> is replaced with the parameters that are passed to the procedure.

Steps 2, 3, and 4, of course, were implemented in Pascal in the previous program; so, you can simply use the group of statements from the previous program starting with the statement that sets Counter to 0 and ending with the END of the BEGIN-END pair associated with the IF-THEN statement here (of course, the statement that writes the word in the previous program should not be included). These are the statements that actually assign characters to the slots in the packed array, thereby "reading" the word. The statement given above that calls SkipBlanks, followed by the statements that appear below the first REPEAT-UNTIL loop (up to the END of the WHILE NOT EOF(TextFile) loop) in the previous chapter's program, constitute the body of the ReadWord procedure. Therefore, these statements are the ones that appear between the BEGIN and END in the declaration of that procedure.

All that needs to be done to complete the ReadWord procedure is to decide which variables will be declared within that procedure and which will be passed as parameters from the main program. (Remember the rule that all variables that appear in a procedure should be declared within that procedure or should appear as parameters in the procedure's Heading.) The following variables appear in the statements within ReadWord: Counter (the integer variable that is used as a subscript for the packed array), Letter (the CHAR variable into which characters are read from the file), Word (the packed array), and TextFile (the input file). Neither Counter nor Letter is used at all in the main program, since they are used only during the process of actually reading an individual word, and so they can be declared within the ReadWord procedure without any problem. Word and TextFile, however, are used in the main program—Word appears in the statement that writes out the word that has just been read by the ReadWord procedure, and TextFile appears in the condition on the WHILE loop and in the RESET statement.

Even if TextFile **were not referenced in the body of the main program, it would still have to be declared in the main program, because in Pascal all file variables must be declared in the main program.**

Because Word and TextFile are used in the main program as well as in ReadWord, these variables must be "shared" with the main program, and consequently, they will have to be passed as parameters from the main program to the ReadWord procedure. In the heading of the ReadWord procedure, pseudonyms will be established for these variables. So, the heading of the ReadWord procedure can look like this:

```
PROCEDURE ReadWord(VAR NextWord : String; VAR InputFile : TEXT);
```

and the call to ReadWord in the main program will then be

```
ReadWord(Word,TextFile);
```

Because Word appears first in the list of parameters in the call to ReadWord from the main program, it is associated with the first parameter in the procedure's Heading—the pseudonym variable NextWord. The second parameter, TextFile, is associated with the second item in the Procedure Heading, InputFile. Therefore, within the ReadWord procedure, Word will be referenced by the name NextWord and TextFile will be called InputFile. This means that all references to Word in the statements in ReadWord that were borrowed from the last chapter's program must now be changed to NextWord, and all references to TextFile must be changed to InputFile, since these are the names by which the variables are known within the ReadWord procedure. Otherwise, the statements from the previous program remain unchanged.

The SkipBlanks Procedure

The SkipBlanks procedure implements the step in the algorithm that reads,

1. Read characters until a non-blank is encountered.

This step was expanded in Chapter Five to be

a. Read a character.
b. If the character is a blank, repeat step a.

which was implemented as the first REPEAT-UNTIL loop in the program. Since SkipBlanks will now take over this task, SkipBlanks will contain as its body the first REPEAT-UNTIL loop from the previous program, which reads blanks until a non-blank character is encountered. This procedure, then, includes references to the variables Letter and TextFile from the previous program. Both of these variables are shared with other parts of the program: Letter is shared with ReadWord, and TextFile is shared with both ReadWord and the main program (although within ReadWord TextFile goes by the name InputFile). Now, since ReadWord is calling SkipBlanks, it should pass both Letter and TextFile (or InputFile, as ReadWord calls it) as parameters to the SkipBlanks procedure.

It does not matter that the declaration for the variable Letter **now appears in the ReadWord procedure; as long as it is "known" to ReadWord it can be passed to SkipBlanks.**

ReadWord can also pass TextFile to SkipBlanks, but since ReadWord knows TextFile by the name InputFile, it will use the name InputFile when it passes the file variable to SkipBlanks. The call to SkipBlanks in ReadWord, then, will be

```
SkipBlanks(Letter,InputFile);
```

and the heading on SkipBlanks will be

```
PROCEDURE SkipBlanks(VAR NextChar : CHAR; VAR InFile : TEXT);
```

This means that within the SkipBlanks procedure, Letter will go by the name NextChar, and InputFile will go by the name InFile. So, all references to Letter in the statements from the last program that now appear in the body of the procedure SkipBlanks must be changed to NextChar, and all references to TextFile must be changed to InFile. This sets up the situation where the main program and each of the two procedures has its own name for the variables they share.

Pseudonyms can be any valid variable name. It is legal to assign as a pseudonym the same name as the variable for which it is a pseudonym (for example, the parameter NextChar **in the Heading of the SkipBlanks procedure could be called** Letter**), but most programmers find it less confusing if the names are different.**

Whether you use the same names for pseudonyms or different ones is up to you; throughout this text, parameters will be given names that are different from the names of the variables with which they are associated.

Having constructed SkipBlanks, the question remains: where should the procedure be declared? In the main program preceding ReadWord? In the main program following ReadWord? Or, since ReadWord calls on SkipBlanks, within ReadWord itself? Only two of these three options can be considered, since SkipBlanks cannot be declared in the main program following ReadWord, because, of course, *a procedure can call another only if the declaration of the "callee" appears before it in the main program or within the calling procedure itself*. This means that SkipBlanks cannot be declared in the main program following ReadWord. But should it be declared within ReadWord or within the main program preceding ReadWord? If it is declared within ReadWord, the main program will not have access to SkipBlanks—the procedure will "belong" to ReadWord and it will be possible to call on SkipBlanks only from within ReadWord. As with variables that are used only within a procedure, it is a good idea to isolate procedures that are not needed elsewhere in the program from the rest of the program—this contributes to the program's *modularity*. Since the process of skipping blanks is a sub-task of the task of reading a word, if ReadWord is removed for use in another procedure you must take SkipBlanks with it, so it makes sense to incorporate SkipBlanks into ReadWord by declaring it inside that procedure.

This is what the declaration of ReadWord and SkipBlanks will look like:

```
PROCEDURE ReadWord(VAR NextWord : String; VAR InputFile : TEXT);
  { Reads the next word from file InputFile }
VAR Letter : CHAR;
  Counter : StringBounds;
PROCEDURE SkipBlanks(VAR NextChar : CHAR: VAR InFile : TEXT);
  { Finds the next non-blank character in file InFile }
  { and puts it in NextChar }
```

```
    BEGIN
      REPEAT
        READ(InFile,NextChar);
      UNTIL (NextChar <> Blank) OR (EOF(InFile));
    END;      { SkipBlanks }
  BEGIN
    SkipBlanks(Letter,InputFile);
    NextWord := Blanks;
    Counter := 0;
    IF NOT EOF(InputFile) THEN BEGIN
      REPEAT
        Counter := Counter + 1;
        NextWord[Counter] := Letter;
        READ(InputFile,Letter);
      UNTIL (Letter = Blank) OR (Counter = StringLength);
    END;      { then begin }
  END;      { ReadWord }
```

This set of statements assumes constants named Blank, Blanks, and StringLength and a subrange type named *StringBounds* are declared in the main program, all of which are described in the Niceties section of Chapter Five.

The Program as a Whole

That takes care of the procedures. However, in terms of the program's overall operation, there is one situation left to consider—what happens if within ReadWord, the end-of-file character is detected, and Word therefore contains only blanks? The WRITELN statement in the main program will print the contents of Word, whatever it may be after ReadWord finishes executing. Do you want to write out the blanks? It will not hurt, but it would be nice to avoid it, and it can be avoided very easily with a small modification to the statement that writes out the word. This is left as an exercise for you.

Here is an outline of the program's overall organization, assuming that the constant and subrange type declarations described in the Niceties section of Chapter Five are incorporated into the program:

```
PROGRAM PrintWords(INPUT,OUTPUT,TextFile);
  Constant Declarations: StringLength, Blank, Blanks
  Type Declarations: String, StringBounds
  Variable Declarations: Word, TextFile
PROCEDURE ReadWord(VAR NextWord : String; VAR InputFile : TEXT);
  Variable Declarations: Letter, Counter
  PROCEDURE SkipBlanks(VAR NextChar : CHAR; VAR InFile : TEXT);
    Variable Declarations: none
  BEGIN     { SkipBlanks }
      .
      .
      .
  END;      { SkipBlanks }
BEGIN      { ReadWord }
      .
      .
      .
END;      { ReadWord }
```

```
BEGIN     { PrintWords }
  RESET(TextFile);
  WHILE NOT EOF(TextFile) DO BEGIN
    ReadWord(Word,TextFile);
    WRITELN(Word);
  END;     { while not eof }
END.     { PrintWords }
```

The overall flow of events in the program is this: the main program begins, and after readying TextFile for reading checks TextFile to see if the next character to be read (the first character in the file, in this case) is the end-of-file character. If not, the loop is entered. The call to the procedure ReadWord causes the statements within the procedure ReadWord to begin executing, temporarily suspending the execution of statements within the main program. ReadWord's variables, constants, and the pseudonyms for the parameters passed to it from the main program are established, and the statements within the procedure begin executing. At this point you can visualize the situation as in the diagram.

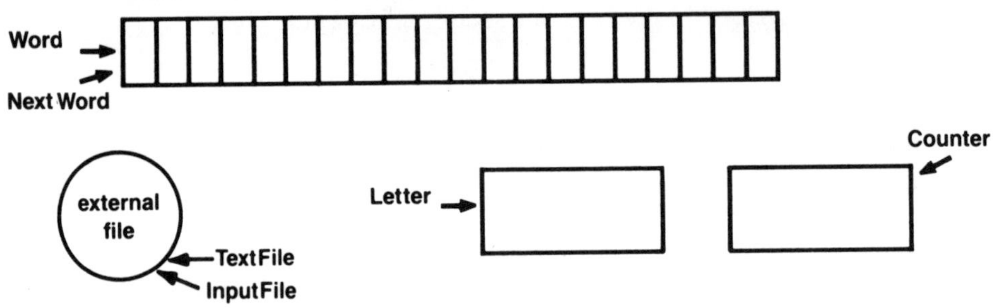

Note that Word and NextWord refer to the same slot in memory, since NextWord is a pseudonym for Word in the ReadWord procedure, and that for the same reason, InputFile refers to the input file known as TextFile in the main program.

The first statement in ReadWord is a call to the procedure SkipBlanks; this statement causes the statements in SkipBlanks to begin executing, temporarily suspending execution of the statements in ReadWord. At this point, then, both the main program and ReadWord are on hold, waiting to continue executing when the procedures they have called finish executing. SkipBlanks' pseudonyms are established, and the statements within the procedure begin to execute. The situation now is this:

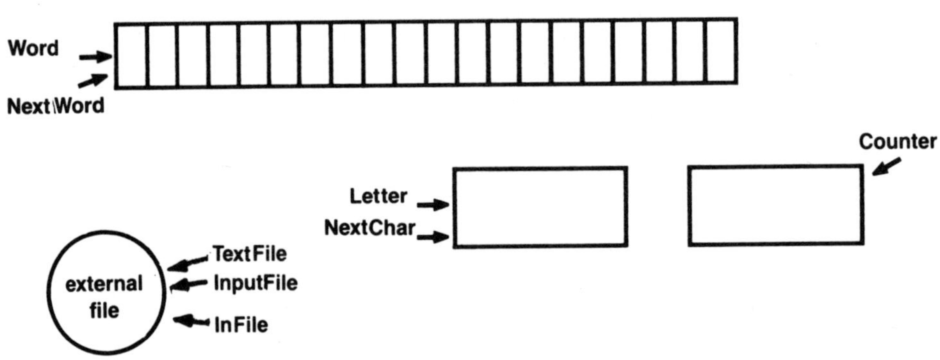

When the procedure finishes executing, the pseudonyms disappear, and control returns to the statement in ReadWord immediately following the call to SkipBlanks. Note that at this point, since NextChar served as a pseudonym for the variable Letter while SkipBlanks was executing, Letter contains the first non-blank character encountered in the input by the SkipBlanks procedure. ReadWord needs this character, of course, in order to assign it to the packed array, and this is precisely why the two procedures need to share the variable Letter.

ReadWord now continues executing, reading characters until it encounters a blank, and filling up NextWord in the process. When ReadWord is finished, all of its constants, variables, and pseudonyms (the names, but not the memory locations to which they refer) are destroyed, and control returns to the main program. However, since within ReadWord NextWord functioned as a pseudonym for Word, the characters that were stored in NextWord are now contained in the variable called Word within the main program. Execution of the statements in the main program then continues with the WRITELN statement following the call to ReadWord, which writes out the contents of Word just assigned within the ReadWord procedure. After this control returns to the top of the loop and the entire process is repeated. This continues until the end-of-file character is detected, and the main program is terminated.

Trace through the steps yourself, keeping track of the contents of all variables and the memory slots to which all variables and pseudonyms refer during the program's execution.

SUMMING UP THE PROGRAM

From now on, every program that you write will involve procedures. You should get used to the idea of thinking about the way a program is structured in terms of the procedures that will make it up. You should conceive of your main program as a general outline of the steps involved in the program, as is the main program in this chapter. In effect, the main program's role should be that of a "manager" that oversees the general flow of events in the program and delegates sub-tasks by calling on various procedures at appropriate points. Your main programs should be relatively short; any time one or two statements are not enough to accomplish a sub-task, the statements should be put in a procedure. So most statements in the main procedure will be calls to procedures. Often, a loop which provides for repeating the steps in the program will be included as well, like the one in the program for this chapter.

Do not be afraid to write short procedures that include only a few statements. If the action of the main program can be made clearer by including a call to a procedure with a descriptive name rather than inserting the statements to accomplish a certain task, by all means use a procedure. You should be careful, though, that your procedures do not get to be too long. Procedures that take up more than about two display screens (and most procedures will be much, much shorter) can probably be broken up into two or more separate procedures. It is probably better to go slightly overboard with procedures than to include long sections of code in your programs.

NICETIES

Comments Within Procedures

Procedures are like miniature programs, and a given procedure might be taken out of one program and inserted into another. Therefore,

---

Each procedure in a program should have a header comment, just like a program, explaining what the procedure does in general terms.

ReadWord, for example, is a procedure that reads the next word from a text file. It should have a header comment that makes this clear. For example, ReadWord should look something like this:

```
PROCEDURE ReadWord(VAR NextWord : String; VAR InputFile : TEXT);
  { Reads the next word from a file }
              .
              .
              .
BEGIN      { ReadWord }
              .
              .
              .
END;     { ReadWord }
```

You might also want to include the date on which the procedure was written or completed. Within a procedure, statements should be commented just as they are in a main program.

Value Parameters

Pascal allows the programmer to pass parameters in two different ways. You have already seen one of them, which provides for a pseudonym to be established for a variable declared in the main program or calling procedure for the duration of a procedure's execution.

The second method of passing parameters works like this: instead of establishing a pseudonym for a variable from the calling procedure, another variable, which belongs to the procedure and behaves like any variable declared within the procedure, is actually set up for the duration of the procedure's execution. At the time the procedure is invoked, the *value* stored in the corresponding variable in the calling procedure's parameter list is copied into this new variable. After that, since the variable within the procedure is separate from the one whose value it took on,

---

Anything that you do to change the contents of the Value parameter variable will not in any way affect the variable in the calling procedure with which it is associated.

Thus the Value parameter variable acts just like any variable that is declared within the procedure, except that it gets its initial value from some variable in the calling procedure.

These parameters are passed in almost exactly the same way as the pseudonym parameters with which you are already familiar. The variable from the calling procedure whose value is being passed appears in a list in the call statement, like this:

```
SomeProcedure(ThisOne);
```

and then the procedure's variable that is to get its initial value from ThisOne appears in the Procedure Heading, along with its type:

```
PROCEDURE SomeProcedure(ThatOne : INTEGER);
```

The keyword VAR does not appear before the variable name in the list when a parameter is passed in this way. This is how the computer knows that this parameter is being passed as a *Value parameter* **rather than as a pseudonym parameter, or, as it is often called, a** *VAR parameter.*

If the setup above is used, this is what will happen when the statement that invokes the procedure SomeProcedure is encountered: a variable named ThatOne is set up—that is, a memory slot with type INTEGER is established in main memory and given the name ThatOne. The current contents of the variable ThisOne are then copied into the newly-established variable ThatOne. After this, ThatOne may be assigned a new value in an assignment statement or READ statement, but this does not affect ThisOne, since it is an entirely separate variable. When SomeProcedure terminates, the variable ThatOne is destroyed, and the variable ThisOne has the same value it had when SomeProcedure was called, regardless of any changes that had been made to ThatOne within SomeProcedure.

When should you pass a parameter as a Value parameter rather than as a VAR parameter? When

1. You use the value of a variable declared in the calling procedure but *do not* change it in the procedure.
2. You use a value of a variable declared in the calling procedure and change it within a procedure, but do not want these changes to affect that variable.

In the second case, you should use a Value parameter simply because this method protects against inadvertent changes to the variable within the procedure. So,

---

If you pass a parameter to a procedure and the associated variable does not appear on the left side of an assignment operator or in a READ statement within the procedure, always pass it as a Value parameter. If it does appear in one of these contexts within the procedure, you must determine whether the new value is to affect the variable in the calling procedure. If yes, pass it as a VAR parameter; if no, pass it as a Value parameter.

Note that none of the parameters passed in the program for this chapter can be passed as Value parameters. The changes to Word and Letter in the procedures to which they are passed must be retained after the procedures terminate. And, although the file TextFile is not changed in any way within the procedures, as noted above, *file names must always be passed as VAR parameters.* This is a special case and the only one to which such a restriction applies.[2]

Another way to determine whether or not a parameter should be passed as VAR or Value is to think of the variable's function in terms of input to, and output from, the procedure. For instance, the variable Word is effectively an "output" variable—the variable has no value or an unneeded value when the procedure is called, but ReadWord gives it a value that the calling program then uses. That is, Word does not contain any information that ReadWord needs or uses (in which case it would provide "input" to the procedure), but ReadWord gives it information that is used by the caller, thus using the variable to supply "output." On the other hand, if you were writing a procedure to print a word and passed a variable containing the word as a parameter to the procedure, then this variable would be "input" to the procedure but would not be an "output" variable. In a third scenario, you might pass a word to a procedure which would capitalize all of the letters in the word (you will, in fact, write a procedure to do this in Chapter Eight). Here, the variable provides both input to the procedure—the word it is to work with—and output from the procedure—the capitalized version of the word.

If you use the input/output analogy for parameters, the following rules apply:

1. Variables that provide *input values only* to a procedure should be passed as Value parameters.
2. Variables that provide output from a procedure, or provide both input to and output from a procedure, should be passed as VAR parameters.

One last difference between VAR and Value parameters is that when a parameter is passed as a Value parameter, that parameter can be a *literal* value rather than a variable. For example, if you have a procedure named SomeProcedure that takes a Value parameter of type String, you can use the following call to the procedure:

```
SomeProcedure('Albatross           ');
```

This call passes the literal string containing the nine letters of the word "albatross" followed by eleven blanks to the procedure. Because the parameter is passed as a Value parameter, the result is that the literal string is stored in the variable named in SomeProcedure's heading. This is possible because a Value

2. The reason for this exception is logical, if you think about it. A variable that functions as a file name does not point to a location in main memory; it simply refers to a file. There is no "value" for a file, in the sense that there is a value stored in a memory slot, and so it would be impossible to give its value to a variable within a procedure. The only possibility is to establish a pseudonym within the procedure.

parameter is basically a new variable, created at the time the procedure is called, which gets its initial value from the corresponding parameter in the call to the procedure. Whether that value is contained in a variable or stated literally does not matter. However, be sure to note that

---

Literal values can be passed to Value parameters only; passing a literal value to a VAR parameter will generate an error.

This is true because a VAR parameter is not a new variable, but simply a pseudonym for a pre-existing one. Therefore a VAR parameter cannot be associated with a literal value.

Literal values of other types, such as INTEGER and REAL, can be passed to Value parameters as well provided their types match. For instance, if a procedure named SomeOtherProc takes an INTEGER-type Value parameter, it can be called with the statement

```
SomeOtherProc(9);
```

Literal values can be intermixed with variables in a call to a procedure that takes more than one parameter, as long as they are associated with Value parameters.

More About Procedure Headings

VAR parameters and Value parameters can be intermixed in a Procedure Heading. The presence or absence of the keyword VAR signals the type of parameter that is being passed. So, if you want to pass a variable ThisOne of type INTEGER as a VAR parameter, a variable Word with type *String* as a Value parameter, and a variable Letter with type CHAR as a VAR parameter, the following statement is valid:

```
SomeProcedure(ThisOne,Word,Letter);
```

and the Procedure Heading will look like this:

```
PROCEDURE SomeProcedure(VAR ThatOne : INTEGER; NextWord : String;
        VAR NextChar : CHAR);
```

The corresponding variables and pseudonyms are determined by position, and the method of passing the parameter is determined by the presence or absence of the keyword VAR.

A Procedure Heading can be split over two or more lines, as long as the break is made at an appropriate point.

If two or more items that have the same type and are being passed by the same method appear successively in the list of a Procedure Heading, their declarations can be combined as follows:

```
PROCEDURE SomeProcedure(VAR W,X : CHAR; Y,Z : INTEGER);
```

This establishes two pseudonyms (VAR parameters) W and X for variables that appear in the corresponding positions in the list in the statement that invokes the procedure, and two variables Y and Z that will get their values from corresponding values in the list in the statement that invokes the procedure. The statement to call the procedure would look like this:

```
SomeProcedure(A,B,C,D);
```

assuming A and B are variables with type CHAR and are to be passed as VAR parameters, and C and D are variables of type INTEGER that are being passed as Value parameters.

If you are passing two variables of the same type, but one is passed as a Value parameter and the other is passed as a VAR parameter, you have to declare them separately in the Procedure heading, like this:

```
PROCEDURE SomeProcedure(VAR ThisOne : INTEGER; ThatOne : INTEGER);
```

The keyword VAR signals that ThisOne is a pseudonym parameter; the absence of VAR signals that ThatOne is a Value parameter. The call to this procedure is unaffected by the method by which the parameters are passed:

```
SomeProcedure(A,B);
```

APPLICATIONS AND CONSIDERATIONS

Since this chapter's program does the same thing as the previous chapter's program does, there are no new applications to discuss. However, you can use your new knowledge about procedures to imagine how programs that you use every day are organized internally. Take the text formatter, for example. If this program enables the user to imbed formatting commands in the text he or she is writing, then it is likely that each command had associated with it a particular procedure. When the text formatter sees a particular command, it simply calls the procedure that corresponds to it. This way, the details of dealing with each particular formatting task are encapsulated and separated from the remainder of the program, and the statements that implement them can be easily found, modified, and debugged. Furthermore, the procedure corresponding to a given command can be called over and over again as needed during the process of formatting the text.

EXERCISES

1. Modify the program along the lines of exercise 3 or 4 from Chapter Five, implementing the portion of the program that does the printing as a procedure. Read the Niceties section of this chapter on Value parameters—how should the parameters to your procedure be passed?

2. (Slightly more difficult.) Notice that just before the procedure ReadWord terminates, the variable **Counter** contains the slot number of the packed array in which the last character in the word was stored. The value of **Counter** at this point, then, actually indicates the length of the word. Of course, when ReadWord terminates, this information is lost, since the variable **Counter** is destroyed at the procedure's end.

Modify the program so that **Counter** is a parameter to ReadWord rather than a local variable declared within the procedure. This way, after the procedure terminates its value will be known by the main program. Then, modify the main program so that following each word that is printed the word's length is printed (on the same line) as well.

3. (More difficult.) Do exercise 2, above, but enhance the program further so that after all the words and their lengths have been printed, the program prints a message telling how many words of length 3 were found in the text. (Of course, you can choose any length you want—or, if you prefer your program to be especially sophisticated, modify the program to ask the user to enter the length.)

4. (More difficult.) Do exercise 2 from Chapter Five using procedures. Besides the procedures outlined in this chapter, the program should include two additional procedures. First, one that performs the incrementing of the letter, sentence, and word counters (some methods of solving this problem would dictate that only the letter and sentence counters be incremented in this procedure, and that the word counter be incremented separately; but in any case the word counter should not be incremented within ReadWord, since ReadWord's function is simply to read a word!). Second, one that computes the average word length and average sentence length for the text, given the number of letters, sentences, and words. This procedure should compute the averages, but it should be left to the main procedure to print them out—again, the procedure should perform a single function, which in this case is computing (but not printing) the averages. Carefully consider which variables need to be passed to these procedures as parameters, and which can be declared locally.

7
Storing the Text in Main Memory

In order for a program to work with data, that data must be stored in main memory while the program is executing. So far, at any given time only individual characters or, in more recent programs, individual words were available to the program, since a character or word existed only when it was stored in main memory. You have seen that you can do some fairly interesting things with individual characters and words, but more sophisticated kinds of text analysis require that the full text be accessible to the program. Having the text in a file is not enough; the entire text must be in main memory at once. With access to the entire text, a program can search for words and configurations of words in the text, and determine their relative locations within the text as well as their contexts. If the whole text is in main memory, it is possible to do repeated searches for different words at the user's request, and, as you will see in later chapters, the text can be reorganized in main memory to speed up the process of locating specific words as well as gather other kinds of information about them. In this chapter the task will be to read in and store each of the words in the text, so that at the end of the process the entire text resides in main memory on a word-by-word basis.

Reading and storing the words in a text in main memory is pointless if the data is not processed further in some way. For the sake of simplicity, the basic program for this chapter will print only the words in the text, but many other interesting possibilities are outlined in the Niceties section of the chapter as well as in the Exercises.

Reading and storing the words of the text in main memory can be seen as a sub-task that sets the stage for the real work of the program: the analysis. The "analysis" in the program for this chapter consists of simply printing the words. Based on this, you can devise an overall algorithm for this chapter's program like the following:

1. Store the text in main memory.
2. Print all of the words in the text.

Each of these steps needs to be broken down further, of course, but as you go through the process of specifying the steps of the algorithm more and more explicitly, remember that each of the steps in the top-down analysis can serve as a model for a piece of the program. In particular, the general outline above will serve as a model for the main program.

Step 1 needs a great deal more elaboration, but actually, most of this work has been done. Storing the text in main memory will involve reading through the file character-by-character, identifying the individual words in the text, and storing each one in a unique location in memory. You have already written programs that read characters from a file and identify and store individual words, and you can borrow the algorithm outlining that process here and tweak it a little to perform the extra step of storing each in a unique location in memory (the programs in Chapters Five and Six re-used the same memory location for each of the words identified). That algorithm is

1. Ready the file for reading.
2. While the character about to be read is not the end-of-file character, repeat the following:
   a. Read a word.
   b. Print the word.

Step 2.b is no longer necessary, since words will not be printed as they are read in but will instead be printed after the entire text has been read and stored in main memory. However, to accomplish the task for this chapter's program, step 2.b can be replaced by a step that provides for storing the word in a unique memory location after it has been read. So the new algorithm will be

1. Ready the file for reading.
2. While the character about to be read is not the end-of-file character, repeat the following:
   a. Read a word.
   b. Store the word in a unique memory location.

Step 2.a has already been expanded in previous chapters and, in fact, the procedure to accomplish this step has been written and can be simply used here to serve the purpose, so there is no point in considering it any further here. Step 2.b requires only a very few Pascal statements; before considering it in more detail, you will need to learn a bit more about Pascal. For the moment, consider the algorithm above to be sufficient to describe the process of storing the text in main memory.

Step 2 in the overall algorithm, printing the words in the text, can be specified more precisely as follows:

1. For each word stored, do the following:
   a. Print the word.

This, too, is specific enough to get started, and in fact corresponds very well to the Pascal steps actually required to print the text. Before considering the actual Pascal implementation of this and the algorithm above for loading the text, you will need to learn more about arrays.

ELEMENTS OF PASCAL

Arrays

As mentioned in the previous chapter, arrays differ from packed arrays only in the way they are stored internally. To the programmer, the two look almost exactly the same—both contain a group of variables of the same type, and both are manipulated in the same ways, by using loops and subscript variables to access their individual slots. The syntax associated with each is the same, except for a slight variation in their declarations, but you will continue to use the array name followed by a subscript in square brackets to refer to a particular slot in the array. Internally, the difference between an array and a packed array is that although you have the illusion that the elements of a *non*-packed array are stored contiguously, in reality they may not be. But the way the elements of an array are stored need not concern you, since the storage scheme is invisible to you; you need only know the differences in the ways arrays and packed arrays are treated in a Pascal program. The differences are these:

1. You cannot assign values to each of the slots in the entire array in a single assignment statement as you can with a packed array. Thus, an array name with no subscript will never appear on the left side of an assignment operator.
2. You cannot compare an entire array with another array, as you can do with packed arrays containing variables of type CHAR.
3. You cannot write out the entire array by simply giving the name of the array in a WRITE or WRITELN statement, as you can with a packed array of type CHAR variables.

If you look at these differences, you can probably see that each one results from the fact that the array cannot be treated as a whole since the elements may not be stored contiguously.

Apart from these differences, arrays are very much like packed arrays. They are declared very similarly:

```
TYPE NumberArray = ARRAY[1..100] OF INTEGER;
```

This statement establishes a new type, in this case an array consisting of 100 slots that hold type INTEGER values, with the name *NumberArray*. The only difference between this declaration and the declaration of a packed array is that the word "packed" is omitted from the type specification. Given this type declaration, the variable declaration

```
VAR Value : NumberArray;
```

establishes Value with the type *NumberArray*. Individual slots in the array are now referenced by the names Value[1], Value[2], Value[3], and so on, just as they are in a packed array.

Arrays of Arrays

The type specification for each slot in an array—INTEGER, in the example above—can be any valid Pascal type, *including user-defined types*. This means that after establishing a type like *NumberArray*, above, you could, if you wanted to, create another ARRAY type like this one:

```
TYPE MoreNumbers = ARRAY[1..50] OF NumberArray;
```

This establishes an ARRAY type consisting of 50 slots, each of which is itself an array of 100 slots containing INTEGER values! Before grappling with this idea, consider the applications of such a setup in terms of the problem for this chapter. All of the words in the text are to be stored. Each word will have to be stored in a packed array. To store many words, then, you will need an array where each element consists of a packed array in which a word is stored. Thus, you need an array of (packed) arrays.

The declaration of such a monster would consist of the following:

```
CONST StringLength = 20;
         MaxWords = 1000;
TYPE String       = PACKED ARRAY[1..StringLength] OF CHAR;
       WordArray = ARRAY [1..MaxWords] OF String;
VAR Words : WordArray;
```

Consider what is going on in this set of declarations. After the constants StringLength and MaxWords are declared, the *String* type is defined in the Type Declarations section of the program, as usual. Once it is defined, this or any other user-defined type can be used to indicate the type of the elements in an array, and in fact, this is what is done in the next type declaration. *WordArray* is defined to be the type name of an array, each of whose elements is a variable of type *String*. The type *WordArray*, then, defines an entity that consists of 1000 packed arrays. Finally, in the Variable Declarations section of the program, a variable named Words is declared and given the type *WordArray*, and this causes an array in which each slot consists of a packed array of 20 characters to be set up in main memory and given the name Words. You can visualize the array as in the figure. Note that with this setup, you won't need the single packed array variable that was called Word in the previous two chapters; now, there are (according to the declaration above) 1000 such slots, and each has its own name. The names, of course, are Words[1], Words[2], Words[3], and so on. Once again, you can think of an array as a quick way to get yourself a lot of variables of the same type without having to declare them individually.

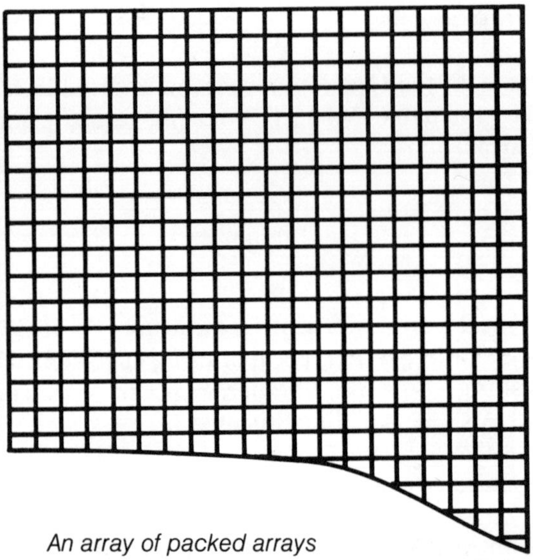

An array of packed arrays

Since each of the elements in the Words **array is a packed array of type CHAR variables, each of these elements can be treated as an entity and therefore written out, compared, and assigned to as a whole, as can any packed array.**

By the way, if the declarations above were made, a variable Word could be also declared in the Variable Declarations section of the program with type *String*, if necessary, and it would be set up and could be used in the program as it was in previous programs.

Once a type is established, even if it is subsequently used as part of another type (as String **is in the example above), it is still a valid type and can be used to define variables in the Declarations section of the program.**

What do you do if you want to refer to a specific slot in one of the packed arrays in the Words array? Suppose, for instance, that you want to refer to the 4th character in the 459th packed array in the Words array. To do so, you would use the name

```
Words[459,4]
```

The first number indicates the slot in the main array, and the second number indicates the slot in the secondary packed array. Words[459,4] is the name of a CHAR-type variable, since the 4th slot of the array in the 459th slot of Words is of type CHAR. So, you can treat this variable in any of the ways that are appropriate for CHAR variables. For instance, you can say

```
Words[459,4] := 's';
```

which stores the letter 's' in the 4th slot of the 459th packed array in **Words**; or you can say

```
Words[459,4] IN ['a'..'z','A'..'Z'] ...
```

which causes the computer to check that **Words[459,4]** is a letter of the alphabet. You can also use INTEGER-type variables as one or both subscripts—for instance, you can refer to

```
Words[Counter,4]
```

or

```
Words[Counter1,Counter2]
```

and in both cases, the value or values of the INTEGER-type variables in the subscript are used to determine the particular element of **Words** that is being referred to.

CONSTRUCTING THE PROGRAM

The Main Program

One of the first things to consider in order to write the program for this chapter is the new variables that will be needed. In this program, you will need to declare an array that is capable of holding all of the words in the text. As indicated in the preceding section, an array of packed arrays is suitable for this purpose. The array will be declared in the main program rather than in a procedure, because it will be used by procedures and the main program alike in both this program and others that you will write in later chapters. The array declaration given earlier is appropriate here; so the declarations section of your main program will look like this:

```
CONST StringLength = 20;
         MaxWords = 1000;
TYPE String = PACKED ARRAY[1..StringLength] OF CHAR;
       WordArray = ARRAY[1..MaxWords] OF String;
       StringBounds = 0..StringLength;
       ArrayBounds = 0..MaxWords;
VAR Words : WordArray;
              .
              .
              .
  Other variable declarations
              .
              .
              .
```

The effects of these declarations should be clear from the preceding discussion. Notice the use of the constants StringLength and MaxWords to specify the upper bounds of the packed array and the Words array—these constants can be used throughout the program, anywhere the upper bounds of the arrays are referenced. Then, if a change is made in the size of either or both of the arrays, only the value assigned to the constant will need to be modified. Notice also that the declarations of the subrange types *StringBounds* and *ArrayBounds* have been added to the earlier example. You are familiar with *StringBounds*, and *ArrayBounds* is very similar. Like *StringBounds*, the type *ArrayBounds* will be given to any variable whose function within the main program or any procedure is to serve as an index into an array—in this case, the Words array.

Some additional variables will have to be declared in the main program; these will be added as the need arises.

Once the Words array has been set up, you can turn to the statements that will appear in the main program. Earlier, the overall algorithm for this chapter's program was given as

1. Load the text into main memory.
2. Print all of the words in the text.

The statements in the main program will follow this outline very closely, because step 1, in particular, can be implemented as a procedure, and therefore step 1 will be replaced by a single Pascal statement that calls the procedure. If this procedure is given the name "Load," then the main program will look something like this:

```
BEGIN
  Load (<parameters>);
            .
            .
            .
  Statements to print the words
            .
            .
            .
END;     { main program }
```

The Load procedure will take over the task of reading the file and storing all of the words from the text in separate slots in the Words array. There is no longer any reason for the main program to concern itself with any of the details of reading the words from the file; when this step needs to be performed, it will simply call on the Load procedure to do it. This means that many of the statements that were included in last chapter's main program will be moved into the Load procedure here.

This is a good time to determine what the parameters to the Load procedure will be. What variables declared in the main program will be needed by Load? Well, since Load reads from TextFile, it will obviously need access to this variable. And if Load is to store the words from the text in the Words array, then the procedure will need access to this variable as well. So, TextFile and Words should be passed to Load as parameters.

There is one other piece of information that needs to be shared between the main program and the Load procedure that bears some consideration. The Words array, as it is declared above, contains 1000 slots. This number of slots is set up because it is assumed that the *actual* number of words in the text is not known before the program executes.[1] It is extraordinarily unlikely that the text will contain exactly 1000 words, and this means that only a portion of the slots in the Words array will be filled. The slots that are unfilled will remain empty—that is, they will most likely contain garbage left over from previous uses of the portions of main memory they occupy—and these slots will have to be ignored throughout the remainder of the program. Thus, only the filled portion of the Words array will be dealt with after the loading process is completed, and so the number of slots filled during the loading process must be known by the main program. It is very typical to allocate an array to some maximum size and then use a variable of type INTEGER (or some subrange of INTEGER) to hold the number of items actually stored in the array. (This number also indexes the last slot filled in the array.) Anytime the information stored in the array is accessed, this variable is used to be sure only the filled portions of the array are referenced.

In order for the main program and the Load procedure to share the variable containing the number of words actually stored in the array, the following can be done: a variable with type *ArrayBounds* (a subrange of INTEGER including the values 0 through MaxWords, as indicated in the set of declarations given above) can be declared in the main program and passed as a parameter to the Load procedure. Since Load determines the number of words that are stored in the Words array, Load can very easily assign to this variable the value that corresponds to the number of words stored in the array. If this variable is passed to Load as a VAR parameter, the value Load assigns to it will be retained after the procedure terminates. Thus the main program will have access to the number of words stored in the array for use in later parts of the program. To enable this, you will have to declare an additional variable in the main program; if it is called NumberOfWords then you will add the declaration

```
NumberOfWords : ArrayBounds;
```

to the VAR Declarations section of the main program. Note that this variable is assigned the type *ArrayBounds*, which defines the range of integer values that can serve as subscripts into the Words array (plus the value 0).

The call to Load in the main program can now be fully specified:

```
Load(Words,NumberOfWords,TextFile);
```

1. It may be that you do know how many words are in the text your program will read, but if you declare the Words array to be exactly big enough to hold the words in your text the program will not be very general—that is, it will not work for texts that are even a few words longer than the one you are using now. It is usual to pick some round number for the size of arrays like Words so that the program can accommodate any text of an approximate size (here, that size is up to a maximum of 1000 words). If you are using much larger or much smaller texts, then you may want to change the value of MaxWords; see the section on "Estimating the size of an array" in the Niceties section of this chapter for more discussion of appropriate values for MaxWords.

Note that aside from the declaration of the array, this is *the only context within a program in which the name of a non-packed array can appear without a subscript.*

The second step in the algorithm for the main program provides for printing each word in the array. As you will see, the statements that accomplish this are very brief, and so instead of writing a separate procedure to write the words, the statements will simply be included in the main program.

To print the words in the array, you need to access each of the words in the array in succession. As soon as you contemplate accessing successive elements of an array of any kind you should immediately think—loop and counter variable. This is exactly what is needed here—a loop that repeats once for each word in the array, and a counter variable starting with value 1 and incremented by 1 each time through the loop, so that it can be used as the array subscript within the loop. Only two more things need to be considered: first, under what condition or conditions is the loop to continue repeating? Obviously, it should continue until all of the words have been printed. What condition signals this? Well, since NumberOfWords will contain the number of *filled* slots in the Words array, the counter variable should be incremented until its value exceeds NumberOfWords, at which point it would be about to reference the first unfilled slot in the array. This is the only condition for stopping the loop: that the counter value exceeds the value in NumberOfWords. Given this, what kind of loop should be used here? WHILE? REPEAT? FOR? Note that the loop needed here will repeat a *definite* number of times, and if you recall the discussion of the FOR loop in Chapter Five, FOR loops are designed for this particular situation. Put another way,

---

If you are writing a loop that increments a variable by 1 on each iteration, and the only condition for stopping that loop is that the variable reaches a certain value, then use a FOR loop.

This is the case here, and so a FOR loop is appropriate.

The form of the FOR loop needed here is

```
FOR Counter := 1 TO NumberOfWords DO BEGIN
  WRITELN(Words[Counter]);
END;      { for }
```

Counter is assumed to be a variable of type *ArrayBounds*, declared in the main program. So you should add the declaration

```
Counter : ArrayBounds;
```

to the Variable Declarations section of the main program.

Putting all this together, you have the main program for this chapter:

```
BEGIN
  Load(Words,NumberOfWords,TextFile);
  FOR Counter := 1 TO NumberOfWords DO BEGIN
    WRITELN(Words[Counter]);
  END;      { for }
END.     { main program }
```

The Load Procedure

The next order of business is to construct the procedure Load. To begin, consider the Procedure Heading—what should it look like? In the call to Load from the main program, three variables are passed to the procedure: Words, NumberOfWords, and TextFile. So three parameters must appear in Load's heading, corresponding one-for-one in type with the variables that appear in the call. How should the parameters be passed, as VAR or Value parameters? To answer, you need to consider whether or not the changes that Load will make in main program variables Words and NumberOfWords need to be retained after the Load procedure terminates. (Recall that because TextFile is a file variable it must be passed as a VAR parameter.) Of course, they do. Before Load executes, neither the array Words nor the variable NumberOf Words is given a value—these variables are "empty" at the time Load is called. It is Load's primary function to assign values to these variables that can be used in later parts of the program. Therefore, these variables function as "output" from the procedure and must be passed to Load as VAR parameters.

Given these constraints, the Procedure Heading for Load should look like this:

```
PROCEDURE Load(VAR FileWords : WordArray; VAR WordsInFile : ArrayBounds;
        VAR WordFile : TEXT);
```

So within Load, FileWords will serve as a pseudonym for the main program variable Words, WordsInFile will serve as a pseudonym for NumberOfWords, and WordFile will be a pseudonym for TextFile.

Turn your attention now to the body of the Load procedure. The variables ments in the procedure are constructed, so discussion of the Variable Declarations section of the procedure will be set aside for the moment. Earlier, you saw that step 1 of the overall algorithm for this chapter's program (load the words from the file into main memory) could be expanded to be

1. Ready the file for reading.
2. While the character about to be read is not the end-of-file character, repeat the following:
   a. Read a word.
   b. Store the word in a unique memory location.

To implement this algorithm, you can borrow the code from last chapter's main program, which implemented a nearly identical algorithm, and change the names around to accommodate Load's terminology. The statements in Load will therefore be something like this:

```
BEGIN
  RESET(WordFile);
  WHILE NOT EOF(WordFile) DO BEGIN
    ReadWord(Word,WordFile);
              .
              .
              .
    Statements to store the word
              .
              .
              .
  END;     { while }
END;     { Load }
```

The references to TextFile in the code from the previous program were here changed to WordFile, since this is the name by which the file from which Load reads is known within the procedure.

Notice that the step to read a word is implemented by calling the ReadWord procedure. You should begin to see the practical benefits of using procedures here—now that the ReadWord procedure is written, it can simply be brought into this chapter's program wholesale and called upon when needed, without further thought about the details of word-reading. You can focus your attention now on higher-level tasks, like loading the text and, later, even more useful tasks.

Note that when Load calls ReadWord, it *passes* the variable Word to ReadWord as a parameter, thus enabling the two procedures to share that variable. This brings up another point—where is the variable Word that is used in Load declared? It was not declared in the main program, nor should it be, since it is not used there. But Load obviously uses it—it is the variable into which ReadWord puts the word it reads each time it is called, and Load will take this word and store it in the array after ReadWord provides it. Word should be declared in Load, and, as in the statements above, passed to ReadWord in the same way that it was passed to ReadWord by the main program in last chapter's program. So, you now know at least one of the variables that will be declared in Load—the variable Word.

The final concern here is step 2.b, which is new. How do you go about storing the word? As ReadWord reads each word from the file, it should be stored in the Words (or FileWords, as it is known within Load) array. You want the first word to be stored in slot 1 of the Words array, the second to be stored in slot 2 of the array, the third to be stored in slot 3, and so on. Since each time through the loop, after ReadWord is called the variable Word holds the word to be stored, you can put it in one of the slots in Words with a statement like

```
FileWords[<slotnumber>] := Word;
```

This works because the item on the right side of the assignment operator is of the same type as the item on the left—both Word and each element of the FileWords array are of type *String*; furthermore, you can assign a whole packed array to another whole packed array in a single assignment like the one above. As for the slot number, this varies each time the loop is executed—that is, it is incremented by one each time another word is stored. You should be able to see that once again, the typical situation is at hand where a counter is initialized and incremented within a loop in which it is used as a subscript to an array. So you will need a variable with type *ArrayBounds* (since it serves as a subscript to the FileWords array) that is given a starting value before the WHILE loop begins and a statement inside the loop to increment the variable.

Before you add the declaration of a variable with type *ArrayBounds* to the Variable Declarations section of Load, consider using NumberOfWords (Load calls it WordsInFile) for this purpose. Whatever variable you use, the value of that variable will be the number of words stored after the loop finishes executing, and this is the value that must be assigned to WordsInFile before the procedure finishes executing. Therefore, the variable WordsInFile can do double duty as a counter variable while its final value is being computed. As for its initial value, like Counter in the ReadWord procedure, it makes sense to start WordsInFile out with a value of 0. Then, if the WHILE loop never executes because the file is empty, the value that NumberOfWords will have back in the main program will reflect exactly the number of words Load stored in the Words array—none.

To implement all of this, you need to insert a statement to set WordsInFile to 0 before the WHILE loop. Within the loop, you will need another statement to increment WordsInFile, and the variable WordsInFile will also be inserted as the subscript variable in the statement given above to store Word in the next available slot of the FileWords array.

This takes care of Load for the most part. Only one thing is left to consider. Under very exceptional circumstances (where one or more blanks precede the end-of-line character that precedes the end-of-file character in the file), ReadWord may fill Word with blanks when it is called. When this happens, you do not want to store the string of blanks in the Words array—for one thing, if you store the string of blanks in the array, the count of the number of words stored will be off by one. And in later programs, a string of blanks in one of the slots in the array would cause problems as well.

The way around storing blanks in Words is simply to include a statement in the Load procedure that checks the word that ReadWord reads each time it is called. If the word is just a string of blanks, then the word will not be stored and WordsInFile will not be incremented. Otherwise, Load will store the word and increment WordsInFile as usual. In terms of the algorithm, step 2.b must be modified as follows:

1. Ready the file for reading.
2. While the character about to be read is not the end-of-file character, repeat the following:
   a. Read a word.
   b. If the word is not a string of blanks, do the following:
      (1) Store the word in a unique memory location.

Now, if the word read in step 2.a is a string of blanks, what is now step 2.b.1 will simply be skipped. The obvious Pascal implementation of step 2.b is an IF-THEN statement (rather than IF-THEN-ELSE, since there is no "else" here) with a condition asserting that the contents of the variable Word is *not* a string of blanks. Such a condition is expressed like this:

```
Word <> '
```

or, if you declared a constant **Blanks** in your program as suggested in the Niceties section of Chapter Five, you can assert

```
Word <> Blanks
```

The IF-THEN statement then will be

```
IF Word <> Blanks THEN BEGIN
  WordsInFile := WordsInFile + 1;
  FileWords[WordsInFile] := Word;
END;     { then begin }
```

If you put everything together, Load will look like this:

```
PROCEDURE Load(VAR FileWords : WordArray; VAR WordsInFile : ArrayBounds;
        VAR WordFile : TEXT);
  { Reads and loads the words from WordFile }
  { into the array FileWords }
VAR Word : String;
BEGIN
  RESET(WordFile);
  WordsInFile := 0;
  WHILE NOT EOF(WordFile) DO BEGIN
    ReadWord(Word, WordFile);
    IF Word <> Blanks THEN BEGIN
      WordsInFile := WordsInFile + 1;
      FileWords[WordsInFile] := Word;
    END;     { then begin }
  END;     { while }
END;     { Load }
```

Notice that **WordsInFile** is given the initial value 0, like **Counter** in the ReadWord procedure, and is incremented just before each word is stored.

The Program as a Whole

The following is an outline of the program's structure, in terms of the way it will look:

```
PROGRAM LoadWords(INPUT,OUTPUT,TextFile);
  Constant declarations: StringLength, MaxWords, Blank, Blanks
  Type Declarations: String, WordArray, StringBounds, ArrayBounds
  Variable Declarations: Words, NumberOfWords, Counter, TextFile
  Procedure Declarations:
  PROCEDURE ReadWord(VAR NextWord : String; VAR InputFile: TEXT);
    Variable Declarations: Letter, Counter
    Procedure Declarations:
    PROCEDURE SkipBlanks(VAR NextChar : CHAR; VAR InFile : TEXT);
      Variable Declarations: none
```

```
    BEGIN     { SkipBlanks }
      .
      .
      .
    END;     { SkipBlanks }
  BEGIN     { ReadWord }
            .
            .
            .
  END;     { ReadWord }
  PROCEDURE Load(VAR FileWords : WordArray;
      VAR WordsInFile : ArrayBounds;
      VAR WordFile : TEXT);
    Variable Declarations: Word
  BEGIN     { Load }
          .
          .
          .
  END;     { Load }
BEGIN     { LoadWords }
  Load(Words,NumberOfWords,TextFile);
  FOR Counter := 1 TO NumberOfWords DO BEGIN
    WRITELN(Words[Counter]);
  END;     { for }
END.     { LoadWords }
```

Notice that ReadWord and Load are declared at the same "level" within the program—that is, both are declared directly within the main program. According to the rules about which procedures can call which, a procedure can call only those "sibling" procedures whose declarations appear earlier. That means that given the setup above, where ReadWord is declared before Load, Load can call ReadWord, but because Load is declared *after* ReadWord, ReadWord cannot call Load. If the declaration of ReadWord appeared after Load's declaration, then when Load attempted to call ReadWord you would get an error message saying that ReadWord was "unknown" at that point in the program.

Note that Load cannot call SkipBlanks, since SkipBlanks is declared inside ReadWord and therefore effectively "belongs" to ReadWord. The main program cannot call SkipBlanks either, for the same reason. The main program can call Load, and because of the setup, it could call ReadWord as well. This brings up a point—why isn't ReadWord declared in Load, since Load is the only procedure that calls on ReadWord? In other words, why make ReadWord accessible to the main program when the main program doesn't call on it? The reason for this is that ReadWord can be used *anytime* a word is to be read from any file, and it will, in fact, be called upon by the main program in many of the exercises for this and later chapters. The process of reading a word that the procedure embodies is potentially a sub-task of a variety of tasks, not just loading the text. Therefore, it makes sense to have it generally available within the program. However, note that for the basic program outlined above, ReadWord could very well be declared inside Load.

SUMMING UP THE PROGRAM

The Load procedure will be included in all of the programs you write in the remainder of this text. Although it will be modified slightly in later programs, by and large you can now forget about the details of loading words into the array and simply call the procedure whenever it is needed. Here again is an example of the advantage of modularizing your programs with procedures.

Notice that in the program above, a variable named Counter is declared in both the main program and the ReadWord procedure. This situation bears comment because you will encounter it several times in later programs. First of all, you should note that the variable Counter in the main program is an entirely separate variable from Counter in the ReadWord procedure. Each refers to a different slot in main memory. The variable Counter declared in the main program is created when the main program begins executing and exists until the entire program terminates. Each time ReadWord starts to execute, a new slot in memory is set up and given the name Counter and each time ReadWord terminates this slot is destroyed. While ReadWord is executing, there are, effectively, two slots in main memory with the name Counter; and since the main program's variables are "known" in all procedures declared within it, ReadWord potentially has access to it. However, *any reference to* Counter *within ReadWord refers to the most local declaration of the variable, and so the main program's* Counter *is not only separate but, in this case, inaccessible to ReadWord.*

Why not let ReadWord use the main program's Counter, rather than declaring another one of its own? It has been said before in a different way: a procedure should not use the variables of another procedure or the main program unless you truly want the variables to be shared. The Counter variable used in the main program and the Counter variable used in ReadWord have no relation to one another—no value stored in one is ever used by the other, and so the two should be separate. If ReadWord used the main program's Counter, it is possible that some value left over from the use of Counter in the main program could be inadvertently used within ReadWord, and vice versa. This is not likely, but when it does happen it causes bugs in a program that are very difficult to find. Furthermore, if ReadWord uses a main program variable, then if ReadWord is extracted from this program for use in another, you will have to be sure that a variable Counter is declared there as well, even if it isn't needed for any other purpose. For these reasons, the wisdom of experienced programmers forbids the use of so-called "global" variables—variables declared outside a procedure. Take advantage of this wisdom—it may save you hours of debugging time.

In general: counter variables are not passed as parameters (although notice that NumberOfWords, which functions as a counter variable in Load, is passed to the procedure), and are therefore declared within the procedures in which they are used. This is because for the most part, a counter variable is given its initial value within the procedure, and its final value is not needed after the procedure terminates. So it has no connection with the variables or values used in other procedures or the main program, and should therefore be known only to the procedure in which it is used.

Another point that should be made here involves the use of WHILE,

REPEAT-UNTIL, and FOR loops to access an array. Of course, you are becoming used to the idea of using a loop and a counter variable to access the elements of an array. But how do you know which kind of loop to use? The answer depends upon whether or not you know how many elements in the array you will access within the loop. In cases where you do not know how many slots in the array you will access—for example, when reading words in, since you have no idea how many words will be read—you must use a WHILE or REPEAT-UNTIL loop. Which of these you choose depends on whether or not the statements in the loop will be executed at least once or not. As mentioned in Chapter Five, when you use a WHILE or REPEAT-UNTIL loop to access the elements of an array, you must initialize a counter variable before the loop begins that will be used as a subscript to the array and increment that variable within the loop. The condition on the loop will almost always invoke a check on the value of the counter variable, to ensure that it does not exceed the number of slots in the array.

When you want to access a set number of slots in the array—for example, when you print the words in the array *after Load has indicated the number of words that are stored in it*—you will use a FOR loop that goes from 1 to the number of items to be accessed. In the main program for this chapter, NumberOfWords holds the actual number of slots that will be accessed within the loop, and so this variable is used as the loop's upper bound. Inside the FOR loop, the counter variable is again used as a subscript to the array. Here, however, the counter variable is given its initial value in the loop's heading, and so it need not be initialized before the loop begins to execute. Furthermore, the FOR loop automatically increments the counter variable for you, so you need not include a statement to do so within the loop. And since the FOR loop will stop automatically when the counter variable reaches the value given as the upper bound in the loop's heading, there is no need to check to be sure it does not go beyond the number of elements in the array.

NICETIES

Error Trapping

In the Load procedure, a potential problem has not been dealt with adequately—the situation in which the number of words in the file exceeds the number of available slots in the Words array. If more words than slots exist, your program will try to store a word in an element of the array that does not exist: the one just beyond the end of the array you defined. As a result, your program will "crash" after an error message has been issued.

As you already know, a well-written program will include the means to handle situations such as these so that in the event of an error, your program can retain control and either terminate gracefully, by stopping itself or adjusting to the situation and continuing on. Within the Load procedure, then, steps should be taken to determine if the program is about to store into a non-existent element of the array, and if so, prevent it from doing so.

The obvious solution is to enhance the condition on the WHILE loop in Load to check that WordsInFile does not exceed or equal the value of MaxWords, the constant that defines the size of the array. So the condition can be modified to read

```
WHILE (NOT EOF(WordFile)) AND (WordsInFile < MaxWords) DO ...
```

Note that to enter the loop, WordsInFile must be less than MaxWords. If WordsInFile is equal to MaxWords when the loop is entered, inside the loop 1 will be added to it and its value will then exceed MaxWords. So when WordsInFile is subsequently used in the loop as a subscript to the FileWords array, it will reference a non-existent slot in the array.

This condition is all that is needed to stop the loop before it attempts to store beyond the end of the array. If the loop stops as a result of the situation that WordsInFile equals MaxWords, any words that remain in the file will not be read. It would be nice to let the user know that this has happened, if possible, so that later results which may be affected by this situation will be understandable.

To do this, all you need to do is to check, after the loop finishes executing, what made the loop stop. You know that if the end of the file has not been encountered, then the reason for stopping the loop must have been that the value of WordsInFile became too large. So after the loop terminates, but before the procedure terminates, you can add a statement that checks to see if the end of the file has *not* been encountered. If not, then a statement can be printed indicating to the user that all of the words in the file have not been read. The following statement will accomplish this:

```
IF NOT EOF(WordFile) THEN BEGIN
  WRITELN;
  WRITELN('*** Warning: your file contains more words');
  WRITELN('     than this program can handle.');
  WRITELN('     The entire file could not be read.');
  WRITELN;
END;     { then begin }
```

Estimating the Size of an Array

As mentioned above, your program will rely on a variable to know how many words have been stored in your array in later parts of the program. Unlike the Word packed array, in which unused spaces are explicitly filled with blank characters, the unused spaces in the array to hold the words in the text will remain undefined—that is, they will probably contain garbage left over from a previous use of the portion of main memory that they occupy. They will never be accessed in later parts of the program.

How big should the array to hold words be? This depends on the *approximate* size of your text. Usually, some round figure like 500, 1000, or 2000 is given in the declaration of the array. You should choose a number that is large enough so that the array can hold all of the words in the text, but if you have a very short text of, say, under 500 words, there is no sense in declaring the array with a size of 2000. If your array is too small, you will get an error message when your program attempts to store more words than there is room for, so at least at first, it is best to err on the side of overestimating the number of slots required than underestimating them. Your array can be too large only if there is not sufficient room in main memory to accommodate it, and, again, you will get an error message if this is the case. If main memory is limited on your computer and you want to be sure not to overestimate the size of your array, you can modify the program outlined in Chapter Five to print out the exact number of words in your text and use this value to determine the size of your array.

More About Array Bounds

The declarations of the array and packed array types in the programs you have been writing have always indicated that individual elements in the arrays are referred to with INTEGER values. That is, slots are numbered from 1 to some number and each element is referred to by providing an INTEGER subscript with the array name. In most situations, INTEGER-type subscripts are appropriate. However, Pascal allows subscripts to be CHAR values as well as INTEGER values, since, like numbers, characters have an implied sequence as well (the collating sequence, of course!). For example, you can declare an array like the following:

```
TYPE CharArray = ARRAY['A'..'Z'] OF INTEGER;
VAR Characters : CharArray;
```

and this sets up an array named Characters that consists of 26 slots, each capable of holding a value of type INTEGER. The first slot has the index 'A,' the second has the index 'B,' and so on.

To access any element of this array, you must, as usual, provide a subscript following the array name, but in this case the subscript must be one of the letters 'A' through 'Z' (capital, not small). So, you can refer to

```
Characters['A']
```

or

```
Characters['O']
```

or

```
Characters[Letter]
```

provided Letter holds one of the characters 'A' through 'Z.'

One interesting use of an array with CHAR-type subscripts is to keep a tally of the number of times each of the letters in the alphabet appears in a text. To do this, you could do the following each time a character is read from the file:

```
IF Letter IN ['A'..'Z'] THEN BEGIN
  Characters[Letter] := Characters[Letter] + 1;
END;      { then begin }
```

This statement first checks the contents of the variable Letter to be sure it contains a value appropriate as a subscript to the Characters array. If so, the element of the Characters array at position Letter is incremented by one (recall that the *elements*—not the subscripts—of the Characters array have the type INTEGER). If this statement is executed as each character is read from the file, then after the file has been read, Characters['A'] will contain the number of capital A's that appear in the file, Characters['B'] will contain the number of B's, and so on. To write out the contents of each slot in the Characters array after the number of times each capital letter appears has been tallied, you can use a FOR loop with CHAR values as stop and starting values, like this:

```
FOR Letter := 'A' TO 'Z' DO BEGIN
  WRITELN(Letter,' appears in the text ', Characters[Letter]:1, 'times.');
END;      { for }
```

This generates output like the following:

```
A appears in the text 132 times.
B appears in the text 16 times.
C appears in the text 9 times.
            .
            .
            .
```

Refer to the Niceties section of Chapter Five for a description of FOR loops with CHAR-type start and stopping values.

Note that the set of statements given above for counting the number of times the capital letters appear in the text assumes that, before 1 is added to any element of the Characters array, all of the elements in the array are set to 0. This can be accomplished with a FOR loop just like the one above, which instead of the WRITELN statement includes the statement

```
Characters[Letter] := 0;
```

Nested Loops Revisited

In Chapter Three, you saw how to use nested WHILE loops in a program. Here is another set of nested loops—FOR loops, in this instance—that will enable you to access each character in the Words array, one-by-one:

```
FOR Counter1 := 1 TO NumberOfWords DO BEGIN
  FOR Counter2 := 1 TO StringLength DO BEGIN
    IF Words[Counter1,Counter2] IN ['A'..'Z'] ...
  END;      { for counter2 }
END;      { for counter1 }
```

Note that this set of loops accesses all 20 characters in each filled slot of the Words array. Counter1 should have the type *ArrayBounds*, since it indicates which of the elements of the Words array is being referred to. Counter2 should have the type *StringBounds,* since it indicates which of the characters in the packed array stored at position Counter2 in the Words array is being referred to.

To understand how the set-up above works, trace through its operation. When the top of the outer FOR loop is first encountered within the program, Counter1 is given the initial value 1, and the statement within the FOR loop is executed. The statement within the FOR loop just happens to be another FOR loop, and this inner FOR loop must complete its entire cycle of execution before control will return to the top of the outer FOR loop. Thus the inner FOR loop starts executing, giving Counter2 the initial value 1. Inside the inner FOR loop for the first time, reference is made to Words[Counter1,Counter2], which is to say Words[1,1], since the value of both Counter1 and Counter2 is 1 at this point. Words[1,1] is a reference to the packed array in slot 1 of Words and to the first slot in that packed array. Thus, this reference is to the first character of the first word stored in the Words array. In this particular example, this character is checked to see if it is an upper case letter—the details of what is done if it is are omitted here since they do not bear on the point of the example.[2] Now, when the end of the inner FOR loop is reached, control returns to the top of the *inner* FOR loop; this causes the value of Counter2 to be incremented to be 2, and then the loop is re-entered. Inside, the reference is now to Words[1,2] since the value of Counter2 is 2. But note that the value of Counter1 is still 1, since it is not incremented until control returns to the top of the outer FOR loop. Before this happens, the inner FOR loop must complete its cycle of execution, taking Counter2 through the values 1 to Stringlength and enabling access within the loop to each of the individual character slots in the first packed array in Words. When the inner FOR loop finally terminates, the end of the outer FOR loop is encountered and control goes to the top of the outer FOR loop, at which point Counter1 is incremented to be 2. Then the whole process begins again: the inner FOR starts to execute, starting Counter2 with the value 1. Inside the inner FOR loop the reference is to Words[2,1] since Counter1 is now 2 but Counter2 is 1 this first time around. Counter2 will go through the values 1 through 20 again while Counter1 stays at 2, thus enabling access to all of the characters in the second packed array in Words.

Obviously, the two loops above will continue executing until when 1 is added to Counter1 at the top of the outer FOR loop, its value exceeds NumberOfWords. At this point the outer FOR will terminate.

If it is not clear to you how these loops work, trace through the operation of the two loops, keeping track of the values stored in Counter1 and Counter2 as you go along.

Linear Search

A linear search is not a Pascal language feature, but rather a method for searching a group of data elements—in this case, words stored in an array—for a particular item. The program outlined in this chapter can be easily modified so

2. Note, however, that the IF statement given in the preceding section, "More About Array Bounds," could be inserted here to count the capital letters in the words in the text after they are stored in the array rather than as they are being read.

that instead of simply printing the words in the text, it performs a linear search for any word of the user's choosing. It can even tell the user where and how many times the word occurs in the text.

The steps in the process are as follows: after the text has been loaded into main memory, the main program will prompt the user for a word. The program will step through the array, word-by-word, comparing the user's word with each word in the array. If a match is found, the program will print a message indicating the position of the word in the text—for instance, it will tell the user if the word is the 395th or 1204th word in the text. Finally, the program will print a message indicating how many times the word was found in the text (zero, if the word was not found at all). The method of searching through an array by looking first at the item in slot 1, then at the item in slot 2, and so on, is called *linear search*. Later, you will see that there are other, much more efficient ways to search an array, provided that the words in the array are in alphabetical order.

One fact should be noted here before going on. If the user enters the word "The" and the text contains the word "the," the two will not be considered to be the same word since the computer distinguishes between upper and lower case when testing for equality. The solution to this problem is the subject of the next chapter.

Reading a Word From the User. The first step in the process outlined above—reading a word from the user—can be accomplished easily by simply calling on the ReadWord procedure from the main program. As usual, ReadWord can be passed a *String*-type variable in which to store the word read. The name of the file from which the procedure is to read must also be passed as a parameter. But note: The name of the file passed to ReadWord from which the word is to be read should not be TextFile, since the word is not being read from that file, but rather from INPUT. Recall that INPUT is the name of the "file" that is the keyboard of a terminal or microcomputer. The file INPUT is automatically declared with type TEXT, and so it will be compatible with the pseudonym declaration in the Procedure Heading for ReadWord that corresponds to it.

In order to provide ReadWord with a *String*-type variable in which to read a word from the user, the variable must be declared within the main program. If you declare a variable named UsersWord with type *String* in the Variable Declarations section of the main program, then in order to read a word from the user at the keyboard the following set of statements can be inserted in the main program just after the call to Load:

```
WRITE('Enter the word you want the program to search for:  ');
ReadWord(UsersWord,INPUT);
```

After ReadWord finishes executing, UsersWord will contain the word the user entered at the keyboard.

You might want to include a set of statements to print a brief description of the program's function just before the prompt and call to ReadWord given above, so that the user will have a better idea why he or she is entering a word.

The Linear Search. The next segment of the program will do the actual searching. As mentioned above, the search consists of a loop to move through the words that Load stored in the Words array, a slot at a time, comparing the contents of that slot to the word the user entered. When a match occurs, a message should be printed indicating where in the array the word was found. This isn't frivolous information: if the word is stored in the 561st slot in the array, it is the 561st word in the text. This is called the word's *linear position* in the text, and it gives some idea of the word's relative location within the text. If the text contains 1000 words, the word at position 561 is near the middle. More interestingly, if the word appears in the text 10 times, and most or all of those occurrences are between positions 400 and 600 in the text, some special use of the word must be being made in that area of the text.

A basic loop to do the searching would look like this:

```
FOR Counter := 1 TO NumberOfWords DO BEGIN
  IF UsersWord = Words[Counter] THEN BEGIN
    WRITELN('The word appears in the text at position ',Counter:1);
  END;      { then begin }
END;      { for }
```

Look this loop over to be sure you understand how it works.

The only additional consideration here is counting the number of times the word is found in the array. To do this, you can set a counter to 0 initially and then add one to it each time the word is found. This is easy; the loop above can be slightly modified to incorporate these steps, as follows:

```
Frequency := 0;
FOR Counter := 1 TO NumberOfWords DO BEGIN
  IF UsersWord = Words[Counter] THEN BEGIN
    WRITELN('The word appears in the text at position ',Counter:1);
    Frequency := Frequency + 1;
  END;      { then begin }
END;      { for }
WRITELN('The word ', UsersWord,' appears ',
          Frequency:1,' times in the text.');
```

Frequency is a variable with type INTEGER (not *ArrayBounds* or *StringBounds*, since it does not serve as an array subscript) that must be declared in the main program. Its use here in conjunction with the counter variable Counter is interesting: Counter is the variable that is used as a subscript to the array, and so it is incremented once each time the loop executes as usual. Frequency, however, is not being used to access the array at all—it is being used to keep track of the number of times a specific event occurs in the program (here, the number of times a match between the user's word and a word in the array occurs). This is another way in which counter variables are often used in computer programs, and you should go over the program segment above to be sure you understand how it works.

Note that if the word does not appear at all in the text, the user will see a message that indicates that the word appeared 0 times, since that is the value that will be contained in the variable Frequency.

APPLICATIONS AND CONSIDERATIONS

Having all the words in the text in main memory at the same time opens the door to a wide range of possibilities for exploring a text, many of which will be treated in the chapters to come.

In the section of the Niceties that describes linear search, you heard mention of the fact that the location of a word in a text can be very important information. The *relative* locations of words in a text are used in the analysis of content in texts of all kinds. In content analysis, two assumptions operate: first, it is assumed that the closer together (in terms of the number of words that intervene) words or character configurations are within a text, the more related they are within that text. So if the word "water" (or any word considered to have the same meaning) appears close to the word "trap" in the text, then the two are in some way related in that part of the text where they appear. A second assumption is that the *frequency* with which a word or configuration appears in a text is related to the strength of its contribution to the text's meaning. So, if "water" appears very frequently in a text, chances are the concept of "water" plays an important role in the content or meaning of the text. Or, if "water" appears very frequently in a certain portion of a text, then "water" is a concept that contributes to meaning at that point.

A great deal is taken for granted in content analysis—for instance, that a word or other character configuration can be seen as indicative of a concept at some level, and that we can determine what number of occurrences constitutes a "frequent" event. Obviously, the kind of meaning that can be determined by these methods is very broad, but it has several applications. For instance, a text can be searched and the very frequent words in the text (apart from function words such as "the," "and," and prepositions, etc.) can be determined, and this can give a general idea of the topic of the text. Programs to do this kind of thing can be quite fancy, if they have the ability to determine that certain words are indicative of the same content or are closely related. The purpose of this kind of program is often to do automatic abstracting or indexing of texts. A second application of content analysis is in the field of psychology, where patient interviews are often analyzed for repetition and association of various concepts that might lend insight into the patient's structure of ideas. The third application is in literary analysis, where content analysis is used to determine themes and patterns of themes and ideas in a text. For instance, if a group of words (e.g., "water," "wet," "liquid") are considered to be indicative of a certain concept, the places in the text where these words occur can be examined to see where the concepts are referenced. Further, if the words are especially frequent in certain parts of the text—say, at the beginning, middle, and end—then you can get an idea of the *structure* of the text in terms of these ideas. Perhaps the recurrence of these images at intervals has something to do with the way that the events in the text are organized, and even further, the reintroduction of these ideas no doubt has some effect on the reader, whatever the context. This can be carried even farther if the locations of a variety of different word groups are determined and the interactions among them considered. Several examples of these methods are cited in the Applications and Considerations section of Chapter Eleven.

EXERCISES

1. Modify the program to print the text out *backwards*.

2. Modify the program in this chapter to perform the linear search, as described in the Niceties section of this chapter.

3. Do exercise 2, but enhance the program so that it will repeat the process of prompting the user and searching for a word as long as the user wants to continue.

4. Do exercise 2 or 3, but include the statements that do the searching and message printing in a separate procedure named Search. The word to be searched for should be read from the user within the main program and passed to the Search procedure.

5. (Slightly more difficult.) Modify the program so that instead of printing the words in the text it prints the number of times each of the letters A through Z (capitals only) appear in the text, as shown in the Niceties section of this chapter.

6. (More difficult.) Modify the program so that it will search for a given word and, when the word is found, it will print the word along with three words that follow it immediately in the text. To do this you should prompt the user for a word and then perform the linear search as described in the Niceties section. When the word is found, print it and then travel down the array to print the words in the next three slots in the array (on the same line).

This is a handy way to examine the use of a given preposition in the text. For instance, if the user enters the word "in," then the output would be

```
in each of the
in any direction. The
in a category headquarters
        .
        .
        .
```

You can modify the program to print more or fewer words of context if you'd like. Test your program on a file containing the text "She went in the room in the red house that her brother was in." The output should be

```
in the room in
in the red house
in.
```

7. (More difficult.) Do exercise 5, but have the output print each occurrence of the word the user enters in the context of five words (or ten or any number you choose) on *both sides* of the word.

To be especially fancy, let the user enter the number of words to appear in the output on either side of the word.

8
Standardizing the Text

In this chapter's program all of the words in the text will be prepared for further analysis by *standardizing* them as they are stored in the array in the following way: all letters will be translated to upper case, and all punctuation will be removed from each word.[1] The reason for this is simply to enable the computer to see all instances of the same word as the same, which, because the computer is a very literal machine, it will not do if the words contain letters of different cases or extraneous punctuation marks. For instance, if you tell the computer to locate all instances of the word "then" in the text, it will look only for instances of the four letters 't,' 'h,' 'e,' and 'n' (followed by sixteen blanks, if the length of the packed array in which the word is stored is twenty). It will not consider words such as "Then", "then", and "then," as instances of the word you specified, since the character 'T' is not the same as the character 't' in the computer's mind, and the string "then" followed by a comma is not the same as "then" followed by a blank. (See the discussion of the way the computer compares packed arrays in

1. Internal punctuation—that is, punctuation that appears within a word, such as the apostrophe in "you'll" and the hyphens in "father-in-law"—will not be eliminated from the words in the text. Note that the periods following abbreviations will be eliminated, however, since there is no way to distinguish the period that ends a sentence from a period that is part of an abbreviation, although a way around this is suggested in the Niceties section of this chapter.

Chapter Four.) So this chapter's program will make what human beings consider to be instances of the same word conform to the computer's idea of sameness.

Each word will be standardized after it is read from the file, but before it is stored in the Words array within the program. This implies an additional step in the loading process, which in turn means that a step to "standardize the word" must be inserted into the algorithm for loading the text that was developed in the last chapter. This changes last chapter's algorithm to be:

1. Ready the file for reading.
2. While the character about to be read is not the end-of-file character, repeat the following:
   a. Read a word.
   b. Standardize the word.
   c. If the word is not a string of blanks, do the following:
      (1) Store the word in a unique memory location.

Because this algorithm describes the Load procedure, Load must be changed to incorporate the new step 2.b. As you can guess, this will amount to a call to a procedure, in which the details of standardizing a word will be dealt with, thus leaving Load to its primary business: loading the text into the array.

One note before going on: why is the standardizing done before the word is checked to see if it consists of blanks, rather than after? After all, there is no need to standardize a string of blanks. The reason is that the standardizing process might turn a "word" that is not a string of blanks into one by eliminating punctuation. That is, if something like '...' appears in the text surrounded by blanks, ReadWord will read it and store it in Word like any other string of non-blanks. Since standardization removes punctuation, '...' will be changed into nothing—a string of blank characters, which of course should not be stored in the Words array; if standardization is done after the check for a string of blanks rather than before this won't be caught. For this reason, standardization should be done before Load checks the word to see if it consists solely of blanks.

As mentioned above, standardizing a word means that punctuation (except internal punctuation) is removed from the word and all of the letters in the word are translated to upper case, if necessary. This process can be broken down into the following three steps:

1. Remove all punctuation that precedes the word.
2. Remove all punctuation that follows the word.
3. Capitalize the letters in the word.

Using this process, a word that is read in as "(Now," will be stripped of the leading left parenthesis and the trailing comma, and the 'o' and 'w' will be capitalized to yield "NOW". Similarly, the word "yet.")" will be stripped of the trailing period, quotation mark, and right parenthesis and capitalized to yield "YET".

Each of these three steps obviously needs some elaboration in order to be implemented in Pascal.

In terms of the character-by-character operation of the computer, you can imagine that step 1 will break down into something like this: starting at the first character in the word, look at that character, and if it is anything but an alphabetic character, get rid of it. Now if that first character was not an alphabetic character, then there may be another non-alphabetic character preceding the word, and so you must keep looking. So you must repeat this process of examining characters at the beginning of the string until you encounter a letter, in which case consider the beginning of the word to be found and stop.

The part of the pseudo-algorithm given above that reads "get rid of it" clearly needs work. You may be able to think of one or two ways to get rid of a character in a word. One thought is to replace it with a blank, which means that the string "(Now" would be changed to " NOW", in which the first character is a blank. This is not a solution, though, because since words are compared on a character-by-character basis, the word "NOW" is just as unequal to " NOW" as it is to "(NOW". Another solution is to move every character in the word over a slot to the left (consider slot 1 to be the "left-most" in the packed array), thus overwriting the undesirable non-alphabetic character. This is the solution that will be used here. Given this, step 1 can be more precisely specified as follows:

1. Set a counter to 1.
2. While the character in the slot of the packed array corresponding to the counter is not an alphabetic character, do the following:
   a. Add 1 to the counter.
3. Replace the word (starting at the first slot) with the portion of the word starting at the position corresponding to the value of the counter.

Step 1 of this algorithm sets a counter that will be used to refer to successive characters in the word to the value 1. Step 2 examines the first character in the word to see if it is an alphabetic character, and if not, provides for adding 1 to the counter in order to reference the next character in the word. When the first alphabetic character is encountered, the counter should indicate its position; so in step 3, the piece of the word starting at the position corresponding to the value of the counter is moved over to start in slot 1, erasing whatever was there and putting this character at the beginning of the word. Thus, if the word is initially ""(That" (a quotation mark followed by a left parenthesis followed by the word itself), when step 2 terminates the counter should be 3, because that is the position in the word where the first alphabetic character was found. Step 3 should then set the word to "That" by moving the character in position 3 into position 1, the character in position 4 into position 2, and so on.

Getting rid of trailing blanks involves a process that is almost the reverse of the one above. That is, instead of starting at the beginning of the word, you must start at the end of the packed array and go along until you find an alphabetic character, in which case the *end* of the word has been found. However, here you can get rid of punctuation marks that may appear at the end of the word as you go along by simply replacing them with blanks (blanks at the end of a word present no problem at all when two words are compared). So an algorithm like the following will suffice here:

1. Set a counter to be equal to the length of the string.
2. While the character in the slot of the packed array corresponding to the counter is not an alphabetic character, do the following:
   a. Replace the character with a blank.
   b. Subtract one from the counter.

Step 2 keeps the process of replacing characters with blanks going until an alphabetic character is encountered in the word. All characters encountered before this happens are replaced by blanks—including blanks that may appear at the end of the word in the packed array.

You might wonder why the algorithm is not modified so that step 2.a is performed only if the character under consideration is not a blank (note that having reached this point in the algorithm, you know it is not an alphabetic character). This could be done, but it would involve more work than simply doing the replacement regardless of whether or not the character is a blank. The reason for this is that it takes about as much effort to check the character to see if it is a blank as it does to actually replace the character with a blank. If, for example, there are four non-alphabetic characters at the end of the word and two of them are punctuation marks, simply replacing them with blanks without checking first requires four operations. Checking each character before replacing them adds four operations (one for each check) to the number performed here, but of course two of the replacements are eliminated since in two cases, discovering a blank causes the replacement process to be skipped. But the total number of operations required is now six (four checks and two replacements) instead of four, so you have increased the amount of work required rather than reduced it.

Note once again that by starting first at the beginning of the word and then at the end to get rid of punctuation ensures that punctuation in the middle of the word remains there.

The final step of the process is to capitalize all of the letters in the word. This can be done by looking at each character in the word, one-by-one, and if the character is a lower case letter, translating it to upper case. An algorithm describing this process is

1. For each character in the word, do the following:
  a. If the character is a lower case letter, do the following:
    (1) translate the letter to upper case.

Step 1.a.1 needs work, but later you will see a clever way to accomplish this step in a single, rather complex statement.

The algorithms given above to accomplish the three steps involved in the standardization process are sufficient to get started. Before considering them in more detail, turn your attention to some new features of Pascal.

ELEMENTS OF PASCAL

BOOLEAN Variables

Pascal includes one more built-in type (as opposed to user-defined types like arrays) in addition to CHAR, INTEGER, and REAL. These variables have type BOOLEAN, and are declared in the usual way in the Variable Declarations section of the program:

```
VAR Found : BOOLEAN;
```

Boolean variables are a bit different from the other types, which hold values that are familiar to us, like numbers and characters.

Boolean variables are variables that can hold only two possible values: the value TRUE, and the value FALSE.

To directly assign the values TRUE and FALSE to a Boolean variable, you can use statements like the following:

```
Found := TRUE;
```

and

```
Found := FALSE;
```

Note that TRUE and FALSE are Pascal keywords which, unlike other keywords, represent values that can be assigned to variables with type BOOLEAN.

Since Boolean variables have a value of either TRUE or FALSE, they can be used in conditions in a unique way. Recall that an assertion within a condition must be some statement that can be determined to be true or false. A Boolean variable can also be determined to be either true or false, based simply on its current value. So, it is possible to have a condition like the following, if Found is a Boolean variable:

```
IF Found THEN BEGIN ...
```

Just as before, the condition is evaluated to determine if it is true or false. Here, the value of the variable Found is simply consulted; if it contains the value TRUE, then the condition is true and the statements following the THEN BEGIN are executed. If it contains the value FALSE, then the condition is false and the statements following the THEN BEGIN are skipped.

Functions

Functions in Pascal are a great deal like the procedures with which you are already familiar. They have the following traits, all of which they share with procedures:

- Functions enable the programmer to set apart a group of statements and invoke them by mentioning the function's name at any point in the program.
- Functions are defined in the Procedure Declarations section of a program.
- Functions are declared with a Function Heading that is very similar to a Procedure Heading.
- Functions take VAR and Value parameters, which are specified in the Function Heading just like they are in a Procedure Heading.
- Variables can be declared in a function under the same rules as those for procedures.

Now, for the major difference between functions and procedures: functions, in the context in which they are invoked, actually *represent a particular value* that is determined within the function. The function reference that invokes the function is effectively replaced by the value computed within the function.

Function calls are not isolated statements like procedure calls, but rather appear in contexts where some value is required—for example, in an expression on the right side of an assignment operator, or in a WRITELN statement.

In this sense, functions are something like variables, since they have values. The difference is that the value of a function is not some value that has been stored in main memory, as it is when you use a variable; rather, this value is computed by the statements within the function at the time the function is called.

Pascal provides several *built-in* functions—that is, functions that are already written and "declared" for you, and whose internal workings you will never see, but which you can invoke at any point in your program. To familiarize you with the way a function works, we will look at built-in functions first and then go on to consider the process of writing your own, *user-defined* functions.

The Built-in Functions ORD and CHR. As you already know, within the computer each character is represented by the numeric code associated with that character in the collating sequence. One of Pascal's built-in functions will, given a character, provide you with that numeric code. The name of the function is ORD, which is short for *ordinal value*. If you want your program to print out the numeric code for the character stored in the variable *Letter*, for instance, you can use this statement:

```
WRITELN(ORD(Letter));
```

ORD(Letter) represents the call to the function ORD. When the call to ORD is encountered, the function is invoked, which means that the statements within the function—which, because the function is built-in, don't appear within your program—are executed at this point. Here the statements within the function compute the numeric code for the character stored in the variable Letter, which is a parameter to the function ORD in this example. The function ORD takes a single parameter of type CHAR.

So far, the operation of a function is just like a procedure. The difference is in how the value computed by the function is sent back to the caller. After the value is computed—in the example above, the value computed is the numeric code for Letter—is is *returned* to the calling procedure.

In effect, the reference to ORD(Letter) **is replaced by the value computed by the function, just as a reference to a variable in this context would be replaced by the value stored in it. Thus a function call always occurs in a context where a variable could occur, except, of course, on the left side of an assignment operator or in a READ statement.**

So, if you want to assign the numeric code for the character stored in the variable Letter to a variable called ThisOne, you can say

```
ThisOne := ORD(Letter);
```

When this statement is executed, the following happens: as usual in an assignment statement, whatever value is represented by the right side of the statement will be assigned to the variable that appears on the left side. To get the value represented by the right side, the function ORD is called, passing to it as a parameter the CHAR-type variable Letter. The statements in the ORD function are executed and the value it computes—the numeric code for the character stored in Letter—is returned, thus effectively replacing the function call in the assignment statement with the returned value. Now that the value represented by the right side of the statement has been computed, this value is stored in ThisOne, which brings up another important point about functions:

Every function returns a value of a specific type, and the function call can be used only in a context where a value of that type is allowed.

Although it takes as a *parameter* a variable of type CHAR, the function ORD *returns* a value of type INTEGER. So in order for the assignment statement above to be valid, ThisOne must be an INTEGER-type variable (or a subrange of INTEGER) since an INTEGER value is being assigned to it.

Pascal provides another function, CHR, that does just the opposite of what ORD does. Given an integer, it returns the character that has that numeric code. So if you want to find out which character has the numeric code 65, simply say

```
WRITELN(CHR(65));
```

and the character will be printed out for you. It works like this: when a WRITELN statement is encountered, the values represented by whatever is inside the parentheses are printed. Usually, a variable name or names appear here, in which case the values stored in the variables are printed. But the appearance of the function name indicates that the function is called to compute a value. So the statements within the function are executed, the value is computed by these statements, and it is returned, replacing the call with the value itself. This value is then printed.

The parameter to the function CHR is type INTEGER, and the type of the value that it returns is CHAR—the opposite of ORD.

User-defined Functions. The functions ORD and CHR are pre-written and can be invoked by calling them, but it is possible to write your own functions as well. To do so, you must declare the function and specify the statements that are to be executed when it is called, just as you do to declare a procedure. As mentioned above, function declarations look very much like procedure declarations, and they appear in the Procedure Declarations section of the program. Function declarations can be intermixed with procedure declarations—that is, it is not necessary to declare all your procedures first, and then your functions, or vice-versa. You can declare a function and then a procedure and then a function, or whatever you find convenient. The only restriction on the order of the declarations within the Procedure Declarations section of a program results from the fact that a procedure can only call procedures and functions that are declared before it, and this rule applies to functions as well:

A function can call other procedures and functions, but it can call only procedures and functions whose declarations precede its declaration in the Procedure Declarations section of a program, procedure, or function.

Although in many respects they are very much alike, function declarations differ from procedure declarations in two ways. First, the Function Heading is slightly different from the Procedure Heading. Its form is

FUNCTION NameIt(<*parameters*>) : <*type*>;

Instead of the keyword PROCEDURE, the keyword FUNCTION is used. As with a procedure, you provide a name for the function (here, the name is NameIt), and within parentheses you may specify one or more VAR and/or Value parameters and their types. The biggest difference in the Function Heading is the colon and type specification on the end of the heading, which are not included in a Procedure Heading.

In a Function Heading, <*type*> is replaced by the type of the value that the function returns.

For instance, the function declaration for ORD would include the specification of type INTEGER here, and the declaration of the function CHR would specify type CHAR.

In standard Pascal, the type of value returned by a function can be INTEGER, CHAR, REAL, or BOOLEAN (see below for a description of the type BOOLEAN), or a subrange of INTEGER or CHAR, but not an array or packed array.

Parameters to a function can be of any built-in or user-defined type, just like the parameters to a procedure. A function can also take any number of parameters.[2]

The second difference between the declaration of a procedure and the function is that within the function, the programmer must indicate the value that the function is to return.

2. Functions can also return values with *enumerated types*, which are described in Appendix D.

To indicate the value that a function is to return, the value is assigned to the function name, as if it were a variable, in an assignment statement.

To see how this is done, consider the following function declaration, which takes as a parameter a variable of type *String*, and determines the actual length of the word—that is, the number of alphabetic characters of which it is composed:

```
FUNCTION Length(LengthWord : String) : StringBounds;
  { Returns the number of contiguous characters in LengthWord }
VAR LastChar : StringBounds;
  EndOfWord : BOOLEAN;
BEGIN
  LastChar := StringLength;
  EndOfWord := FALSE;
  WHILE (LastChar > 0) AND (NOT EndOfWord) DO BEGIN
    IF LengthWord[LastChar] IN ['a'..'z','A'..'Z'] THEN BEGIN
      EndOfWord := TRUE;
    END     { then begin }
    ELSE BEGIN
      LastChar := LastChar - 1;
    END;    { else begin }
  END;    { while }
  Length := LastChar;
END;    { Length }
```

Note that the *type* returned by the function is provided in the function heading; in this case, the function type is *StringBounds*, a sub-range of the INTEGER type, since the value returned by the function—that is, the length of the word—is an integer value between 0 and StringLength.

You can look over the statements within the function yourself to see how they go about determining the length of the word (note the use of the BOOLEAN-type variable). The point here is that at the end of the function, when the value that corresponds to the position in the packed array where the first blank appears has been determined, this value (which is stored in the variable LastChar) is assigned to Length, the function name. Here, once again, a function name is treated something like a variable. However,

You cannot assign a value to a function name anywhere in a program except within the statements section of the function with that name.

The assignment statement above gives the function the value that is returned to the caller when the function terminates. Therefore, it is almost always the last statement to appear within the body of a function.

Given the function declaration above, the following statement could appear in the main program or any procedure that has access to the function:

```
ThisOne := Length(Word);
```

where Word is a variable of type *String*, and ThisOne is a variable of type *StringBounds* or INTEGER. This statement assigns to the variable ThisOne the value that indicates the slot number of the last alphabetic character that appears in the packed array Word.

Two notes about functions:

Functions should be used in situations where a single value of type CHAR, INTEGER, REAL, or BOOLEAN is computed and returned to the caller. If several values are returned, or if the value of a variable is simply modified (as is the case with Word and Letter in the procedures in the preceding chapter), then use a procedure.

Functions should not modify the values of the variables that are passed as parameters to them, and so all parameters passed to a function should be Value parameters.

It is perfectly legal in Pascal to pass VAR parameters to a function, but for the most part, when VAR parameters are necessary (which they are only if the procedure needs to modify the value of the variable for which the VAR parameter is a pseudonym), a procedure should be used instead of a function.

CONSTRUCTING THE PROGRAM

The main program for this chapter will not see any changes at all—it will call on Load and print the words in the text, one per line, as in the previous chapter. However, when the words are printed they will appear in their standardized form.

The standardization of the words will be overseen by Load as the words in the text are read in. As mentioned earlier, a statement will be added to Load to call on a procedure that will perform the standardization, and this statement will appear in Load just after the call to ReadWord and before the IF statement in Load. Assuming the procedure is named Standardize, Load will be modified as follows:

```
WHILE NOT EOF(WordFile) DO BEGIN
  ReadWord(Word, WordFile);
  Standardize(<parameters>);
  IF Word <> Blanks
      .
      .
      .
    etc.
```

What variable or variables should be passed to Standardize? Standardize's function is to take the word just read by ReadWord and eliminate leading and trailing punctuation and capitalize the lower case letters in the word. So the "input" to the procedure is Word, the string ReadWord just read, and the "output" is the Word variable in standardized form. Clearly, Standardize needs the variable

Word, and since Standardize's action is to modify Word, that variable provides both input to and output from the procedure, and no other variables need to be shared between Load and Standardize. The call to Standardize, then, will be

```
Standardize(Word);
```

The Standardize Procedure

Since the standardizing procedure modifies the contents of Word, and since the effects of the modification need to be retained after the standardizing procedure finishes executing, Word should be passed as a pseudonym, or VAR parameter to Standardize. So the heading for the Standardize procedure will look like this:

```
PROCEDURE Standardize(VAR StandardWord : String);
```

Within the procedure, then, the name StandardWord will serve as a pseudonym for the variable called Word in the Load procedure.

Earlier, the process of standardizing a word was broken down into three steps: getting rid of leading punctuation, getting rid of trailing punctuation, and translating all lower case letters into upper case. Standardize will include the statements necessary to perform each of these tasks, which will be considered in turn.

The algorithm for the first task, getting rid of leading punctuation in the word, is

1. Set a counter to 1.
2. While the character in the slot of the packed array corresponding to the counter is not an alphabetic character, do the following:
   a. Add 1 to the counter.
3. Replace the word (starting at the first slot) with the portion of the word starting at position Counter.

Much of this algorithm can be implemented fairly easily in Pascal. The first step indicates that a counter variable is required, and step 1 can be implemented with a simple assignment statement that sets this counter variable to 1. Step 2 is a WHILE loop, inside which a statement to add 1 to the counter will appear.

Although at first glance it seems straightforward, the implementation of this algorithm deserves considerable attention because it involves some fundamental programming problems and uses a general structure that you will see again and again in programs within this book, and in most programs that manipulate arrays.

It seems from the algorithm above that the statements to implement steps 1 and 2 should be something like this:[3]

3. You should make note of the way the parentheses are used in the condition on the WHILE loop in this statement. The parentheses surround the positive assertion that the character stored in StandardWord is among the alphabetic characters. The NOT precedes this entire assertion and negates it, so that it can be read to say something like "while it is not the case that the character stored in StandardWord is an alphabetic character do ...". If the parentheses were left out of this condition, the NOT would be taken to negate only StandardWord rather than the entire assertion about the value of StandardWord, which makes no sense to the computer and will therefore generate an error.

```
Counter := 1;
WHILE NOT(StandardWord[Counter] IN ['a'..'z','A'..'Z']) DO BEGIN
  Counter := Counter + 1;
END;     { while }
```

This set of statements will work for most cases, but as always, when constructing any piece of code you should consider the exceptional case. Here, the exceptional case occurs when there are *no* alphabetic characters in StandardWord. In this circumstance, one will be added to Counter repeatedly (since there is nothing to stop this process), and eventually Counter will be given the value 21. Assuming StringLength is 20 and Counter is declared with type *StringBounds,* an error will result at this point because the value assigned to Counter is outside its range (*StringBounds* ranges from 0 to StringLength). But even if the subrange is extended, or Counter is declared as an INTEGER-type variable, the loop above won't work: when control returns to the top of the WHILE loop, the value of StandardWord[Counter] will be checked, and the program will be attempting to examine StandardWord[21]. This also causes an error, because the program has attempted to access a part of main memory outside the boundaries of the array. So the statements above must be modified to be sure that the value of Counter never exceeds that of StringLength. This seems easy to do; the condition on the WHILE loop can be broadened to specify that the loop should continue as long as the character in position Counter is not alphabetic and the value of Counter does not exceed that of StringLength. This would mean modifying the condition on the WHILE loop to be

```
WHILE (NOT(StandardWord[Counter] IN ['a'..'z','A'..'Z']))
  AND (Counter <= StringLength) DO BEGIN
```

With this condition, both assertions must be true in order for the loop to continue, so if the character at position Counter is an alphabetic character or the value of Counter is not less than or equal to the value of StringLength, the loop will stop. But this does not solve the problem, because in order for the condition Counter <= StringLength to be false, the value of Counter must be 21. When this is the case, an error will result either because the value of Counter exceeds the range defined within the *StringBounds* type, or, if Counter is INTEGER-type, the part of the condition that reads StandardWord[Counter] IN ['a'..'z','A'..'Z'] will refer to StandardWord[21]. So an error will result if the condition is re-stated this way as well.[4]

The way around the problem is to remove the reference to StandardWord[Counter] from the condition altogether. This leaves the part of the condition above that checks the value of Counter against that of StringLength in the

4. On some systems you can circumvent this problem by declaring Counter as INTEGER and re-stating the condition in reverse, as WHILE (Counter <= StringLength) AND (NOT(StandardWord[Counter] IN ['a'..'z','A'..'Z'])). In this case the first assertion is checked, and if it is false, the second assertion is not checked at all, because only one of the assertions needs to be false in order to stop the loop. So when Counter is 21 the loop will stop because Counter is greater than StringLength, and no attempt will be made to evaluate the part of the condition that references StandardWord[21]. However, it is not good programming practice to rely on peculiarities of a particular computer system.

heading of the WHILE loop, as it should be to prevent going outside the bounds of the array. However, you also want the loop to stop if an alphabetic character is encountered, and so you need some means to indicate whether or not StandardWord[Counter] contains an alphabetic character *without* referencing this variable in the loop's heading. The way to accomplish this is to use a BOOLEAN-type variable as a "flag."

Consider the following variation on the WHILE loop given above:

```
Counter :=0;
FirstLetter := FALSE;
WHILE (Counter < StringLength) AND (NOT FirstLetter) DO BEGIN
  Counter := Counter + 1;
  IF StandardWord[Counter] IN ['a'..'z','A'..'Z'] THEN BEGIN
    FirstLetter := TRUE;
  END;      { then begin }
END;      { while }
```

The BOOLEAN variable FirstLetter is given the initial value FALSE before the loop begins. Looking at the statements inside the loop, you should be able to see that the value of FirstLetter will remain FALSE until an alphabetic character is encountered in the word, in which case its value will be switched to TRUE, thus "flagging" the situation that an alphabetic character has been encountered in the word. Now, instead of checking the value of StandardWord[Counter] in the loop's heading, the value of FirstLetter can be checked instead. When FirstLetter is FALSE, the assertion NOT FirstLetter is true, since NOT in front of any assertion negates it. Similarly, when FirstLetter is TRUE, NOT FirstLetter is false. So, as long as the value of FirstLetter remains FALSE, the assertion within the condition will be true and the loop will continue to execute, provided the other part of the condition concerning the value of Counter remains true as well.

Moving the part of the condition that refers to StandardWord[Counter] out of the heading of the WHILE loop also enables Counter to be given the initial value 0 rather than 1. This is preferable primarily because it means that this loop now conforms to the format of the other loops within the program, which typically set counter variables to an initial value of 0. Adopting a conventional strategy for similar programming situations can help prevent errors, because familiarity with the routine will make it less likely that you forget to perform certain steps.

Another advantage of the setup above is that Counter can now be declared with type *StringBounds*, which specifies a range of values between 0 and 20 (in the earlier set-up, the value of Counter ranged from 1 to 21), and so it, too, conforms to other counter variables that are used to access packed arrays in the program. Note that setting Counter to 0 initially changes the condition on the loop so that it now checks that Counter is *less than*, rather than *less than or equal to*, StringLength.

You should note that the parentheses in the condition on the WHILE loop above are extremely important because they tell Pascal how to group the parts of the condition. Specifically, the parentheses ensure that Counter < StringLength is seen as one assertion and NOT FirstLetter is seen as another, separate assertion, and that these two entities are joined by the AND. Without the parentheses, Pascal will try first to join StringLength AND NOT FirstLetter, which makes no sense to the computer and will cause an error.

You should familiarize yourself thoroughly with the overall structure of the set of statements above, because you will see it again and again. Specifically,

---

A set of statements similar to those above will be used any time you need to access successive slots of an array and may want to stop the process before the end of the array is reached. The characteristics of this set of statements are that (1) a counter variable is used to access successive slots in an array within a WHILE loop, (2) the counter's value is checked in the condition in the loop's heading to be sure it does not go outside the range of index values for the array, and (3) a BOOLEAN-type variable is used as a flag to stop the loop for some reason other than reaching the end of the array.

This takes care of steps 1 and 2 in the process of stripping leading punctuation, and only step 3 remains. To accomplish this part of the task, a procedure will be written that will set a given *String*-type variable to equal some piece or *substring* of another *String*-type variable.[5] In the usual top-down fashion, the statements that will appear in this procedure will be considered later, and for now, you can simply insert the procedure call in Standardize to take care of step 3 of the algorithm above. If the procedure is named SubString, then step 3 will be implemented with the statement

```
SubString(<parameters>);
```

The parameters will be filled in after the procedure itself has been written. You can assume that by calling this procedure, StandardWord will be set to be equal to a piece or substring of itself starting at position Counter. Counter, of course, will contain the position of the first alphabetic character in StandardWord after the loop above finishes executing.

This takes care of the first step in the overall process of standardizing a word—getting rid of leading punctuation. Trailing punctuation must now be eliminated. The algorithm for this is

1. Set a counter to be equal to the length of the string.
2. While the character in the slot of the packed array corresponding to the counter is not an alphabetic character, do the following:
   a. Replace the character with a blank.
   b. Subtract one from the counter.

5. A procedure to pull out a substring of a *String*-type variable is a very common string manipulating procedure and one which is built in to many programming languages as well as many versions of Pascal. Because a substring procedure is not part of standard Pascal, the procedure will be written here; if your version of Pascal includes such a procedure then you may want to use it instead. Even if you use a pre-written version of the procedure, considering its construction will give you an understanding of its inner workings.

When you look at this algorithm, it should become clear that this set of statements can be implemented in almost exactly the same way as the previous algorithm stripped leading punctuation. The only difference between this algorithm and the earlier one is that the counter is initially set to StringLength rather than 1, and within the loop its value is decremented rather than incremented. Also, there is an additional step within the WHILE loop here that replaces characters in the word with blanks. But the overall situation—moving through an array, slot-by-slot, and potentially stopping before the end of the array is reached—is the same as in the algorithm above, and this is the situation for which the general structure of statements given above is suited. The following statements implement this algorithm, and you should note the similarities between this set of statements and the one above:

```
Counter := StringLength;
FirstLetter := FALSE;
WHILE (Counter > 0) AND (NOT FirstLetter) DO BEGIN
  IF StandardWord[Counter] IN ['a'..'z','A'..'Z'] THEN BEGIN
    FirstLetter := TRUE;
  END     { then begin }
  ELSE BEGIN
    StandardWord[Counter] := Blank;
    Counter := Counter - 1;
  END;     { else begin }
END;     { while }
```

These statements will appear below the ones given above to strip leading punctuation and therefore the variables Counter and FirstLetter can be re-used here because their usefulness in terms of the preceding loop has ended.

To get an idea of how these statements work, consider what will happen if the variable StandardWord contains the string 'cross-examined),   ' (16 characters followed by 4 blanks) when these statements are encountered. At the outset the variable Counter is set to equal StringLength, which is assumed to have a value of 20 for this example. Then the WHILE loop is encountered for the first time. For the entire condition to be true, it must be true that the variable Counter contains a value greater than 0, *and* that an alphabetic character has not been encountered—a condition that is true when the value of FirstLetter is FALSE. Both assertions are true, and so the loop is entered. Inside the loop, the contents of position 20 (the current value of Counter) in the StandardWord packed array are examined, and since that character is a blank and not an alphabetic character, the statements between the ELSE BEGIN and END of the IF-THEN-ELSE statement are executed. The first of these statements sets slot 20 of StandardWord to blank, replacing the blank that had been stored there before. The next statement *subtracts* one from the value currently stored in Counter, yielding 19, and then stores this value in Counter, eradicating the old value of 20. Control returns to the top of the loop, and the condition is re-evaluated. Again, Counter is greater than 0 and FirstLetter is still FALSE, so the loop is entered again. The result is exactly the same as in the previous pass through the loop's statements, except that Counter will end up with the value 18.

You can see that this same set of steps will continue as long as the character in StandardWord that is being examined is a blank. You can also see that every time the loop executes the value of Counter is decreased by one, so that by using it as a subscript into the StandardWord packed array, the program can look at each slot in the packed array from the last to the first. Now consider what happens when Counter finally reaches the value 16. When control returns to the top of the loop, the value of Counter is checked to determine if it is greater than 0, and that of FirstLetter is checked to be sure it is still FALSE. The condition on the loop is true, and the statements in the loop are executed once again. Inside the loop, slot 16 of StandardWord is determined not to be alphabetic, and so slot 16 of StandardWord is assigned the value stored in the constant Blank, which eradicates the old contents of that slot, the comma. The entire packed array now contains the string 'cross-examined)   '. After this, Counter is again decremented by one, so that it has the value 15. At the top of the loop, Counter is determined to be greater than 0 and FirstLetter is still FALSE, and so the entire condition is true and the loop is entered again. Slot 15 in StandardWord is determined not to be an alphabetic character, and it is therefore set to blank, eradicating the parenthesis that had been there. StandardWord now contains 'cross-examined   '. Finally, 1 is subtracted from Counter, which is then assigned the value 14.

After it is determined that Counter is greater than 0 and FirstLetter is still FALSE, the loop is entered again. This time, however, the character in slot Counter is an alphabetic character, and this causes the statement between the THEN BEGIN and END to be executed for the first time. This, of course, sets FirstLetter to TRUE. Control then returns to the top of the loop; Counter is still greater than 0, but the assertion NOT FirstLetter is now FALSE because FirstLetter is TRUE. Again, only one of two assertions joined by an AND need be false to make the entire condition false, and so the loop is terminated. The hyphen in the middle of the word is left untouched, but all of the punctuation that appeared at the end of the word has been translated to blanks.

The statements above take care of step 2 of the standardizing process, getting rid of trailing punctuation. It only remains to translate all of the alphabetic characters in the word to upper case. The algorithm for this part of the standardization process is

1. For each character in the word, do the following:
  a. If the character is a lower case letter, do the following:
    (1) Translate the letter to upper case.

To implement step 1.a, a function will be written that takes as a parameter a variable of type CHAR and also returns a value of type CHAR. The function will check the character that is passed to it as a parameter, and if it is a lower case letter, the function will return its upper case equivalent; otherwise, the character returned by the function will be the same as the character that was passed to it. If the name of this function is Capitalize, the character in the fifth slot of StandardWord can be translated to its upper case equivalent with the statement

```
StandardWord[5] := Capitalize(StandardWord[5]);
```

This statement calls on the Capitalize function, passing it the character in the fifth slot of StandardWord. The statements within the function examine the character and translate it to upper case if it is a lower case character. It will then return the (possibly) modified version of the character to the calling procedure. As you recall from the earlier description of a function call, this effectively replaces the call to the function with the value it returns. So the right side of the assignment statement above will be evaluated to yield the character the function returns, and this result will then be assigned to the fifth slot of StandardWord, erasing the old contents.

As indicated in the algorithm, each of the characters in StandardWord can be replaced in this way by simply calling the function repeatedly, each time passing it another character in StandardWord until the entire packed array has been processed. Step 1 of the algorithm can be implemented with a FOR loop, as follows:

```
FOR Counter := 1 TO StringLength DO BEGIN
  StandardWord[Counter] := Capitalize(StandardWord[Counter]);
END;      { for }
```

This loop enables the program to access each of the slots in StandardWord successively. One by one, the characters in the packed array are passed to the function Capitalize, which will return the upper case equivalent of the character in StandardWord[Counter] if it is a lower case letter, and it will return the same character as the character stored in StandardWord[Counter] otherwise.

The function Capitalize itself does not modify the contents of StandardWord[Counter]. **This is accomplished after the function terminates, by assigning the function result back into** StandardWord[Counter].

Each time through the loop, the result of the function call is stored in StandardWord[Counter], thus replacing lower case characters in the packed array by their upper case equivalents, and other characters by copies of themselves.

Note that the variable Counter is used here for a third time in the standardizing procedure. Since its value from the previous operation is no longer needed, the variable can be used again without losing any information.

This completes the work that is to be done by the standardizing procedure. Three variables are used within the procedure: StandardWord, which is passed to it from the calling procedure and thus appears as a parameter in the Procedure Heading, the variable with type *StringBounds* named Counter, and the BOOLEAN variable FirstLetter. These last two variables function only within the procedure; they get their starting values within Standardize and not from the calling procedure, and their values need not be known when Standardize terminates. So these variables should be declared locally in the Variable Declarations section within the standardizing procedure.

Putting all of this together, the standardizing procedure looks like this:

```
PROCEDURE Standardize(VAR StandardWord : String);
  { Strips leading and trailing punctuation and }
  { capitalizes letters in StandardWord }
VAR Counter : StringBounds;
  FirstLetter : BOOLEAN;
BEGIN
  { Strip leading punctuation }
  Counter := 0;
  FirstLetter := FALSE;
  WHILE (Counter < StringLength) AND (NOT FirstLetter) DO BEGIN
    Counter := Counter + 1;
    IF StandardWord[Counter] IN ['a'..'z','A'..'Z'] THEN BEGIN
      FirstLetter := TRUE;
    END;      { then begin }
  END;      { while }
  SubString(<parameters>);
  { Strip trailing punctuation }
  Counter := StringLength;
  FirstLetter := FALSE;
  WHILE (Counter > 0) AND (NOT FirstLetter) DO BEGIN
    IF StandardWord[Counter] IN ['a'..'z','A'..'Z'] THEN BEGIN
      FirstLetter := TRUE;
    END      { then begin }
    ELSE BEGIN
      StandardWord[Counter] := Blank;
      Counter := Counter - 1;
    END;      { else begin }
  END;      { while }
  { Capitalize all letters in the word }
  FOR Counter := 1 TO StringLength DO BEGIN
    StandardWord[Counter] := Capitalize(StandardWord[Counter]);
  END;      { for }
END;      { Standardize }
```

To complete the work of standardizing a word, the procedure SubString and the function Capitalize must be implemented.

The SubString Procedure

The SubString procedure will take as a parameter a *String*-type variable and store a specified piece or sub-string of that variable in another "target" variable, also with type *String*. To specify the piece of the original string to be stored in the target string, the starting and ending positions of the substring must be passed as parameters as well. For instance, if a packed array of type *String* contains the characters "("This   " (a left parenthesis, a quotation mark, the characters 'T', 'h', 'i', and 's', followed by 14 blanks), and you specify that the substring to be extracted from it starts at position 3 and goes through position 6, then the substring to which you refer consists of the four characters "This". The SubString procedure will take these four characters, store them in the first four slots of the target string, and pad the remainder of the target string with blanks.

Therefore SubString needs four parameters: the string from which the substring is to be extracted, the starting position of the substring, the ending position of the substring, and the target string. SubString uses the values of the first three of these four parameters as "input" with which it works, but it does not modify their values or use them for output in any way, and so they should be passed as Value parameters. The target string, however, is not used as input to the procedure but instead serves to hold the output of the procedure—the substring itself. Thus the target string variable must be passed as a VAR parameter.

Given all of this, the heading of the SubString Procedure will be

```
PROCEDURE SubString(FromWord : String; Start, Stop : StringBounds;
        VAR ToWord : String);
```

FromWord, Start, and Stop are all variables that are newly-created each time the SubString procedure is called, but which get their initial values from the parameters to which they correspond in the procedure call. ToWord is a pseudonym for the parameter in the call to which it corresponds, and as such is just the name by which the parameter variable in the call is known within the procedure.

To extract a substring of one *String*-type variable and put it in another, all that really needs to be done is to go to the slot in the original string corresponding to the start position specified, copy the character in that slot to slot 1 of the target string, go to the next slot of the original string, copy it into the second slot of the target string, and so on until you reach the slot in the original string corresponding to the stop position given. To implement this, you can use a simple FOR loop that starts at the value in Start and stops at the value in Stop, which will provide access to the slots from Start to Stop (the first and last characters in the substring to be extracted) in the original string. A separate counter can be initialized to 1 and incremented by hand within the FOR loop to access slots in the target string, like this:

```
ToPos := 0;
FOR Counter := Start TO Stop DO BEGIN
  ToPos := ToPos + 1;
  ToWord[ToPos] := FromWord[Counter];
END;      { for }
```

The starting INTEGER value specified in the heading of a FOR loop need not be 1—it can be any INTEGER value.

The loop above uses the variable Counter to access each of the successive positions in FromWord, in order to copy the characters into ToWord, the target string. ToPos is used to access successive slots of ToWord, starting at position 1. Counter and ToPos, of course, are variables local to SubString and must be declared in the Variable Declarations section of the procedure. Because these variables serve as subscripts into packed arrays of type *String*, they should be given the subrange type *StringBounds*.

If FromWord contains the string "("Now" followed by 15 blanks, Start holds the value 3 and Stop holds the value 5, then the first time through the FOR loop above, Counter will have the value 3. ToPos is 0 to start; inside the loop, it is incremented to be 1, and so in the subsequent statement, the character in position 3 of FromWord is copied into slot 1 of ToWord. After this, at the top of the FOR loop, Counter is automatically incremented to be 4, and the next time the loop is entered, ToPos is incremented so that it is 2, and then the character in slot 4 of FromWord is copied into slot 2 of ToWord. On the third and final time through the loop, ToPos is incremented to be 3 and the contents of slot 5 of FromWord is copied into slot 3 of ToWord. So that when the loop terminates, ToWord contains the specified substring.

Of course, ToWord contains something else as well in the 17 remaining slots of the packed array—garbage, since nothing else was ever put in this part of the string. Needless to say, these slots should be filled with blanks, and ReadWord's method for ensuring that the unoccupied slots of NextWord contain blanks can be borrowed here to meet the need. So, before the loop above you should add the statement

```
ToWord := Blanks;
```

which sets the entire string to blanks so that slots left unfilled in the subsequent FOR loop will not contain garbage.

The whole of the SubString procedure is

```
PROCEDURE SubString(FromWord : String; Start, Stop : StringBounds;
        VAR ToWord : String);
  { Puts the characters in positions }
  { Start through Stop in ToWord }
VAR Counter, ToPos : StringBounds;
BEGIN
  ToWord := Blanks;
  ToPos := 0;
  FOR Counter := Start TO Stop DO BEGIN
    ToPos := ToPos + 1;
    ToWord[ToPos] := FromWord[Counter];
  END;    { for }
END;    { SubString }
```

Now that the procedure has been written you can fill in the parameters in the call to SubString that appears in the Standardize procedure. SubString takes a *String*-type variable in which the substring is to be found, the start and stop positions, and the target string. Recall that the call to SubString in Standardize is made in order to replace the current contents of StandardWord with the piece of StandardWord that starts with the first alphabetic character, known to be at position Counter, and ends at the last character of the word. This means that the variable StandardWord is both the string containing the substring *and* the target string, and therefore the call to SubString should look like this:

```
SubString(StandardWord,Counter,StringLength, StandardWord);
```

It may seem a little strange to specify a variable twice among the parameters to a procedure, but in this case it makes sense to do so. This is clear if you consider what happens when SubString is called: because FromWord is a Value parameter, when SubString is called a new memory location is set up and given the name FromWord, and then *the contents of the parameter with which it is associated—StandardWord, in this case—are copied into that memory location.* Similarly, the values stored in Counter and StringLength are copied into new memory locations with the names Start and Stop. ToWord, on the other hand, becomes a pseudonym for StandardWord, which means that it simply refers to the same location that StandardWord does—no new memory location is set up for ToWord. Now, as SubString executes, ToWord is completely blanked out, obliterating the contents of the memory location to which it refers, which is to say that it blanks out StandardWord. But no matter; a copy of the contents of StandardWord is in FromWord, and the specified piece of FromWord is then copied into ToWord. Thus the old contents of StandardWord are replaced by the piece of StandardWord specified by the values of Start and Stop, which is exactly what is needed.

Note that by writing SubString so that the target variable is at least potentially different from the variable from which the sub-string is to be extracted makes it general and useful in a variety of contexts.

The Capitalize Function

The item passed to the function Capitalize in the Standardize procedure is an element or single slot in the packed array. You have already seen that an entire array can be passed to a procedure. Individual elements can also be passed, *as long as the corresponding parameter in the Procedure or Function Heading has the same type as the element.* In this case, the type of the elements in the packed array is CHAR; so the type of the variable in the Function Heading for Capitalize will also be CHAR. The Function Heading should look like this:

```
FUNCTION Capitalize(LowerLetter : CHAR) : CHAR;
```

Here, the variable LowerLetter corresponds to the parameter passed to it by the calling procedure. LowerLetter is a variable of type CHAR, and is therefore completely compatible with the corresponding parameter, StandardWord[Counter], which also has type CHAR.

Finally, the statements within the Capitalize function need to be determined. Only a single IF-THEN-ELSE statement will be needed to accomplish the entire task. The condition on the statement will examine the character passed to the function to determine if it is a lower case letter or not. If it is, it will be translated to its upper case equivalent using the CHR and ORD functions, and returned to the calling procedure. If not, the character itself will be returned to the calling procedure.

The translation of a lower case letter to its upper case equivalent can be accomplished in a single, concise arithmetic expression, but the inner workings of the expression are relatively complex. If you have a variable of type CHAR named **LowerLetter** in your program and it contains a lower case letter, you can translate this letter to upper case, and store the upper case equivalent back in the same variable (**LowerLetter**) with the following statement:

```
LowerLetter := CHR((ORD(LowerLetter)-ORD('a'))+ORD('A'));
```

Look at this statement carefully. What happens is this: the part of the statement that reads **(ORD(LowerLetter) – ORD('a'))** is dealt with first, since, by virtue of the parentheses in the expression, it is most closely grouped. **ORD(LowerLetter)** calls on the ORD function, which returns the numeric code for the character stored in the variable **LowerLetter**. Suppose that the letter 'c' is stored in **LowerLetter**, and suppose that the numeric code for 'c' is 99. **ORD(LowerLetter)**, then, is effectively replaced in the expression by the value 99, the value returned by the ORD function in this instance. **ORD('a')** will be replaced by the numeric code for 'a', which, whatever its value may be, is a fixed distance from 99, the code for 'c'. If in the collating scheme on your computer, the code for 'a' is 97, subtracting the code for 'a' from the code for 'c' yields 2. After this result is computed, it is added to the value returned by the function call **ORD('A')**. Now, whatever the code for 'A' is, it is a fact that *the difference between the code for 'c' and the code for 'a' is the same as the difference between the code for 'C' and the code for 'A'*. This is simply a result of the way the ASCII and EBCDIC coding sequences are set up.[6] So, by *adding* the difference between the code for 'c' and the code for 'a' to the code for 'A', the result is the code for 'C'. If the code for 'A' is 65, then adding 2 (the difference between the codes for 'c' and 'a') to it will yield 67, which must be the code for 'C'.

The example above uses actual ASCII codes, and here is another one that uses EBCDIC codes. Suppose you want to translate 'w' to 'W', and suppose that the code for 'w' is 166 and the code for 'a' is 129. Performing the subtraction in the statement above yields the value 37. Now, if the code for 'A' is 193, then the result of adding 37 to it is 230. In the coding scheme, 230 will be the code for 'W'.

This arithmetic trick for translating lower to upper case works whether your system uses the ASCII or EBCDIC set of codes. Therefore, it is "machine-independent," and any program that includes the Capitalize function as given above will run on any machine that uses one of these coding schemes.

The CHR function, as you recall, will take any number passed to it as a parameter and return the character for which that number is the numeric code. The parameter to the CHR function in this example is the entire expression that appears within the parentheses that follow the word CHR. The expression is evaluated first, yielding, in this case, the numeric code for the character 'C', and this value is then passed to the CHR function. CHR will then return the cor-

6. The numeric codes for the lower case letters in the ASCII scheme are sequential, as are the codes for the upper case letters. In EBCDIC, the codes are not always sequential, but the code is arranged so that any upper case letter is the same "distance" from 'A' as its lower case equivalent is from 'a.' See Appendix C for a listing of the actual ASCII and EBCDIC codes.

responding character, and this character is finally stored in the variable LowerLetter as a result of the assignment operation.

This method of converting lower case to upper case letters is one of those clever tricks of the trade that very few people discover on their own, but instead learn in the way you learned it, simply by being told. You should understand how it works, and take advantage of the method whenever you need it.

The method above will not work at all, of course, if the character stored in the variable LowerLetter is anything but a lower case letter. So it is absolutely essential to verify this before using it. This can be done with an IF-THEN statement within the function Capitalize, as follows:

```
IF LowerLetter IN ['a'..'z'] THEN BEGIN
  Capitalize := CHR((ORD(LowerLetter)-ORD('a'))+ORD('A'));
END;      { then begin }
```

Notice that this statement assigns the character ultimately yielded by the expression on the right of the assignment operator not to LowerLetter, but to the function name Capitalize. Within a function, such an assignment provides the value that is to be returned by the function to the calling procedure.

What happens if LowerLetter does not contain a lower case letter? The function Capitalize will not be assigned a value, and the function will consequently have no value to return to the calling procedure. This will result in an error. So the IF-THEN statement above should be modified to be an IF-THEN-ELSE statement, thus providing some value for Capitalize if the character is not in the lower case alphabet. What value should be given to Capitalize in this event? The function is to return the upper case equivalent if the character passed to it is a lower case letter, but it is to return the character itself in any other situation. So, the statement within the function Capitalize should be

```
IF LowerLetter IN ['a'..'z'] THEN BEGIN
  Capitalize := CHR((ORD(LowerLetter)-ORD('a'))+ORD('A'));
END      { then begin }
ELSE BEGIN
  Capitalize := LowerLetter;
END;      { else begin }
```

Capitalize will now be given a value to return to its caller in any event.

Note that the statement above is the only statement necessary within the function Capitalize.

The only parameter to the function Capitalize is the character it will translate to upper case. The function uses this character, but it does not modify it—the upper case equivalent, if it is derived, is assigned not to the variable in which the character originally resided, but to the function name. So the parameter passed to the function Capitalize should be passed as a Value parameter.

Capitalize does not use any variables of its own and so the Variable Declarations section of the function can be omitted. The final form of the function is

```
FUNCTION Capitalize(LowerLetter : CHAR) : CHAR;
  { Returns the upper case equivalent of LowerLetter }
BEGIN
  IF LowerLetter IN ['a'..'z'] THEN BEGIN
    Capitalize := CHR((ORD(LowerLetter)-ORD('a'))+ORD('A'));
  END     { then begin }
  ELSE BEGIN
    Capitalize := LowerLetter;
  END;     { else begin }
END;     { Capitalize }
```

The Program as a Whole

The structure of this chapter's program is

```
PROGRAM StandardWord(INPUT,OUTPUT,TextFile);
  Constant declarations: StringLength, MaxWords, Blank, Blanks
  Type Declarations: String, WordArray, StringBounds, ArrayBounds
  Variable Declarations: Words, NumberOfWords, Counter, TextFile
  Procedure Declarations:
    PROCEDURE ReadWord(VAR NextWord : String; VAR InputFile : TEXT);
      Variable Declarations: Letter, Counter
      Procedure Declarations:
      PROCEDURE SkipBlanks(VAR NextChar : CHAR; VAR InFile : TEXT);
        Variable Declarations: none
      BEGIN     { SkipBlanks }
        .
        .
        .
      END;     { SkipBlanks }
    BEGIN     { ReadWord }
      .
      .
      .
    END;     { ReadWord }
    PROCEDURE SubString(FromWord : String; Start, Stop : StringBounds;
              VAR ToWord : String);
      Variable Declarations: Counter, ToPos
    BEGIN     { SubString }
      .
      .
      .
    END;     { SubString }
    FUNCTION Capitalize(LowerLetter : CHAR) : CHAR;
      Variable Declarations: none
    BEGIN     { Capitalize }
      .
      .
      .
    END;     { Capitalize }
    PROCEDURE Standardize(VAR StandardWord : String);
      Variable Declarations: Counter, FirstLetter
```

```
        BEGIN      { Standardize }
           .
           .
           .
        END;     { Standardize }
        PROCEDURE Load(VAR FileWords : WordArray;
                  VAR WordsInFile : ArrayBounds; VAR WordFile : TEXT);
          Variable Declarations: Word
        BEGIN      { Load }
           .
           .
           .
        END;      { Load }
    BEGIN      { StandardWords }
      Load(Words,NumberOfWords,TextFile);
      FOR Counter := 1 TO NumberOfWords DO BEGIN
        WRITELN(Words[Counter]);
      END;     { for }
    END.     { StandardWords }
```

Standardize must be declared before Load, since Load calls Standardize, and both Capitalize and SubString must be declared before Standardize because Standardize, in turn, calls them. Capitalize and SubString are declared outside of Standardize rather than within Standardize, even though Standardize is the only procedure that calls them, for the same reasons ReadWord is declared outside of Load—that is, these are general-purpose procedures that may be called upon in other contexts later on.

SUMMING UP THE PROGRAM

The program is growing in complexity, but by breaking up the program into procedures the complexity is kept under control. You should trace through the program's action by hand, using a short sample file, to understand the order of the procedure calls and how variables are shared among procedures.

NICETIES

More About Boolean Variables

Earlier in this chapter, you saw how to assign the values TRUE and FALSE to a Boolean variable. Actually, any assertion that can be evaluated as either true or false can be assigned to a Boolean variable. You are already familiar with assertions of this type, which you used as conditions in WHILE and REPEAT-UNTIL loops, and in IF-THEN and IF-THEN-ELSE statements. For example, all of the following assertions can be evaluated to be either TRUE or FALSE.

```
Letter IN ['A'..'Z','a'..'z']
ThisOne < ThatOne
NOT (Word[Counter] IN ['A'..'Z'])
NOT Found
Word = Words[Counter]
```

Since the "value" of these assertions is determined to be TRUE or FALSE, they can appear on the right side of an assignment operator *if the variable on the left side of the assignment operator is a Boolean variable*. If the assertion is true, the value TRUE is assigned to the variable; if the assertion is false, the value FALSE is assigned to the variable.

Some examples will make this clearer. Suppose a CHAR variable Letter contains the character 'D'. The following assignment will give the variable CapitalA, which is assumed to have been declared with type BOOLEAN, the value FALSE:

```
CapitalA := Letter = 'A';
```

Similarly, the value TRUE will be assigned to the Boolean variable Alphabetic by the following statement, if Letter contains the character 'D':

```
Alphabetic := Letter IN ['A'..'Z','a'..'z'];
```

You should begin to get the idea. Any assertion that can be determined to be TRUE or FALSE—in other words, any assertion that can appear as a condition in a WHILE or REPEAT-UNTIL loop or in an IF-THEN or IF-THEN-ELSE statement—can appear on the right side of an assignment operator if the variable on the left of the assignment operator is a Boolean variable.

Boolean Functions

It was mentioned above that a function can return to its caller a value of any built-in Pascal type (except REAL) or a subrange of INTEGER or CHAR. The types are INTEGER, REAL, CHAR, and BOOLEAN; so it is possible to have a function that returns a BOOLEAN value—that is, a value of either TRUE or FALSE. When this is the case, the function call can appear in any context where an assertion that is determined to be true or false can appear—that is, in the conditions in WHILE and REPEAT-UNTIL loops and IF-THEN and IF-THEN-ELSE statements, and on the right side of an assignment operator if the variable on the left is a Boolean variable.

Suppose, for example, that you want to write a function that takes as a parameter a variable of type CHAR, and returns TRUE if the character is a letter of the alphabet and FALSE otherwise. The function might look like this:

```
FUNCTION Alphabetic(Character : CHAR) : BOOLEAN;
  { Determines if Character is a letter }
BEGIN
  Alphabetic := Character IN ['A'..'Z','a'..'z'];
END;
```

This function's single statement will determine whether or not the assertion that the contents of the variable Character is one of the letters of the alphabet is true or false; if it is true, the value TRUE will be assigned to Alphabetic, which, because it is the name of a Boolean function, acts as a Boolean variable in this context. If the assertion is false, the value FALSE will be assigned to Alphabetic. This value will then be returned to the caller.

A call to such a function could appear in the following contexts:

```
IF Alphabetic(Letter) THEN...
```

and

```
WHILE NOT (Alphabetic(Word[Counter])) DO...
```

Incidentally, if such a function were included in your program, the following condition could appear on the IF-THEN statements in the WHILE loops in the Standardize procedure:

```
IF Alphabetic(StandardWord[Counter]) THEN...
```

since this condition is exactly equivalent to

```
IF (StandardWord[Counter] IN ['A'..'Z','a'..'z']) THEN...
```

Similarly, the condition on the REPEAT-UNTIL loop in SkipBlanks could be changed to

```
UNTIL (Alphabetic(NextChar)) OR (EOF(InFile));
```

Boolean functions are useful when you have long or complicated conditions to express, or when you use the same conditions in many places throughout a program. Since determining whether or not a certain character is a letter of the alphabet is common within the programs you are and will be writing, and since the statement is awkward to type, you might find including such a function in your programs useful. Be sure to declare it in the main program, and declare it at the beginning of the Procedure Declarations section, so that it is accessible to all procedures and the main program.

Linear Search Revisited

The linear search shown in the Niceties section of last chapter's program works considerably better when the text it searches is standardized, because now all occurrences of a given word, whatever its various forms in the original text, are seen as the same. So, whereas last chapter's linear search may not have found some instances of a word, now that the text is standardized all occurrences will be found.

The statements to do the searching need no modification at all to work with the standardized text, but you will have to add a statement to the main program following the call to ReadWord that reads the user's word. Since the user may enter the word in lower case or partially in lower case, in order to make the user's word conform to the form of the words in the **Words** array, the user's word should be standardized as well. All you need to do to accomplish this is to add a call to Standardize to the main program, so that the statements that prompt the user and read the word entered are now

```
WRITE('Enter the word you want the program to search for: ');
ReadWord(UsersWord,INPUT);
Standardize(UsersWord);
```

Some Additional String-Manipulating Procedures

The SubString procedure written in this chapter and the Length function that was used as an example are two common string manipulating operations that are very useful in programs such as the ones in this text. They are so common, in fact, that many implementations of Pascal build them into the Pascal language so that they need not be written by the user.

Two other useful string manipulations are *concatenation*, which takes two strings and joins them together into a single string, and *indexing*, which locates the position at which one string begins in another. Procedures to perform these two functions are given below. Even if your implementation of Pascal provides these functions, you may be interested to see how they work or you may want to tailor these functions to your particular needs.

Concatenation. The procedure below takes as parameters two variables of type *String*, and stores the non-blank characters in the first string followed by the non-blank characters in the second string in a third *String*-type variable called Result. For example, if you pass a *String*-type variable containing 'Joan ' and another containing 'Jones ' to the procedure, the variable you associate with Result will contain 'JoanJones ' when the procedure terminates. Note that no blank intervenes between the two.

```
PROCEDURE Concatenate(FirstString,SecondString : String;
        VAR Result : String);
  { Attaches the word in SecondString to the end of FirstString }
  { and puts the resulting string in Result }
VAR Length1,Length2,Counter : StringBounds;
  Length3 : INTEGER;
BEGIN
  Length1 := Length(FirstString);
  Length2 := Length(SecondString);
  Length3 := Length1 + Length2;
  Result := Blanks;     { If string is too long the result contains blanks }
  IF Length3 <= StringLength THEN BEGIN
    FOR Counter := 1 TO Length1 DO BEGIN
      Result[Counter] := FirstString[Counter];
    END;     { for }
    FOR Counter := (Length1+1) TO (Length1+Length2) DO BEGIN
      Result[Counter] := SecondString[Counter-Length1];
    END;     { for }
  END;     { then begin }
END;     { Concatenate }
```

Notice that this procedure calls the Length function given earlier in this chapter.

Index. Index is a function that takes as parameters two strings, and returns a value with type *StringBounds* corresponding to the position in the *first* string where the nonblank characters in the second string begin. If the second string does not appear in the first string, the function returns 0. For instance, if you pass as the first string a variable containing the string 'STIRRING   ' and as the second the string 'ING   ', the function will return the value 6, since the string 'ING' begins in the sixth position of the first string. If the second string were 'ED' rather than 'ING', 0 would be returned because the second string does not appear in the first.

```
FUNCTION Index(FirstString,SecondString : String) : StringBounds;
  { Returns the location in FirstString where SecondString }
  { begins, or 0 if it does not appear }
VAR First,Last,LengthFirst,LengthSecond : StringBounds;
  Found,Lasted : BOOLEAN;
BEGIN
  LengthFirst := Length(FirstString);
  LengthSecond := Length(SecondString);
  First := 0;
  Found := FALSE;
  WHILE ((First+LengthSecond) <= LengthFirst) AND (NOT Found) DO BEGIN
    Lasted := FALSE;
    Last := 1;
    WHILE (Last <= LengthSecond) AND (NOT Lasted) DO BEGIN
      IF FirstString[First+Last] = SecondString[Last]
        THEN Last := Last + 1
        ELSE Lasted := TRUE;
    END;     { while }
    IF Last > LengthSecond
      THEN Found := TRUE
      ELSE First := First + 1;
  END;     { while }
  IF Found
    THEN Index := First + 1
    ELSE Index := 0;
END;     { index }
```

This function calls Length as well.

The Index function is very handy for programs that do morphological or syntactic analysis, since it can be used to search for given prefixes, suffixes, and root forms.

A WriteWord Procedure

When a WRITE or WRITELN statement is used to print the contents of a packed array of type *String* as defined in the programs in this text, the entire contents of the packed array is printed—including trailing blanks that may fill up the array at the end of the actual word that is stored there. In certain situations, you might want to print only the non-blank characters in the packed array—for instance, when the word is to be embedded in a line of text, like this:

```
WRITELN(UsersWord,' appears in the text ',Frequency:1,' times.');
```

If UsersWord is a variable of type *String* that contains the word 'AND' followed by 17 blanks, the resulting output line is

```
AND                    appears in the text 26 times.
```

It would be nice to be able to print the word 'AND' without the trailing blanks in this situation.

The answer to the problem is to write a short procedure that can be called WriteWord, whose task it is to print only the non-blank characters in a packed array. The procedure will simply start at the first slot in the packed array, print the contents, and continue to print the contents of the remaining slots in order until a slot containing a blank is encountered.

The structure of the statements required for this operation will follow the familiar pattern set by the loops in the Standardize procedure. As in the situations in Standardize, WriteWord will access (and print) successive slots in an array, but it may want to stop the process before reaching the end of the array—that is, if a blank is encountered. So a WHILE loop, a counter variable initialized to 0, and a BOOLEAN variable are required. Thus the WriteWord procedure is

```
PROCEDURE WriteWord(OutWord : String);
VAR Counter : StringBounds;
  EndOfWord : BOOLEAN;
BEGIN
  Counter := 0;
  EndOfWord := FALSE;
  WHILE (Counter < StringLength) AND (NOT EndOfWord) DO BEGIN
    Counter := Counter + 1;
    IF OutWord[Counter] <> Blank THEN BEGIN
      WRITE(OutWord[Counter]);
    END     { then begin }
    ELSE BEGIN
      EndOfWord := TRUE;
    END;     { else begin }
  END;     { while }
  WRITELN;
END;     { WriteWord }
```

Several things should be noted about this procedure: first, OutWord is passed to the procedure as a Value parameter because it serves as input to the procedure and is not modified by the procedure in any way. Second, you should be aware that if for some reason OutWord contains a string in which a blank is embedded between non-blank characters, only the characters up to the blank will be printed. For example, if OutWord contains the string "HARRY SMITH   ", only "HARRY" will be printed since the loop stops when the *first* blank is encountered.

Finally, the procedure above writes its output to the default output device (usually the display screen of the terminal or microcomputer) automatically. The procedure could easily be generalized to write to any file by modifying it to be

```
PROCEDURE WriteWord(OutWord : String; VAR OutFile : TEXT);
VAR Counter : StringBounds;
      EndOfWord : BOOLEAN;
BEGIN
  Counter := 0;
  EndOfWord := FALSE;
  WHILE (Counter < StringLength) AND (NOT EndOfWord) DO BEGIN
    Counter := Counter + 1;
    IF OutWord[Counter] <> Blank THEN BEGIN
      WRITE(OutFile,OutWord[Counter]);
    END     { then begin }
    ELSE BEGIN
      EndOfWord := TRUE;
    END;     { else begin }
  END;     { while }
  WRITELN(OutFile);
END;     { WriteWord }
```

Now the procedure writes to a file that it calls **OutFile** and the caller of the procedure indicates the actual name of the file when WriteWord is called. You can still use the procedure to write a word to the default output device by using the call

```
WriteWord(Word,OUTPUT);
```

and during the course of the procedure's execution, all output will go to the file named OUTPUT; otherwise, use a call like

```
WriteWord(Word,MyOutFile);
```

and all output will go to the file named **MyOutFile**. (See the Niceties section of Chapter Three for more details about writing to files other than OUTPUT.) This second variation on the procedure is more flexible, but if you don't write to files other than the default output device, then you may want to save the trouble of specifying the file name in every call to WriteWord by using the first version given above.

APPLICATIONS AND CONSIDERATIONS

Standardizing a text brings up several considerations, because by eliminating punctuation and translating everything to upper case, certain kinds of information about the text are lost. Some of this information may be uninteresting or irrelevant to the purpose, in which case the loss has no consequences. But sometimes, standardizing a text yields peculiar results or causes things to appear to be what they are not.

The most obvious problem concerns abbreviations. If your text contains a word like "U.S.A.", the program will modify that to be "U.S.A" (without the final period), which is not necessarily desirable. Worse yet, something like the abbreviation for the state of Maine, "Me." will be translated to "ME", and therefore treated as an instance of the pronoun. If the punctuation is left in, on the other hand, the word "me" in the sentence, "Give it to me." will be seen as the same as the abbreviation for the state of Maine.

There is no easy way to enable the computer to distinguish between periods at the end of abbreviations and periods at the end of sentences. If all of the periods that end sentences are followed by two blanks, and all periods that are part of abbreviations are followed by one blank, you could come up with a somewhat complicated set of statements to distinguish between the two. A simpler solution is to *code* the text in such a way that periods that are part of abbreviations are represented by a different character from the one used to indicate the end of a sentence. The program could then provide for leaving these characters alone when it goes about translating trailing punctuation to blanks. It could even translate the character used to indicate the abbreviation, if it is not the period, to a period.

In general, considerations such as these require a bit of manipulating, both within the program that processes the text and within the text itself. Most often, a special situation—such as a period that is part of an abbreviation rather than an indication of the end of a sentence—is designated within the text with a special character, one that does not appear in any other context. Then the program is modified to recognize the character and accommodate whatever situation it signals.

EXERCISES

1. Modify the program to include a function named Alphabetic, as outlined in the Niceties section of the chapter, and replace all conditions that check that a character is alphabetic with a call to this function.

2. Modify your program to include a function named EndOfWord that will replace the condition on the REPEAT-UNTIL loop in the ReadWord procedure. The condition on the loop should then look like this:

```
UNTIL EndOfWord;
```

3. Do exercise 3, but include another function called BeginWord to replace the entire condition on the REPEAT-UNTIL loop in SkipBlanks as well.

4. Many versions of a procedure that extracts a substring take as parameters not the positions at which the string starts and stops, but rather the position at which the string starts and the *length* of the substring to be extracted.

Modify the SubString procedure given in this chapter to take the length of a substring rather than the position at which the string stops as a parameter. This will require that you do some additional arithmetic within the procedure to ensure that the specified string does not overshoot the end of the packed array.

5. (A bit more difficult.) Modify the program so that after loading the array, it counts and prints the number of words with each of the lengths 1 through 20. The output should look like this:

```
15 words in the text have a length of 1 character
39 words in the text have a length of 2 characters
.
.
.
```

6. (A bit more difficult.) Modify the program so that it will distinguish abbreviations as discussed in the Applications and Considerations section of this chapter. Your file, of course, must contain special coding for abbreviations, and the program must know what the special symbol for abbreviations is. For instance, all abbreviations in the file could be followed by the symbol '#' rather than a period, in which case the program must look in all words as they are read for the '#' and treat them specially. If, for example the program encounters Mr# in the text, the program should store the word as 'MR.' rather than simply 'MR'.

7. (More difficult.) Modify the program to prompt the user for a string (for example, 'ING') and to print only the words from the text that contain that string. Then print the number of words that contain that string.

8. (Even more difficult.) Do exercise 7, but enhance the program so that it prints words in which the user's string is a *suffix*. Do not forget to consider the possibility that the word is **StringLength** characters long. An alternative is to do the exercise for *prefixes* rather than suffixes.

9. (For the adventurous programmer.) Write a program along the lines of exercises 7 and 8, but ask the user if he or she is interested in words in which the string entered is a suffix, prefix, or simply appears anywhere in the word. Then print only those words in which the string appears as the user specifies.

You can make the program more useful by enabling the user to repeat the process of entering a string and specifying its function in the words to be printed as long as he or she wants to.

10. (For the very adventurous programmer.) Write a program to look for patterns of assonance and/or alliteration in a text. Specifically, for any word in the text the program should look to see if adjacent words share common consonants, vowels, or consonant or vowel pairs. Where two or more adjacent words do share certain features, print the words in the sequence in which they appear in the text. Examine the output to determine how many of the cited instances are actual instances of alliteration or assonance.

9
Sorting the Text

In this chapter the problem to be attacked is that of rearranging the words that have been loaded into an array so that they are in alphabetical order—or, as it is called in the computing world, *sorting* the words in the array. As in the last two chapters, the main program's job in the basic program will be to simply print the words in the array, but this time they will appear in the output in alphabetical order.

The reason for sorting the words in the array is simply that if the words are arranged in alphabetical order, it is much easier and faster for the computer to find a particular word in the list, as you will see in Chapter Ten. This is true for humans as well. You rely on the ordering of the words in a dictionary or index, or the ordering of names in the telephone directory, in order to find the item in which you are interested. Without an ordering system you would have to search through the dictionary or directory item by item to find what you want, the same way the computer does in the linear search algorithm described in last chapter's Niceties section. For both humans and computers, a linear search is time consuming, and for humans, it can be frustrating as well. By alphabetizing the list of words, the amount of time and effort required to search for a given word can be reduced enormously.

Information can be sorted according to any criteria, not just by alphabetical sequence. A list of numbers can be ordered so that the larger numbers appear at the top of the list, or so that the smaller numbers appear at the top. If, for example, numeric codes indicating a word's part of speech or derivation were associated with each of the words in a list, the words could be ordered on this basis rather than alphabetically. Or words could be sorted into alphabetical sequence on the basis of their endings rather than the first letters in the words—this would yield a list where all the words *ending* in 'a' appear first, then all the words ending in 'b', and so on. This kind of ordering is often used in programs designed to analyze suffixes and word endings, and a discussion of the ways to accomplish this is included in the Niceties section of this chapter. The applications of sorting information are varied, and so the process outlined in this chapter can be used in a wide variety of contexts.

A program that will sort the words in an array according to the method outlined in this chapter requires no new Pascal language features to write. Instead, the focus here is on the algorithm to accomplish the sorting itself. As you will see, the computer's method of sorting words into alphabetical order is for the most part analogous to the way you would accomplish the task yourself. The difference, as usual, is that you are probably only dimly aware of each of the steps you go through, whereas for the computer, each step has to be spelled out explicitly.

If someone gave you a stack of index cards, each of which had written on it a word, and you were then asked to put the stack in alphabetical order, how would you go about it? If the stack were relatively small, you might do something like this: you would go through the stack a card at a time, and as you encountered a card that should belong closer to the beginning or end of the stack, you would move it in that direction. You would probably jump around in the stack, moving cards to their approximate ultimate location in the stack. As the stack became more and more ordered, the process would become more precise, so that your method would eventually be something like this: as you looked at each card, you would compare its word with the word on the card before it. If the second card belongs in front of the first, you would switch the cards. Of course you might combine several such steps into one step and switch the card you are looking at with several that precede it, if necessary.

The part of this method that involves moving from one section of the stack to another, based on your conception of how far back or forward in the stack the proper spot for a given word is located, is too imprecise for a computer. But the part of the process that involves comparing two words, and switching them around if they are out of order, is something that a computer can do.

Based on this idea, a method for programming the computer to sort a list has been developed by computer scientists, which they have dubbed the *Bubble Sort*. The name is indicative of the fact that by means of this method, items that belong at the beginning of a list tend to "bubble" to the top, while items that belong at the end sink rapidly to the bottom.

The process underlying the bubble sort is simple. It can be easily demonstrated by using a short list of words like the following:

```
KIWI
BANANA
```

MANGO
GUAVA
AVOCADO

To put this list in alphabetical order, you can go through the list, comparing successive pairs of words as you go along. When two words are out of alphabetical order, they are switched. After going through the list once, the words will not be in alphabetical order, but they will be closer to it. So the process can be repeated, starting at the beginning of the list, comparing successive pairs of words and switching them when they are out of order. If they are still out of order, the process can be repeated again. Eventually, as you will see, the list will be in alphabetical order.

Try the method on the list above. First, the words KIWI and BANANA are compared; because they are out of order the two words are switched. The list now looks like this:

BANANA
KIWI
MANGO
GUAVA
AVOCADO

Next KIWI and MANGO are compared, but they are not out of order, so the words are left where they are, and the list remains as it appears above. Now MANGO and GUAVA are compared, and because they are out of order, they are switched, yielding

BANANA
KIWI
GUAVA
MANGO
AVOCADO

Finally, MANGO is compared to AVOCADO, and again, the two are switched so that they are in the proper order. So at the end of the first pass through the list, the words are in the following order:

BANANA
KIWI
GUAVA
AVOCADO
MANGO

Obviously, more work needs to be done. A second pass through the list will leave BANANA and KIWI untouched, but then comparing KIWI and GUAVA will cause a switch. The next pair to be compared is then KIWI and AVOCADO, which are again switched. Comparing KIWI to MANGO results in no change. The list after the second pass is

BANANA
GUAVA
AVOCADO
KIWI
MANGO

You should begin to see a pattern developing. At the end of the first pass through the list, MANGO, which is the word that is highest in the alphabetical sequence, made its way to the bottom of the list, where it belongs. On the second pass, KIWI, the next highest in alphabetical sequence, made its way to its proper location. As you will see, this happens on every pass: the word highest in alphabetical sequence that is not already in its proper location will "sink" to the position in which it belongs. This means that after the first pass, the bottommost word will be in its proper position; after the second pass, the *two* bottommost words will be in their proper position, and so on. By this logic, on the next pass GUAVA should sink to where it belongs in the list.

This is exactly what happens. Comparing BANANA and GUAVA yields no change; but comparing GUAVA and AVOCADO results in a switch. Subsequent comparisons produce no change, since, as expected, the bottom three words are in their proper order. So the list is now

BANANA
AVOCADO
GUAVA
KIWI
MANGO

On the next pass, BANANA and AVOCADO are switched, but that is all, yielding

AVOCADO
BANANA
GUAVA
KIWI
MANGO

The process is repeated once again, but this time no switches are made at all. Therefore, the list must be in order, and the sorting process is completed.

The process outlined above is one of the most straightforward strategies that is used to sort words by computer. It can be stated algorithmically as follows:

1. For successive pairs of words in the list, do the following:
  a. If the words are not in alphabetical order, do the following:
    (1) Switch their positions.

2. If the list is not in alphabetical order, repeat step 1.

Your programming skills are sophisticated enough at this point to move directly into the construction of the program that sorts the words in the array without considering any additional Pascal language constructs.

CONSTRUCTING THE PROGRAM

The sorting algorithm will be implemented as a procedure which can be called on by the program after the text has been loaded into the array. The main program will therefore call on the sorting procedure just after it calls on Load.

The main program will pass an unsorted array of words to the procedure and get back a sorted version of the array. So the Words array will be sent to the sorting procedure as a pseudonym or VAR parameter, since the changes the sorting procedure will make in the array must remain in effect after the procedure finishes executing. The sorting procedure will also need to know the number of words that are actually sorted in the array, since it works only with the filled portion of the array. Therefore, the main program must pass NumberOfWords to the procedure as well. However, NumberOfWords should not be changed by the sorting procedure—the number of words in the array remains the same after sorting—and so the value stored in NumberOfWords should be the same before and after the sorting procedure executes. Consequently, the variable that contains the number of words stored in the array should be sent to the sorting procedure as a Value parameter. So the statement to call the procedure will be

```
Sort(Words,NumberOfWords);
```

if the procedure is named "Sort." This statement should be inserted in the main program immediately following the call to Load.

Notice that Sort does not need the file in which the text is stored on disk. Once the loading process is complete, the file is no longer a concern, because the words in the text are now in main memory where they can be sorted and manipulated further in any way desired. So in general, after Load is finished executing you can forget about the file in which the original text is stored.

The Sort Procedure

The Procedure Heading for the sorting procedure will look like this:

```
PROCEDURE Sort(VAR SortWords : WordArray; WordsInSort : ArrayBounds);
```

This sets up SortWords as a pseudonym for Words in the procedure, and establishes a variable named WordsInSort within the Sort procedure that will be given, as its initial value, the value stored in NumberOfWords at the time of the call.

The statements within Sort will be based on the algorithm outlined at the beginning of this chapter. To translate the steps in the algorithm into Pascal, the process can be broken into its components. The Pascal statements required to make one pass through the array can be determined first, and then the rest of the algorithm can be implemented. So, in effect, this algorithm will be developed from the inside out.

The part of the algorithm that deals with a single pass through the array says

1. For successive pairs of words in the list, do the following:
   a. If the words are not in alphabetical order, do the following:
      (1) Switch their positions.

This algorithm needs some refinement before it can be translated into Pascal.

Consider step 1, above. How can successive pairs of words in an array be accessed? The first thing that comes to your mind should be—a loop. When you want to look at everything in an array, use a loop.

The loop can enable going through the array and comparing each word to the one that follows it. Since the loop will execute a known number of times (enough times to process all the words in the array), a FOR loop can be used. The FOR loop conveniently has a built-in counter variable, and this counter variable can be used as a subscript to access each word in the array and compare it to the word in the slot that follows. Stated more precisely, each time the loop goes around, the word stored in SortWords[Counter] will be compared to the word stored in SortWords[Counter+1]. The heading on the FOR loop can therefore be something like

```
FOR Counter := 1 TO WordsInSort DO ...
```

The only problem with this is that when Counter finally gets to have the value of WordsInSort, inside the loop, SortWords[Counter+1] will refer to an undefined slot in the Words array—the slot immediately following the last word that was stored in the array. So, instead, the FOR loop should specify that its counter variable attain a maximum value of *one less* than the number of words in the array. To accomplish this, the heading of the FOR loop could be modified to read

```
FOR Counter := 1 TO WordsInSort - 1 DO ...
```

Alternatively, one could be subtracted from WordsInSort *before* the FOR loop begins to execute, and the original heading above could still be used.

For reasons that will become clear later, the method that involves subtracting one from WordsInSort before the loop executes and leaving the heading in its original form, is the one that will be used here. Notice that the change made to WordsInSort here does not affect in any way the contents of its corollary, NumberOfWords, in the main procedure, because NumberOfWords was passed as a Value parameter. WordsInSort receives its initial value from NumberOfWords, but beyond this the association ends. So you can confidently meddle with the contents of WordsInSort within the Sort procedure and be sure that once back in the main procedure, the number of words stored in the array will still be stored in NumberOfWords.

The heading established, the statements within the FOR loop can be determined. These statements are to *compare* a word with the one that follows it in the array. But the notion of comparing has to be refined a bit to be expressed in Pascal. What is really being done? What you really need to find out is whether or not the word in SortWords[Counter] has a numeric code value that is *greater than* the numeric code value for the word in SortWords[Counter+1]. Recall the way in which the computer internally determines whether or not one string of characters is greater than another. It looks at the first character of each, and if the numeric code for the first character of word number one is greater than the code for the first character in word number two, then word number one is greater than word number two. If the reverse is true—the character in the first slot of word number one is less than the character in the first slot of word number two—then word number one is determined not to be greater than word number two. But if the two characters are equal, the computer goes on to compare the characters in slot two of word number one and word number two. The process above is repeated. If the computer reaches the ends of the words and all characters were found to be equal, word number one is determined not to be greater than word number two. By this scheme of comparison, the computer's idea of which words are greater than others corresponds to our notion of which words are higher in alphabetic sequence. So if the computer sees one word as greater than another, it is higher in alphabetic sequence.

What needs to be done within the FOR loop, then, is to assert that if, indeed, SortWords[Counter] is greater than SortWords[Counter+1], the two should be switched. This requires an IF-THEN statement based on the following model:

```
IF SortWords[Counter] > SortWords[Counter+1] THEN BEGIN
   Switch the words
END;
```

The next step is to figure out how to switch the words.

On first consideration, you might assume that the following statements will accomplish the switch:

```
SortWords[Counter] := SortWords[Counter+1];
SortWords[Counter+1] := SortWords[Counter];
```

But this will not work at all. By assigning the contents of SortWords[Counter+1] to SortWords[Counter], the previous contents of SortWords[Counter] are destroyed and replaced by a copy of whatever is stored in SortWords[Counter+1]. At this point, both slots have the same contents. When the next statement is executed, the contents of SortWords[Counter] are copied into SortWords[Counter+1], but what is being stored there is not the word that was originally in SortWords[Counter], but simply a copy of what is already in SortWords[Counter+1].

The solution can be arrived at by imagining what you would do if you had two bottles, each filled with a liquid of your choice, and you wanted to switch the contents of the bottles. The solution? Get a third bottle! The contents of the first bottle are poured into the third bottle, the contents of the second bottle are poured into the first, and the contents of the third bottle are poured into the second. This is exactly how to switch the contents of the array slots in the sorting procedure. You will not actually use bottles, of course, since memory slots are better suited to holding the contents of a variable. But the principle is the same.

You will need a variable that can hold the contents of a slot in the array. This means that the variable must have the same *type* as a slot in the array. The type of the slots in the array is *String;* so within the Sort procedure, a variable of type *String* should be declared, to be used as a third bottle. The variable can be given an unimaginative name like "Temp," since it is being used to temporarily store the word that is being switched.

The statements to accomplish the switch, then, are these:

```
Temp := SortWords[Counter];
SortWords[Counter] := SortWords[Counter+1];
SortWords[Counter+1] := Temp;
```

In the first statement, the contents of the first bottle, SortWords[Counter], are poured into the third bottle, or Temp, where they are put for safekeeping. Then, the contents of the second bottle, SortWords[Counter+1], are poured into the first bottle, destroying the old contents (but remember that a copy of the contents is in Temp). Finally, the contents of the third bottle, Temp, are poured into the second bottle, and the feat is accomplished.

Inserting these statements within the IF-THEN statement outlined above, and inserting the IF-THEN statement inside the FOR loop yields the following:

```
WordsInSort := WordsInSort - 1;
FOR Counter := 1 TO WordsInSort DO BEGIN
  IF SortWords[Counter] > SortWords[Counter+1] THEN BEGIN
    Temp := SortWords[Counter];
    SortWords[Counter] := SortWords[Counter+1];
    SortWords[Counter+1] := Temp;
  END;     { then begin }
END;     { for }
```

Recall that the first statement subtracts one from WordsInSort before the FOR loop executes to ensure that the loop accesses only filled slots in the Words array.

The FOR loop above takes care of a single pass through the array. Now the part of the algorithm that provides for repeating this process as long as switches are made must be implemented. Repeating, of course, is accomplished by a loop as well, and so the entire FOR loop will be surrounded by another loop. Since this outer loop is to execute an indefinite number of times—as many times as necessary to sort the array, which varies depending upon the original order of the words—it will be a WHILE or REPEAT-UNTIL loop. And because the statements within the loop must be executed *at least once*—since it takes at least one pass to determine whether or not the words are sorted—a REPEAT-UNTIL loop is appropriate.

The overall organization of the statements within the procedure is this:

```
REPEAT
  WordsInSort := WordsInSort - 1;
  FOR Counter := 1 TO WordsInSort DO BEGIN
    IF SortWords[Counter] > SortWords[Counter+1] THEN BEGIN
      Temp := SortWords[Counter];
      SortWords[Counter] := SortWords[Counter+1];
      SortWords[Counter+1] := Temp;
    END;     { then begin }
  END;     { for }
UNTIL the array is sorted
```

The remaining problem is how to determine when the array is sorted. This is not as difficult as it may seem at first. Specifically, if it is the case that the FOR loop in the segment of code above completes its execution without switching *any* of the words in the array, then the array must be sorted. So each time the FOR loop executes, you can keep track of whether or not any two words are switched. How can you do this? There is one thing that always happens when even one switch is made, but never happens if no switch is made, during a pass through the array: the statements within the BEGIN-END pair associated with the THEN part of the IF-THEN statement are executed. What needs to be done, then, is to set some sort of signal that indicates whether or not this part of the procedure is reached during the execution of the FOR loop. For this purpose, a BOOLEAN variable is appropriate.

Consider this: suppose that just prior to the execution of the FOR loop, a BOOLEAN variable is set to TRUE. Within the BEGIN-END pair associated with the THEN part of the IF-THEN statement, a statement is inserted to set the variable to FALSE. Now, if the FOR loop finishes executing, and the value of the BOOLEAN variable is FALSE, a switch must have been made, since the only way the variable can be set to FALSE within the loop is by executing the statements that are within the BEGIN-END pair associated with the THEN part of the IF-THEN statement. These statements are executed only if two words are out of order, in which case a switch is made. But if the FOR loop finishes executing and the BOOLEAN has the value TRUE, it must be that no switch was made. So this BOOLEAN variable can be used to signal whether or not a switch was made during a pass through the array. This in turn indicates whether or not the sorting process has been completed; if no switches are made on a pass through the array, the words are in alphabetical order.

Suppose that the BOOLEAN variable is given the name "Sorted." The statements above should be modified to be:

```
REPEAT
  Sorted := TRUE;
  WordsInSort := WordsInSort - 1;
  FOR Counter := 1 TO WordsInSort DO BEGIN
    IF SortWords[Counter] > SortWords[Counter+1] THEN BEGIN
      Temp := SortWords[Counter];
      SortWords[Counter] := SortWords[Counter+1];
      SortWords[Counter+1] := Temp;
      Sorted := FALSE;
    END;     { then begin }
  END;     { for }
UNTIL Sorted;
```

When the REPEAT-UNTIL loop is first entered, Sorted is immediately set to TRUE, anticipating that no switches will be made. The FOR loop is then entered, and assuming at least one pair of words are switched, Sorted is set to FALSE. When the FOR loop finishes executing and control reaches the bottom of the REPEAT-UNTIL loop, Sorted is FALSE, and so the REPEAT-UNTIL loop is executed again. Again, Sorted is set to TRUE, in case no switches are made, and the FOR loop is entered. This process continues until the FOR loop finishes executing without making any switches at all, thus leaving Sorted with its original value of TRUE. When control reaches the bottom of the REPEAT-UNTIL loop at that point, the condition on the loop will be TRUE (since Sorted contains the value TRUE) and the loop will not be executed again.

Notice that the statement that subtracts one from WordsInSort is *inside* the REPEAT-UNTIL loop, which means that each time the REPEAT-UNTIL loop executes the value of WordsInSort is decreased by one. At first glance this seems undesirable, but as it turns out, subtracting one from WordsInSort just before each execution of the FOR loop enables the sorting procedure to run more efficiently than it would if the statement were moved before the REPEAT-UNTIL loop. The reason is this: recall that after one pass through the array, the bottom element is always in place. There is really no sense in comparing the bottom element to the one that precedes it in the array on the next pass, since it is known to be in its proper place. And after the next pass, the next-to-the-last word is in place as well, so both can be ignored the next time around. In fact, after each pass through the array, one less word need be dealt with. Obviously, if fewer words are compared, the program will run faster. If your text is at all large, you can save a noticeable amount of time by eliminating extra comparisons.

The first time the FOR loop is executed, WordsInSort is one less than the number of words in the array. So in the final iteration of the FOR loop, the word in the second-to-last position in the array is compared to the word in the last position in the array. On the next pass, one is subtracted from WordsInSort and so its value is now *two* less than the number of words in the array. So this time, the final value of Counter is two less than the number of words in the array, and the loop stops after comparing the word in the *third-to-last* position in the array with the word in the *second-to-last* position. Thus, the last word in the array is ignored this time around, which is fine since it is known to be in its proper position. The following time, WordsInSort is *three* less, and so on. So by subtracting one from WordsInSort each time the FOR loop completes executing, one less word is considered in the comparison process, as desired. That is, by reducing WordsInSort by one each time, the list of words that is being considered actually becomes, conceptually, one word shorter.

If it is not clear to you why WordsInSort should be decreased by one on each pass through the array, go back to the example list of words in the beginning of this chapter and go through the sorting process again. This time, however, do not bother with the last word in the list on the second pass through, and on subsequent passes, ignore the bottommost word of the list that was considered in the previous pass. This should prove to you that one less word can be compared on each pass through the array in the sorting procedure.

The final form of the Sort procedure is

```
PROCEDURE Sort(VAR SortWords : WordArray; WordsInSort : ArrayBounds);
    { Alphabetizes the words in array SortWords }
VAR Counter : ArrayBounds;
  Sorted : BOOLEAN;
  Temp : String;
```

```
BEGIN    { Sort }
  REPEAT
    Sorted := TRUE;
    WordsInSort := WordsInSort - 1;
    FOR Counter := 1 TO WordsInSort DO BEGIN
      IF SortWords[Counter] > SortWords[Counter+1] THEN BEGIN
        Temp := SortWords[Counter];
        SortWords[Counter] := SortWords[Counter+1];
        SortWords[Counter+1] := Temp;
        Sorted := FALSE;
      END;    { then begin }
    END;    { for }
  UNTIL Sorted;
END;    { Sort }
```

Counter, Sorted, and Temp are all variables used solely within Sort and so are declared locally.

The Program as a Whole

The program outline from last chapter can be extended to be

```
PROGRAM Alphabetize(INPUT,OUTPUT,TextFile);
  Constant declarations: StringLength, MaxWords, Blank, Blanks
  Type Declarations: String, ArrayBounds, StringBounds, WordArray
  Variable Declarations: Words, NumberOfWords, Counter, TextFile
  Procedure Declarations:
  PROCEDURE ReadWord(VAR NextWord : String; VAR InputFile : TEXT);
    Variable Declarations: Letter, Counter
    Procedure Declarations:
    PROCEDURE SkipBlanks(VAR NextChar : CHAR; VAR InFile : TEXT);
      Variable Declarations: none
    BEGIN    { SkipBlanks }
      .
      .
      .
    END;    { SkipBlanks }
  BEGIN    { ReadWord }
    .
    .
    .
  END;    { ReadWord }
  PROCEDURE SubString(FromWord : String;
            Start, Stop : StringBounds; VAR ToWord : String);
    Variable Declarations: Counter, ToPos
  BEGIN    { SubString }
    .
    .
    .
  END;    { SubString }
  FUNCTION Capitalize(Lowerletter : CHAR) : CHAR;
    Variable Declarations: none
```

```
BEGIN    { Capitalize }
  .
  .
  .
END;    { Capitalize }
PROCEDURE Standardize(VAR StandardWord : String);
  Variable Declarations: Counter, FirstLetter
BEGIN    { Standardize }
  .
  .
  .
END;    { Standardize }
PROCEDURE Load(VAR FileWords : WordArray;
        VAR WordsInFile : ArrayBounds; VAR WordFile : TEXT);
  Variable Declarations: Word
BEGIN    { Load }
  .
  .
  .
END;    { Load }
PROCEDURE Sort(VAR SortWords: WordArray; WordsInSort : ArrayBounds);
  Variable Declarations: Counter, Sorted, Temp
BEGIN    { Sort }
  .
  .
  .
END;    { Sort }
BEGIN    { Alphabetize }
  Load(Words,NumberOfWords,TextFile);
  Sort(Words,NumberOfWords);
  FOR Counter := 1 TO NumberOfWords DO BEGIN
    WRITELN(Words[Counter]);
  END;    { for }
END;    { Alphabetize }
```

Since the main program calls Sort, it does not matter where among the procedures already declared in the main program the declaration of Sort is inserted. It is inserted after Load in the set-up above simply because the call to Sort follows the call to Load in the main program.

SUMMING UP THE PROGRAM

The program for this chapter requires no new Pascal language features to write. At this point you are familiar with the fundamentals of computer programming, and so from now on the emphasis will be not on language features, but on the algorithms and methods used in the various programs you will write. This is an important part of programming, and one that is all too often given little attention. Simply being aware of certain language features does not a program or a programmer make (as the saying should go). So since you are now familiar with most of the features of the Pascal language, you can turn your attention more toward the mental processes and the techniques that are required to write computer programs. These mental processes will serve you not only in writing programs, but in approaching problems (in the very broadest sense of the term) of all kinds. The quantitative approach to problem solving that you have been using to write the programs in this text is often unfamiliar to humanists, and if so, familiarizing yourself with it can help you look at the materials with which your discipline is concerned in new ways. This new approach nicely complements the humanist's traditional approach, which often focuses more on broad concepts and context than on detail.

NICETIES

Reversing Words

In some circumstances a listing of words in order by their endings can be useful. For instance, if you are interested in the use of various syntactic forms, a reverse listing of the words in a text can show you quickly all of the words in a text with common suffixes. Words with the same suffix—for example, words ending in "ing," "ed," "able," or "tion"—often fall into the same syntactic category. Words with the same ending also rhyme, and so a reverse listing of the words in a text (if that text is a poem) can show which words might be used for rhyming. (A reverse concordance is more useful for this purpose—see Chapter Thirteen.)

A reverse sorted listing of the words in a text can be generated by first reversing *each* word within the packed array in which it is stored in the Words array, using the Sort procedure developed earlier in this chapter to Sort the array, and then printing the array's contents. The only step for which you have not already written a procedure or segment of code is the step of reversing each of the words.

A simple procedure can be written that will take a packed array of type *String* and reverse the word contained in it, so that if the variable originally contained "DERIVATION ", after reversal the variable will contain "NOITAVIRED ". This procedure can then be called once for each of the words in the Words array. Of course, the procedure could be written so that it takes the array as a parameter and reverses all of the words in it. But by writing the procedure to deal with one *String*-type variable only, the procedure becomes more flexible, since it can be called to reverse a single word or *String*-type elements of arrays with types other than *WordArray*. This is another example of making procedures "single-minded" so that they can be used in other situations.

In general, if you perform a process on each of the elements of an array, make the process a procedure and call it repeatedly.

The reversing procedure will take as a parameter the *String*-type variable that it is to reverse and include another *String*-type variable in which the reversed version is placed. Even though you want the reversed version to be put back in the same variable, returning a separate string makes the procedure potentially useful in a wider range of situations. (This logic was applied for the same reason when the parameters for SubString were determined.) The original word can therefore be sent as a Value parameter, and the variable in which the result is stored must, of course, be passed as a VAR parameter. The whole of the procedure is

```
PROCEDURE Reverse(OriginalWord : String; VAR BackWord : String);
  { Reverses word stored in OriginalWord and stores }
  { the resulting string in BackWord }
VAR LengthWord, ToPos : StringBounds;
BEGIN     { Reverse }
  LengthWord := Length(OriginalWord);
  BackWord := Blanks;
  ToPos := 0;
  FOR Counter := LengthWord DOWNTO 1 DO BEGIN
    ToPos := ToPos + 1;
    BackWord[ToPos] := OriginalWord[Counter];
  END;     { for }
END;     { Reverse }
```

Reverse calls on the Length function (Chapter Eight) to locate the last non-blank character stored in OriginalWord. Notice that the FOR loop uses the DOWNTO option, which causes the value of the loop control variable, Counter, to be *decremented* by one rather than incremented by one each time the loop iterates. ToPos is incremented by one each time the FOR loop executes, and so the characters in OriginalWord are copied one by one, starting with the last, into successive slots of BackWord, starting with the first. The result is that BackWord contains a reversed version of the contents of OriginalWord.

One note of interest: the procedure above could be written without the variable ToPos as follows:

```
PROCEDURE Reverse(OriginalWord : String; VAR BackWord : String);
  { Reverses word stored in OriginalWord and stores }
  { the resulting string in BackWord }
VAR LengthWord : StringBounds;
BEGIN     { Reverse }
  LengthWord := Length(OriginalWord);
  BackWord := Blanks;
  FOR Counter := LengthWord DOWNTO 1 DO BEGIN
    BackWord[(LengthWord-Counter)+1] := OriginalWord[Counter];
  END;     { for }
END;     { Reverse }
```

This set-up computes the position in BackWord into which the contents of OriginalWord[Counter] are to be copied, rather than specifying it explicitly with ToPos. In terms of efficiency, the amount of effort as a result of the number of calculations that must be performed is about the same for both methods. The first approach seems to require an extra variable and therefore extra storage, but if the second set-up is used, internally the computer uses an extra memory location to compute and store the result of the calculation in the brackets anyway, so not much is gained. The first set-up has the advantage of clarity, in the sense that the slot into which the contents of OriginalWord[Counter] is stored is immediately obvious.[1]

A FOR loop can be used to call Reverse repeatedly from the main program, in order to reverse every word in the Words array, as follows:

```
FOR Counter := 1 TO NumberOfWords DO BEGIN
  Reverse(Words[Counter],Words[Counter]);
END;     { for }
```

Note that Words[Counter] is passed twice to Reverse, to correspond to both the Value parameter OriginalWord and the VAR parameter BackWord. This strategy was used in the call to SubString in Standardize.

The set of statements above should appear *before* the call to Sort, which, if it follows this FOR loop, will sort the words into alphabetical order by their endings. If the main program then prints out the contents of the Words array, a reverse alphabetical listing of the words in the text will appear.

APPLICATIONS AND CONSIDERATIONS

Efficiency of the Bubble Sort

The Bubble Sort is not terribly efficient. The efficiency of a sorting technique is measured by the number of operations it performs. In the case of a Bubble Sort, an "operation" can be regarded as a comparison of two words. If there are 100 words in the array, then going through the array *once* (the process described by the inner FOR loop of the Sort procedure) requires 99 comparisons. If the array is in its worst possible configuration (from the sorting procedure's point of view), then the procedure will have to go through the array 99 times (that is, the REPEAT-UNTIL loop will execute 99 times). The total number of comparisons is therefore 99 × 99, or 9801. In general, in the worst case a Bubble Sort requires n^2 comparisons, where n is the number of items that are being sorted. (In this example, $100^2 = 10{,}000$.)

Computer scientists have developed sorting procedures that perform far better than the Bubble Sort. It may therefore seem that the Bubble Sort is a bad strategy to adopt, but there are three reasons why this may not be so: (1) The data in the programs in the text are sorted only once during the course of the program. Therefore, the sorting strategy is not as crucial to the overall performance of the program as it would be if the data needed to be sorted a number of times. (2) The Bubble Sort behaves badly (making n^2 comparisons) when the words in the array are in the worst possible order to start. The number of comparisons a Bubble Sort makes *on average* is not as bad as the worst case given above, since fewer iterations of the REPEAT-UNTIL loop are made if the data

1. Note that the variable *ToPos* can be eliminated from the SubString procedure as well, by replacing the subscript on ToWord with (Counter−Start) + 1.

require only a few passes through the FOR loop in order to get the words in alphabetical order. (3) The Bubble Sort has the clear advantage that it is easy to write. Sorting strategies that are more efficient are typically much more complex and often require additional main memory to implement. Bubble Sort requires no additional memory except for the temporary variable, which is negligible.

In Chapter Twelve another sorting strategy will be implemented.

Using the Alphabetical Word Listing

Sorting the words in the text opens the door to many interesting possibilities, as you will see in the chapters to come. In general, by putting the words in the text in alphabetical order you remove them from their context, and this enables looking at the words in the text as *words* in isolation. In many instances this is desirable, for context can obscure word use for the reader. It is very difficult to notice when you are reading a text how many different words of a certain form or with certain meanings are used, but in a sorted listing such things are often immediately obvious.

For instance, suppose you are interested in an author's use of negatives such as "no," "not," "never," and so on. An alphabetical listing of the words in the text would show you immediately if these words occur in the text, how many times they occur, and would also show other words you had forgotten to include like "nothing" and "neither," which would appear in adjacent sections of the list. You could easily scan the list to extract other words of negation, or use a reverse listing like the one described in the Niceties section of this chapter to readily show all words ending in "not" or "n't." Or suppose you are interested in an author's use of images of darkness. An alphabetical listing will readily show all of the forms of the word "dark" that appear in the text—such as "darkened," "darkening," "darker," and so on—and once again, an alphabetical listing is easy to scan for words with related meanings (perhaps "night," "shadow," "dim," etc.). An alphabetical listing will also help you if you are interested in words with common prefixes (or suffixes, if you generate a reverse listing), which can be interesting in syntactic studies.

An alphabetical listing is possibly most useful when you do not know what you are looking for in a text. When words are isolated from their contexts in such a list, the use of words that was not apparent from reading the text often reveals itself. For instance, a listing might reveal that images of darkness play a role in a text because a variety of forms of the word "dark" appear in the list and/or appear several times. Because the words are scattered around the text, and because the reader's attention is usually on units of meaning larger than the word when he or she reads the text, the large number of forms of "dark" used in the text might not be apparent until the list is consulted. Similarly, the listing might reveal that the author tends to use words with certain forms a great deal, which could be of interest in stylistic studies.

Often it is useful to have a *dictionary* of the words in the text rather than simply an alphabetical listing of all words. A dictionary lists each word only once, rather than listing all occurrences of each word. In most cases such a dictionary will include the *frequency* of each word along with the word itself, indicating how many times it appears in the text. This presents the material in a more readable and compact form for the researcher. One of the exercises at the end of the chapter calls for generating a dictionary of the words in the text.

EXERCISES

1. Modify the program so that it prints only words beginning with the letter 'C'. Since the text is in alphabetical order, your program need not look through the entire array for words beginning with 'C'. Instead, the program should stop looking through the words in the array when it determines that all words beginning with 'C' have been encountered and printed.

2. Do exercise 1, but prompt the user for the letter with which the words to be printed begin. Include a function that can be called on to determine that what the user entered is indeed an alphabetic character after it has been read in. Also, ensure that the letter is in upper case before using it to determine which words to print.

3. Modify the program to print a reverse alphabetical listing of the words in the text, as shown in the Niceties section of this chapter.

4. Modify the program to prompt the user for a word, search the array for the word, and print a message indicating how many times the word appears in the text. To do this, you should modify the linear search algorithm from Chapter Seven so that it takes advantage of the fact that the words are now in sorted order and does not search any more of the array than it has to. The positions at which the word is found should not be printed, since now that the text is sorted these positions have no meaning.

5. (A bit more difficult.) Modify the program so that its output is a *dictionary* of the words in the text—that is, a listing of each distinct word in the text. To do this, you must go through the array, but avoid printing duplicate entries of the same word.

6. (A bit more difficult.) Do exercise 5, but enhance the dictionary to print each word's frequency following the word itself in the listing.

7. (A bit more difficult, but easier than it looks.) Modify the program so that the words are sorted not in alphabetical order, but in order according to their length. That is, words of length one should appear first in the array, then words of length two, etc.

8. (More difficult.) Do problem 7, but arrange the data so that all the words of length one are in alphabetical order, the words of length two are in alphabetical order, and so on.

10
Searching the Text

In the Niceties section of Chapter Seven, you saw how to search an array by looking at each element, one after another. This is a very inefficient method of searching a text, because if the text is large, the search can take quite a long time. However, with a list of elements that is in no particular order, a linear search is the only type of search possible. With an ordered list of items, on the other hand, much more efficient search methods can be applied, which is easy to understand if you consider how you go about looking up a word in the dictionary. Because you know the words are in order, you do not have to look at every word to find the one you are interested in. Instead, you open the dictionary, look at the words on the page you opened to, and if the word you are looking for occurs before these words in alphabetical sequence, you open to another page closer to the front of the dictionary; if the word occurs after the words in alphabetical sequence, you move toward the back of the book. You repeat this process until you find the page on which your word appears, and then you use the same method within the words on that page to find the word you are interested in.

The search method you will implement in this chapter is called a *binary search*, and as you will see, the method is not very different from the one you use to search the dictionary. The name is derived from the fact that the search is performed by successively dividing the list that is being searched into halves ("binary" means "by two"), thus yielding smaller and smaller lists of items to be searched. The process is used in a simple guessing game that works like this: you ask someone to pick a number between, say, 1 and 100, and you assert that you will guess the number in only a few tries, by asking only questions that can be answered with "yes" or "no." Suppose that the number chosen is 78. First, you ask if the number is greater than 50. The answer is "yes," so you can (mentally) narrow your search down to the numbers between 51 and 100. The lower half of the 1-to-100 sequence can be eliminated from consideration, and so you have halved the size of the list you must search. Next, you ask if the number is greater than 75. The answer is "yes" again, and so once again, you throw out the bottom half of the list—the numbers between 51 and 75. Your new list consists only of the numbers between 76 and 100. Now you ask if the number is greater than 88 (halfway between 75 and 100); the answer is "no." So you throw out the top half of your list, yielding a list only of the numbers 76 through 88. You ask if the number is greater than 82, and the answer is "no," so the list is pared again to contain only the numbers 76 through 82. Now you ask if it is greater than 79, and the answer is "no," so the new list contains only the numbers 76, 77, 78, and 79. Now you can ask if the number is greater than 77, which it is, and narrow the list to 78 and 79. The next question would be, is the number 78 (or 79)? If the answer is "yes," you have the number, if the answer is "no," you then know the number is the other one on the list. You have managed to guess the number in seven or eight tries, which, given the fact that there were 100 possibilities, is rather impressive. This method works only if the list of items to be searched is an ordered list, which, of course, the list of numbers between 1 and 100 is.

The binary search algorithm you will implement in this chapter is exactly the same as the one outlined above. Obviously, it will save a great deal of time by reducing drastically the number of comparisons that have to be made to search a list linearly. Of course, since the list must be ordered, computer time must be spent to sort the list in the first place before a binary search can be attempted, but the savings in search time far exceed the time spent sorting if the text is at all large. For instance, if you have a text of 1000 words, the average number of comparisons that must be made to find a given word in the text using the linear search method is 500. With a binary search, the maximum number of comparisons that will be made is ten. If you search the text for 20 words, with a linear search the program will make, on the average, 10,000 comparisons, versus a maximum of 200 with a binary search. The savings in time is obvious.

In the main program for this chapter's problem the user will be prompted for a word. The main program will then call on the search procedure to determine whether or not the word appears in the text and print a message indicating the result. No new Pascal language features are required for this problem: you have all the tools you need. However, the development of the precise algorithm for the search procedure requires some attention.

The two main ingredients of the search are the sorted array of words and a search word—that is, the word that will be searched for in the text. This word will be obtained from the user at the terminal and passed to the searching procedure. Now, to go about searching for this word in the array by the method outlined above, what needs to be done is to determine whether or not the word in the *middle* of the array is greater than the search word. How is the word in the middle of the array referred to? Well, if the procedure knows how many words are in the array, the middle word is at the position that is *half* of the number of words in the array. For instance, if the number of words in the array is 738, the word at the mid-point of the array is at position 369. The search word, then, can be compared to the word at position 369 to determine if the search word is greater than that word, according to the computer's internal method of numeric coding. If so, then the search will continue, considering only the words in positions 370 through 738 in the array. The middle word in this new list must be determined, and so the program will have to calculate the midpoint between 370 and 738, which is actually the *average* of the numbers. Then the search word can be compared with this word, and the process will continue in this manner until the word is located in the array.

To illustrate the process, consider the following example. Suppose that the array contains the following words:

[1] AID
[2] ALL
[3] COME
[4] FOR
[5] GOOD
[6] IS
[7] NOW
[8] OF
[9] PARTY
[10] PEOPLE
[11] THE
[12] THE
[13] THEIR
[14] TIME
[15] TO
[16] TO

(The numbers indicate the positions of the words in the array.) Suppose that the search word is PEOPLE. When the search begins, the entire array is under consideration. Since there are 16 words in the array, the word at the midpoint is in position 8; so the search word PEOPLE is compared to OF, the word at position 8 in the array. The first thing to ascertain is whether or not the search word has been found—that is, if PEOPLE is *equal* to the contents of the array at position 8. Since it is not, the next thing to do is to determine in which half of the array the word does appear, which can be discovered by determining whether or not the search word is *greater than* the word at position 8. It is, and so for the next phase of the search, only words greater than OF need be considered. To do this, the list is conceptually divided in half; the first half is ignored, and only the second half figures into the next stage of the search. The beginning of the new list is the position one beyond the position of the word with which the search word was just compared, which is position 9. The end of the list is still position 16. Now, this new list must be divided in half, so that the word at the midpoint of the new list can be compared to the search word. To determine the midpoint between 9 and 16, the average of 9 and 16 must be computed. To find the average, 9 and 16 are added, yielding 25, and the result is divided by 2, which yields

12.5. Since positions in an array are indicated by integer values, it is impossible to regard position 12.5 as the midpoint; the only solution is to ignore the digits to the right of the decimal point and use only the whole part of the number. So the word at position 12, THE, is next compared to the search word, PEOPLE, and it is found not to be equal to it. Since it is not, another comparison is made, and the search word is determined *not* to be greater than THE. Once again, based on this information a new list must be established, the first position of which is the same as that of the previous list, position 9, and the last position of which is one *less* than the position of the word just compared to the search word. (If the search word is not equal to or greater than the word to which it is being compared, it must be less than the word, so that word can be eliminated from consideration.) So the new list consists of positions 9 through 11. The midpoint of this list is, again, determined by averaging 9 and 11, which yields 10. The word at position 10 is compared to the search word, a match is found, and the search stops.

Note that when the array is "divided in half," this is done only conceptually; words are not actually eliminated from the array. Instead, the boundaries of the list, which are initially set at 1 and 16 in the example above, are simply changed. After the first set of comparisons, the boundaries of the list are 9 and 16; after the next set of comparisons, the boundaries are 9 and 11. The midpoint of any list can be determined by finding the average of its boundaries—this is just as true for the boundaries 1 and 16 as for any other set of boundaries.

What happens if the word does not occur in the array? Suppose, for instance, that instead of the word PEOPLE, the word MEN was being searched for in the group of words listed above. On the first attempt, MEN would be compared with the word in position 8, and since it is not equal, the word would be determined not to be greater than OF. The second half of the list should then be discarded, beginning with the word at position 8, so that the list under consideration consists only of words 1 through 7. The average of 1 and 7 is 4; so MEN would next be compared to FOR. Since MEN is not equal to FOR, but is greater than FOR, the list should be pared down again to include only the second half of the list under consideration. The new list consists of positions 5 through 7; the midpoint between them is 6 (again, ignoring digits beyond the decimal point), and so MEN is compared to IS. The two are not equal, and it is further determined that MEN is greater than IS, so the first half of the list is moved up again to one greater than the position of the word to which the search word was just compared. This makes the first position in the list 7, which is the same as the last position in the list; the average of 7 and 7 is 7, so the word in position 7 is compared to the search word. Because MEN is less than NOW, the last position is now set to 6, which makes it one less than the first position in the list—which is an indication of an empty list. At this point, the search must be stopped, since it is obvious that the search word does not appear in the array.

What has happened here is that the list to be searched shrank and shrank in an attempt to close in on the matching word, until the values of the first and last positions in the list actually *crossed*, and the first became larger than the second. This situation can be used as a signal to indicate that the words in the array have been exhausted without success.

The following is an algorithmic outline of the steps involved in the binary search:

1. While the list to be searched is not empty and the word has not been found, do the following:
   a. Compute the midpoint of the list by finding the average of the first and last positions in the list.
   b. If the search word is equal to the word at the midpoint, do the following:
      (1) Stop the search.
   c. Otherwise, if the search word is greater than the word at the midpoint, do the following:
      (1) Set the first position in the list to be 1 greater than the midpoint.
   d. Failing the conditions in both of steps 1.b and 1.c, do the following:
      (1) Set the last position in the list to be 1 less than the midpoint.

CONSTRUCTING THE PROGRAM

The overall design of the main program for this problem is this: first, the program will call Load to load the words from the file into the array, and then it will call Sort to alphabetize them. After this, the program will prompt the user to enter a word at the display screen. ReadWord can be called upon to do the actual reading of the word (remember that the file name passed to ReadWord when it is to read from the display screen is INPUT), and then Standardize can be called on to ensure that the word is in a form compatible with that of the words in the array, as shown in the Niceties section of Chapter Eight. After this, the main program will call on the search procedure to search the array for the user's word. Finally, the main program will print a message to the user indicating whether or not the word was found in the array.

The binary search procedure must be given the array to be searched, the number of words stored in the array, and the word to be searched for, in order to perform its task. Should these things be passed as VAR or Value parameters? The binary search procedure uses these variables, but it does not change them; consequently, they should be sent as Value parameters. The binary search procedure must send something back to the main program, however—an indication of whether or not the word was found in the array, since it is the job of the main program, and not the search procedure, to print the message to the user. The search procedure's only job is to search; whether or not to print a message indicating that the word is found, or to use the information provided by the search procedure in some other way, should be left up to the calling procedure.

It is just as easy to have the search procedure do more than just indicate whether or not the word is found—it can indicate *where* in the array the word is found. This can be done by returning the *position* in the array of the word it finds to be equal to the word for which it is searching. If the word is not found, the procedure can return the value 0, since 0 is not a valid position in the array. All of this brings up an important point: the search procedure will take several variables as Value parameters, but it is returning only one, simple value to its caller.

When a procedure returns a single result to its caller, and when the result has a simple type (a built-in or sub-range type) the procedure should be implemented as a function instead.

This is the case with the searching procedure. So, instead of a searching procedure, you will have a searching *function* in your program, the result of which is the position in the array at which the word is found or 0 if it is not found.

What type of value will the searching function return? Since the value it returns is between 0 and the value of the constant MaxWords, it can return a value of type *ArrayBounds*.

Having read the word in which the user is interested and having standardized it, the main program can invoke the searching function to provide the information about its location in the text, if any. The main program can store the value returned by the searching function in a variable, where the value will then be examined and appropriate action taken. To invoke the searching function (assuming its name is "Search"), use the statement

```
Position := Search(Words,NumberOfWords,UsersWord);
```

where Position has the same type as the value returned by Search—that is, Position has the type *ArrayBounds*.

Once the value has been returned to the main program indicating if the word was found and where, all that remains to be done is to examine the value and act accordingly. If the value is not 0, then the word was found and a message to that effect can be printed. Otherwise a message that the word does not appear in the text should be printed. This can be accomplished with a simple IF-THEN-ELSE statement whose condition asserts that Position is greater than 0; if true, one message is printed, and if false, another is printed.[1]

Given all of this, the statements in the main program will be

```
BEGIN
  Load(Words,NumberOfWords,TextFile);
  Sort(Words,NumberOfWords);
  WRITE('Enter a word, and I will tell you if it appears in the text:   ');
  ReadWord(UsersWord,INPUT);
  Standardize(UsersWord);
  Position := Search(Words,NumberOfWords,UsersWord);
  IF Position > 0 THEN BEGIN
    WRITELN('The word was found in the text at position ',Position:1);
  END    { then begin }
  ELSE BEGIN
    WRITELN('The word was not found in the text');
  END;    { else begin }
END.    { main program }
```

1. You could just as easily use the condition Position = 0 and reverse the order of the statements that write the messages within the IF-THEN-ELSE statement.

The Search Function

The heading on the Search function will be

```
FUNCTION Search(SearchWords : WordArray; Last : ArrayBounds;
        WordToFind : String) : ArrayBounds;
```

To determine the statements within the Search function, consider the binary search process as it was outlined in the previous section. The basic action involves *repeatedly* examining the word at the middle of the current list, first to determine if it is equal to the search word, and if not, to determine if the search word is greater than the word at the middle of the list. Since the same basic step is repeated over and over, a loop is obviously appropriate. The loop will surround the statements required to perform the necessary comparisons of the search word to a word in the array at each step along the way.

What kind of loop should be used? The exact number of times the loop will execute is unknown; it depends on when (and if) the word is found. Consequently, a WHILE or REPEAT-UNTIL loop should be used instead of a FOR loop, so that the loop can be stopped when the word is found, if this happens before the list that is being searched becomes empty. To choose between the WHILE loop and the REPEAT-UNTIL loop, you will have to consider whether or not a condition will be checked before the statements inside the loop, which will compare the search word to the word at the midpoint of the current list, are executed, in which case a WHILE loop is appropriate. If the statements inside the loop should be executed once before checking the condition, a REPEAT-UNTIL loop will be used. In this case, the condition should be checked before the loop executes even a single time. The reason for this is not immediately obvious, but should be noted because it will apply in most cases involving an array: *the loop in the Search function must not execute at all if the array is empty—that is, if no words have been stored in the array—for if it does, the program will crash since it will access non-existent slots in the array.* Therefore, the check for an empty list must be made before the statements inside the loop are executed for the first time as well as before all subsequent executions.

It is unlikely that when Search is called the Words array will be empty, since the program will always call on Load first to fill the array. However, it is always possible that for some reason Load does not read words into the file (for instance, if the file is for some reason empty when Load is called), and of course, no procedure should assume its caller passes good data to it. Consequently, a WHILE loop is appropriate here.

Always check that an array is not empty before accessing any element within it, even when the chances the array is empty are remote.

You might ask here why a check for an empty array was not made in Sort, if such a check is so important. The reason is that if the array is empty when Sort is called, the FOR loop (in which references to elements of the array are made) will never execute. If NumberOfWords is 0 when the procedure is called, the heading on the FOR loop will say, in essence, FOR Counter := 1 TO −1..., and therefore the loop will never execute and no elements of the array will be accessed.

Looking back at the algorithm for the searching process, two conditions signal that the searching process being carried out within the WHILE loop should be stopped: if the list that is being searched is empty or if the word has been found in the array. The first condition, that the list is empty, is signalled by the fact that the last position in the list currently being searched is *less than* the first position in the list. Recall the situation in the example in the previous section, where the word MEN was not found in the list. The list continued to shrink by closing in on the position where the word MEN ought to have been, until by adding one to the midpoint value, the first position in the list being formed came to be farther down in the list than the last value. So the first condition on the WHILE loop will check the first and last positions in the list being searched, and the loop will not execute when the first exceeds the last in value.

The second condition, that the word is in fact found in the array, will require a BOOLEAN variable. This variable will be set to FALSE before the WHILE loop executes, and if the word is then found in the array, it will be set to TRUE. The value of the variable can be checked in the condition on the WHILE loop to determine whether or not to continue the search process.

In Pascal, the condition on the WHILE loop can be expressed like this:

```
WHILE (First <= Last) AND (NOT Found) DO ...
```

where First is the variable holding the value that indicates the first position in the current list, Last is the variable holding the value that indicates the last position in the list, and Found is a BOOLEAN variable that is set to FALSE before the loop executes. Note that First and Found are declared locally within Search, but that Last is a Value parameter in the Procedure Heading, and therefore gets its initial value from NumberOfWords. Because it is a Value parameter, changes to Last will not affect the value of the variable NumberOfWords in the main program. Note also that the initial value of First must be assigned within the function, and that its initial value is, of course, 1, since the original array is from 1 to NumberOfWords, or Last, as it is known within Search. Like Last, First can be declared with the type *ArrayBounds*.

If either condition on the WHILE loop is true, the search will be stopped. Note that if the array is empty, NumberOfWords and hence Last will have the value 0, and so the loop will never execute if for some reason no words have been stored in the array since in that case First[1] will not be less than or equal to Last[0].

Inside the loop, the first task is to compute the midpoint of the list. If the variable First holds the first position in the list, and Last holds the last position in the list, then the midpoint is computed by adding First to Last and dividing by 2. Recall that when the division of the sum of First and Last is an odd number, the result of dividing this value by 2 is a number with digits to the right of the decimal point. However, these digits should be ignored and only the whole part of the number should be used to indicate a position in the array. Now back in Chapter Three it was pointed out that Pascal includes two division operators:

the familiar slash, which provides for retaining fractional results of a division, and DIV, which provides for retaining only the whole part of the result and throws digits to the right of the decimal point away. DIV, then, provides exactly what is needed here. So the statement to compute the midpoint value will be

```
MidPoint := (First+Last) DIV 2;
```

This statement assigns the result of the computation in a variable called MidPoint, which can be declared with type *ArrayBounds*. The values of First and Last must be known in subsequent statements, and so the results of the arithmetic cannot be assigned to one of those variables. Note the use of the parentheses in the statement: the parentheses are essential in this context to ensure that the computer performs the addition before the division. Otherwise, the value stored in Last would be divided by 2, and *then* the value stored in First would be added to this result, yielding an incorrect value.

The remaining statements within the loop perform the actual comparisons, and, where necessary, adjust the first and last positions to delineate the list to be searched the next time through the loop. Looking at the algorithm, you can see that the first thing to do is to compare the search word with the word at the midpoint in the array for equality. If it is true that they are equal, the variable Found should be set to TRUE, which will stop the loop from executing another time. However, if it is not true that they are equal, the search word should be compared to the word at the midpoint of the list to see if it is greater than that word. Note that this comparison should be made *only* if the search word and the word at the midpoint are not equal. If it is true that the search word is greater, then the first position in the list to be searched should be set to *one greater* than the midpoint value. If it is both false that the two words are equal and false that the search word is greater, then and only then should the last position in the list be set to a value that is *one less* than the midpoint value.

Obviously, IF-THEN-ELSE statements are required to handle this situation. The idea is to set them up so that comparisons are made only when necessary. If the words are found to be equal, then there is no sense comparing them to see if the search word is greater. If the word is greater, there is no sense in comparing the words to see if the search word is less. You can set up the statements within the loop so that *if* the search word is equal to the word at the computed midpoint of the array, *then* Found is set to TRUE; *else* the program will check to see if the search word is greater or less than the word at the midpoint of the array. The basic structure here is

```
IF the search word is equal the word at the midpoint THEN BEGIN
  Set Found to TRUE
END     { then begin }
ELSE BEGIN
  Determine whether the search word is greater or less
  than the word at the midpoint
END;     { else begin }
```

With this structure, only if the search word is *not* equal to the word at the computed midpoint of the array is the ELSE part of the statement executed; if it *is* equal, the statements within the ELSE BEGIN and END are skipped, avoiding needless checking.

What about the statements that should be inserted within the ELSE BEGIN and END? Here again, you have an IF-THEN-ELSE situation: *if* the word is greater than the word at the midpoint, *then* the value of First (the lower bound of the piece of the array being searched) needs to be adjusted; *else* the value of Last (the upper bound of the array being searched) needs to be changed. So you will need a statement like this:

```
IF the search word is greater than the word at the midpoint THEN BEGIN
  Set First to midpoint plus 1
END     { then begin }
ELSE BEGIN
  Set Last to midpoint minus 1
END;    { else begin }
```

The whole of the IF-THEN-ELSE structure inside the WHILE loop is therefore

```
IF the search word is equal the word at the midpoint THEN BEGIN
  Set Found to TRUE
END     { then begin }
ELSE BEGIN
  IF the search word is greater than the word at the midpoint THEN BEGIN
    Set First to midpoint plus 1
  END     { then begin }
  ELSE BEGIN
    Set Last to midpoint minus 1
  END;    { else begin }
END;    { else begin }
```

Look carefully at this setup to see how the flow of events is controlled by the IF-THEN-ELSE statements to avoid redundant checking of the search word against the word at the midpoint of the array.

The whole of the WHILE loop, including the statement to calculate the midpoint, will be

```
WHILE (First <= Last) AND (NOT Found) DO BEGIN
  MidPoint := (First+Last) DIV 2;
  IF WordToFind = SearchWords[MidPoint] THEN BEGIN
    Found := TRUE;
  END     { then begin }
  ELSE BEGIN
    IF WordToFind > SearchWords[MidPoint] THEN BEGIN
      First := MidPoint + 1;
    END     { then begin }
    ELSE BEGIN
      Last := MidPoint - 1;
    END;    { else begin }
  END;    { else begin }
END;    { while }
```

Assuming that First and Found are properly initialized before the loop above executes, this constitutes the bulk of the body of the Search function. However, one final consideration remains: if the word is found, Search is supposed to return the position at which the word is found to the calling procedure. As the statements above stand, no value is returned by the procedure at all, which makes the function rather solipsistic. Something must be assigned to Search before the function ends in order for the function to return its result. But what? And where? Looking at the WHILE loop above, you should see that after the loop terminates, one of two situations exists: either Found is TRUE, in which case the word is in the array, or it is FALSE, in which case it is not. Furthermore, if Found is TRUE then the position at which the word was found is in the variable MidPoint, since the condition that WordToFind = SearchWords[MidPoint] caused Found to be given the value TRUE, and because Found was TRUE, the loop stopped before changing MidPoint's value. So *after* the WHILE loop terminates, *if* Found is TRUE *then* Search should be assigned the value contained in MidPoint—the position of the word in the array. If Found is FALSE, on the other hand, Search should be assigned the value 0. Another IF-THEN-ELSE is in order, with the following form:

```
IF Found THEN BEGIN
  Search := MidPoint;
END     { then begin }
ELSE BEGIN
  Search := 0;
END;     { else begin }
```

Note that because Found is a BOOLEAN variable you can use it as a condition on the IF statement, since it can be evaluated to be TRUE or FALSE. You do not have to specify Found = TRUE.

Putting all of this together, the Search function is as follows:

```
FUNCTION Search(SearchWords : WordArray; Last : ArrayBounds;
          WordToFind : String) : ArrayBounds;
  { Returns the position at which WordToFind appears }
  { in SearchWords or 0 if it does not appear }
VAR First, MidPoint : ArrayBounds;
      Found : BOOLEAN;
BEGIN
  First := 1;
  Found := FALSE;
  WHILE (First <= Last) AND (NOT Found) DO BEGIN
    MidPoint := (First+Last) DIV 2;
    IF WordToFind = SearchWords[MidPoint] THEN BEGIN
      Found := TRUE;
    END     { then begin }
    ELSE BEGIN
      IF WordToFind > SearchWords[MidPoint] THEN BEGIN
        First := MidPoint + 1;
      END     { then begin }
      ELSE BEGIN
        Last := MidPoint - 1;
      END;     { else begin }
    END;     { else begin }
  END;     { while }
```

```
    IF Found THEN BEGIN
      Search := MidPoint;
    END     { then begin }
    ELSE BEGIN
      Search := 0;
    END;     { else begin }
  END;     { Search }
```

The Program as a Whole

In terms of the overall program format, this program requires only the addition of a function declaration and some modifications to the main program.

```
PROGRAM SearchForWords(INPUT,OUTPUT,TextFile);
  Constant declarations: StringLength, MaxWords, Blank, Blanks
  Type Declarations: String, ArrayBounds, StringBounds, WordArray
  Variable Declarations: Words, NumberOfWords, Position, TextFile
  Procedure Declarations:
  PROCEDURE ReadWord(VAR NextWord : String; VAR InputFile : TEXT);
    Variable Declarations: Letter, Counter
    Procedure Declarations:
    PROCEDURE SkipBlanks(VAR NextChar : CHAR; VAR InFile : TEXT);
      Variable Declarations: none
    BEGIN     { SkipBlanks }
      .
      .
      .
    END;     { SkipBlanks }
  BEGIN     { ReadWord }
    .
    .
    .
  END;     { ReadWord }
  PROCEDURE SubString(FromWord : String; Start, Stop : StringBounds;
           VAR ToWord : String);
    Variable Declarations: Counter, ToPos
  BEGIN     { SubString }
    .
    .
    .
  END;     { SubString }
  FUNCTION Capitalize(Lowerletter : CHAR) : CHAR;
    Variable Declarations: none
  BEGIN     { Capitalize }
    .
    .
    .
  END;     { Capitalize }
  PROCEDURE Standardize(VAR StandardWord : String);
    Variable Declarations: Counter, FirstLetter
  BEGIN     { Standardize }
    .
    .
    .
  END;     { Standardize }
```

```
    PROCEDURE Load(VAR FileWords : WordArray;
           VAR WordsInFile : ArrayBounds; VAR WordFile : TEXT);
      Variable Declarations: Word
    BEGIN     { Load }
       .
       .
       .
    END;     { Load }
    PROCEDURE Sort(VAR SortWords : WordArray; WordsInSort : ArrayBounds);
      Variable Declarations: Counter, Sorted, Temp
    BEGIN     { Sort }
       .
       .
       .
    END;     { Sort }
    FUNCTION Search(SearchWords : WordArray; Last : ArrayBounds;
         WordToFind : String) : ArrayBounds;
      Variable Declarations: First, MidPoint, Found
    BEGIN     { Search }
       .
       .
       .
    END;     { Search }
  BEGIN     { SearchForWords }
    Load(Words,NumberOfWords,TextFile);
    Sort(Words,NumberOfWords);
    WRITE('Enter a word, and I will tell you if it appears in the text: ');
    ReadWord(UsersWord,INPUT);
    Standardize(UsersWord);
    Position := Search(Words,NumberOfWords,UsersWord);
    IF Position > 0 THEN BEGIN
      WRITELN('The word was found in the text at position ',Position:1);
    END     { then begin }
    ELSE BEGIN
      WRITELN('The word was not found in the text');
    END;     { else begin }
  END.     { SearchForWords }
```

SUMMING UP THE PROGRAM

All of the programming constructs and statements required to complete the program are very familiar to you by now, and so you should have little trouble writing the program. The important concept in this chapter is not the language features necessary to write the program, but the algorithm underlying the binary search and the means by which it is implemented in Pascal.

This is a good place to remind you that your program should be well commented and provide friendly and informative messages for the user. Be sure to set up your program so that it offers a brief explanation to the user of what it does, and prints a clear and friendly message at the end of the search indicating whether or not the word was found in the text.

NICETIES

Determining Frequency

While the binary search procedure indicates whether or not a word is found in the text, it gives no idea how many times the word occurs. However, it is easy to determine the frequency with which a word occurs in the text once it has been found, since now that the words in the array are in aphabetical order, all of the occurrences of a given word appear together in the array.

In this section you will see how to write a procedure named "Occurrence" that will enable the program to determine the frequency of a word in the array. This procedure will call on Search to determine if the word appears in the text and then find the first and last positions in the array at which the search word appears. Given this information, it is easy to determine the frequency by a simple subtraction operation. For the sake of generality, the procedure will provide the positions of the first and last occurrence of the search word to the calling procedure, and let the calling procedure do the arithmetic to determine the frequency. As you will see in the next chapter, the locations of the first and last occurrence of the word in the array is information that can be used in other ways as well.

Like the function Search, the Occurrence procedure needs the array, the search word, and the number of words in the array, to be sent to it as parameters by the main program (if only because the Occurrence procedure must pass them along to the Search procedure); and since it uses these variables but doesn't alter them, they can be passed as Value parameters. In addition, parameters in which the information that the Occurrence procedure provides to *its* caller must be included. The procedure, of course, will provide to its caller the locations of the first and last occurrences of the word in the array, and so two parameters of type *ArrayBounds* are necessary. These must be VAR parameters, since the values given to them within the Occurrence procedure must be available to the caller after the Occurrence procedure finishes executing.

The call to the Occurrence procedure will look like this:

```
Occurrence(Words,NumberOfWords,UsersWord,First,Last);
```

and the heading on the procedure will be

```
PROCEDURE Occurrence(OccurrenceWords : WordArray;
        WordsInOccurrence : ArrayBounds; WordToCount : String;
        VAR FirstOccurrence,LastOccurrence : ArrayBounds);
```

If the search word is found, then after Occurrence terminates First and Last will contain the slots in the Words array at which the first and last occurrences of the word are stored. If the search word is not found in the array, Occurrence will have set First and Last to 0 to indicate this fact.

Within the Occurrence procedure, the very first thing that needs to be done is to invoke Search to find out where the search word appears in the array, if at all. The statement to invoke Search is

```
Position := Search(OccurrenceWords,WordsInOccurrence,WordToCount);
```

where **Position** is a variable of type *ArrayBounds* that is declared locally within Occurrence. After Search finishes executing, control returns to Occurrence, and the position at which the word was found in the array (or 0 if it was not found) is stored in the variable **Position**. The Occurrence procedure must now determine whether or not the search word was found in the array. If it was not found, the variables **FirstOccurrence** and **LastOccurrence** should also be given the value 0, and Occurrence should terminate. Otherwise, the Occurrence procedure can proceed to determine the number of times the search word appears in the array.

Assuming that the word is found, what steps need to be taken? Two facts are important here: first, all occurrences of the same word in the array will appear contiguously, and if more than one occurrence exists, Search may not find the first one first. Consider the following situation. A portion of a sorted array might look like this:

```
.
.
.
[23] BALLOON
[24] BAMBOO
[25] BAMBOO
[26] BAMBOO
[27] BANDANA
.
.
.
```

If the array is searched for the word BAMBOO, and the entire array contains 464 words, the word will be found at position 25 and not at position 23, where it first appears, since the search will proceed as follows:

Pass	First	Last	Position of word examined (MidPoint)
1	1	464	232
2	1	231	116
3	1	115	58
4	1	57	29
5	1	28	14
6	15	28	21
7	22	28	25 ← *found*

Given all this, how does the Occurrence procedure go about finding the first and last occurrence of the word in the array? The solution is brute force: the program must first go *backwards* through the array from the position at which the word was found to find the first appearance, and then go *forwards* from the position at which the word was found to find the last appearance.

In order to go backwards through the array to find the first occurrence, the computer must compare the search word to the words at successively lower positions in the array until it finds the first word that *does not* match the search word. Only then does it know that the first appearance of the search word in the array is the *next* word in the list.

The programming statements to accomplish this appear below:

```
FirstOccurrence := Position - 1;
StillEqual := TRUE;
WHILE (FirstOccurrence > 0) AND (StillEqual) DO BEGIN
  IF WordToCount = OccurrenceWords[FirstOccurrence] THEN BEGIN
    FirstOccurrence := FirstOccurrence - 1;
  END     { then begin }
  ELSE BEGIN
    StillEqual := FALSE;
  END;     { else begin }
END;     { while }
FirstOccurrence := FirstOccurrence + 1;
```

Notice that this loop follows the familiar pattern for moving through an array when you may want to stop before reaching the end—a check that the subscript does not move beyond the end of the array plus a BOOLEAN flag to stop the loop if certain conditions are met before reaching the end of the array constitute the condition on the loop.

The rationale behind the set of statements above needs to be understood, because it is derived from careful consideration of all the possibilities. First of all, since it is known that the word appears at position Position in the array, the search for the first occurrence can begin with the word at the position *prior* to Position in the array (Position − 1). So a counter variable (FirstOccurrence) is set to that value, to be used as a subscript to the array. A BOOLEAN variable, StillEqual, is set to TRUE, and will be set to FALSE within the loop when the word in the array does not equal the search word; this technique should begin to be familiar by now. You might think that a REPEAT-UNTIL loop should be used here, since you will want to compare at least one word with the search word, and so the loop will be executed at least once. But there *is* a situation in which the loop should not execute: where Position is 1. This would make FirstOccurrence equal to 0 the first time through the loop, and when the program attempts to access OccurrenceWords[0], an error will result, since OccurrenceWords[0] does not exist. So the condition must be checked *before* the loop is entered, even for the first time.

Within the loop, if the word in the indicated position in the array equals the search word, one is subtracted from FirstOccurrence. Again, this makes it necessary to check that FirstOccurrence is greater than 0 each subsequent time the loop is entered, because it is possible that if the search word is found at, say, position 3 in the array, but the words in positions 1 and 2 are also equal to the search word, FirstOccurrence could become 0. For the same reasons given above, this situation must be avoided within the loop.

StillEqual is used to provide a means to know when the word being compared to the search word within the loop does not equal the search word. When this happens, the loop should stop, since this indicates that the first occurrence of the search word in the array must be the previous word checked. StillEqual, then, simply gives the program a way of knowing when a word other than the search word has been encountered in the array. When this happens, of course, FirstOccurrence will have as its value the position of the word that did not equal the search word. This means that the word in the *next* position in the array—the one below the word most recently compared to the search word—is the first occurrence of the search word in the array. So after the loop terminates, one is added to FirstOccurrence, so that it can be used as a subscript to get to this first occurrence of the search word in the array.

After the first occurrence of the search word in the array has been found, it remains to find the last occurrence. The process for doing so is the reverse of the process above: it simply moves in the opposite direction in the array. The statements are as follows:

```
LastOccurrence := Position + 1;
StillEqual := TRUE;
WHILE (LastOccurrence <= WordsInOccurrence) AND (StillEqual) DO BEGIN
  IF WordToCount = OccurrenceWords[LastOccurrence] THEN BEGIN
    LastOccurrence := LastOccurrence + 1;
  END     { then begin }
  ELSE BEGIN
    StillEqual := FALSE;
  END;     { else begin }
END;     { while }
LastOccurrence := LastOccurrence - 1;
```

Of course, now the concern is not that FirstOccurrence might become 0, but that LastOccurrence might exceed WordsInOccurrence, and, again, allow for an attempt to access an element of the array that has not been filled. One is added to LastOccurrence instead of subtracting one from it each time through the loop, and after the loop terminates, one is subtracted since the search word will have been overshot by one position.

The whole of the Occurrence procedure looks like this:

```
PROCEDURE Occurrence (OccurrenceWords : WordArray;
            WordsInOccurrence : ArrayBounds; WordToCount : String;
            VAR FirstOccurrence, Last Occurrence : ArrayBounds);
VAR Position : ArrayBounds;
  StillEqual : BOOLEAN;
BEGIN
  Position :=Search(OccurrenceWords,WordsInOccurrence,WordToCount);
  IF Position = 0 THEN BEGIN { word not found }
    FirstOccurrence := 0;
    LastOccurrence := 0;
  END     { then begin }
```

```
        ELSE BEGIN      { word found }
          FirstOccurrence := Position - 1;
          StillEqual := TRUE;
          WHILE (FirstOccurrence > 0) AND (StillEqual) DO BEGIN
            IF WordToCount = OccurrenceWords[FirstOccurrence] THEN BEGIN
              FirstOccurrence := FirstOccurrence - 1;
            END      { then begin }
            ELSE BEGIN
              StillEqual := FALSE;
            END;      { else begin }
          END;      { while }
          FirstOccurrence := FirstOccurrence + 1;
          LastOccurrence := Position + 1;
          StillEqual := TRUE;
          WHILE (LastOccurrence <= WordsInOccurrence) AND (StillEqual) DO BEGIN
            IF WordToCount = OccurrenceWords[LastOccurrence] THEN BEGIN
              LastOccurrence := LastOccurrence + 1;
            END      { then begin }
            ELSE BEGIN
              StillEqual := FALSE;
            END;      { else begin }
          END;      { while }
          LastOccurrence := LastOccurrence - 1;
        END;      { else begin }
      END;      { Occurrence }
```

To be sure you understand how these statements work, consider the following trace of what would happen if, given the array shown earlier, BAMBOO were found in position 25 by Search. Since Position is not 0, the statements given above to find the first and last occurrences of the search word in the array will be executed. FirstOccurrence is then set to Position − 1, which is 24, and StillEqual is set to TRUE. Then, the condition on the WHILE loop is checked. FirstOccurrence is greater than 0, *and* StillEqual is set to TRUE, so the whole condition is determined to be true and the loop is entered. The search word is now compared to the word at position 24, which is BAMBOO. Because the condition on the IF-THEN-ELSE statement is true, the THEN part of the statement is now executed, thus subtracting 1 from FirstOccurrence and giving the value 23. The ELSE part of the statement is skipped, so control returns to the top of the loop, where the condition is checked again. FirstOccurrence is still greater than 0, and StillEqual is still true; so the loop is entered again. This time, however OccurrenceWords[23], which is BALLOON, does not equal the search word, BAMBOO, and so the ELSE part of the IF-THEN-ELSE statement is executed. This sets StillEqual to FALSE. At the top of the loop once again, the condition is determined to be false, since StillEqual is now FALSE. So, the loop terminates. One is then added to the current contents of FirstOccurrence, which is 23, thus giving FirstOccurrence a final value of 24, which is the position of the first occurrence of BAMBOO in the array. Next, LastOccurrence gets the value 26, StillEqual (which, having completed its work in the loop above, can be re-used here) is set to TRUE, and the second WHILE loop is encountered. The condition is determined to be true, and the loop is entered. Since the search word equals the word stored in OccurrenceWords[26], 1 is added to LastOccurrence, giving it the value 27. At the top of the loop, the condition is still true, and so the loop is entered once again. But WordToCount is not equal to OccurrenceWords[27], which is BANDANA, so instead of adding 1 to LastOccurrence, StillEqual is set to FALSE. When the condition on the loop is checked this time around, the FALSE value of StillEqual causes the loop to terminate. Finally, 1 is subtracted from LastOccurrence so that it contains the value 26, which is the last position in the array at which the word BAMBOO occurs.

This completes the action of the procedure Occurrence. When the procedure terminates, and control returns to the main program, how does the main program go about determining the frequency of the search word in the array, given the first and last positions? First of all, after the main program calls Occurrence, it must check to be sure that the word was found at all. If it was not, First and Last will have the value 0, and so the program can simply check the contents of First or Last—there is no need to check both—to be sure the word is found. If so, it will print the frequency. Now the frequency can be easily determined from the positions of the first and last occurrences with the formula

```
(Last-First) + 1
```

In the BAMBOO example above, this would yield (26 − 24) + 1, which is 3, the proper number. An expression like this one can appear in a WRITELN statement, so the main program can include a statement following the call to Occurrence like

```
WRITELN('The word appears in the text ',(Last-First) + 1:1,' times. ');
```

Recursion

Recursion is a fundamental concept in computer science. In terms of programming, recursion is the situation in which a *procedure calls itself.*

Recursion is a difficult concept but one which is readily exemplified by the binary search. Note that in the process of performing the binary search, the same search process (finding the middle element and checking its value against the search word) is performed over and over again. The only difference between one search and the next is the portion of the array that is searched; the process remains the same.

To see how the recursive version of the binary search works, consider first a modification of the statements you have already seen to perform the search:

```
IF First > Last THEN BEGIN
  Search := 0;
END     { then begin }
ELSE BEGIN
  MidPoint := (First+Last) DIV 2;
  IF WordToFind = SearchWords[MidPoint] THEN BEGIN
    Search := MidPoint;
  END     { then begin }
```

```
    ELSE BEGIN
      IF WordToFind > SearchWords[MidPoint] THEN BEGIN
        search for WordToFind in
          SearchWords[MidPoint+1] to SearchWords[Last]
      END     { then begin }
      ELSE BEGIN
        search for WordToFind in
          SearchWords[First] to SearchWords[MidPoint-1]
      END;     { else begin }
    END;     { else begin }
  END;     { else begin }
```

Given First and Last, the boundaries of the array to be searched, this piece of code first examines their values to ensure that the array is not empty. If it is, the word has not been found and Search (the function name) is set to 0 to indicate this fact. Otherwise, the search proceeds along the lines outlined earlier in this chapter. The difference here is that when the search word is not equal to the word at position MidPoint, rather than adjusting the value of First or Last, the instructions are to perform the search again on the appropriate section of the array.

Suppose that the statements above constitute the body of the Search function. Since these statements perform a *single* search of the array, these same statements can be invoked again in order to perform the parts of the code above that state "search for WordToFind in SearchWords[MidPoint+1] to SearchWords[Last]" and "search for WordToFind in SearchWords[First] to SearchWords[MidPoint−1]." This means that the Search function would be

```
FUNCTION Search(SearchWords : WordArray; WordToFind : String;
      First,Last : ArrayBounds) : ArrayBounds;
VAR MidPoint : ArrayBounds;
  BEGIN
    IF First > Last THEN BEGIN
      Search := 0;
    END     { then begin }
    ELSE BEGIN
      MidPoint := (First+Last) DIV 2;
      IF WordToFind = SearchWords[MidPoint] THEN BEGIN
        Search := MidPoint;
      END     { then begin }
      ELSE BEGIN
        IF WordToFind > SearchWords[MidPoint] THEN BEGIN
          Search := Search(SearchWords,MidPoint+1,Last);
        END     { then begin }
        ELSE BEGIN
          Search := Search(SearchWords,First,MidPoint-1);
        END;     { else begin }
      END;     { else begin }
    END;     { else begin }
END;     { Search }
```

This version of the Search function is recursive because it calls itself. By considering how this version of the Search function works, you can get an idea of what recursion is all about.

Consider an invocation of the Search function above, using the example from the beginning of this chapter in which the word PEOPLE is searched for in the following list:

[1] AID
[2] ALL
[3] COME
[4] FOR
[5] GOOD
[6] IS
[7] NOW
[8] OF
[9] PARTY
[10] PEOPLE
[11] THE
[12] THE
[13] THEIR
[14] TIME
[15] TO
[16] TO

The function above can be called with the statement

```
Position := Search(Words,UsersWord,1,NumberOfWords);
```

Notice that in this version of the Search function, the slot number of the first item in the array to be examined must be passed to the function as well as the slot number of the last item.

In this example, Words contains the 16 words given above, UsersWord contains the word PEOPLE, and NumberOfWords is 16. When the function is first called, then, within the function Search, First contains the value 1 and Last contains 16. The function checks that First is not greater than Last and then proceeds with the search. MidPoint is 8, and WordToFind (which contains PEOPLE) does not equal SearchWords[8] (OF), so the function goes on to determine if WordToFind is greater than SearchWords[8]. It is, and so the following happens: the value assigned to the Search function (the value it will return to the original caller) is set to be the value returned by the Search function, *with the parameters indicated*. At this point, the execution of Search is suspended and the function that it calls—which just happens to be Search itself—begins executing.

When a procedure or function calls itself, the call works just as a call to any other procedure or function would. Execution of the caller is suspended and the callee takes over. When the callee terminates, control is returned to the caller and its execution resumes.

So Search begins executing again, but this time its parameters are different. Specifically, this time First gets the value 9 instead of 1. Then the function starts executing as usual. First is less than Last and so the function continues on to compute a value for MidPoint, which comes out to be 12; WordToFind is compared to THE, found not to be equal, and then found not to be greater. So the statement inside the final ELSE-BEGIN-END pair is executed, setting the value to be returned by *the current invocation of Search* to be whatever result is returned by the function call on the right of the assignment operator. That call happens to be Search, so this next incarnation of Search's execution is suspended and Search starts executing again. This time First is 9 (its value in the calling function) and Last is MidPoint – 1, which is 11. Search determines that First is not greater than Last, and so computes the new midpoint value of 10. WordToFind is found to be equal to SearchWords[MidPoint]. What happens here is that 10 is assigned as the value returned by the function. Now, for the first time, an incarnation of Search terminates (the rest of the calls are suspended, waiting for results from the function they, in turn, called). This means that the value 10 is returned to its caller. Its caller, you recall, is the *second-to-last* incarnation of Search, which called the function with First at 9 and Last at 11. Now that the result of this call has been obtained, this incarnation of Search continues executing. The value returned by the call to Search is thus assigned as the value to be returned from *this* incarnation of the Search function, and then this incarnation terminates since the end of the function is reached. Its result, in turn, is returned to its caller, the first incarnation of Search. The first incarnation of Search takes this value and of course assigns it as its return value, returns it and terminates. Finally, back in the original calling program, the value returned by the first incarnation of Search (10) is assigned to Position, and the process is complete.

The graphic representation of the sequence of events may help to understand the process outlined above. The arrows show the flow of control through various calls to the Search function.

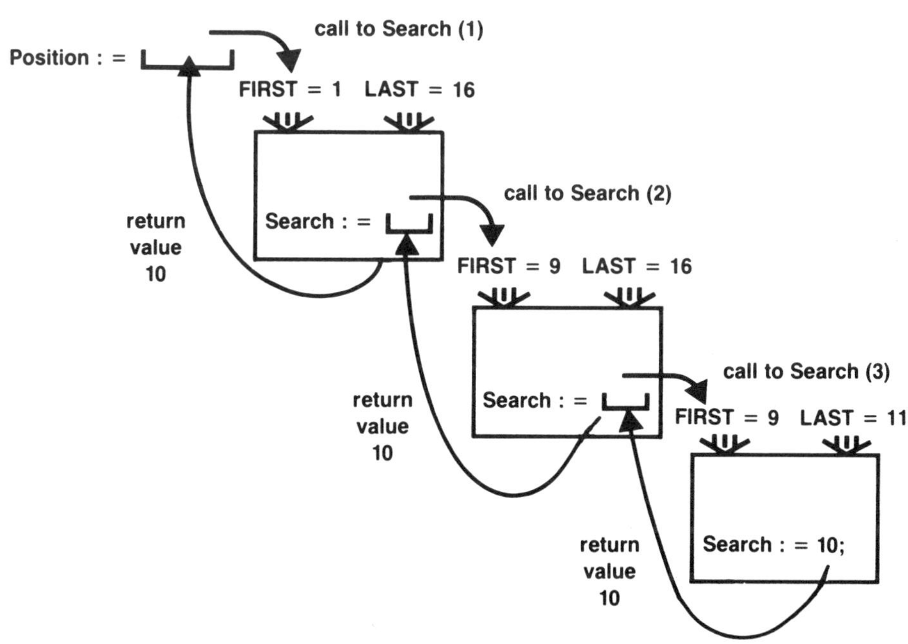

Be aware that recursion is a difficult concept to grasp the first time around.

The example above shows *direct recursion*, a situation where a procedure or function calls itself. *Indirect recursion* is also possible: if procedure (or function) P calls procedure Q, and procedure Q in turns calls procedure P, the recursion is said to be indirect. Indirect recursion requires a special Pascal construct to implement, since in this situation it is impossible to declare a procedure prior to the declaration of a procedure that calls it (that is, you can define P before Q or Q before P, but not both, as the situation described above would require). See Appendix D for a description of the FORWARD statement, which provides a way around this.

APPLICATIONS AND CONSIDERATIONS

Efficiency Considerations

A primary consideration when searching any large body of data is the efficiency of the algorithm that does the searching. The binary search, happily, is one of the most efficient methods for searching ordered data that exists. The efficiency of a searching (like a sorting) algorithm is generally measured in terms of the average number of comparisons required to locate an item. For a binary search, the number of comparisons that must be made can be calculated by determining the $log_2 n$, where n is the number of items that are being searched. For those of you who have forgotten what logarithms are, $log_2 n$ is simply the power to which 2 is raised to yield n. So if your **Words** array contains 100 words, then the maximum number of comparisons required to find a given word will be 7, since 2^7 is 128 (the value closest to and greater than 100 that is a power of 2). If you have 1000 words in your array, then the maximum number of comparisons required to find any item is 10, since 2^{10} is 1024 (the value closest to and greater than 1000 that is a power of 2). As the number of items to be searched gets larger and larger, the number of comparisons required inches up more and more slowly, and so a binary search is very efficient for large amounts of data.

Search methods that are more efficient than the binary search (and there are not many) are typically very complex and require additional storage to implement. Thus the binary search is one of the best search strategies available, both in terms of efficiency and ease of programming.

Spelling Checkers

Now that you are familiar with the binary search and searching in general, you can imagine how many general utility programs are implemented. For instance, many computer systems have available to their users a program to do a spelling check on any document that the user has stored on disk. These programs work very much along the lines of programs you have already written. The program will have available to it a dictionary of words, possibly stored in an array very much like the **Words** array. Typically, these dictionaries contain only a sub-set of the words in the English language because of the large amount of storage required to represent every word in the language in main memory.[2] Then the program reads the user's file, just as the programs in this text read a file, word by word. As each word is read in, it is used as a "search word" into the dictionary. If the word is found in the dictionary, it is assumed that the word is spelled correctly. If it is not found, then the word is assumed to be spelled incorrectly and some message to this effect is given to the user. The output of some spelling checkers consists of a listing of potentially misspelled words, whereas fancier programs will reprint the text and highlight misspelled words in some way.

Most spelling checkers allow the user to add words to the dictionary. The user typically stores the words he or she wants to add to the dictionary in a file, and the spelling checker program then reads this file and adds each of the words in it to the dictionary. The words may be inserted into the dictionary in their proper alphabetic sequence, or they may be held in a second array that can be searched later when some word is not found in the original list. This facility is convenient because texts often contain jargon words, place and proper names, and other specialized words that would not appear in a conventional dictionary.

Since many texts that are entered into machine-readable form are intended as input to a text formatter, often the text will contain formatting commands. Many spelling checkers see these commands as misspelled words and generate reams of useless output. Other spelling checkers are more sophisticated and can recognize certain input items as text formatting commands (at least, the formatting commands of a particular text formatter).

EXERCISES

1. Modify the program outlined in this chapter to prompt the user for search words and issue a message that the word was or was not found in the text, until the user signals that he or she wants to stop.

2. Modify the program outlined in this chapter to incorporate the Occurrence procedure described in the Niceties section. The program should prompt the user for a search word and print the frequency or else a message that the word does not appear in the text.

3. Do exercise 2, but have the program continue the process as long as the user wants to.

4. Modify the program to implement the Search function as a recursive function, as shown in the Niceties section of the chapter.

5. (A bit more difficult.) Modify the program to print a *frequency dictionary* of the words in the text, using the Occurrence procedure outlined in the Niceties section of the chapter.

A frequency dictionary is a listing of each *distinct* word in the text, together with its frequency. To do this, you will need to call Occurrence repeatedly, each time passing it as the search word parameter the next distinct word in the text; this would be an element of the **Words** array. Start with the word in position 1. After the call to Occurrence, print the word and its frequency. On the next call to Occurrence, pass as the search word the word

2. There are sophisticated programming techniques that allow a program to search through data stored on disk without bringing it into main memory, and many spelling checkers use these methods to avoid storing an entire dictionary in main memory.

in position Last + 1, where **Last** is the value provided by Occurrence on the previous call. Since **Last** would at this point indicate where the last occurrence of the first word appears in the array, the word in the next slot must be the next distinct word in the text. Continue this process until all of the distinct words in the text have been processed.

6. (More difficult.) Modify the program so that it reads in *two* texts, and provides a list of all the words that appear in the first text but not in the second. To do this, the words in the first text should be used as search words into the second text. Print any word that is not found in the second text. Be sure to indicate *only once* that a given word does not appear in the second text.

7. (Still more difficult.) Do exercise 6, but print the words that are not found in the second text in alphabetical order.

8. (More difficult.) Modify the program so that it reads a file that contains *pairs* of words. Each pair consists of a word in two different languages—thus, the file contains a small "dictionary." Then read in a second file containing a text in one of these two languages, and provide a word-by-word translation of the text into the second language. (At worst, you will get a sense of the difficulties involved in machine translation by doing this exercise!)

9. (More difficult.) If you have a machine-readable dictionary available to you, use it to implement the spelling checker program discussed in the Applications and Considerations section of this chapter. Note that the program will read the dictionary into the array, but not the user's text—only a word at a time needs to be available from the latter.

You can enhance the program by enabling the user to specify a list of his or her own words for the dictionary. These can be read in and stored in a second array, and the sort and search routines can then be used for this array as well. Note that this means that the second array must have type *WordArray* (since Sort and Search both require an array of type *WordArray*), and so the second array must be as large as the first one. This is fairly wasteful since it is doubtful the user will specify a large number of words. A way around this is to add the user's words to the end of the original listing of words in the array **Words** and then call Sort, which will alphabetize the array and thus incorporate the user's words into the original dictionary.

10. (More difficult.) Do exercise 9, but implement the procedure outlined below to enable you to reduce the size of the dictionary.

To reduce the amount of memory required for storage, many dictionaries contain only the singular form of nouns whose plurals are formed regularly. When the program searches the dictionary for words from the user's input, if the word is not found the program applies procedures to remove endings from the word (if the endings are present) and then use the modified version of the word as a search word to see if its "root" form exists in the dictionary. For instance, a word such as "book," which forms its plural regularly (by adding *-s*), would be stored in the dictionary only in the singular form. If "books" is read in from the user's text, it is not found in the dictionary. However, seeing the *-s* ending, the program can remove it and search for the resulting string ("book"), which it will find. A general procedure for suffix removal can be applied for words that form plurals by adding *-s, -es* ("couches"), or by deleting a final *-y* and adding *-ies* ("jellies"). That procedure is (1) search for the input word; if not found, (2) remove *-s,* search for the word; if not found, (3) remove *-e,* search for the word; if not found, (4) change *-i* to *-y,* search for the word; if not found, fail.

Verbs whose present and past participles are formed regularly can be stored in their infinitive form and procedures similar to the one above can be applied to remove *-ed* and *-ing* endings. When a word is not found in the dictionary and it ends with *-ed,* do the following: (1) remove *-d,* search for the word (this will find "bake"); if not found, (2) remove *-e,* search for the word; if not found, (3) change *-i* to *-y,* search for the word; if not found, (4) remove the second consonant of a doubled consonant at the end of the word, search for the word; if not found, fail. If the word not found in the dictionary ends with *-ing,* do the following: (1) remove *-ing,* add *-e* (this will find "bake"), search for the word; if not found (2) remove *-e,* search for the word; if not found, (3) remove the second consonant of a doubled consonant at the end of the word, search for the word; if not found, fail.

You may want to add some constraints for suffix removal—for instance, never remove a suffix from a word when removal will yield a string of two or fewer characters. This will prevent removing *-ing* from "sing" and *-s* from "as." But note that to ensure that the procedures do not improperly remove endings, your dictionary should contain words like "sing," "as," and others in which *-s, -es, -ed,* and *-ing* are not proper suffixes. These words will then be found in the preliminary search and the program will never attempt to remove the suffixes. The dictionary must also contain irregular forms, such as "sang," so that these will not be regarded as misspelled words when the searching process fails.

Note that the Length and SubString procedures given in Chapter Eight are very useful for this exercise.

11
Generating a Word Frequency Graph

In the last few chapters you have learned how to store, standardize, sort, and search a text. Given these tools, you are now prepared to begin extracting information about the text that can be used to help formulate and substantiate hypotheses about its form and content. In this chapter and the chapters that follow, you will learn methods for extracting several types of information from a text by building on the basis provided by the loading, sorting, and searching procedures.

This chapter deals with word distribution. The output of the program you will write will be a graph that shows the number of times a user-chosen word appears in different segments of the text. The idea behind such an operation is that by looking at the pattern of a word's distribution across a text, shifts in the importance of the word in various parts of the text are revealed. What this says about the text is dependent upon what it is the user feels the word represents. For instance, a word or group of words might be regarded as indicative of a particular theme. To use a simple example, suppose that the user were interested in exploring the theme of death in a text. He or she would then identify the words in the text that evoke that theme—perhaps words such as "death," "dying," "grave," "shroud," and the like.[1] A distribution of these words across the text

1. A dictionary of the words in the text could provide the starting point for determining words that are indicative of a certain theme. A *concordance,* which is described in Chapter Thirteen, would provide an even better basis.

might show that early in the text words in this group appear relatively frequently, but that their use then drops off until some later point in the text, where they appear again in relatively large numbers. Following this, their use may drop off again, and they may reappear in large numbers near the text's conclusion. Looking at this pattern, the user can first of all conclude that the theme of death is probably more important in the segments of the text where the words appear frequently than in the remaining segments of the text. This in itself can tell the user something that he or she did not know, or perhaps only suspected, about the way in which the theme is used within the text. Furthermore, the pattern may reveal something about the *structure* of the text as a whole. If the theme of death is important in the text, and it appears, say, at the beginning, middle, and end, this might indicate that the text is built around three key scenes or passages that are distributed symmetrically across it.

The words involved in a distribution need not be only theme words. You might, for instance, be interested in the way images, which often create mood and atmosphere in a text, are used. For example, you could examine a distribution of all words that function within a text as images of darkness, such as "dark," "darkness," "blackness," and the like. It might also be interesting to compare the distribution of such images to a distribution of images of light or brightness, to see if they occur at different places in the text, or in the same places, or near to or far from one another in the text. This kind of information can help to reveal the way in which the author manipulates mood and atmosphere in the text and how changes in mood and atmosphere affect the reader.

Similarly, words which belong to a particular word class or type can be distributed in ways that reveal linguistic or stylistic shifts within a text. A distribution of action verbs might show that these words occur more prevalently in one or more segments of the text, which in turn might indicate something about style and theme in those segments. A distribution of verbs in general might show that they occur more frequently in certain portions of the text, indicating that sentences are probably shorter and description is less prevalent. Concentrations of adjectives or adverbs in certain parts of the text also indicate a shift in style and tone. The types of words or word classes that can be distributed are limitless and depend solely on what the researcher is interested in examining in a text.

While examination of the text by hand can reveal the same things as a computer-generated distribution can, nonetheless the rapidity with which the analysis can be performed, especially for large texts, means that it is more likely that it will be performed at all. Many times it is difficult to see overall patterns of usage in a text, and it is here that computer-generated distributions can contribute most to the researcher's examination of a text. Of course, the method has certain constraints—for the program outlined in this chapter, all elements must be individual words, and no distinction is made between *homographs* (words that are spelled the same but have different meanings), such as "spring" and "leaves," both of which function as both noun and verb. However, a slightly more sophisticated program could handle phrases as well as words and provide some means to distinguish homographs. The Applications and Considerations section at the end of this chapter provides more information about the problem of homographs and word distribution in general.

Before going on to consider the new Pascal language features that are required for this program, several aspects of the problem for this chapter need to be discussed.

Dividing Up the Text

For the purposes of the distribution analysis, the text must be divided up into segments. The distribution analysis will indicate how many times the word or words under consideration occur in each segment. The first concern in writing this program, then, is determining just exactly what constitutes a segment of the text.

There are two ways to do this. First of all, the text can simply be divided into several segments of equal length, in terms of the number of words contained in each. The number of segments into which the text is divided can either be fixed within the program or indicated by the user when the program is running. This is the simplest solution to dividing the text, but it obviously ignores "natural" divisions within the text, such as chapters, paragraphs, and even sentences. With this method, it is likely that the dividing line between one segment and the next will fall in the middle of a sentence, and it would be a rare coincidence if a division fell at the end of a chapter. For a large text, and for the purposes of determining general patterns across the text, the exact point at which a segment ends is not overly important, since the idea is to see where a given word or group of words crop up.

Quite often, however, the researcher is interested in looking at the text in terms of its individual chapters, or wants the divisions to occur at specified points in the text so that each segment contains a definable scene or stanza, or whatever. The best way to enable the user to specify exactly where the divisions occur is to have him or her insert some symbol into the text file at these points, which the program can then regard as a signal that a segment is ending. This requires more work on the part of the user, but gives him or her more control over the process of dividing the text.

Because it is easy to implement, the basic program for this chapter will use the first method, which divides the text into segments of equal length. The means to implement the second method are discussed in the Niceties section at the end of the chapter.

Linear Position

The location of a word in the text can be defined by many means: it can be said to appear in the first chapter, or the fifth paragraph, or the sixty-third sentence, or it can be indicated by simply saying that it is the 462nd word in the text. This last method of locating a word is based on what is called its *linear position*, or its position in the "line" or string of words which, if placed side by side in ticker-tape fashion, would constitute the text in its original form. As each word is read into the program, its linear position is known, since the first word read in has linear position 1, the second word has linear position 2, and so on.

In this program, the linear position will be used to determine the location of a word in the text. Of course, when the array is sorted, it is no longer possible to determine the linear position of a word simply by noting its position in the array of words, and so the linear position of each word will have to be noted explicitly and stored along with the word. The means to do this are discussed in the section of this chapter on Elements of Pascal.

Histograms

The output of the program for this chapter is a graph depicting the distribution of a word across the text. It would be possible to simply print out the number of times the word appears in each segment of the text, but a graphic representation of the frequencies will show much more clearly and rapidly the fluctuations in the word's frequency among the various text segments. Clusters of occurrences will show themselves immediately, and the user can easily *see* the contrast in frequency between one segment and the next.

A histogram is a suitable type of graph for depicting word distribution across a text. A histogram is basically a bar graph, but it is laid on its side so that the top line or bar represents the frequency for the first text segment, the next line indicates the frequency for the second text segment, and so on. For example, suppose the word under consideration is determined within the program to appear the following number of times in the indicated segment (assuming the text is divided into ten segments):

Segment Number	Frequency
1	14
2	6
3	23
4	2
5	4
6	16
7	26
8	9
9	7
10	12

The following graph will be printed:

```
 1|**************
 2|******
 3|***********************
 4|**
 5|****
 6|****************
 7|**************************
 8|*********
 9|*******
10|************
```

In this histogram, each occurrence is represented by an asterisk, but you can use any symbol you like.

The Algorithm

The process of generating a frequency distribution graph will require loading and sorting the text, as you have already done, and then prompting the user for the word for which the graph is to be generated. Once it is ascertained that the word appears in the text, the next step is to determine how many times the word appears in each of the segments of the text. This accomplished, the graph can be generated. A more precise outline of the steps for this program is

1. Load the words in the text and their linear positions into the array of records.
2. Sort the words in the array into alphabetical order.
3. Read a word from the user and standardize it.
4. Determine the number of times that the word appears in each segment of the text.
5. Print a histogram representation of the frequency information (a distribution graph).

Steps 1, 2, and 3 have been implemented already. Implementing steps 4 and 5 will be the focus of this chapter.

To determine the segment of the text in which a given occurrence of a word appears (assuming the text is divided into segments of equal length), you can use the linear position of the word. In fact, you will see later that given the linear position of an occurrence of a word, you can perform some simple arithmetic to determine the segment in which the word falls. Of course, the text segment has to be determined for *each* occurrence of the word in the text. So an algorithm for step 4, above, is

1. For each occurrence of the word in the text, do the following:
   a. Calculate the text segment in which the word appears.
   b. Add one to a counter that is keeping track of the number of times the word appears in that segment.

This set of steps is specific enough to get started.

Step 5 of the general algorithm involves actually printing a histogram graph representing the number of occurrences of the word in each of the text segments. Assuming that a counter for each segment contains the number of occurrences for that segment, what needs to be done here is simply to print the number of asterisks indicated in each of the counters on a separate line. That is, if the counter for the first segment contains the value 14, then 14 asterisks should be printed on the first line; and if the counter for segment two contains the value 7, then 7 asterisks are printed on the second line; and so on for each text segment in order. More specifically, the algorithm is

1. For each text segment, do the following:
   a. For each occurrence tallied for this segment, do the following:
      (1) Print an asterisk.
   b. Go to a new line.

Neither of these algorithms is particularly complicated, and you will see that the programming statements required to implement them are similarly concise and straightforward.

ELEMENTS OF PASCAL

Records

An array is a means by which information that is of the same type can be grouped. For instance, you have seen arrays consisting of items of type CHAR and arrays consisting of items of the user-defined type, *String*. A *record* in Pascal is a means to group information as well, but instead of grouping a series of items all of the same type, a record groups items that are of different types. Unlike an array, a record does not create a series of identical items, but is used simply for grouping.

A record, like an array, is established in the Type Declarations section, in the following way:

```
TYPE WordRecord = RECORD
                    Word : String;
                    LinearPosition : ArrayBounds;
                  END;
```

This type declaration establishes a type of object that consists of two parts: a variable of type *String*, and a variable of type *ArrayBounds*.[2] In the Declarations section of the program, a name can be specified and given this type, as follows:

```
VAR WordInfo : WordRecord;
```

Like the declaration of an array name, this declaration establishes a name, Word Info, that refers to the *entire* object that consists of the two elements defined as parts of the type *WordRecord*. Also, like an array, you will rarely refer to the entire record all at once, but instead will refer to its individual pieces. With an array, of course, individual elements are referred to by giving the array name and a subscript indicating the position of the element in the array. With a record, individual elements are referred to by giving the record name, followed by a period, followed by the name assigned to that part of the record within the record definition in the Type Declarations section. So to refer to the *String* variable part of the record, you would use the name

```
WordInfo.Word
```

and to refer to the part of the record with type *ArrayBounds* you would use the name

```
WordInfo.LinearPosition
```

Each of these names refers to a specific variable of a particular type which may be manipulated like any variable of that type.

2. This example assumes that the types *String* and *ArrayBounds* have already been established in the Type Declarations section.

Given this, you may wonder what the advantage of using a record is. After all, Word and LinearPosition could be declared in the Declarations section of the program just as easily, and the only difference would be that the WordInfo prefix would not need to be added to their names to refer to these variables. The advantage of using records is basically twofold: first, records enable the programmer to explicitly group information that is associated, and second, records can be used in array declarations, as you will see below.

By the way, the record defined above is exactly what will be needed for this program. Each word must have associated with it its linear position, and by grouping the word and its linear position, the two become, conceptually, one item. However, variables of any type can be grouped into records, including, of course, variables with user-defined types such as records and arrays. All of this is explained more fully in the Niceties section at the end of this chapter.

One final note:

The name given to a variable that is part of a record can be the same as the name given to a variable in the Variable Declarations section of the program, with no confusion.

The reason there is no confusion is that the variable that is part of a record requires the prefix that is the record name to identify it, and the variable declared in the variable Declarations section of the program does not. So if you have the record definition given above and also declare a variable named Word in the VAR section, the first would be called WordInfo.Word and the other, simply Word.

Arrays of Records

The record defined above is sufficient for holding one word and its linear position, but of course the program must be able to accommodate perhaps thousands of words and their associated linear positions. But since a record is a user-defined type, and an array can consist of elements of any user-defined type, it is possible to set up an array of which each element is a record.

Suppose that you had defined the *WordRecord* type shown above in your program. Now, you can define another type like this:

```
WordArray = ARRAY[1..MaxWords] OF WordRecord;
```

This establishes a type that is an array consisting of individual elements, each of which itself is a record with two parts: a variable of type *String* and a variable of type *ArrayBounds*. Then the following can be specified within the Declarations section:

```
VAR Words : WordArray;
```

This declaration is identical to the one you have been using, except that *WordArray* is now defined as an array of records rather than an array of only *String*-type variables.

Note that when a record type is used to define the elements of the array, as *WordInfo* is in the example above, it may be the case that no variable in the VAR Declarations section of the program is given this type.

As you might guess, the first record in the array declared above has the name

```
Words[1]
```

The individual pieces of this record are referred to as

```
Words[1].Word
```

and

```
Words[1].LinearPosition
```

So, the only difference here is that the name of the record is the name of an array element. Again, Words[1].Word refers to a *String*-type variable and Words[1].LinearPosition refers to a variable with type *ArrayBounds*, and these may be used in any context where variables of their respective types are allowed.

CONSTRUCTING THE PROGRAM

The Main Program

To determine the location of the word in the text, the linear position must be known, and since the words in the array are rearranged into alphabetical order by the Sort procedure, the linear position must be kept with each word in the text so that it is available after the sorting is completed. This means that the linear position must be stored before the sorting is done, and that in the process of sorting the linear position must be kept with the word it is associated with.

Records can be used to keep a word associated with its linear position. That is, instead of storing only the word in the Words array, the word and its linear position will be stored together and later moved as a unit during the sorting process. So instead of an array of *String*-type variables, this program requires an array of elements each of which consists of a *String*-type variable *and* a variable of type *ArrayBounds*. Thus a record should be defined in the Type Declarations of the main program, as shown earlier:

```
TYPE WordRecord = RECORD
                    Word : String;
                    LinearPosition : ArrayBounds;
                  END;
```

and then the type *WordArray* should be re-defined as

```
WordArray = ARRAY[1..MaxWords] OF WordRecord;
```

The declaration of the **Words** array in the Variable Declarations section of the program remains the same, but it now describes a different object—an array of records.

Note that the variable **NumberOfWords** can still be used to keep track of the number of slots filled in the array.

The main program will, as usual, oversee the overall processes required to accomplish the task of generating a word frequency graph. As shown earlier, the steps to do this are

1. Load the words in the text and their linear positions into the array of records.
2. Sort the words in the array into alphabetical order.
3. Read a word from the user and standardize it.
4. Determine the number of times that the word appears in each segment of the text.
5. Print a histogram representation of the frequency information (a distribution graph).

This general outline describes the main program and as before, most of these steps will be implemented as separate procedures.

Implementing steps 1, 2, and 3 in the algorithm above presents no problem, since procedures already exist to perform steps 1 and 2, and step 3 is familiar enough by now. (Be sure that your program provides a message to the user that lets him or her know exactly what the program is doing.) Each of steps 4 and 5 can be handled with a separate procedure. The first of these, the procedure to determine the frequencies in each segment of the text, will provide to its caller the frequencies themselves, which will then be passed on to the graphing procedure and used to create a histogram graph. Some variable will have to be declared in the main program in which to store these frequencies. What sort of variable will be needed for this purpose? Well, the frequencies will be integer values, and so a type INTEGER variable is appropriate. But there will be a frequency value for each segment of the text, and so several integer variables will be needed. This suggests an array, which, you will find, is even more appropriate for the task since the frequencies for the first segment of the text can be stored in the first slot in the array, the frequencies for the second segment can be stored in the second slot, and so on. Thus an array of INTEGER-type variables, which has one slot for each segment of the text, will be shared by the main program and the procedure that determines the frequencies. The main program will send the empty array and expect it to be filled with the frequency information when the procedure terminates.

How many segments of the text will there be? This is up to the programmer, but whatever number is decided upon, it is a good strategy to declare the value as a constant at the beginning of the main program. Since the number of segments will be used to define the size of the array in which the frequencies will be stored and will appear at several other points in the program, it is worthwhile to make the number of segments a constant value so that it can be easily changed without requiring modifications to several statements within the program.

In general, the number of segments should be few enough to provide for a sufficient number of words in each segment so that clusters of occurrences will show up readily. For a text of a thousand words, ten segments of a hundred words each is reasonable, whereas dividing the text into 50 segments of 20 words each would probably yield a distribution where the frequencies are too dispersed to be very meaningful. But again, the number of segments is determined by how finely-tuned you want the distribution to be; for a word that appears very frequently in the text, 50 segments might not be too many at all.

The type of the array to hold the frequencies can be declared within the main program as follows:

```
TYPE TallyArray = ARRAY[1..NumberOfSegments] OF INTEGER;
```

where NumberOfSegments is a constant declared in the Constant Declarations section of the main program, defining the number of segments into which the text is divided. The array to actually hold the frequencies can then be declared in the Variable Declarations section of the program as

```
Tally : TallyArray;
```

Having called Load and Sort to read and alphabetize the array, and having read a word from the user and called Standardize to get it in a form appropriate for searching the array, the main program can move to steps 4 and 5 in the outline above by calling two procedures. The procedure to determine the frequency with which the user's word occurs in each segment of the text will need the Words array, the variable NumberOfWords, the user's word (stored in UsersWord), and the array Tally defined above, in order to operate. If the procedure to determine the frequencies is named Distribute, the call to the procedure will be

```
Distribute(Words,NumberOfWords,UsersWord,Tally);
```

The procedure to generate the frequency distribution graph will need only the Tally array in order to print the histogram, and so if this procedure is named Histogram, its call is

```
Histogram(Tally);
```

The whole of the main program is

```
BEGIN     { main program }
  Load(Words,NumberOfWords,TextFile);
  Sort(Words,NumberOfWords);
  WRITE('Enter a word for which a distribution graph will be printed: ');
  ReadWord(UsersWord,INPUT);
  Standardize(UsersWord);
  Distribute(Words,NumberOfWords,UsersWord,Tally);
  Histogram(Tally);
END.      { main program }
```

Before considering how to go about implementing the Distribute and Histogram procedures, some changes must be made to the Load, Sort, and Search procedures to accommodate the use of records in the Words array. This program will also use the Occurrence procedure outlined in the Niceties section of the previous chapter; similar changes must be made to this procedure.

Changes to the Load Procedure

The first thing that must be considered in Load and in all of the procedures in the program is that the type *WordArray* now refers to a different sort of object. The declaration in the Procedure Heading can remain as it is since the type has been redefined, but within the procedure, references to items within the array must be changed to refer to pieces of a record rather than simple array elements. This means that if the pseudonym for the Words array is FileWords within Load, the reference to FileWords[WordsInFile] (assuming WordsInFile is the pseudonym for NumberOfWords) that now exists within the procedure must be changed to FileWords[WordsInFile].Word, since when a word is stored in the array you are storing it in the Word piece of the record that is named FileWords[WordsInFile], not in the entire record. So you will use the statement

```
FileWords[WordsInFile].Word := Word;
```

instead of

```
FileWords[WordsInFile] := Word;
```

Note that when an array of records is passed to a procedure or function as a parameter, the fields of the component records are not re-named in the Procedure Heading. So, although the array itself may have a new name within the procedure or function, the names of the fields within the records are the same as in the original declaration of the component record type.

As pointed out earlier, there is no conflict between the name Word that is given to the *String*-type variable declared within the Load procedure and the name Word that represents part of a record in the FileWords array—the prefix is a part of the name for the piece of the record and clearly distinguishes it from the variable Word that is declared separately.

The perfect time to store the linear position of each word is as it is read in, since the linear position of the word is readily available at this point in the program. Therefore it is appropriate to perform this operation as the words are read and stored within the Load. All that needs to be done is to assign the linear position of the word to the LinearPosition part of the record in which the word is being stored. What is the linear position? It is indicated by the variable WordsInFile, since this variable counts the words as they are read in. So to store the linear position, the statement

```
FileWords[WordsInFile].LinearPosition := WordsInFile;
```

can be used. This statement should be inserted within the loop, at a point just after the word itself is stored in the array. Remember that while at this point the information stored in FileWords[WordsInFile].LinearPosition is redundant (the number stored there is the value of WordsInFile itself), after the array is sorted the linear position number will no longer be the same as the slot number in which a given word is stored.

These are the only changes that need to be made within Load.

Changes to the Sort Procedure

As in Load, it is necessary within Sort to realize that SortWords is now a pseudonym for an array of records, and that references to only the word part of those records must be specified in the appropriate way.

Within the innermost loop in the Sort procedure, each word is compared to the word that follows it in the array. Obviously, only the Word part of the record should be compared here, and so the statement that performs the comparison should be changed to reflect this:

```
IF SortWords[Counter].Word > SortWords[Counter+1].Word THEN ...
```

This does *not* apply to the statements that switch the words around, however.

When Sort switches words in the process of alphabetizing the Words array, both the words and their linear positions must be switched, and not just the words.

If this were not done, the whole point of storing the linear position in the first place would be lost. The idea of storing the linear positions is that if the words are rearranged, the linear position is still known because it is explicitly stored along with the word. If only the words were moved and not the linear positions, the numbers that are stored in the same array elements as the words would be meaningless.

What needs to be done is to move *both* the word and the linear position when a switch is made in the Sort procedure. In Pascal, this can be done quite easily, as follows:

```
Temp := SortWords[Counter];
SortWords[Counter] := SortWords[Counter+1];
SortWords[Counter+1] := Temp;
```

Now that SortWords refers to an array of records, the name SortWords[Counter] refers to *the entire record*, including both the Word and LinearPosition parts. But as always, such a statement is valid only if the variable on the left of the assignment operator has the same type as the variable on the right of the assignment operator. Now, the type of SortWords[Counter] is *WordRecord*, since each element of the array known as SortWords in this procedure has the type *Word-*

Record. In this case, the type does not match because Temp has been declared with type *String*, which was appropriate when the items being assigned to it were *String*-type variables. So *the declaration of* Temp *must be changed to give* Temp *the type WordRecord rather than String*, in order for the set of statements above to work. If Temp is left as a *String*-type variable, an error will be issued telling you something about type incompatibility.

A record may be referred to in its entirety only in a few contexts, and the set of assignment statements above illustrates one of them.

A whole record can be assigned to another record of the same type. It is not necessary to assign each of the fields within the record separately.

It is also possible to compare a whole record with another record of the same type, which would result in each piece of the first record being compared to its counterpart in the second. In Sort, only the Word part of a record is compared to the one that follows it in the array, since the only concern is that one word might be greater than the other. It is irrelevant whether or not the linear position stored in one record is greater than that stored in another; so it would be inappropriate to compare records here.

A word must be said about which records are considered to be of the same type. As with arrays,

---

In Pascal, only records whose type names are the same are considered to be of the same type, even if those records are structured exactly the same way.

So in the Sort procedure Temp must have the type *WordRecord* in order to be considered to be of the same type as SortWords[Counter]. You could not, for example, define a type such as

```
TYPE AnotherRecord = RECORD
                        Word : String;
                        LinearPosition : ArrayBounds;
                      END;
```

and then go on to assign Temp the type *AnotherRecord*, even though the records look alike and even contain internal names that are exactly the same.

Changes in the Search Function and Occurrence Procedure

The only changes that must be made to the Search function and Occurrence procedure are to the variable names, as shown above for Load and Sort. In both procedures, the search word is being compared not to the entire record, which contains both a word and an integer indicating the word's linear position, but to the Word part of the record only. So if the name SearchWords is the pseudonym for Words in the Search function, references to SearchWords[MidPoint] should be replaced by SearchWords[MidPoint].Word. Similarly, in Occurrence, references to OccurrenceWords[Counter] should be replaced by Occurrence-Words[Counter].Word.

The Distribute Procedure

Given the call shown above, the heading for Distribute will be

```
PROCEDURE Distribute(ListOfWords : WordArray; WordsInList : ArrayBounds;
        WordToDistribute : String; VAR TallyKeeper : TallyArray);
```

Note that the only VAR parameter is the TallyKeeper array, since it is the only variable to which modifications are made within the Distribute procedure that must be available to the main program after the procedure finishes executing.

The Distribute procedure implements step 4 in the overall algorithm, which was given earlier as

1. For each occurrence of the word in the text, do the following:
   a. Calculate the text segment in which the word appears.
   b. Add 1 to a counter that is keeping track of the number of times the word appears in that segment.

Within the Distribute procedure, then, the segment in which each occurrence of the user's word appears in the text must first be determined. To do this, the procedure must examine the linear position of each occurrence of the word. How does the program access each occurrence of the word in the array? First of all, the word must be found in the array. Then all of the instances of the word that appear in the array must be examined to determine their linear positions, which, of course, are stored with the words. As it turns out, procedures already exist not only to find the word, but also to determine the positions of the first and last occurrences of the word in the array.[3] The Distribute procedure, then, can simply call on Occurrence (which in turn calls on Search) to find the word and determine the positions of its first and last occurrence in the array. After this, it must determine that the values provided by Occurrence representing the positions of the first and last occurrences of the word are not 0, which would indicate that the word was not found in the array. If the word is found, however, it can look at the linear positions associated with each occurrence of the word and determine the segment in which the word appears.

If the first thing that Distribute does, then, is to call Occurrence, the value of the first and last positions of the word in the Words array can be used to enable access to each of the linear positions at which the word occurs, since the linear position is stored in the same record as the word itself. The linear posi-

3. The Occurrence procedure was set up to provide the positions of the first and last occurrences of a word rather than the frequency so that it would be generalizable to other tasks such as this one. It is sometimes difficult to foresee the potential uses of a procedure, but whenever possible, you should design a procedure so that it provides "raw" information to its caller so that the caller can decide what to do with it.

tions can then be used to determine the text segment in which each occurrence of the word appears.

How is the segment determined from the linear position? Suppose that you have a text of 1085 words, and have divided the text into 10 segments. By simply dividing 10 into 1085 it is easy to determine that each segment of the text contains 108 words (with a few left over—this will be discussed in a moment). So if the linear position of some occurrence of the word is between 1 and 108, the word falls in segment 1; if it is between 109 and 216, it is in segment 2, and so on. Fortunately, a tricky bit of arithmetic can compute the segment from the linear position in a single statement, so that you will not need a string of IF-THEN statements to determine the segment number. To do so, the program must know the number of words in each segment; so far, only the number of segments is available, in the constant NumberOfSegments. The first step, then, is to do the division necessary to provide the program with this information:

```
WordsInSegment := WordsInList DIV NumberOfSegments;
```

Note that the DIV operator is used instead of "/" so that any remainder from the division will be thrown out; this is necessary because the number of words in a given segment must be a whole number. WordsInSegment should be declared within the Distribute procedure with the INTEGER sub-range type *ArrayBounds*, since its value cannot validly exceed this range.

Given the number of words in each segment, the following statement can be used to calculate the segment in which a word stored in ListOfWords[58].Word (for example) appears:

```
Segment := (ListOfWords[58].LinearPosition DIV WordsInSegment) + 1;
```

Segment is another integer variable that is declared in Distribute. This is the tricky bit of arithmetic referred to above, and it deserves some attention to see how and why it works. The best way to figure out how it works is to try a few examples. Suppose that the linear position of the word is 272, which means that it appears in the second segment, using the 1085 word text and the 10 segments described above. 272 divided by 108 yields 1 when the remainder is thrown away as a result of the DIV operation. Adding 1 to this value yields 2, the number of the proper segment. If the linear position is 66, the result of (66 DIV 108) is 0, which added to 1 yields 1—again, the proper segment. Try this with any number between 1 and 1085, and you will see that the result is always correct.

Well, almost always. There is one situation for which this trick does not work. If the linear position is any of the numbers between 1081 and 1085, the segment will be determined to be segment number 11, which does not exist. In this case, you will have to fudge the result slightly so that these few extra words will be regarded as part of the final segment.[4] After the calculation above is per-

4. In reality, they are not, if each segment is looked upon as having 108 words. But there will never be more than nine extra words—or, more generally, one less than the number of segments—tacked onto the last segment, and this slight discrepancy should not skew the distribution very much.

formed, the program will simply have to check if the segment number determined by the calculation is greater than the number of segments into which the text is divided, and if it is, reset it to be the last segment. In Pascal, this is stated as follows:

```
IF Segment > NumberOfSegments THEN BEGIN
  Segment := NumberOfSegments;
END;     { then begin }
```

Having determined the segment in which the word occurs, the information must be recorded. Recall that the Tally array, which is known as TallyKeeper in the Distribute procedure, consists of a series of type INTEGER variables that are to keep track of the number of times the word appears in each segment of the text. The first slot in the array will hold the number of times the word appears in the first segment, the second slot will hold the number of times the word appears in the second segment, and so on. Once it is determined that an instance of a word appears in a given segment, then, the thing to do is to add one to the counter that is keeping track of the number of times the word appears in that segment. How does the program know which element of the TallyKeeper array to increment? If the word has been found to appear in segment five, then the fifth element of the array should be incremented; if it is found to appear in segment eight, the eighth element should be incremented. This means that the variable Segment itself can be used as a subscript to indicate the element of the array that should be incremented. Thus, once the value of Segment has been determined by statements like those above, you can say

```
TallyKeeper[Segment] := TallyKeeper[Segment] + 1;
```

and this will add 1 to the appropriate counter.

This brings up an important point. When the value 1 is first added on to any element of the Tally array, that element must have some value already or an error or erroneous results will ensue. Therefore, *the elements of the* Tally *array must be initialized to zero.* You should be used to the idea of initialization by now, especially for variables that serve as counters. Initializing an array is simple—you need a FOR loop to enable accessing the successive elements of the array, and a statement inside the loop that sets the elements to 0:

```
FOR Counter := 1 TO NumberOfSegments DO BEGIN
  Tally[Counter] := 0;
END;     { for }
```

Where should the initialization of the Tally array be done? Your first thought may be to initialize Tally at the beginning of the Distribute procedure. However, in this case *the initialization should be done in the calling procedure*—here the calling procedure is the main program, and so the FOR loop above should appear in the main program. This is done to keep the Distribute procedure as general as possible, so that if you want to call Distribute repeatedly with a series of words, and calculate a *cumulative* set of frequencies, you will not wipe out the previous contents of the **TallyKeeper** array each time you enter the Distribute procedure.[5]

You now have the appropriate statements to determine the text segment in which a *single* occurrence of a word appears and to increment a counter of occurrences in that segment. However, this process must be repeated for each occurrence of the word that exists in the array. Now, after the Distribute procedure calls the Occurrence procedure, the Distribute procedure has available to it the location in the array of the first and last occurrences of the word in question. Distribute first checks that the values stored in the variables containing the locations of the first and last occurrences are not zero, which would indicate that the word does not exist in the array. But if it does exist, the process of determining the segment and incrementing the counter must be performed for *each* occurrence of the word. In other words, the statements outlined above should be repeated for each occurrence of the word. This means that a loop will be needed. A FOR loop can be used since the number of times the loop will execute is known (one time for each occurrence of the word). The counter variable in the FOR loop will be used within the loop to access each of these occurrences, and so its initial value should be the value that indicates the location of the first occurrence of the word in the array, and its final value should be the value indicating the location of the last occurrence. So the heading of the loop should be

```
FOR Counter := First TO Last DO ...
```

where **First** is the variable in which the location of the first occurrence of the word in the array is stored, and **Last** is the variable in which the location of the last occurrence is stored. The entire loop to access all of the occurrences of the word in the **Words** array look like this:

```
FOR Counter := First TO Last DO BEGIN
  Segment := (ListOfWords[Counter].LinearPosition DIV WordsInSegment) + 1;
  IF Segment > NumberOfSegments THEN BEGIN
    Segment := NumberOfSegments;
  END;     { then begin }
END;     { for }
```

Note that the statement given earlier to compute the value of **WordsInSegment** should *not* be placed inside the loop, since there is no need to perform this computation more than once.

Avoid including statements within a loop that compute the same result over and over. In general, computations within a loop should involve at least one variable that is changed within the loop or (in a FOR loop) the loop control variable itself.

---

5. A problem in which this technique would be used is outlined in the first of the Exercises at the end of this chapter. Note that it is for this reason also that the Distribute procedure does not do the actual printing of the histogram.

Note also that First and Last are declared within the Distribute procedure rather than in the main program, since they are not used in the main procedure, and that they are sent as parameters to the Occurrence procedure.

The final form of Distribute is therefore

```
PROCEDURE Distribute(ListOfWords : WordArray; WordsInList : ArrayBounds;
        WordToDistribute : String; VAR TallyKeeper : TallyArray);
  { Counts the number of times WordToDistribute appears in each }
  { segment of the text and stores the result in TallyKeeper }
VAR Counter, First, Last, WordsInSegment : ArrayBounds;
  Segment : TallyBounds;
BEGIN     { Distribute }
  WordsInSegment := WordsInList DIV NumberOfSegments;
  Occurrence(ListOfWords,WordsInList,WordToDistribute,First,Last);
  IF First > 0 THEN BEGIN
    FOR Counter := First TO Last DO BEGIN
      Segment := (ListOfWords[Counter].LinearPosition DIV WordsInSegment)+1;
      IF Segment > NumberOfSegments THEN BEGIN
        Segment := NumberOfSegments;
      END;     { then begin }
    END;     { for }
  END;     { then begin }
END;     { Distribute }
```

One or two additions have been made to the procedure: first, Segment has been declared with type *TallyBounds,* which should be defined in the Type Declarations section of the main program as follows:

```
TallyBounds = 0..NumberOfSegments;
```

Second, an IF-THEN statement has been included in the procedure, surrounding the FOR loop that computes the segment numbers for all of the occurrences of the word in the Words array. This IF-THEN statement prevents the loop from executing if the word is not found in the Words array, in which case Occurrence sets First and Last to 0. Otherwise, an error would result when within the FOR loop an attempt is made to access ListOfWords[0].LinearPosition.

This is all there is to the Distribute procedure. When the procedure terminates, the Tally array will hold the frequency with which the word stored in UsersWord occurs in each text segment. The main procedure can now use this information to print a histogram representation of the word's distribution across the text.

The Histogram Procedure

After the Distribute procedure finishes executing, the main program will call on the Histogram procedure, passing it the Tally array as a parameter. The procedure is sent only the Tally array; it needs no other information from the main program in order to print the histogram. And since the Histogram procedure uses the information from the Tally array in order to print the graph, but does not alter it in any way, the array should be passed as a Value parameter. So the heading for Histogram will be

```
PROCEDURE Histogram(GraphValues : TallyArray);
```

where GraphValues is the name given to the array whose initial values within the procedure will be obtained from the main program's Tally array.

The algorithm for printing the histogram is

1. For each text segment, do the following:
   a. For each occurrence tallied for this segment, do the following:
      (1) Print an asterisk.
   b. Go to a new line.

To implement step 1, a loop can be used that has a counter starting at one and terminating at the number of elements in the array, which is the number of divisions in the text. Since the number of times the loop will execute is known, a FOR loop like the following can be used:

```
FOR Counter := 1 TO NumberOfSegments DO ...
```

To implement step 2, you need to know how many times the word occurs in segment number Counter (the index on the FOR loop). Then for each of these occurrences you need to print an asterisk. How can this be accomplished? What you can do is this: set up a FOR loop in which one asterisk is printed each time through. The loop will execute GraphValues[Counter] times—that is, as many times as the value stored in the element of the GraphValues array currently under consideration indicates. This way, if GraphValues[Counter] contains the value thirteen, thirteen asterisks will be printed. This loop, of course, goes inside the other FOR loop that enables accessing each element of the GraphValues array, and its heading could be

```
FOR Counter2 := 1 TO GraphValues[Counter] DO ...
```

Inside the loop, a simple WRITE statement can be included that prints a single asterisk. The final result is

```
FOR Counter := 1 TO NumberOfSegments DO BEGIN
  FOR Counter2 := 1 TO GraphValues[Counter] DO BEGIN
    WRITE('*');
  END;     { for }
  WRITELN;
END;     { for }
```

Notice that a WRITELN is included among the statements above in order to issue a line eject after a line of asterisks has been printed. As indicated in the algorithm above, this must be done for each text segment, and so the WRITELN appears within the outer FOR loop.

The whole of the Histogram procedure is

```
PROCEDURE Histogram(GraphValues : TallyArray);
  { Prints a histogram representation of the data }
  { in the array GraphValues }
VAR Counter : TallyBounds;
      Counter2 : INTEGER;
BEGIN     { Histogram }
  WRITELN('Frequency Distribution Graph');
  WRITELN;WRITELN;
  FOR Counter := 1 TO NumberOfSegments DO BEGIN
    WRITE(Counter:1,' | ');
    FOR Counter2 := 1 TO GraphValues[Counter] DO BEGIN
      WRITE('*');
    END;     { for }
    WRITELN;
  END;     { for }
END;     { Histogram }
```

Some cosmetic WRITE and WRITELNs have been added here to make the output pretty. In particular, a label for the graph has been added and the segment number is printed to the left of each line of asterisks and separated from it with a vertical bar. You can make your output as fancy as you like—consider this an exercise in formatting, and feel free to experiment.

The Program as a Whole

In this program two procedures are added (plus Occurrence) within the main program:

```
PROGRAM FrequencyGraph(INPUT,OUTPUT,TextFile);
  Constant declarations: StringLength, MaxWords, Blank, Blanks,
          NumberOfSegments
  Type Declarations: String, StringBounds, ArrayBounds, WordRecord,
          WordArray, TallyBounds, TallyArray
  Variable Declarations: Words, NumberOfWords, Tally, UsersWord, TextFile
  Procedure Declarations:
    PROCEDURE ReadWord(VAR NextWord : String; VAR InputFile : TEXT);
      Variable Declarations: Letter, Counter
      Procedure Declarations:
        PROCEDURE SkipBlanks(VAR NextChar : CHAR; VAR InFile : TEXT);
          Variable Declarations: none
        BEGIN     { SkipBlanks }
          .
          .
          .
        END;     { SkipBlanks }
    BEGIN     { ReadWord }
      .
      .
      .
    END;     { ReadWord }
```

```
PROCEDURE SubString(FromWord : String;
        Start, Stop : StringBounds;
        VAR ToWord : String);
  Variable Declarations: Counter, ToPos
BEGIN     { SubString }
   .
   .
   .
END;     { Substring }
FUNCTION Capitalize(Lowerletter : CHAR) : CHAR;
  Variable Declarations: none
BEGIN     { Capitalize }
   .
   .
   .
END;     { Capitalize }
PROCEDURE Standardize(VAR StandardWord : String);
  Variable Declarations: Counter, FirstLetter
BEGIN     { Standardize }
   .
   .
   .
END;     { Standardize }
PROCEDURE Load(VAR FileWords : WordArray;
        VAR WordsInFile : ArrayBounds;
        VAR WordFile : TEXT);
  Variable Declarations: Word
BEGIN     { Load }
   .
   .
   .
END;     { Load }
PROCEDURE Sort(VAR SortWords : WordArray; WordsInSort : ArrayBounds)
  Variable Declarations: Counter, Sorted, Temp
BEGIN     { Sort }
   .
   .
   .
END;     { Sort }
FUNCTION Search(SearchWords : WordArray; Last : ArrayBounds;
        WordToFind : String) : ArrayBounds;
  Variable Declarations: First, MidPoint, Found
BEGIN     { Search }
   .
   .
   .
END;     { Search }
PROCEDURE Occurrence(OccurrenceWords : WordArray;
        WordsInOccurrence : ArrayBounds;
        WordToCount : String;
        VAR FirstOccurrence, LastOccurrence : ArrayBounds);
  Variable Declarations: Position, StillEqual
BEGIN     { Occurrence }
   .
   .
   .
END;     { Occurrence }
```

```
    PROCEDURE Distribute(ListOfWords : WordArray;
            WordsInList : ArrayBounds; WordToDistribute : String;
            VAR TallyKeeper : TallyArray);
       Variable Declarations: Counter, First, Last,
            WordsInSegment, Segment
    BEGIN      { Distribute }
       .
       .
       .
    END;      { Distribute }
    PROCEDURE Histogram(GraphValues : TallyArray);
       Variable Declarations: Counter, Counter2
    BEGIN      { Histogram }
       .
       .
       .
    END;      { Histogram }
    BEGIN   { FrequencyGraph }
       Load(Words,NumberOfWords,TextFile);
       Sort(Words,NumberOfWords);
       { Initialize the Tally array }
       FOR Counter := 1 TO NumberOfSegments DO BEGIN
          Tally[Counter] := 0;
       END;      { for }
       WRITE('Enter a word for which a distribution ',
             ' graph will be printed: ');
       ReadWord(UsersWord,INPUT);
       Standardize(UsersWord);
       Distribute(Words,NumberOfWords,UsersWord,Tally);
       Histogram(Tally);
END.      { FrequencyGraph }
```

SUMMING UP THE PROGRAM

The only potential problem with this program is the case in which the number of occurrences within a text segment for some word is very large—specifically, over about 110. When this happens the line of asterisks you generate may exceed the length of the output line on your screen. One of two things will happen in this situation: an error will result, because your line is too long, or the computer will wrap the line of asterisks around on to the next line of the screen. Neither is a desirable result.

There are two solutions to the problem. First, you can check the value of GraphValues[Counter] *before* generating the line of asterisks within the Histogram procedure, and if the value exceeds the line length, you can generate only a line's worth of asterisks and provide a signal to the user that the real number of occurrences was greater. You might, for instance, put a special symbol at the end of the line to indicate that the line was truncated.

The second solution is to represent more than one occurrence of a word with a single asterisk. For instance, instead of printing an asterisk for each occurrence, you might instead print an asterisk for every two occurrences. The resulting graph would give a good sense of the relative distribution of the word across the text segments, which is the primary purpose of the graph. To do this you can DIVide the value of GraphValues[Counter] by 2 or whatever value suits your data before generating the line of asterisks in Histogram.

The program outlined in this chapter is only a simple example of the kinds of things you can do with the programming tools you've developed throughout the preceding chapters in this book. Several variations and elaborations on this program are suggested in the Niceties section of this chapter and in the Exercises, but even these suggestions only skim the surface of what you are now capable of doing. You should start to think of other applications of your programming skills and develop algorithms and programs that suit your particular needs. You are familiar with all of the basics of programming at this point; only a few elaborations will be presented in the remaining chapters.

NICETIES

More About Records

The parts of a record can be variables of any type, including user-defined types. This means that a part of a record can be an array, or another record. For example, suppose that you want to store only one instance of each word in the text in your array, but want to maintain a list of all the linear positions at which a word appears in the text and store it with the word. You can declare a record structure like this:

```
TYPE LPArray = ARRAY[1..20] OF INTEGER;
  WordRecord = RECORD
                 Word : String;
                 LinearPosition : LPArray;
               END;
```

This includes in the record an array that can hold up to twenty linear position numbers. You can then define an array whose elements are of type *WordRecord*, as in the program for this chapter, and each element of *that* array will consist of a type *String* variable and an array capable of holding twenty integers. Thus, if the larger array were defined to have 1000 elements, you will have created 1000 twenty-element integer arrays.

Similarly, a record can be a part of another record. Suppose you were setting up a record to hold bibliographical information. You might proceed like this:

```
TYPE Name = RECORD
              Firstname : String;
              Lastname : String;
            END;
  Publish = RECORD
              House : String;
              Location : String;
            END;
  Book = RECORD
           Title : String;
           Author : Name;
           Publisher : Publish;
           Date : INTEGER;
         END;
```

The record type *Book* now contains two sub-records, with types *Name* and *Publish*. You can create a variable with this type by declaring

```
VAR MyText : Book;
```

Now, to refer to the **Firstname** part of the **Author** part of the record named **MyText**, you use the name

```
MyText.Author.Firstname
```

Thus for each sub-record, a period is added and the name of the sub-record indicated, until you reach the bottom level of the definition. Pieces of the record that are not at the lowest level can be referred to and used like any variables of their type as well. For instance, suppose that given the type declarations above, the following declarations appear in the program:

```
VAR MyText : Book;
  MyName : Name;
```

Then, within the program, a statement like

```
MyText.Author := MyName;
```

could appear.

The WITH Construct

Occasionally, when you are dealing with records you will make several references to various fields within a record in a block of code. In these cases it is troublesome to repeat the record name over and over again, and Pascal provides a way around this.

Suppose you declare a variable named **MyText** like the one in the example in the preceding section. To initialize its fields you can use the WITH construct, as follows:

```
WITH MyText DO BEGIN
  Title := 'All About Pascal     ';
  Author.Firstname := 'Nicklaus                ';
  Author.LastName := 'Wirth                   ';
  Publisher.House := 'Univ. of Penn.          ';
  Publisher.Location := 'Philadelphia            ';
  Date := 1987;
END;      { with }
```

By enclosing the statements within the **WITH MyText DO BEGIN** and **END**, the prefix **MyText** is assumed for all names that appear there. Other statements can appear as well that don't reference the record.

You can use multiple WITH statements for multi-leveled records, like this:

```
WITH MyText DO BEGIN
  Title := 'All About Pascal      ';
  WITH Author DO BEGIN
    Firstname := 'Nicklaus          ';
    LastName := 'Wirth              ';
  END;     { with }
  WITH Publisher DO BEGIN
    House := 'Univ. of Penn.    ';
    Location := 'Philadelphia     ';
  END;     { with }
  Date := 1987;
END;     { with }
```

Letting the User Determine the Text Segments

As mentioned in the beginning of this chapter, it is possible to let the user mark the places in the text where the divisions between segments are to occur, rather than simply letting the program divide the text into segments of equal length. To implement this strategy, the user would have to insert some symbol, such as "@@@" or some other string that would never appear as part of the text, at the points in the text where the divisions are to occur. Then as the program reads words from the text, it would have to determine if the "word" read in is "@@@," or whatever symbol is used. If so, it would know that another text segment is to begin.

Because the text segments can no longer be determined from the linear position of the word in the text, the number of the segment in which the word appears must be stored along with the word as the word is read in. So the record structure that defines the elements of the array in which the words are stored must be modified to accommodate this extra bit of information.[6] A counter can be initialized to one before words are read in; as each word is read, the value stored in this counter variable will be assigned as the text segment for the word. When the program encounters the string "@@@" in the text, the string is not stored as a word, but instead the text segment counter variable is incremented by 1, thus indicating that a new segment is being processed.

Within the Distribute procedure, the statements to calculate the text segment in which the word appears can be eliminated, since the segment number is provided in the record with the occurrence of the word. So this information can simply be retrieved from the array of records and used to increment the appropriate element of the TallyKeeper array.

Note that the number of segments into which the text is divided is no longer determined by setting up a constant at the beginning of the main program, but is instead determined by the number of times the marker (for example, "@@@") appears in the text. So the variable containing the number of segments should be passed as a parameter to the Distribute and Histogram procedures.

Note also that the size of the Tally array is now variable. The number of elements in the array is determined by the number of segments the user indi-

6. If the linear position is not needed elsewhere in the program, it can be eliminated from the record.

cates. Since there is no way of knowing how many segments the user will divide the text into, your program should define the Tally to contain some maximum number of elements. Alert your user to this maximum, and if the number of segments exceeds the maximum allowed, *give your user a message to this effect and terminate the program.* In this way your Tally array will now be treated as your main array is—a variable will indicate the number of elements that are being used in the array, although the array may contain several unused elements. This is analogous to the use of only part of your Words array, and the use of NumberOfWords to indicate how many elements are actually filled.

APPLICATIONS AND CONSIDERATIONS

Word Distribution Studies

Several literary studies have used word frequency distribution graphs as their basis, and in many cases new insights into the text have been obtained. Perhaps the earliest study of this kind is John Smith's analysis of James Joyce's *Portrait of the Artist as a Young Man.*[7] Smith looked at the distribution patterns for several of the novel's major images and noticed that the frequency of specific images increased dramatically in the six sections of the novel long recognized as describing the main character's "epiphanal" moments. This pattern had not been detected by traditional methods of analysis. Smith also determined that images that appear frequently but separately in earlier portions of the text re-appear in dense concentrations together in many of the epiphanal passages, and as a result, he was able to draw conclusions about the way elements of earlier experiences fuse and contribute to the epiphanal scenes.

The author of this textbook looked at distribution patterns for 167 images in William Blake's prophetic poem *The Four Zoas,* and in addition to identifying concentrations of images that contribute to the effect of many of the poem's passages, saw a broad pattern of distribution for the images that defined a five-part structure for the poem that had not been noticed by critics in the past.[8] In another case (and in fact in the process of playing with word distribution for the first time), this author generated a graph for words of negation in Sylvia Plath's *The Bell Jar,* and found that the number of negatives *decreased* dramatically in the chapter in which the main character resolves to commit suicide. Clearly, in these instances and in Smith's study, the computer enabled insights into a text that would have been nearly impossible to gain without it.

Determining Word Class

Many applications of computers to the analysis of literature and language require that the *word class,* or part of speech, for each word or some words in the

7. See John B. Smith, "Image and Imagery in Joyce's *Portrait:* A Computer-Assisted Analysis." In *Directions in Literary Criticism: Contemporary Approaches to Literature,* ed. Stanley Weintraub and Philip Young. University Park, Pa.: Pennsylvania State University Press, 1973, pp. 220–227.

8. See Nancy M. Ide, "Patterns of Imagery in William Blake's *The Four Zoas,*" Diss., Pennsylvania State University, 1982.

text be identified. Unfortunately, this is a difficult task for the computer. There is no way that it can look at a word and know absolutely by its form whether it is a noun, verb, adjective, adverb, or any other part of speech. For this reason, even in sophisticated programs for parsing natural language, the computer usually relies on a dictionary that indicates the part of speech for each word in the language to determine word class. As the words in a text are read in, the dictionary is consulted and the part of speech for the word extracted. When a word is found to serve in more than one word class, the surrounding words are examined to resolve the problem—for instance, if a word can function as both a noun and a verb, but the word that precedes it in the text is an article, then the word must be a noun.

It would be easy to modify the program outlined in this chapter to use such a dictionary to determine parts of speech if this information were needed. The dictionary could be read in as a series of word/word-class pairs, perhaps consisting of a word followed by an integer indicating word class, and stored in an array of records designed to hold this information. If the words are not already in alphabetical order, the dictionary could be sorted. To determine the part of speech for any word in the text, then, the Search procedure could be called with the word as the search word, and the dictionary as the array to be searched. The word class information associated with the word in the dictionary could then be easily extracted.

There have, of course, been attempts to write computer programs that determine word class. The most well-known of these is EYEBALL, written by Donald Ross and others at the University of Minnesota. Two criteria are used in this and similar programs to determine word class: word form and context. The form of a word is sometimes indicative of its class—for example, adverbs often end in -ly, and many verbs end in -ing. The problem is that many adverbs do not end in -ly, and some words that end in -ly, such as "belly" and "only," are not adverbs. Likewise, not all words ending in -ing are verbs. Many complex algorithms have been developed to determine word class on the basis of word form, and some have achieved as much as 90% accuracy.

Context can be used to determine word class in situations where the word class of some words in a text is known. One approach is to have available a dictionary of *function words* and their word classes. Function words are words such as articles—a, an, the—and prepositions, which appear very frequently in texts but constitute, in themselves, a small list. Thus the storage required for such a dictionary is quite small. Given the word class of the function words in a text, others can be determined quite reliably from context—a word of unknown class following a preposition is probably a noun; if two words follow a preposition, they are probably an adjective and a noun.

Again, this method is not entirely reliable, and the most successful algorithms for determining word class have used a combination of word form and context to determine word class. However, given the increased availability of cheap and plentiful memory, it is likely that dictionary look-up will remain the dominant method for determining word class in the future. It is not overly optimistic to assume that in the years to come such dictionaries will be built-in or readily available on most personal computers.

The Trouble with Homographs

Earlier in this chapter the problem of homographs—words that are spelled the same but mean different things—was discussed briefly. Homographs are a problem in computer-assisted analyses such as studies based on word distribution graphs because it is not certain you are getting what you want in the distribution. If, for instance, you are looking at images involving vegetation or trees and include the word "leaves" among the words you are considering, you may well see several occurrences of that word in the distribution graph that represent its use as a verb rather than a noun.

The only way to distinguish homographs is by looking at context. Most homographs have different word classes—for instance, "leaves" is a noun or a verb, and so homographs can be distinguished if word class can be determined for every use of the word in the text. The difficulties of determining word class mechanically were discussed in the preceding section. Word class could be determined more easily for homographs if dictionary look-up determined word class for all of the other words in the text, but even so, at least a partial syntactic analysis of the sentence in which each occurrence of the homograph appears would have to be performed. Syntactic analysis with dictionary look-up has been accomplished by machine, but most "parsers," as they are called, are not sophisticated enough to handle the complex and varied syntactic constructions found in most literary texts. Even if they were, the amount of computing effort required to parse a text is enormous at this point and hardly seems worth doing to resolve the relatively small problem of homographs.

For these reasons, at present most researchers deal with homographs by hand. Often the researcher uses a concordance (see Chapter Thirteen) to examine each word in its context and identify the uses of a word in which he or she is interested. Then either the researcher removes the unwanted occurrences from the graph by hand or somehow marks or identifies the words in the text so that the distribution can be re-run with the desired words only.

EXERCISES

1. Modify the program in this chapter to enable the user to indicate where the divisions in the text occur, as discussed in the Niceties section of this chapter.

2. Modify the program to enable the user to see a distribution for a *group* of words if he or she so desires. The user should be able to enter words until he or she wants to stop. The frequencies for these words in each of the text segments are accumulated in the **Tally** array, and the resulting histogram shows their *collective* distribution across the text.

3. Do exercise 2, but enhance the program even further to enable the user to see as many histograms for as many words or groups of words as he or she wants to.

4. Modify the program so that the user specifies the number of segments of equal length into which the text is divided. This means that the value of **NumberOfSegments** is read from the user rather than fixed within the program by establishing a constant. It also means that the size of the **Tally** array is variable (but note that a maximum must be specified)—see the discussion on "Letting the User Determine the Text Segments" in the Niceties section of this chapter to learn how to deal with this.

5. (A bit more difficult.) Modify the program so that it provides a histogram depicting the distribution over the text of words of a certain length. The user should enter the length desired, and your program must determine which words have this length and where these words occur in the text. This will involve going through the array word-by-word and determining the length of each word, and incrementing the appropriate element of the **Tally** array when a word of the desired length is encountered. You can use the Length function given in Chapter Seven to determine the lengths of the words in the array.

Note that if you allow the user to repeat the process of generating such a graph, you will reference the lengths of the words in the **Words** array several times, and so it is efficient to compute and store each word's length along with it in the array as the word is read in.

6. (A bit more difficult.) Modify the program so that in addition to noting the linear position of the word in the text, it also notes which sentence the word appears in (sentence 1, sentence 2, sentence 3, etc.). This program will use the method for detecting the end of a sentence that is outlined in Chapter Four. The output of this program should be a listing of the sentence numbers and linear numbers for the word the user is interested in, rather than a histogram.

7. (A bit more difficult.) Do exercise 6, but also note the paragraph and chapter number in which the word appears. To know when a new paragraph or chapter begins, some symbol must be inserted by the user into the text, as discussed in the Niceties section for letting the user determine the points of text segmentation.

8. (More difficult.) Modify the program so that it is capable of producing distribution graphs for all words that contain a prefix entered by the user in response to a prompt from the program. Since the words in the text are in alphabetical order, you can easily find words with a particular prefix (if they exist) in the array.

9. (More difficult.) Do exercise 8, but have the program handle suffixes instead of prefixes. Here, of course, you cannot take advantage of the fact that the array is in alphabetical order, and so you must look at each word in the array to determine if it has a particular suffix.

An alternative method would be to store each word in the array *backwards* before the words are sorted. This would entail implementing the Reverse procedure outlined in the Niceties section of Chapter Nine.

10. (More difficult.) Write a program that collapses the word list in the array so that it contains only one occurrence of each word, but still retains all of the linear positions at which a word appears in the text as part of the information associated with a word. (See the Niceties section under More About Records for some ideas about this.) The program should then read in a user-specified word and generate a histogram depicting its distribution across the text.

11. (More difficult.) If you have a dictionary with part-of-speech available, write a program that will generate a distribution of words in a certain word *class*—for example, a distribution for all adverbs. See the Applications and Considerations section of this chapter for more about this.

12
Generating a Word Index

A word index is an alphabetic listing of each *discrete* word that appears in a text, together with an indication of all of the places the word appears in that text. Usually, the word's *frequency*—that is, the number of times the word appears in the text—is given as well. The specific form of the information in the word index that indicates the location or locations at which the word appears varies, depending on the kind of text the index is derived from. For poetry, an indication of verse or stanza number, line number and, perhaps, where in the line the word occurs is appropriate; whereas for a novel, chapter number, paragraph number, sentence number, and the location of the word within the sentence is suitable information to enable the user of the index to find the word in a printed version of the text.

In this chapter you will see how to modify the word frequency program to enable the user to see a word index for any word he or she chooses. Word indexes often are produced for all of the words in a text at once rather than for individual words of the user's choosing. But like all of the programs in this text, the word index program that will be developed here is *interactive,* thus enabling the user to "interact" with the text to extract only the information desired. The exercises at the end of the chapter call for modifying the program to enable the user to enter words repeatedly and to be able to request a word index for the entire text.

Instead of simply adding on to the previous program, as you have done for most of the programs so far, in this chapter you will effectively "scrap" the Occurrence, Distribute, and Histogram procedures,[1] completely rewrite the Sort procedure, and add a great deal to the Load procedure. You will not need to learn any new features of the Pascal language, but instead you will learn techniques for *organizing* or "structuring" your data (that is, the words in the text and the information that is associated with them) to increase the efficiency of the program. In Chapter Nine you saw that organizing data in a certain way—by sorting it, in that instance—enabled a much more efficient means to search that data. Here you will see more elaborate kinds of data organization, designed to both reduce the amount of time required to find a particular item and minimize the amount of storage space (memory) the data uses.

The Organization of the Data

The first scheme you saw for organizing the data with which the programs in this text are concerned (the individual words in a text) involved the use of an array of *String* variables. Later this scheme was modified so that records were used within the array in order to associate additional information with each word. The word index program will require associating even more information with each word in the text, since information concerning the chapter, verse, sentence, line, and so on must be available. Since you are already familiar with records, you can envision a straightforward means to set up space in which to store this additional information—more fields can simply be added to the definition of the record structure. The record structure described in last chapter's program includes only two fields, one to hold the word itself and one in which to store the word's linear position. If, say, a chapter number, sentence number, and word-in-sentence number are to be associated with each word as well, the definition of the *WordRecord* type from the previous chapter's program could be changed to

```
TYPE WordRecord = RECORD
                    Word : String;
                    LinearPosition : INTEGER;
                    Chapter : INTEGER;
                    Sentence : INTEGER;
                    WordInSentence : INTEGER;
                  END;
```

If each element of the array Words consists of such a record, you will be able to store all of the required information with each word in the text.

The record structure described above will serve the purposes of the word index program very well. But notice that if records of this type are used, each word in the text will be stored along with its location information even when many of the words are duplicates. This is clearly a waste of storage; it would be

1. Exercise 3 at the end of the chapter calls for modifying these procedures to work within the word index program, and so these procedures need not be thrown away altogether.

far more efficient to store only one copy of every *distinct* word in the text. In this program you will implement a scheme in which only one copy of a word is stored, even when that word appears several times within a text. Note that it will still be necessary to retain the information that indicates linear position and chapter number, sentence number, word-in-sentence number, or other information that suits the text for *each instance* of a word. That is, if the word "the" appears in the text 200 times, you must store 200 sets of information about the locations of these instances of the word "the" in the text since this information is different for each instance, but it is not necessary to hold on to 200 copies of the word "the." Instead, only one copy of the word "the" will be stored.

Implementing a storage scheme where only a single copy of each distinct word is retained means that the record structure described above is inappropriate, since there will no longer be one word stored per set of location information about linear position, chapter, sentence, and word-in-sentence. In fact, there will be far fewer words than sets of location information. So it makes sense to take the word field out of the record structure described above, and to create a separate (and smaller) array to hold the distinct words in the text. Without the word field but with the remaining fields still included, the record structure described above can be used for the location information for the words; so, as before, an array of such records will be created. Because the word field is no longer part of the record structure, the amount of storage required to accommodate this extra field in each record in the array is eliminated. The smaller array that holds only words will reclaim some of this storage space, but not all of it—in fact, you will probably find that you need less than two-thirds the number of spaces for words than you did when each word in the text was stored.[2] Given the two arrays, one to hold the words and one to hold location information about each instance of each of the words in the text, the only thing that remains is to find a way to associate the words in the first array with the location information in the second array. That is, for a given word in the word array, you must be able to find the set or sets of location information in the second array that describe the places where that word appears in the text. To do this, you will implement a new data structure called a *linked list*.

Linked Lists

An array is a data structure that provides for grouping data items together in an ordered list. For example, the Words array that you have been using is a collection of words (and, in Chapter Eleven, linear positions as well) grouped into a list. The words in the list are ordered in the sense that the first word in the list is in slot 1 of the array, the second word is in slot 2, the third in slot 3, and so on. The numbers of the slots function as "addresses" for the items in the array. Now suppose that within a computer program you want to retain a list of items, so that you know which is first in the list, which is second, etc., but that you do not have an array at your disposal. Suppose further that each item is stored some-

2. This is usually the case because it is a fact that a small fraction of the distinct words in a text—notably, function words such as "in," "of," "the," and "and"—often account for as much as 50% of the total number of words.

where in memory, but since the items are not stored in an array, their addresses are random rather than numbered sequentially. But suppose that you know the address of each item that you want to put in your list. Without worrying about the form of this address or how you come to know it, imagine forming a list from this group of items as follows: along with each item in the list, you store the address of the item that *follows* it in the list. So with the first item you store the address of the second item, with the second item you store the address of the third item, and so on. You maintain the address of the first item in the list separately. Then, anytime you want to access the items in the list (and know their order), you retrieve the address of the first item and use this to access that item; having done so, you have access to the address for the second item, since it is stored with the first item, so you can access the second item; and once you have accessed the second item, you can get the address of the third item, and so on. In this way you can access the items in a list, starting with the first and proceeding through the list in order, item by item, as you can by using a FOR loop with an array.

One way to envision a linked list is to imagine the items in the list as containing two pieces of information: the data (for the programs in this text, the data could be a word or a record containing a word and/or some associated information such as its linear position, etc.) and the address of the next item in the list. If you think of the address as a pointer to the next item, you can picture the list like this:

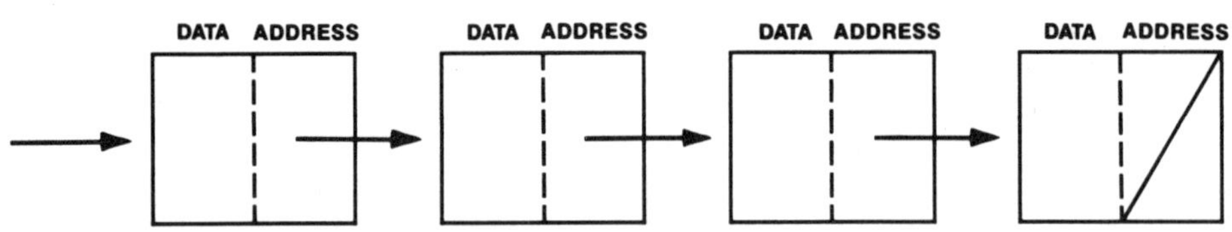

The arrow pointing to the first item in the list is the address of the first item, which is maintained separately. Note that the last item has no address associated with it, since no item follows it in the list.

Another way to think about linked lists is to consider how (and why) a linked list might be implemented in a Pascal program. Since you do not ordinarily have access to the addresses of variables, this might be difficult to imagine. However, you do have access to the location of a variable when it is stored in an array, because the number of the slot in which the variable is stored is effectively its address. Now suppose that you set up an array like the Words array described in Chapter Seven—that is, an array that consists of *String* variables (rather than records as in Chapter Eleven)—and that your program reads words from a file, as usual, and stores them in the array. Suppose that you want to maintain an actual list of the words in their original order—the order in which they were read in—but that you also want to maintain the list of words in alphabetical order. You could duplicate the Words array and then sort it, thus keeping two copies of the words in memory. However, linked lists can be used to create a sorted list of the words without duplicating the original array: instead of sorting the list by rearranging the words in the array and thereby losing track linear sequence, you can create a second list *within* the first, by maintaining it as a linked list. This can be done by associating an integer with each word in the array. This is accomplished by making each element in the array a record just like the one described in Chapter Eleven, except that here, the field "Linear-Position" has the name "Link." The record structure will look like this:

```
TYPE WordRecord = RECORD
                    Word : String;
                    Link : ArrayBounds;
                  END;
```

Now the Link field of each record in the array can be used to hold the address of the next word in the *sorted* list of words. The ordering of the words with respect to the array arrangement will not be changed, and so the linear sequence in which the words were read in and stored will not be lost.[3] But when you want to look at the *sorted* list, you can ignore the sequential array arrangement and follow the links instead.

To understand the linked list better, consider this example:

	DATA	ADDRESS
[1]	MY	0
[2]	DOG	4
[3]	HAS	1
[4]	FLEAS	3

The words in this array have been standardized and stored in the array in their original order. The alphabetic list is maintained as a linked list within the original list, and contains the words in the following order: DOG, FLEAS, HAS, MY. The alphabetic list is obtained by using the Link field associated with each word to determine the word that follows it in the list, rather than simply going through the array from slot 1 through the last slot as usual. It works like this: first, you must obtain the address (position in the array) of the first item in the list. The position of the *first* item in a linked list is usually stored in an independent INTEGER-type variable called a *list header*. Here the list header variable

3. You may wonder why, if a field that holds an integer value is added to the list, it is more space-efficient to use the linked list scheme than to create another copy of an array. The reason is that integer values generally occupy four bytes (32 bits) of storage, with some variation on different machines, and that a single character occupies one byte (8 bits). A *String*-type variable therefore takes up twenty bytes of storage, which is far more than the amount of space required to store an integer.

contains the number 2. This value is used as a subscript of the Words array to get to the word DOG, which is the first word in the alphabetic list of the words in the array. The remainder of the list is accessed by using the Link fields of successive items in the list. The Link field of the record that holds the word DOG contains the number 4, which is the position of the record containing FLEAS. FLEAS is the word that follows DOG in alphabetic sequence. The number 3 is stored with the word FLEAS, and 3 is the position of HAS, the word that follows FLEAS in alphabetic sequence. HAS is stored along with the number 1, which indicates where the word MY appears in the array. MY is the last word in the alphabetic sequence, and so its Link field contains a 0, to indicate the end of the list.[4]

The point of this is that once you have access to a word, you can easily get to the word that follows it in the list by "following the links"—that is, by accessing the word that is stored at the position in the array indicated in the Link field. So once you know where the first word in the linked list is, you can get to all the other words in order. In the example above, once you access the word DOG, you can easily get to the next word in the alphabetic list by using the contents of the Link field of the record in which DOG is stored as a subscript. You access DOG by using the list header variable as a subscript into the array. Suppose that the list header variable is called "Header." Then the word DOG can be accessed with the name

```
Words[Header].Word
```

and the position of the *next* item in the list is stored in Words[Header].Link. Accessing the next word in the list can be regarded as a two-step process, where the first step is to obtain the position of the next item with an assignment statement like the following:

```
Next := Words[Header].Link;
```

Next now becomes the "address" of the word that is next in the alphabetic list—here, Next gets the value 4, since that is what is stored in Words[Header]Link. The second step of the process uses this address to actually access the variable, with the name

```
Words[Next].Word
```

Since Next is 4, Words[Next].Word is clearly FLEAS, the second word in the alphabetic list.

How do you get to the next word in the list—that is, the word following FLEAS? The process is the same: you can get the address of the next word from the Link field of the record containing the word FLEAS. Since Next contains the

4. Any value could be used to indicate the end of the list as long as it is not a value that could function as a valid address for an item on the list. The use of 0 is conventional with an array with a lower bound of 1.

address of FLEAS, the address of the word that follows FLEAS in alphabetic sequence is stored in Word[Next].Link; you can assign this value to Next (thus erasing its old contents, which are not needed any longer) and then use Next to get to the desired word. So you can use the statement

```
Next := Words[Next].Link;
```

which will take the contents of the Link field associated with FLEAS (3, in this example) and store it in the variable Next. Now Next can again be used as a subscript to the array, this time accessing the word HAS with the name Words[Next].Word.

The process of using the Link field to get to the next item in a linked list can be repeated over and over until you reach the end of the list, and in this way all of the items can be accessed. In fact, a simple loop can be used for this purpose. Consider the following:

```
Next := Header;
WHILE (Next <> 0) DO BEGIN
  WRITELN(Words[Next].Word);
  Next := Words[Next].Link;
END;      { while }
```

This loop will print out the alphabetic listing of the words in the array above by using the linked list that is contained within it. To see how, consider what happens when this set of statements executes: since Header contains 2, the first thing that will happen is to assign the value 2 to the variable Next. Next is obviously going to serve as the holder of the address for the word in the list that is currently being printed. The WHILE loop checks that Next is not 0—recall that when we reach the end of the list, the Link field associated with the last word will contain the number 0. Also, if the list were empty for some reason, Header would be 0, and hence Next would be 0 the first time the loop is encountered. So the condition on the WHILE loop prevents attempting to process an empty list and, if the list is not empty, it stops the loop when the end of the list is encountered.

In our example, Next will contain the value 2 the first time the WHILE loop is encountered, and so the loop will be entered. So Words[Next].Word will be printed, and since Next is 2, the word DOG will be printed. After that, Next will be assigned the value contained in Words[Next].Link; that value is 4, and so Next now contains the value 4. Control then returns to the top of the loop, and the value of Next is checked again to ensure that it is not 0. It is not, and so the loop is re-entered, and now that Next has the value 4, the word FLEAS, which is stored in the fourth slot in the array, is printed. Again, Next is given the value stored in the Link field of the record at position Next in the array; since Next is 4, Words[Next].Link is 3, and so Next now contains the value 3. At the top of the loop the condition that Next is not 0 is again satisfied, and the loop is re-entered. HAS is printed, and Next is then assigned the value 1. The top of the loop is again encountered, Next is determined not to be 0, the loop is entered yet again, and MY is printed. Next is then assigned the value that is stored in Words[1].Link, which is 0. Finally, when the top of the loop is reached, the condition that **Next** is not 0 is *not* met, and this stops the loop. All of the words in the array have been printed in alphabetical order, and the loop stops when the end of the list is encountered.

Note that the statement

```
Next := Header;
```

is used to put the address of the *first* item in the list into the variable **Next**, whereas the addresses of subsequent items in the list are put into **Next** with the statement

```
Next := Words[Next].Link;
```

This is standard procedure for traversing a linked list; accessing the first item in the list is always a special case.

The simple loop given above is the standard means for sequentially accessing the items within a linked list. If it is not exactly clear how it works, spend some time going over the steps involved, because it is the key to understanding the linked list representation.

The WordTypes and Tokens Arrays

Armed with an understanding of linked lists, you can now consider how to implement the scheme outlined earlier for organizing the information associated with the words in the text. Two arrays will exist: one that holds the distinct words in the array, in alphabetical order so that the array can be efficiently searched, and one that holds the location information for each word that appears in the text. The location information can be stored in the order corresponding to the order in which the words appear in the original text, so that the information for the first word in the text is stored in slot one, the information for the second word in the text is in slot two, and so on. Note that this will eliminate the need to store the linear position for the words, since the slot number in the array will indicate the linear position of the word with which the information is associated. Each word that appears in a text is called a "token," and each distinct word that appears in a text is called a "type"; therefore, the array containing the alphabetical listing of the words can be called a "type list," and although the words themselves do not appear in the second array, since it contains the information for each word in the text (whether it is a duplicate or not), it is effectively a "token list." These terms are commonly used when discussing the "type/token ratio" in a text—that is the ratio of distinct words to total words. This ratio is indicative of the richness of the author's vocabulary, since the higher the ratio of types to tokens, the more different words appear in the text. Vocabulary richness, like average word and sentence length, is an indicator of style and is occasionally used in authorship analyses. To conform to the terminology, the array that holds the alphabetical listing of distinct words in the text will be called "WordTypes" and the one that holds the location information will be called "Tokens."

The purpose of organizing the data according to the plan just outlined is to enable the rapid retrieval of all of the location information for a given word. Since the words in the WordTypes array are in alphabetical order, a word can be easily found in this list with a binary search, but there must be a means by which this word can be associated with the location information that appears in the Tokens array. There may be only one entry in the token list for a given word, or there may be hundreds. The solution to the problem is this: together with each word in the WordTypes array, a link will be stored that points to the *first* set of location information in the Tokens array that is associated with that word. So, if the first word in the text is THE, the location information for that instance of the word THE will be stored in slot one of the Tokens array. The word THE will be stored in its proper alphabetical position in the WordTypes array. Along with the word THE, in a link field within the same record, the number 1 will be stored, thus providing the address *within the* Tokens *array* of the location information associated with the word THE. So to get the information for the word THE, the WordTypes array can be searched to find the word, and then the field containing the link to the Tokens array is used as a subscript into the Tokens array, thus enabling access to the associated set of location information that is stored there.

There will no doubt be many sets of location information stored in the Tokens array that pertain to the word THE. These sets of information will not be located sequentially in the Tokens array, since the location information is stored according to the linear sequence of the words in the original text. So how do you get to the location information for other occurrences of the word THE, if only the address of the first set of information is stored with the word in the WordTypes array? The answer, of course, is a linked list. Specifically, all of the sets of location information for a given word will be linked together in a linked list *within* the Tokens array. This means that if the word THE appears at positions 1, 25, 36, and 124 in the original text, the location information for each of these occurrences will be stored in slots 1, 25, 36, and 124 of the Tokens array; and a linked list of these items can be maintained. When the information needs to be accessed, the word THE is found in the WordTypes list, and the Link field associated with it will point to the first set of location information for that word. Within the record in the Tokens array that contains the first set of location information for the word THE, a link field will contain the position at which the second set of information is stored in the Tokens array, and so on through the end of the list. You can envision this setup as in the figure. The arrows reinforce the idea that the information contained in the link field of a given record "points to" the next record in the list.

Note that in this scheme the link field that is stored with a word in the WordTypes array functions as the list header for the linked list records containing the sets of location information for that word. Note also that within the Tokens array, you will actually have many little linked lists, each corresponding to a different word from the WordTypes list.

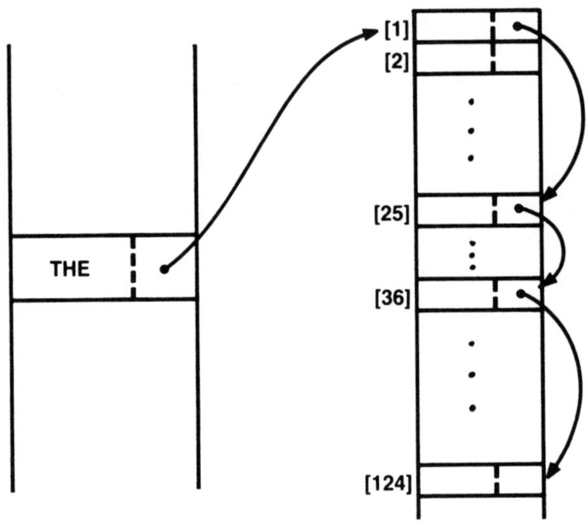

Insertion Sort

As the words are read in from the text, they will be stored in the WordTypes array. The WordTypes array will contain only one copy of each word, and this means that either duplicate entries must be eliminated after the text has been loaded and sorted, or that only one copy of any word is stored in the WordTypes array in the first place. The second alternative is preferable, because it means that instead of setting up an array large enough to hold the total number of words in the text, a smaller array can be used. Since the number of word types in a text is usually no more than two-thirds the number of tokens, a substantial amount of storage can be saved.

In order to store only a single copy of every word, it must be determined as each word is read in from the file whether or not it is already in the WordTypes array. If it is, then the word itself will not be stored, and only its location information will be stored in the Tokens array; if it is not, then the word will be stored in the WordTypes array (its location information will be stored in the Tokens array in this case as well). This means that the WordTypes array must be searched every time a word is read in. Now if the words in the WordTypes array are not in alphabetical order, a linear search will be necessary, and this could become very costly in terms of time. It would be ideal if the words were in alphabetical order, in which case a binary search could be used and the efficiency of the program improved considerably. The only way to maintain a sorted list as the array itself is being created is to insert the words into their alphabetized positions in the array as they are read in. This is possible using what is called an *Insertion Sort*. A procedure to insert a word into its proper position in the Words array will replace the Bubble Sort procedure in your program. This routine will be called every time a word is to be inserted into the array—that is, every time a word is read from the text that does not appear in the array already. In order to ascertain whether or not the word is already in the array, the array must be searched, but note that since words are always inserted into the array in their alphabetized positions, even in the process of being loaded the array is sorted and can be searched efficiently with a binary search.

The Insertion Sort works as follows: when a word is to be inserted into the array, all of the words already in the array that follow it in alphabetical sequence are moved down one slot, in order to make room for the new word. For instance, suppose that you have the following list:

[1] AID
[2] ALL
[3] COME
[4] FOR
[5] GOOD
[6] IS
[7] NOW
[8] OF
[9] PEOPLE
[10] THE
[11] THEIR
[12] TIME
[13] TO

Suppose the word PARTY is to be inserted into the list above. PARTY should be inserted in slot 9 of the array—that means that the current contents of slot 9 must be moved to slot 10, the current contents of slot 10 must be moved to slot 11, and so on through the end of the list. The insertion procedure will do just this, but since the contents of slot 9 cannot be stored in slot 10 until the contents of slot 10 have been moved, the insertion algorithm begins at the *end* of the list and moves each word one position closer to the end of the array until it finds the slot in which the word to be inserted belongs.

The algorithm for the Insertion Sort is

1. Set **Counter** to be equal to the number of words currently in the array.
2. While the place in the array where the word is to be inserted has not been found, do the following:
   a. If the word to be inserted *precedes* the word at position **Counter** in alphabetical sequence, do the following:
      (1) Move the word at position **Counter** in the array down one slot, closer to the end of the array.
      (2) Subtract 1 from **Counter**.
   b. Otherwise, if the word to be inserted does *not* precede the word in the array in alphabetical sequence, do the following:
      (1) Indicate that the place where the word is to be inserted has been found.
3. Insert the word in the slot in the array indicated by **Counter** +1.
4. Add 1 to the number of words in the array.

Follow this algorithm through for the example given above, where PARTY is to be inserted into the array. Step 1 will give the value 13 to the counter, since there are currently 13 words in the array. Step 2 checks that the place to insert the word has not been found. Since this is not the case, PARTY is compared to TO, the word in slot 13. Since PARTY precedes TO in alphabetical sequence, steps 2.a.1 and 2.a.2 are taken. In step 2.a.1, TO is copied into slot 14 of the array, thus effectively moving it down one slot. Note that the original copy of TO is still in slot 13 at this point. Step 2.a.2 subtracts 1 from the counter, making it

12, and then the algorithm returns to step 2. Since the place in the array where the word is to be inserted has not been found, PARTY is compared to TIME, since TIME is in slot 12. Once again, PARTY precedes the word in the array in alphabetical sequence. So TIME is copied into slot 13, obliterating the word TO that was stored there previously. Both slots 12 and 13 now contain the word TIME, and slot 14 holds the word TO that was copied into it earlier. Next, the counter is decremented to 11, and the algorithm returns to step 2 again. The point of insertion has not been found, and so PARTY is compared to THEIR in slot 11 and again found to precede the word in alphabetic sequence. THEIR is copied into slot 12 (erasing TIME) and the counter is decremented to 10. Back in step 2, it is once again ascertained that the insertion point has not yet been found. So PARTY is compared to THE, which is currently in slot 10. Because PARTY is less than THE, THE is copied into slot 11, and the counter is set to 9. After returning yet again to step 2, PARTY is compared to PEOPLE, PEOPLE is copied into slot 10, and the counter is set to 8.

The next time through the sequence of steps, PARTY is compared to OF in slot 8, and for the first time, the word to be inserted is found *not* to precede the word in the array in alphabetical sequence. So OF is not copied into the next slot in the array, and step 2.b.1 indicates that the place at which the word is to be inserted into the array has been found. The algorithm returns to step 2 again, but since the point of insertion has now been found, steps 2.a, 2.b, and 2.c are skipped and the algorithm proceeds to step 3. Here PARTY is copied into slot 9, the slot that corresponds to the current value of the counter *plus* 1. One is added to the counter here because when the repetition of step 2 terminates, the counter will contain the slot number for the first word encountered that should come *before* the word that is to be inserted.

Finally, in step 4, the number of words (which had been 13) is now incremented by one to be 14. The final result is an alphabetized array in which the word PARTY appears in its proper position and for which the proper number of words has been recorded.

Getting the Location Information from the Text

The next thing to consider before writing the program to generate a word index is how the location information is to be extracted from the text. In the last chapter, you extracted location information of one kind from the text when you recorded each word's linear position. However, the word index will provide several different kinds of location information, and, as mentioned earlier, the information will be different for different kinds of texts. The stanza number, the line number within the stanza, the word number within the line, and the linear position (word number within the entire poem) might be appropriate, but some long poems are divided into larger units which would be noted in a word index.[5] Many poems are not segmented into stanzas, and in some contemporary poetry there is no division by lines. Clearly, the kind of information a word index pro-

5. For example, Wordsworth's *Prelude*, Milton's *Paradise Lost*, and Spenser's *Faerie Queene* are divided into Books, and Tennyson's *In Memoriam* is broken into numbered segments.

gram provides must be suited to certain kinds of texts. This must be taken into consideration when the program is designed.

In the program for this chapter, the input text will be regarded as prose. The information that will be provided for each word will be the linear position at which it appears, along with the chapter number, sentence number, and the position within the sentence. All of this information will be gathered during the process of reading the words from the input file, since all of the location information can be determined as the words are read in. As you have already seen, this is especially true for information about a word's linear position, since the linear position is simply the number a word is given as words are read in and counted.

Gathering the rest of the location information requires a bit more effort, but not much. You can probably already see how to determine the number of the sentence a word appears in if you think back to Chapter Four. All that will have to be done is to keep a counter for sentences. The counter will be set to 1 initially. Then, as in the program for Chapter Four, the counter will be incremented each time a period, question mark, or exclamation mark is encountered.[6] When words are read in, the current value of the sentence counter will be stored to indicate the sentence number in which the word appears. The position of a word within the sentence in which it appears will also be noted, and this information can be obtained by keeping yet another counter that is set to 1 every time a new sentence is encountered and incremented each time a new word is encountered thereafter. Then this counter will contain the position of a word within the current sentence as the word is read in, and once again, this information can be stored at that time.

The number of the chapter in which a word appears is nearly impossible to determine from a text in its usual format. This problem is usually circumvented in a brute force way, by requiring that the input text be *marked* to indicate the places where one chapter (or any other text segment) ends and another begins. There are no set conventions for marking a text in this way, and no clearly advantageous or generally accepted scheme exists. In the program for this chapter it will be assumed that chapter markers appear *between* chapters—that is, no marker appears at the beginning of the text. A constant will be established within the program that contains the string of characters that will function as a chapter marker—for instance, the constant might be declared like this:

```
CONST ChapterMarker = '@@@                 ';
```

This would mean that the appearance of three '@'-characters in a row (which will be read by the program as a word and padded with seventeen blanks) will be inserted into the text at the end of each chapter. ChapterMarker is set up as a constant so that the name can be used throughout the program instead of the string itself, thus making it easy to change the marker. As words are read in, they

6. As before, this means that periods appearing in abbreviations like "Mr." and "A.M." will be taken as indications that a new sentence is beginning unless special provisions are made. See the Applications and Considerations section in Chapter Eight for a discussion of this problem.

can be compared to this string, and if the word read in is equal to the chapter marker, then a counter keeping track of the chapter number will be incremented, the "word" will be discarded, and the reading process will continue. The chapter counter will be used to indicate the number of the chapter in which each word that is read appears.

Note that other markers could easily be included in a text as well, and the record structure containing the location information for each word could be modified to accommodate these additional text divisions. Or the chapter marker could be used to signal any other division that occurs within a text.

Setting Up the WordTypes and Tokens Arrays

The final consideration before setting out to write the word index program is how the WordTypes and Tokens arrays will be set up. This task belongs to Load, which, as in earlier programs, is responsible for loading the words from the file into main memory. As it reads the words, Load has access to information about the location of each word, and so this information can be recorded in the Tokens array during the loading process. Load will also establish the linked lists that connect words with sets of location information in the Tokens array.

While Load's new jobs seem complicated, they are actually relatively simple. Load contains a loop that executes once for every word that is read in from the file. Location information for each word will be stored in successive locations in the Tokens array in much the same way that Load stored successive words in the Words array in earlier programs. This means establishing a counter to keep track of the last slot in which information was stored in the Tokens array and incrementing this variable each time through Load's WHILE loop. Load will maintain the counters for chapter number, sentence number, and word-in-sentence number described above, and each time through the loop their current values will be assigned to the appropriate fields of the next open slot in the Tokens array. This takes care of storing location information. As for gathering the location information, Load will also have to include statements to check for the chapter marker and for the end of a sentence and increment the chapter and sentence counters and reset the word counter accordingly.

Handling the Tokens array will be similar to handling the Words array, since information is stored for successive words in successive slots of the array. Handling the WordTypes array is even simpler, given the insertion routine outlined above. Recall that a word is stored in the WordTypes array only if it does not appear there already. So each time a word is read, all that needs to be done is to search the WordTypes array for that word, and if it does not appear, call the insertion routine to insert it. That takes care of the WordTypes array. Now the only thing left to consider is establishing the links between the WordTypes and Tokens arrays and between elements of the Tokens array containing information pertaining to the same word.

If the word that has just been read is *not* in the WordTypes array, then that means that this is the first occurrence of that word that has been encountered. So the set of location information that is stored in the Tokens array this time through the loop is the first set of location information for that word. This makes the task of setting the link from the WordTypes to the Tokens array easy: the link is simply set to point to the element of the Tokens array in which location information is currently being stored. The Link field for this element of the Tokens array can also be set at this time; since this is the only set of location information for the word, it is the last in the linked list of sets of location information for the word, and so its link is set to 0, to indicate the end of the list.

If the word that has just been read *is* in the WordTypes array, the word is not stored. Its location information is stored in the next open slot of the Tokens array, and the only thing to do is to "attach" this set of location information to the end of the linked list of information sets for that word. Since the search for the word will yield the position of the word in the WordTypes array, you have access to the beginning of the linked list of location information for the word (the link field in the entry for that word in the WordTypes array gives the position of the first set of location information for that word in the Tokens array). It is simply a matter of following the list to its end, using a loop like the one given above in the section on linked lists, in order to find the set of location information that is currently last on the list. Having done this, *its* link field can be set to point to the slot in the Tokens array in which information has just been stored, which has the effect of tacking this new set of information on to the end of the linked list. The Link field for the current token is set to 0, as above.

The process outlined above can be described with the following general algorithm:

1. As each word is read in, do the following:
   a. Store the current values of the chapter counter, sentence counter, and word-in-sentence counter in the appropriate fields in the next available slot in the Tokens array.
   b. Set the Link field for the last element in the Tokens array to 0.
   c. Search the WordTypes array to determine if the word is in the array.
   d. If the word is not in the WordTypes array, do the following:
      (1) Call the insertion routine to insert the word in the WordTypes array.
      (2) Set the Link field for the word to the current value of the token counter.
   e. Otherwise, if the word is in the WordTypes array, do the following:
      (1) Get the position for the first set of location information for the word from its entry in the WordTypes array.
      (2) Follow the links through the Tokens array to find the last item in the list.
      (3) Set the Link field for this item to the current value of the token counter.

Steps 1.a through 1.c can be accomplished within Load, but steps 1.d and 1.e will actually be included in a separate procedure called "SetTokenLink," which Load will call from within its WHILE loop. This leaves Load only the tasks of maintaining the various counters and storing location information in the Tokens array and removes a relatively complex and cumbersome set of statements out of the procedure, where they can be dealt with separately.

CONSTRUCTING THE PROGRAM

This program will not use the procedures Occurrence, Distribute, and Histogram, nor will it use the Bubble Sort procedure. All of the other procedures remain the same as before, except for Load, to which statements will be added to record the location information for each word as it is read and to store the words and location information according to the new organization scheme.

The Main Program

Declaring the WordTypes and Tokens Arrays. The WordTypes array and Tokens array will be declared in the main program, as usual. For each, you will define a record structure in the Type Declarations section of the program appropriate for holding information relevant to a particular word, and then define another type consisting of an array of these records.

The type declaration for *WordRecord* in the previous chapter's program can be modified to serve the purposes of the WordTypes array. The record structure describing the elements of the WordTypes array must include a field of type *String* in which a word can be stored, since one copy of each word in the text will be stored in this array. Each of these records must also contain a variable that can serve as a pointer to the Tokens array, to indicate the position in the Tokens array of the first set of location information for the word stored in that record. Assuming that a subrange of INTEGER type is defined for variables that are used to index the Tokens array, this will be the type given to this variable. So at a minimum, the records in the WordTypes array will consist of two fields, one of type *String* and one of type *TokenBounds* (assuming *TokenBounds* is the name of the sub-range type defining indices into the Tokens array); this is obviously similar to the old declaration of *WordRecord*.

A third field could be added to the record to hold the frequency of the word—that is, the number of times the word appears in the text. Since only one copy of the word is retained in the WordTypes array, information about a word's frequency is not readily available, and since the frequency for every word will be printed as part of the word index it might be nice to have it on hand. Of course, the number of times a word appears in a text can be ascertained by counting the number of sets of location information for that word in the Tokens array, and so it is not essential to maintain the frequency in the WordTypes array. The amount of work in terms of computer time required to determine the word's frequency must be weighed against the "expense" of adding to the space required for the WordTypes array in order to decide whether or not to include a field for frequency in the WordTypes array. Your decision will depend on your computer: if space is limited, as it is in many microcomputers, you may opt to compute the frequency by counting the number of sets of location information for a given word. If space is not a problem (which is more likely if you are using a main frame computer) then you can probably afford the convenience of having the frequency information readily available in the WordTypes array. In the examples for this chapter, a field for frequency will be included in the WordTypes array and filled as words are stored in the array; the program statements to compute the frequency will be covered in the Niceties section at the end of the chapter.

The definition of the type *WordRecord*, then, will be changed to

```
WordRecord = RECORD
               Word : String;
               Frequency : INTEGER;
               TokenLink : TokenBounds;
             END;
```

The definition of the array type will be the same as before:

```
WordArray = ARRAY[1..MaxWords] OF WordRecord;
```

Remember that this array can be smaller than the Words array in previous programs because only one copy of each word will be stored in it, and so you may want to reduce the value given to MaxWords in the Constant Declarations section of the program. The WordTypes array itself can then be declared in the VAR declarations section of the program with the statement

```
VAR WordTypes : WordArray;
```

The Tokens array requires defining an additional record structure, one capable of holding all of the location information for a word. Here the number of the chapter and sentence in which a word appears will be stored, as well as the position of the word within the sentence in which it appears. The word index program will also print out the linear position of each instance of a word within the text, but this information need not be stored within the Tokens array. This is because the location information for each word in the text will be stored in the Tokens array in the order in which the words are encountered; therefore, the number of the slot in which the location information is stored is the linear position for the word to which it pertains. The only other piece of information that must be retained in the records within the Tokens array is the link that will enable maintaining linked lists of location information for the distinct words in the text. As before, this is a variable of type *TokenBounds* that will hold the slot number of the next item in the list. The record structure for the Tokens array will therefore be

```
TokenRecord = RECORD
                Chapter : INTEGER;
                Sentence : INTEGER;
                WordInSentence : INTEGER;
                NextToken : TokenBounds;
              END;
```

NextToken is the field in which the link to the next set of location information for a word will be held. The definition of the array type for the Tokens array is

```
TokenArray = ARRAY[1..MaxTokens] OF TokenRecord;
```

MaxTokens is assumed to be a constant defining the size of the Tokens array. This value will be the same as the value you used for MaxWords in the previous program, because like the Words array, the Tokens array requires enough slots to accommodate every word in the text. The declaration of the Tokens array is

```
Tokens : TokenArray;
```

The Main Program Statements. The main program for the word index problem will call on Load, as usual, to store the words in the input file in main memory. Of course, now Load will store words and associated information in a very different configuration, but *how* Load goes about its work is no concern of the main program's—it only cares that the task is done. However, the main program will have to send different information to Load, since the procedure now works with two arrays rather than one. So the call to Load will be modified to be

```
Load(WordTypes,Tokens,TextFile,NumberOfTypes,NumberOfTokens);
```

The main program passes both the WordTypes array and the Tokens array to Load, as well as TextFile as it has always done. Note that instead of a single variable to keep track of the number of filled slots in the array, as in earlier programs, the main program passes two variables named NumberOfTypes and NumberOfTokens, which will contain the number of words stored in the WordTypes array and the number of elements filled in the Tokens array, respectively, when Load finishes executing. These two variables must, of course, be declared in the declarations section of the main program, and will replace the declaration of NumberOfWords from the previous program. Note that NumberOfTypes will have the type *ArrayBounds* as NumberOfWords did before, but that NumberOf Tokens will have the type *TokenBounds.*

Unlike earlier programs, this one will require no call to the Sort procedure in the main program, since the words will be inserted into the WordTypes array in alphabetical order as they are read from the file. This means that the sorting of the WordTypes array is a sub-task of the Load procedure, and therefore Load must manage the calls to the sorting procedure.

The remaining statements within the main program will prompt the user for a word, read the word, standardize the word, and then print the word index for that word—if that word appears in the text. Before calling on a procedure to print the index, the main program must ascertain whether or not the word is in the text, and for this it can call on the Search function. Instead of Words, the main program will pass the array WordTypes, which contains the words in the text, to the Search function. Since the WordTypes array is declared with the type *WordArray,* it is compatible with the array parameter that appears in the heading of the Search function. Note that it makes no difference to the Search function that the WordTypes array contains only one copy of each word, rather than multiple copies as the Words array did. Note also that changing the way the type *WordArray* is defined has no effect on the statements within the Search function, since the Search function deals only with the Word field of the record.

Within the main program, the call to Search will look just as it always has, except that the main program will pass WordTypes and NumberOfTypes to Search instead of Words and NumberOfTypes. So the call to Search will look like this:

```
Position := Search(WordTypes,NumberOfTypes,UsersWord);
```

This assumes that UsersWord is the word in which the user's word is stored and that both UsersWord and Position are appropriately declared in the VAR declarations section of the main program.

When the Search function finishes executing, the variable Position will either contain the value 0 or the number that indicates the position at which the word was found in the array. As in the program for Chapter Ten, the value of Position can be checked at this point; an IF-THEN statement can be used to check if the value is greater than 0, and if it is, a procedure to print the word index for the appropriate word should be called. This procedure will be named "ShowIndex," and the call to ShowIndex will look like this:

```
ShowIndex(WordTypes,Tokens,Position);
```

ShowIndex will need the WordTypes array, the Tokens array, and the position at which the word was found in the array. ShowIndex does not need the word itself, since it can get to the copy of the word in the WordTypes array by using Position as a subscript to that array. Nor does it need to know how many elements in the WordTypes and Tokens array are filled, since it accesses only the word in WordTypes at position Position, and the procedure will not go through the Tokens array *as an array*—that is, it will not step sequentially from one slot to the next in the Tokens array. Elements within the Tokens array will be accessed instead by traversing the linked lists upon which they appear, and the ends of any of these lists have no relationship to NumberOfTokens. The end of a linked list is reached when the NextToken field of one of the items on the list contains the value 0, not when its slot number equals NumberOfTokens.

If, after Search terminates, it is determined that Position is 0, the program should print a message saying that the word does not appear in the text. This is handled by adding an ELSE clause to the IF-THEN statement described above. So the main program looks like this:

```
BEGIN
  Load(WordTypes,Tokens,NumberOfTypes,NumberOfTokens,TextFile);
  WRITE('Enter a word for which a word index will be generated: ');
  ReadWord(UsersWord,INPUT);
  Standardize(UsersWord);
  Position := Search(WordTypes,NumberOfTypes,UsersWord);
  IF Postion > 0 THEN BEGIN
    ShowIndex(WordTypes,Tokens,Position);
  END     { then begin }
  ELSE BEGIN
    WRITELN('The word ',UsersWord,' does not appear in the text.');
  END;     { else begin }
END.     { main program }
```

Changes to Load

The Load procedure needs to be modified to handle both the new configuration of the arrays and the additional information that must be gathered about each word as it is read in. Specifically, the following changes will be made:

1. The heading of the procedure will be modified to accept both the WordTypes and Tokens arrays and the variables that are used to note the last slot in each of these arrays.
2. Variables to keep track of the current chapter, sentence, and word-in-sentence number as words are read in from the file must be declared and initialized, and statements to increment them at the appropriate times must be added.
3. As each word is read in, location information must be stored in the next available slot in the Tokens array.
4. Words must be stored in the WordTypes array, if necessary, and links between the WordTypes and Tokens arrays or between elements within the Tokens array must be established.

As noted earlier, as far as Load is concerned step 4 will involve only a call to a procedure to perform the tasks indicated. So you can devote your attention to the other three tasks for the time being.

To accommodate the new WordTypes and Tokens arrays, the heading of the Load procedure should be modified to look like this:

```
PROCEDURE Load(VAR FileTypes : WordArray; VAR FileTokens : TokenArray;
        VAR WordsInFile : ArrayBounds; VAR TokensInFile : TokenBounds;
        VAR WordFile : TEXT);
```

The parameter TokensInFile is a pseudonym for NumberOfTokens, which is declared in the main program, and it will hold the number of elements in the Tokens array that are actually filled by the Load procedure. Like WordsInFile, TokensInFile should be given the initial value 0 at the beginning of the statement part of the Load procedure. Note that it is now TokensInFile, not WordsInFile, that will be incremented each time through the WHILE loop in Load—that is, each time a word is read—because location information for each word read is stored in successive slots in the Tokens (FileTokens) array. WordsInFile, on the other hand, is incremented only when a word is inserted into the WordTypes (FileTypes) array, and so this task will be taken over by the procedure SetTokenLink.

To keep track of the current chapter, sentence, and the word-in-sentence numbers, Load will need several new variables. As mentioned earlier, determining the chapter number, sentence number, and word-in-sentence number for each word involves establishing counters that are incremented at appropriate times as the words in the text are read. So three new INTEGER-type variables—ChapterNumber, SentenceNumber, and WordNumber—must be declared in Load. Like WordsInFile and TokensInFile, these three variables should be given their initial values before the beginning of the WHILE loop. ChapterNumber and SentenceNumber should be given the starting value of 1 because these variables are incremented at the *end* of each chapter and sentence, respectively.[7] If these variables were given an initial value of 0, all of the words that appear in the first sentence would have a sentence number of 0, and the words in the first chapter

7. Remember that this program assumes that the chapter marker appears at the *end* of each chapter.

would have a chapter number of 0. WordNumber, however, can be given a starting value of 0 because it is incremented as each word is read in, and before its value is assigned to the WordInSentence field of the Tokens (FileTokens) array.

Once the variables that will do the counting of chapters, sentences, and word-in-sentence are declared and initialized, the only work that remains is to see that they are incremented at the appropriate times during the process of reading and storing the words from the text. ChapterNumber, you will recall, should be incremented by 1 when the chapter marker is encountered in the text. When the chapter marker is encountered, ReadWord will simply read it as a word and pass it back to Load, and so in order to determine whether or not the chapter marker has been encountered, Load can simply check to see if the word just read by ReadWord is, in fact, the chapter marker. If it is, two things need to be done: first, the ChapterNumber variable must be incremented, and second, another word must be read. The latter step is necessary because the chapter marker should not be stored; instead, another word should be read and the process of loading the array should continue. What needs to be done if the chapter marker is encountered, then, is to *skip* the statements that standardize and load the word into the array—that is, skip the set of statements beginning with

```
Standardize(Word);
IF Word <> Blanks THEN BEGIN
                  .
                  .
                  .
```

and terminating with the END that matches the BEGIN in this IF statement. If ChapterMarker is a constant declared in the main program as shown above in the section on "Determining Divisions in the Text," this can be accomplished by inserting the statements to check and increment ChapterNumber within the WHILE NOT EOF loop, as follows:

```
WHILE NOT EOF(WordFile) DO BEGIN
  ReadWord(Word,WordFile);
  IF Word = ChapterMarker THEN BEGIN
    ChapterNumber := ChapterNumber + 1;
  END
  ELSE BEGIN
    Standardize(Word);
    IF Word <> Blanks THEN BEGIN
                  .
                  .
                  .
      Statements to Load the word
                  .
                  .
                  .
    END;     { then begin }
  END;     { else begin }
END;     { while }
```

This will accomplish skipping the statements that load the word when the chapter marker is read. When this happens, control will return to the top of the loop after ChapterNumber is incremented, and if the end of file is not encountered, another word will be read by ReadWord and the process of reading words and loading the array will resume.

As mentioned above, WordNumber will be incremented each time a word is read in, and so the statement

```
WordNumber := WordNumber + 1;
```

can be inserted among the group of statements that is executed each time a word is processed—that is, the group of statements that appears within the IF Word <> Blanks THEN BEGIN . . . END statement. Obviously, the statement to increment WordNumber must appear before it is used to fill the WordInSentence field of the Tokens array. The best place to insert the statement that increments WordNumber is just after TokensInFile is incremented—note that the statement that used to increment WordsInFile must now be changed to increment TokensInFile instead. Thus the statement that adds 1 to TokensInFile and the statement that adds 1 to WordNumber will be the first two statements to appear following the check that Word is not equal to Blanks.

The placement of the statement to increment the SentenceNumber variable, which keeps track of the current sentence number, is more problematic. This variable is incremented only when the end of a sentence has been detected, and therefore a check must be made before incrementing the variable to determine if this has occurred. The end of a sentence is signalled by the appearance of a period, question mark, or exclamation point in the text. However, Load does not see each character as it is read in, as did the sentence-counting program in Chapter Four, and so it must look in each word read by ReadWord to see if a period, question mark, or exclamation point appears within the word.[8] To do this, Load can call on the Index function described in Chapter Eight; this function, if you recall, takes two *String*-type variables as parameters and finds the position within the first string where the second string appears. For example, if the string 'him.   ' is the first parameter, and the string '.   ' is the second parameter, the function returns the value 4, because the second string "starts" at position 4 in the first string. However, if the second string does not appear at all in the first, then the function returns the value 0—and this fact can be used to determine whether or not one string appears within another. That is, if the function returns a value greater than 0, then it is the case that the second string appears within the first. Otherwise, the string does not appear. So within Load, the Index function can be called each time a word is read and used to

8. It is possible, of course, to put the statements to detect the end of a sentence in ReadWord, where each character is seen as it is read in. However, modifying ReadWord to detect the end of a sentence would violate the one-task-per-procedure approach that underlies good programming style. If ReadWord were modified, it would no longer be a general procedure that can be used to read words from a text or from the user at the terminal, as you have done in previous programs. Furthermore, the task of keeping track of location information belongs, conceptually, to Load, and it should not be spread around among a variety of procedures.

determine if a period, question mark, or exclamation point appears in the word. For example, to determine if a period appears in the word, the statement

```
IF Index(Word,Period) > 0 THEN BEGIN ...
```

assuming that Period is a constant declared as follows:

```
CONST Period = '.                   ';
```

Note that since both parameters to Index are *String*-type variables, and therefore consist of twenty characters, the period must be padded with nineteen blanks to be compatible with the variable in the header of Index to which it corresponds.

The question mark and exclamation point can be handled similarly by adding two more constants to the declaration above:

```
CONST Period             = '.                   ';
      Questionmark       = '?                   ';
      ExclamationPoint   = '!                   ';
```

These constants can be declared in Load, since they are used only in that procedure and, unlike ChapterMarker, they will never be changed. Given the declaration above, Index can easily be called to search the word for the question mark and exclamation point as well. In fact, since the program will take the same action if the period *or* the question mark *or* the exclamation point is found to appear within the word, you can modify the condition given above within the IF statement to read

```
IF (Index(Word,Period) > 0) OR
   (Index(Word,QuestionMark) > 0) OR
   (Index(Word,ExclamationPoint) > 0) THEN BEGIN ...
```

This condition will be determined to be true if any of its component conditions is true.

The only things left to determine in order to keep track of the sentence number are what should be done if, in fact, the condition in the IF-statement above is satisfied and the statement or statements following the THEN BEGIN are executed, and where the IF-statement should be placed. Determining what to do is easy: obviously, the SentenceNumber counter must be incremented and the WordNumber variable must be set back to 0. But where should the IF-statement be placed? The calls to the Index function must appear *before* the call to Standardize, since Standardize eliminates punctuation. This seems to indicate that the IF-statement should be placed just before the call to Standardize. But this will not work. If the statement appears before the call to Standardize, then 1 will be added to SentenceNumber before storing the location information for the word that was just read in the Tokens array. But the current word—the one containing the end-of-sentence punctuation—is part of the same sentence as the words that precede it. So the information about sentence number must be stored in the Tokens array *before* the IF-statement checks for end-of-sentence.

We would like to keep the call to Standardize above the **IF Word <> Blanks...** statement, because this ensures that if something like '. . .' appears in the text surrounded by blanks, after it is standardized it will not be stored in the array.

This situation is ripe for the use of a BOOLEAN-type flag. We have a circumstance where you need to determine at some point in a program whether or not something else happened earlier. In this case, you need to know *after* you store the location information in the **Tokens** array whether or not the end of a sentence was found in the check that was made above the call to Standardize. The solution to the problem, then, is to set a BOOLEAN variable that can be named "EndOfSentence" to FALSE, and set it to TRUE inside the IF-statement that checks for the end of the sentence. The statements that add one to **SentenceNumber** and reset **WordNumber** to 0 can then be included in another IF-THEN statement that appears later, after the location information has been stored. The condition on this IF-THEN statement will check to see if the end of a sentence was detected earlier.

All of the statements that store location information for the current word—the one just read by ReadWord—in the **Tokens** array appear within the **IF Word <> Blanks THEN BEGIN** ... construct. These statements simply assign the current chapter number, sentence number, and word-in-sentence number to the next available slot in the **Tokens** array; assuming the variable **TokensInFile** is keeping track of the next available slot in the array, then the following statements are needed:

```
FileTokens[TokensInFile].Chapter := ChapterNumber;
FileTokens[TokensInFile].Sentence := SentenceNumber;
FileTokens[TokensInFile].WordInSentence := WordNumber;
FileTokens[TokensInFile].NextToken := 0;
```

The **NextToken** field of the current record in the **Tokens (FileTokens)** array is always set to 0, whether the word has already been stored in the **WordTypes** array or not. If the word to which this set of location information pertains has been seen already and therefore has been stored in the **WordTypes** array, then this location information record will be added to the *end* of the linked list of sets of location information for that word. If the word has not yet been seen and must now be stored in the **WordTypes** array, this set of location information will be the *only* set (so far) on the linked set for that word, and so it will be at the end of the list in this case as well. A 0 in a record's **NextToken** field indicates that this item is the end of the list, and since the record **FileTokens[TokensInFile]** is always at the list's end at the point when the word with which it is associated is read in, the **NextToken** field is always set to 0.

This takes care of the first three modifications to Load that were given at the beginning of this section. The fourth step will simply be a call to SetTokenLink. SetTokenLink will take the **WordTypes (FileTypes)** and **Tokens (FileTokens)** arrays, **WordsInFile** and **TokensInFile**, and the current word as parameters, and it will set up the required links and store the word in the **WordTypes** array, if it is not already in there. So the call to SetTokenLink will look like this:

```
SetTokenLink(FileTypes,FileTokens,WordsInFile,TokensInFile,Word);
```

This statement can be the last to appear within the IF Word <> Blanks THEN BEGIN ... END; statement, and so Load's loop will look like this:

```
EndOfSentence := FALSE;
WHILE NOT EOF(WordFile) DO BEGIN
  ReadWord(Word,WordFile);
  IF Word = ChapterMarker THEN BEGIN
    ChapterNumber := ChapterNumber + 1;
  END
  ELSE BEGIN
    IF (Index(Word,Period) > 0) OR
        (Index(Word,QuestionMark) > 0) OR
        (Index(Word,ExclamationPoint) > 0) THEN BEGIN
          EndOfSentence := TRUE;
    END;      { then begin }
    Standardize(Word);
    IF Word <> Blanks THEN BEGIN
      TokensInFile := TokensInFile + 1;
      WordNumber := WordNumber + 1;
      FileTokens[TokensInFile].Chapter := ChapterNumber;
      FileTokens[TokensInFile].Sentence := SentenceNumber;
      FileTokens[TokensInFile].WordInSentence := WordNumber;
      FileTokens[TokensInFile].NextToken := 0;
      IF EndOfSentence THEN BEGIN
        SentenceNumber := SentenceNumber + 1;
        WordNumber := 0;
        EndOfSentence := FALSE;
      END;      { then begin }
      SetTokenLink(FileTypes,FileTokens,WordsInFile, TokensInFile,Word);
    END;      { then begin }
  END;      { else begin }
END;      { while }
```

Notice the way the check for the end of the sentence is implemented, according to the plan described above. The BOOLEAN variable EndOfSentence is set to FALSE to begin, and its value is checked after the location information has been stored. If the word just read was the last in the sentence, EndOfSentence will be TRUE and so the appropriate counters are given new values and EndOfSentence is set back to FALSE.

The SetTokenLink Procedure

Corresponding to the call given above for SetTokenLink, the heading of the procedure will be

```
PROCEDURE SetTokenLink (VAR TypesList : WordArray;
        VAR TokensList : Token Array; VAR TypesInList : ArrayBounds;
        TokensInList : TokenBounds; WordJustRead : String);
```

The WordTypes array is passed as a VAR parameter because SetTokenLink changes the contents of the WordTypes array. If SetTokenLink inserts a word in WordTypes, NumberOfTypes will also be changed, and so it, too, must be passed as a VAR parameter. Tokens is passed as a VAR parameter because SetTokenLink changes the contents of a record that exists in the array if the newest set of location information must be added to a linked list that is already established. However, SetTokenLink does not add to the **Tokens** array, and so **NumberOfTokens** is passed as a value parameter, as is **Word**.

SetTokenLink is called from Load each time a word is read in from the file. When the call to SetTokenLink is made from Load, the location information for the word just read in will have been stored in the last open slot in the **Tokens** array—that is, in the slot whose value is currently in Load's variable **TokensInFile**. It is SetTokenLink's job to store the word in the **WordTypes** array if it does not already appear there, and set the appropriate links within the **WordTypes** and **Tokens** arrays. Recall that the algorithm outlining the steps required within SetTokenLink is the following:

1. Search the **WordTypes** array to determine if the word is in the array.
2. If the word is not in the **WordTypes** array, do the following:
   a. Call the insertion routine to insert the word in the **WordTypes** array.
   b. Set the **TokenLink** field for the word to the current value of the token counter.
   c. Set the **Frequency** field for the word to 1.
3. Otherwise, if the word is in the **WordTypes** array, do the following:
   a. Get the position for the first set of location information for the word from its entry in the **WordTypes** array.
   b. Follow the links through the **Tokens** array to find the last item in the list.
   c. Set the Link field for this item to the current value of the token counter.
   d. Set the Frequency field for the word to its current value plus 1.

This algorithm adds two steps to the algorithm outlined earlier, in order to provide for storing and maintaining a count of the word's frequency in the **WordTypes** array. Implementing these steps is relatively easy. A call to the Search function will accomplish step 1, assuming that the **WordTypes (TypesList)** array (rather than the **Words** array, as in previous chapters) and **WordJustRead** are sent to Search as parameters. So the first statement in SetTokenLink will be

```
Position := Search(TypesList,TypesInList,WordJustRead);
```

Position, of course, is the variable in which Search will store the location of the word in the **TypesList** array, if the word is found, or a 0 if the word is not found. Because this variable is used only within SetTokenLink, it should be declared there. Note that another variable named **Position** is declared in the main program and used to store Search's result when it is called from the main program. Although they have the same name, these two variables are completely different, since the one declared in SetTokenLink is created each time SetTokenLink begins executing and is destroyed each time SetTokenLink terminates. Any reference to **Position** within SetTokenLink refers to the "most local" variable with that name, and so it refers to the one declared within that procedure.

To implement the remaining steps in the algorithm, two sets of statements are needed—one to handle the case where the word is not found in the **WordTypes** array, and one to handle the case where it is found. An IF-THEN-ELSE statement will be used to ensure that the appropriate set of statements is executed, depending on the results from the Search function. As usual, the value of the variable Position can be checked to determine whether or not the word is found, and so the IF-THEN-ELSE construct will be something like this:

```
IF (Position = 0) THEN BEGIN
          .
          .
          .
     Statements to handle the case
     where the word is not in WordTypes
          .
          .
          .
END     { then begin }
ELSE BEGIN
          .
          .
          .
     Statements to handle the case
     where the word is in WordTypes
          .
          .
          .
END;     { else begin }
```

The set of statements within the THEN BEGIN and END will implement the part of the algorithm that states

a. Call the insertion routine to insert the word in the WordTypes array.
b. Set the TokenLink field for the word to the current value of the token counter.
c. Set the Frequency field for the word to 1.

Implementing step a is easy: it simply involves a call to the Insert procedure. Insert will take as its parameters the WordTypes (TypesList) array, the number of words currently stored in the WordTypes array (TypesInList), and the word to be searched for (WordJustRead). It must also have a parameter in which to store the position at which it inserts the word; the variable Position can be used for this purpose. When Insert is called, Position will always hold the value 0, as a result of the action of the Search function. Insert will insert the word in the proper slot in the WordTypes array and store in Position the number of the slot in which the word is stored. This information is needed in steps b and c, where access to the word's record within the WordTypes array is necessary. Step b involves setting the TokenLink field in the record in which the word is stored within the WordTypes array to the current value of the token counter, which is called TokensInList in SetTokenLink, and step c sets the Frequency field for this record to 1. So the set of statements that will appear within the THEN BEGIN and END are

```
Insert(TypesList,TypesInList,WordJustRead,Position);
TypesList[Position].TokenList := TokensInList;
TypesList[Position].Frequency := 1;
```

After these steps are executed, the word will be inserted in its proper alphabetical position within the WordTypes array; the TokenLink field for the record in which the word is stored will point to the location information that pertains to that word, and which is the last set of such information to have been stored in the Tokens array at this point in the program; and the Frequency field within the record will indicate that so far, the word appears within the text once.

If the word is already stored in the WordTypes array, then these steps will be taken:

a. Get the position for the first set of location information for the word from its entry in the WordTypes array.
b. Follow the links through the Tokens array to find the last item in the list.
c. Set the NextToken field for this item to the current value of the token counter.
d. Set the Frequency field for the word to its current value plus 1.

Steps a and b can be implemented by slightly modifying the loop to traverse a linked list given in the section entitled "Linked Lists." Here the "header" for the list is obtained from the TokenLink field of the record for the word in question, which, of course, points to the *first* set of location information stored in the Tokens array for that word. Once the position of this set of location information is obtained, the end of the list can easily be found by traversing the list until the last item—the one whose NextToken field contains the value 0—is encountered. So the statements required for steps a and b are

```
Next := TypesList[Position].TokenLink;
WHILE (TokensList[Next].NextToken <> 0) DO BEGIN
  Next := TokensList[Next].NextToken;
END;      { while }
```

Next, of course, must be declared within SetTokenLink.

The only difference between this loop and the one given earlier (apart from the absence of a WRITELN statement in this version) is the condition on the WHILE loop. The loop given earlier stopped when Next, which served as the position indicator for the next item in the list, was assigned the value contained in the NextToken field of the last item in the list and thus contained the value 0. Here the loop must stop when Next contains the value of the position of the last item in the list, since the position of the last item is what is needed in order to set its NextToken field to TokensInList. So here the loop must stop just after Next is assigned the value contained in the NextToken field of the *next-to-last* item in the list. Just after Next has been assigned the value contained in the NextToken field of the next-to-last item in the list, Tokens[Next].NextToken will be 0, since Next points to the last item in the list and the last item's NextToken field always contains the value 0. So the condition on the WHILE loop provides for stopping the loop when TokensList[Next].NextToken is 0.

Once Next is known to contain the position of the last item in the list, the NextToken field for that item can be set to point to the last set of location information stored in the Tokens array with the statement

```
TokensList[Next].NextToken := TokensInList;
```

This statement accomplishes adding the last set of location information stored in the Tokens array to the end of the linked list containing all the sets of location information for the word passed to SetTokenLink. It does this by setting the

NextToken field for the item that was last on the list to point to the set of location information just stored. The **NextToken** field of the token just stored is set to 0 in Load, to indicate that it is now the end of the linked list to which it has just been added.

To increment the frequency count for the word just read, the **WordTypes** array must be accessed. Search has stored the position within the **WordTypes** array where the word was found in the variable **Position**, and so **Position** can be used to access the word's record and increment the frequency count:

```
TypesList[Position].Frequency := TypesList[Position].Frequency + 1;
```

The entire set of statements within the ELSE BEGIN and END is therefore

```
Next := TypesList[Position].TokenLink;
WHILE (TokensList[Next].NextToken <> 0) DO BEGIN
   Next := TokensList[Next].NextToken;
END;      { while }
FileTokens[Next].NextToken := TokensInList;
TypesList[Position].Frequency := TypesList[Position].Frequency + 1;
```

And the whole of SetTokenLink is

```
PROCEDURE SetTokenLink(VAR TypesList : WordArray;
        VAR TokensList : TokenArray; VAR TypesInList : ArrayBounds;
        TokensInList : TokenBounds; WordJustRead : String);
VAR Position : ArrayBounds;
      Next : TokenBounds;
  { Connects WordJustRead to its list in the Tokens array. }
  { Calls Insert to add word to the Types array }
  { if it is not already in there. }
BEGIN      { SetTokenLink }
  Position := Search(TypesList,TypesInList,WordJustRead);
  IF Position = 0 THEN BEGIN
    Insert(TypesList,TypesInList,WordJustRead,Position);
    TypesList[Position].TokenLink := TokensInList;
    TypesList[Position].Frequency := 1;
  END      { then begin }
  ELSE BEGIN
    Next := TypesList[Position].TokenLink;
    WHILE (TokensList[Next].NextToken <> 0) DO BEGIN
      Next := TokensList[Next].NextToken;
    END;      { while }
    TokensList[Next].NextToken := TokensInList;
    TypesList[Position].Frequency := TypesList[Position].Frequency + 1;
  END;      { else begin }
END;      { SetTokenLink }
```

You should begin to see the value of breaking a task down into small procedures, each designed to perform a specific task, when writing a computer program. The job of establishing the **WordTypes** and **Tokens** arrays seems awesome when this program is first described, but here you see that the steps required to do the bulk of that work are straightforward and relatively simple, once they are isolated and dealt with without thinking about the rest of the program.

The Insert Procedure

Insert takes the same parameters as Search: the array in which the word is to be inserted (the WordTypes array), the number of items currently in the array, the word to be inserted. Unlike Search Insert is not a function, so a variable in which to store the position at which the word is stored is also passed as a parameter. Because the array is modified by the procedure, the array must be passed as a VAR parameter. Also, after the word is inserted into the array, the variable containing the number of items currently in the array is incremented by one to reflect the addition of a new item, and therefore this variable, too, must be passed as a VAR parameter. The word to be inserted into the array is not changed by the procedure; it serves as *input* to the procedure, and its contents are assigned to a field within a record in the WordTypes array, and so it should be passed as a Value parameter. The variable in which the position in the array at which the word is inserted by the procedure must be passed as a VAR parameter, since it is given its value in the procedure and serves as *output* from the procedure. So the heading of the Insert procedure will look like this:

```
PROCEDURE Insert(VAR InWords : WordArray; VAR TotalWords : ArrayBounds;
          NewWord : String; VAR NewPosition : ArrayBounds);
```

The statements within the procedure implement the algorithm outlined above for the Insertion Sort. To refresh your memory, the algorithm for the insertion is the following:

1. Set Counter equal to the number of words in the array.
2. While the place at which the word is to be inserted has not been found, do the following:
   a. If the word to be inserted *precedes* the word at position Counter in alphabetical sequence, do the following:
      (1) Move the word at position Counter in the array down one slot, closer to the end of the array.
      (2) Subtract 1 from Counter.
   b. Otherwise, if the word to be inserted does *not* precede the word in the array in alphabetical sequence, do the following:
      (1) Indicate that the place where the word is to be inserted has been found.
3. Insert the word in the slot in the array indicated by Counter+1.
4. Add 1 to the number of words in the array.

Step 1 is easy to implement. To do so, you must declare a variable with type *Array Bounds* in the Insert procedure that will serve as a counter. If this variable is given the name Counter, then the first statement in the procedure will be

```
Counter := TotalWords;
```

Step 2 specifies a sequence of actions that are to be performed repeatedly, until the place where the word is to be inserted is found. Two circumstances indicate that the place where the word is to be inserted has been found: (1) a word is encountered that is less in alphabetical sequence than the word to be inserted, as indicated in step 2.b.1 of the algorithm, or (2) Counter becomes 0, in which case none of the words in the array were "less than" the word to be inserted. In the case of (2), the word should be inserted in the first slot in the array, since it should appear prior to all of the other words in the list.

To implement step 2, then, a loop will be needed that continues as long as a word less than the word to be inserted is not encountered *and* Counter is greater than 0. A BOOLEAN flag can be used to indicate whether or not the point of insertion has been found. This flag can be set to FALSE before the loop begins, to indicate that the point of insertion has not yet been found. If the name given to the BOOLEAN flag is Found, the following statement should appear just after the statement that assigns Counter the value contained in TotalWords (the number of words in the WordTypes array):

```
Found := FALSE;
```

Note that Found is local to the procedure Insert and should be declared within that procedure.

Once Counter and Found have been given their initial values, a WHILE loop with the following heading can be used to implement step 2:

```
WHILE (Counter > 0) AND (NOT Found) DO BEGIN...
```

Steps 2.a and 2.b are implemented inside the loop. Obviously, an IF-THEN-ELSE statement is needed here to provide for the two alternatives; the assertion on the IF-THEN-ELSE statement will be that the word to be inserted is less than the word in the array slot corresponding to Counter. A set of statements that implement steps 2.a.1 and 2.a.2 of the algorithm can be inserted between the THEN BEGIN and END to handle the case where the word to be inserted is less than the word in the slot corresponding to Counter, and a statement that accomplishes the step 2.b.1 can appear within the ELSE BEGIN and END. So the overall structure of the statements within the WHILE loop is

```
IF NewWord < InWords[Counter].Word THEN BEGIN
   Statements corresponding to steps 2.a.1 and 2.a.2
END
ELSE BEGIN
   Statement corresponding to step 2.b.1
END;
```

Step 2.a.1 requires that the word in position Counter in the array be copied into the position below position Counter—namely, position Counter + 1. This is accomplished simply, with the statement

```
InWords[Counter+1] := InWords[Counter];
```

Notice that in the condition on the IF statement, the word to be inserted is compared to only the Word field of the record that is stored at position Counter in the WordTypes (InWords) array. But when a word is moved to the succeeding slot in the array, its entire record is copied. Obviously, it would make very little sense to copy the word without its frequency and the pointer to the list of tokens corresponding to it in the Tokens array. Step 2.a.2 involves decrementing the value of Counter by 1, which requires the statement

```
Counter := Counter - 1;
```

In step 2.b.1, an indication that the word's position is found must be made. Recall that a BOOLEAN flag, named Found, is given the value FALSE just prior to the WHILE loop, and so step 2.b.1 can be implemented by simply changing the value of Found to TRUE. This will, of course, cause the loop to terminate when control returns to the top.

Given all of this, the WHILE loop should look like this:

```
WHILE (Counter > 0) AND (NOT Found) DO BEGIN
  IF NewWord < InWords[Counter].Word THEN BEGIN
    InWords[Counter+1] := InWords[Counter];
    Counter := Counter - 1;
  END
  ELSE BEGIN
    Found := TRUE;
  END;      { else begin }
END;      { while }
```

Note that this loop follows the basic structure for moving through an array that is outlined in Chapter Eight.

Steps 3 and 4 appear after the WHILE loop. Step 3 inserts the word in position Counter + 1 in the array:

```
InWords[Counter+1].Word := NewWord;
```

Only the Word field of InWords[Counter+1] is filled in this statement; SetTokenLink takes care of filling the Frequency and TokenLink fields of the record. Step 4 increments TotalWords, which was passed as a VAR parameter so its value could be modified by Insert:

```
TotalWords := TotalWords + 1;
```

The only thing that the algorithm does not provide for is sending the position at which the word was inserted in the WordTypes array back to the calling procedure (SetTokenLink, in this case). Recall that a VAR parameter named NewPosition was established for this purpose. Since the word was inserted at position Counter + 1, adding the statement

```
NewPosition := Counter + 1;
```

will assure that SetTokenLink knows where the word was inserted in the WordTypes (InWords) array.

The complete set of statements required for the Insertion sort procedure is

```
PROCEDURE Insert(VAR InWords : WordArray; VAR TotalWords : ArrayBounds;
            NewWord : String; VAR NewPosition : ArrayBounds);
  { Inserts NewWord in proper alphabetical sequence in the array InWords }
VAR Counter : ArrayBounds;
  Found : BOOLEAN;
BEGIN     { Insert }
  Counter := TotalWords;
  Found := FALSE;
  WHILE (Counter > 0) AND (NOT Found) DO BEGIN
    IF NewWord < InWords[Counter].Word THEN BEGIN
      InWords[Counter+1] := InWords[Counter];
      Counter := Counter - 1;
    END     { then begin }
    ELSE BEGIN
      Found := TRUE;
    END;     { else begin }
  END;     { while }
  InWords[Counter+1].Word := NewWord;
  NewPosition := Counter + 1;
  TotalWords := TotalWords + 1;
END;     { Insert }
```

Note that the insertion will work for the first word that is inserted into the array. In that case, the value of Counter will be 0 (the current number of words in the array) when the WHILE loop is first encountered. Therefore, the WHILE loop will be skipped entirely and the statements corresponding to steps 3 and 4 will be executed. In step 3, the word to be inserted is placed in the slot numbered with the value of the counter—zero, in this case—plus 1, which will place the word in the first slot of the array.

The ShowIndex Procedure

The only procedure that remains to be written is the one that actually uses the information in the WordTypes and Tokens arrays to produce a word index for a given word. Recall that the main program prompts the user for a word, calls on the Search function to determine whether or not the word is in the WordTypes array, and if it is, it calls ShowIndex. The main program passes the word's position in the WordTypes array to ShowIndex to enable the procedure to access the word and all of the information associated with it.

The heading to ShowIndex will look like this:

```
PROCEDURE ShowIndex(IndexWords : WordArray; IndexInfo : TokenArray;
            WordPosition : ArrayBounds);
```

None of the parameters are VAR parameters, since ShowIndex only accesses information that is already stored in the WordTypes and Tokens arrays.

ShowIndex will actually print the word index. The word index will consist of a listing of each set of location information for the word at position WordPosition in the WordTypes array. Of course, to get at the sets of location information for a given word, one need only traverse the linked list of location information for that word in the Tokens array. As usual, this means using the basic loop for linked list traversal given earlier in the chapter in the section on linked lists. That loop has the general form

```
Next := Address of first item in the list;
WHILE Next <> 0 DO BEGIN
            .
            .
            .
  Statements that access the item at position Next
            .
            .
            .
  Next := ArrayName[Next].Link;
END;
```

Here the "address of the first item in the list" is contained in the TokenLink field of the record at position WordPosition (the location of the word for which the index is to be produced) in the WordTypes array, and the "statements that access the item at position Next" will print out the location information—chapter number, sentence number, word-in-sentence number, as well as linear position—in the element of the Tokens array at that position. All of this information is stored in various fields in each element of the Tokens array, except, of course, the linear position of the word. Recall that the location information for each word in the text is stored in the Tokens array in the order encountered, and so the position at which the location information is stored in the Tokens array is the linear position for the instance of the word to which it corresponds. Therefore, if Next indexes the location information for a given word token, Next itself is the linear position for that word token in the text. So the skeletal loop above can be filled out to be

```
Next := IndexWords[WordPosition].TokenLink;
WHILE Next <> 0 DO BEGIN
  WRITELN(IndexInfo[Next].Chapter,IndexInfo[Next].Sentence,
          IndexInfo[Next].WordInSentence,Next);
  Next := IndexInfo[Next].NextToken;
END;
```

in order to access the information desired.

This loop is really the substance of the ShowIndex procedure. As written above, it will access and print all of the sets of location information for the word stored at position WordPosition in the WordTypes array, which is all ShowIndex is intended to do. But clearly, the output will not be attractive or particularly readable. Some consideration must be given to the output format for the word index.

You can decide what the output of your word index should look like and modify the ShowIndex procedure so that you get what you want. Here are a few suggestions and hints:

1. The word and its frequency should be printed along with the location information for the word.
2. One option for output format is to print a header for the index, like the following:

WORD	FREQUENCY	POS'N	CHAPTER	SENTENCE	WORD-IN-SENT
HOUSE	3	26	1	4	3
		127	1	12	5
		454	1	53	16

   If you choose something like this, you should consider putting the statements that print the header in a separate procedure. This way, if you modify the program to generate an index for more than one word or for the entire text, you can move the call to the procedure that prints the header from inside ShowIndex to the main program, where it can be called so that the header is printed only once.
3. Remember that Pascal takes a width specification following any item in the list in a WRITE or WRITELN statement, and that if the item does not take up all the space requested, Pascal will *pad out* the remaining space with blanks. It pads on the left for numbers and on the right for characters or strings of characters. For example, suppose you use the following WRITELN statement:

```
WRITELN(IndexInfo[Next].Chapter:6,IndexInfo[Next].Sentence:8);
```

   If IndexInfo[Next].Chapter contains the value 2, then 2 will be printed with five spaces to its *left*. The field width specification for this output item is 6, and so six spaces will be used to print the number. Since it actually occupies only one space, the remaining five are made blank. Numbers are always *right-justified* in their fields, so the five spaces appear to the left of the number. If IndexInfo[Next].Chapter contains the value 12, four blanks will appear to its left when it is printed. Similarly, if IndexInfo[Next].Sentence contains the value 145, then 145 will be printed with five spaces to its left. In this way any amount of space you want can be left between items in an output list.

   If a width specification is given for a character or a variable containing a string of characters, then the blanks are added to the *right* of the characters that are printed. For example, if you use the statement

```
WRITELN(IndexWords[WordPosition].Word:35);
```

   then all 20 slots of IndexWords[WordPosition].Word will be printed (including the ones that are blank), followed by 15 blanks to pad out the field to 35 characters, as specified. If you say

```
WRITELN(' ':35);
```

   then you will get the 1 blank that appears between the single quotation marks followed by 34 blanks to fill out the field. This is a simple trick to print a sequence of a specified number of blanks without typing a literal string of blanks. Remember that since the program contains a constant named Blanks that contains twenty blanks, twenty blanks can be had in the output by simply saying

```
WRITE(Blanks);
```

4. You can generate any number of blank lines by issuing a series of WRITELN statements; for example, to get 3 blank lines say

```
WRITELN;WRITELN;WRITELN;
```

The Program as a Whole

In this program many of the old familiar procedures are eliminated and some new ones are inserted. There are also several new variables, constants, and word types declared within the main program, and Load declares three new constants as well. The overall structure is

```
PROGRAM WordIndex(INPUT,OUTPUT,TextFile);
  Constant declarations: StringLength, MaxWords, Blank, Blanks,
          MaxTokens
  Type Declarations: String, StringBounds, ArrayBounds, WordRecord,
          WordArray, TokenArray, TokenBounds
  Variable Declarations: WordTypes, NumberOfWords, Tokens,
          NumberOfTokens, Position, TextFile
  Procedure Declarations:
  PROCEDURE ReadWord(VAR NextWord : String; VAR InputFile : TEXT);
    Variable Declarations: Letter, Counter
    Procedure Declarations:
      PROCEDURE SkipBlanks(VAR NextChar : CHAR; VAR InFile : TEXT);
        Variable Declarations: none
      BEGIN    { SkipBlanks }
        .
        .
        .
      END;    { SkipBlanks }
  BEGIN    { ReadWord }
    .
    .
    .
  END;    { ReadWord }
  FUNCTION Length(LengthWord : String) : StringBounds;
    Variable Declarations: LastChar, EndOfWord
  BEGIN    { Length }
    .
    .
    .
  END;    { Length }
  FUNCTION Index(FirstString,SecondString : String) : StringBounds;
    Variable Declarations: First, Last, LengthFirst, LengthSecond, Found, Lasted
  BEGIN    { Index }
    .
    .
    .
  END;    { Index }
```

```
PROCEDURE SubString(FromWord : String;
          Start, Stop : StringBounds; VAR ToWord : String);
  Variable Declarations: Counter, ToPos
BEGIN     { SubString }
   .
   .
   .
END;    { SubString }
FUNCTION Capitalize (Lowerletter : CHAR) : CHAR;
  Variable Declarations: none
BEGIN     { Capitalize }
   .
   .
   .
END;    { Capitalize }
PROCEDURE Standardize (VAR StandardWord : String);
  Variable Declarations: Counter, FirstLetter
BEGIN     { Standardize }
   .
   .
   .
END;    { Standardize }
FUNCTION Search(SearchWords : WordArray; Last : ArrayBounds;
          WordToFind : String) : ArrayBounds;
  Variable Declarations: First, MidPoint, Found
BEGIN     { Search }
   .
   .
   .
END;    { Search }
PROCEDURE Insert(VAR InWords : WordArray;
          VAR TotalWords : ArrayBounds;
          NewWord : String; VAR NewPosition : ArrayBounds);
  Variable Declarations: Counter, Found
BEGIN     { Insert }
   .
   .
   .
END;    { Insert }
PROCEDURE Load(VAR FileTypes : WordArray;
          VAR FileTokens : TokenArray; VAR WordsInFile : ArrayBounds;
          VAR TokensInFile : TokenBounds; VAR WordFile : TEXT);
  Constant Declarations: Period, QuestionMark, Exclamation
  Variable Declarations: Word, EndOfSentence,
          ChapterNumber, SentenceNumber, WordNumber
  Procedure Declarations:
  PROCEDURE SetTokenLink(VAR TypesList : WordArray;
       VAR TokensList : TokenArray; VAR TypesInList : ArrayBounds;
       TokensInList : TokenBounds; WordJustRead : String);
    Variable Declarations: Position, Next
  BEGIN     { SetTokenLink }
     .
     .
     .
  END;    { SetTokenLink }
```

```
    BEGIN     { Load }
      .
      .
      .
    END;     { Load }
    PROCEDURE ShowIndex(IndexWords : WordArray;
              IndexInfo : TokenArray; WordPosition : ArrayBounds);
         Variable Declarations: Next
    BEGIN     { ShowIndex }
      .
      .
      .
    END;     { ShowIndex }
  BEGIN     { WordIndex }
    Load(Words,NumberOfWords,TextFile);
    WRITE('Enter a word for which a word ',
              'index will be printed: ');
    ReadWord(UsersWord,INPUT);
    Standardize(UsersWord);
    Position := Search(WordTypes,NumberOfWords,UsersWord);
    IF Position > 0 THEN BEGIN
      ShowIndex(WordTypes,Tokens,Position);
    END     { then begin }
    ELSE BEGIN
      WRITELN('The word ',UsersWord,' does not appear in the text.');
    END;     { else begin }
  END.     { WordIndex }
```

Note that the function Index is included in the program and that it must be declared before Load since this is the procedure that calls it. And since Index calls on the Length function, this function must be included in the program and declared before Index.

SetTokenLink is a sub-task of the loading process, and is therefore declared within Load. Unlike functions such as Standardize, SubString, Index, and Length, SetTokenLink is so specialized that it would never be used in another context, and so it need not be available to other procedures in the program. Note that SetTokenLink calls Insert, which, because it can be used in other contexts (see the Exercises), is declared in the main program. This points out a fact about which procedures can call which in a program: a procedure can call its parents' siblings, if they are declared *before* the parent procedure.

SUMMING UP THE PROGRAM

The word index program requires substantial changes to the program that the text is developing. However, restructuring the data enables far more flexibility in the way the information about the words in a text can be accessed. Furthermore, by following through the algorithms and the Pascal statements that implement these algorithms, you have learned some of the basics of data structuring techniques. Linked lists are the most important data structuring technique in the field of computer science, and now that you are familiar with them, you can understand, in general terms, how data in large data bases such as library catalogs, on-line dictionaries, and in data bases such as those used by banks to monitor all their accounts, is organized internally. Most techniques that could be said to be more advanced than the linked list are variations and elaborations on this basic plan. So your understanding of computing and computers is now relatively sophisticated.

NICETIES

Computing Word Frequency

If space is at a premium, then you may not want to store the frequency for each word in the WordTypes array. This could result in a substantial savings in the amount of main memory your program requires to run. Recall that on most computer systems, INTEGER variables take up four bytes of storage. So if your WordTypes array contains a thousand records then you will save 4,000 bytes, or 4K, of storage by not storing the frequency for each word. If your WordTypes array is bigger, then obviously even more space will be saved. On the other hand, if you omit the Frequency field then your program will have to compute the frequency for a word when a word index for that word is generated. This will add to the time that your program takes to run because it will add to the number of statements that are executed in the program. In general, there is always a trade-off between time and space in a computer program: if you minimize the space required to hold the data the program manipulates, then the program almost always has to perform additional steps to do its job.

If you are working with limited memory, but the time your program takes to run is not a factor or is less of a factor than space, then you can omit the frequency field in the definition of *WordRecord*, the type of the records that make up the WordTypes array. These records will then contain only two fields, the Word field and the TokenLink field. When it comes time to print the frequency for a word in ShowIndex, the program can compute the word's frequency by simply counting the number of sets of location information for that word. This is done by traversing the linked list in the Tokens array that is associated with the word and counting the number of sets of location information on the list as you go along. So you will need the standard WHILE loop for linked list traversal to go through the list in the Tokens array in order to compute the word's frequency.

Recall that when the word index is generated within the procedure ShowIndex, the linked list of sets of location information for the word in question is traversed in order to print each set of location information that is on the list. So instead of traversing the linked list twice, once to compute the frequency and once to print the sets of location information, the existing loop can be modified to do both things at once. Of course, this means that the frequency for the word cannot be printed until *after* all of the sets of location information, since obviously the final frequency count is not known until the entire linked list has been traversed. This seems a small price to pay for a significant reduction in the amount of work the program has to do, and so this approach will be described.

Note, however, that if you really want to print the frequency first, you can do so by traversing the linked list twice.

All that is needed to compute the frequency is an INTEGER-type variable in which to keep count of the frequency, a statement initializing this variable to 0, and a statement within the WHILE loop that traverses the linked list to add 1 to this counter variable each time the loop executes. The variable, which can be given the name Frequency, should be declared within the ShowIndex procedure because the value it holds is not used elsewhere in the program. After assigning the value 0 to Frequency before the WHILE loop, the statement

```
Frequency := Frequency + 1;
```

should be placed within the WHILE loop so that the variable is incremented once for each iteration of the loop. Note that it does not matter if this statement precedes or follows the statements within the WHILE loop that print the location information, because incrementing the frequency counter and printing the location information are two processes that do not bear directly on one another.

After the loop has completed execution, the value of the variable Frequency can be printed with a WRITELN statement. You may want to print a label along with the number, like the following:

```
Frequency = 12
```

You can do this easily with the statement

```
WRITELN('Frequency = ',Frequency:1);
```

Counting Lines

If your text happens to be a poem, you may well be interested in line numbers rather than sentence numbers within the text. Unfortunately, way back in Chapter Three a decision was made to see the text stored in the file as a ticker-tape-like stream of characters and to ignore lines altogether. To modify the current program to count lines, you will have to do the unthinkable: change ReadWord so that instead of performing the single task of reading a word, it counts lines as well. This is necessary because ReadWord is the only procedure that has an opportunity to check the input for the end-of-line character.

A line number counter will have to be declared within Load and used just like the sentence counter and the chapter counter to assign a value to a field within the Tokens array, but Load will not increment the variable. Instead, Load will pass the variable to ReadWord when it is called. If Load calls the variable LineNumber, then the call to ReadWord will now be

```
ReadWord(Word,TextFile,LineNumber);
```

ReadWord's heading will have to be modified to include a new variable as well. This variable should have the type INTEGER and be passed as a VAR parameter, since ReadWord alters its contents and the modifications must be known to Load.

To complete the job, an IF-THEN statement must be added to both ReadWord and SkipBlanks. Before the statement

```
READ(InputFile,Letter);
```

in ReadWord the following statement should be added:

```
IF EOLN(InputFile) THEN BEGIN
  LineNum := LineNum + 1;
END;     { then begin }
```

assuming that LineNum is the name of the pseudonym for LineNumber that appears in ReadWord's heading. A similar statement must be added to SkipBlanks, but this means that LineNum will have to be passed to SkipBlanks from ReadWord as well. If SkipBlanks calls the variable Line, then the statement

```
IF EOLN(InFile) THEN BEGIN
  Line := Line + 1;
END;     { then begin }
```

should be added to SkipBlanks inside the REPEAT-UNTIL loop, just before the statement

```
READ(InFile,NextChar);
```

This will accomplish the purpose, provided Load initializes LineNumber to 0 before its WHILE loop and assigns the current contents of LineNumber to an appropriate field in each record in the Tokens array as the words are read in. Note that when ReadWord is called from the main program, some variable must be added to the list of parameters to correspond to LineNum. It does not matter what variable is passed, since what ReadWord does to it, if anything, is irrelevant to the main program. One alternative is to maintain the original version of ReadWord as a separate procedure and use it to read from the keyboard. This is probably as good a *negative* example as any of why it is a good idea to keep procedures single-minded. Counting lines is not a simple matter in standard Pascal, regardless of how your procedures are structured.

Another alternative is to have ReadWord pass a special string of characters back to Load in Word when the end of a line is encountered. This string would serve as a signal to Load to increment LineNumber, just as ChapterMarker does. This scheme eliminates the extra parameter on ReadWord but involves considerable re-structuring of ReadWord and SkipBlanks. Its implementation is left as an exercise.

APPLICATIONS AND CONSIDERATIONS

One of the first computer-assisted text projects ever involved generating a word index: Father Roberto Busa used the computer to generate a word index for the entire corpus of St. Thomas Aquinas. It is interesting to note that Father Busa hand-marked each word with its location information and used the computer mainly for photocomposing the final output, rather than having the computer determine the location of each word as you have done in the program for this chapter.

The idea behind a word index is obviously to give the researcher easy access to information about how many times a word appears in a text and where it appears. In this sense, the word index is just another way of providing the information displayed in a frequency distribution graph. And there are many of the same problems in generating a word index as in generating a frequency distribution graph, especially the problem of homographs, discussed at the end of Chapter Eleven. In a word index you will see location information for *all* occurrences of the word "spring" in the text, regardless of whether it is used as a verb, as a noun indicating the season, or as a noun indicating part of a mattress, unless the text is pre-processed to enable the program to distinguish among these three homographs.

Another problem that crops up in generating a word index or, for that matter, a frequency distribution, involves *lemmas*. Lemmas are the dictionary headings under which a variety of word forms fall. For instance, the lemma for "love," "loves," "loved," "lover," and "loving" is "love"—the dictionary heading under which these words would be listed. The lemma for "is," "are," "was," "were," "be," and "am" is "be."

The problem that arises here with lemmas is that it makes sense to arrange words within the word index according to the lemma under which they fall. For instance, if you wanted to see a word index for "love," it is likely that the other forms of the word are of interest as well. It would be nice if the word index program were able to retrieve all forms of a word that fall under the same lemma automatically. So when the user asks for a word index for "is," he or she would be able to get a word index for all forms of the word "be" if desired. Or if a full word index for the text is generated (see the Exercises for a description of this), all words are listed under their lemma. This is especially useful—consider the case of "be," where, if the output were not lemmatized, the forms of "be" would be spread all over the index and difficult to view as a group. Worse yet, if the text is not lemmatized then the burden is on the user to come up with the list of all forms of the word, a process that is not always error-free.

How does one provide a lemmatized word index? The difficulty arises in determining the lemma for each word in the text. There are three ways to do this:

1. Preprocess the text by hand so that each word is accompanied by its lemma. The program can then be modified to read both the word and its lemma.
2. Write a procedure to determine the lemma for a given word.
3. Give the program access to a dictionary, probably stored in main memory while the program is running, that contains every word in the language and its lemma. Each time a word is read in, the dictionary is searched and the lemma determined.

Once the lemma for each word is determined, the program can be augmented to store additional information so that each word is connected to its lemma.

None of these methods for determining lemmas is easy. Method 1 was the first method devised and used, but it requires tedious human effort. Method 2 has been worked on steadily over the years and some good routines for lemmatizing texts in English have been devised, but the programs are very complex. Obviously, the major task is prefix and suffix removal, but for English, which is not an inflected language, this is not straightforward for a computer program. To get a feel for the complexity of the task, consider an attempt to determine whether "ing" is or is not a suffix in a given word. The letters "ing" form a suffix in "aping" but not in the words "king" or "bring," so one would have to establish a rule that "ing" can be a suffix only when at least two letters precede it, and then, one of these letters must be a vowel. But then note that "ing" is a suffix after double consonants in words like "barring" but not in the word "earring," which defies any attempts to make a rule except one that states, "the string 'ing' is not a suffix when it follows 'earr.'" The same is true for distinguishing the fact that "ing" is a suffix in "eating" but not necessarily in "outing." Obviously, the exceptions are many, and for suffixes other than "ing" things only get worse. (See exercise 10 at the end of Chapter Eleven for a brief discussion of methods for suffix removal.) Therefore, you should not plan to write a program to lemmatize a text without allowing for a long period of time to develop it.

You might think that the third alternative, using a dictionary of lemmas, is not the best means to determine lemmas, but it is becoming an increasingly reasonable option. The drawback of using such a dictionary, if it is held in main memory while the program executes, is the space required to store it. As mentioned earlier, space is becoming less and less a problem on both main-frame and microcomputers. The time required to search such a dictionary is not much of a factor either. Probably the main drawback to this approach is that while several machine-readable dictionaries of lemmas exist, they are not readily available. As soon as this changes, the problem of lemmatization will cease to be a problem at all.

EXERCISES

1. Modify the program in this chapter to give the user the option of seeing a word index for a single word *or* for the entire text.

2. Do exercise 1, but if the user chooses to see a word index for a single word, enable him or her to repeat the process for as many words as desired.

3. Modify the program so that the user has the option of generating a word index *or* a frequency distribution graph for the word entered. To do this, the procedures involved in producing the histogram from the last chapter must be incorporated into the current program and modified to work with the new organization of the data, as follows: (1) the Occurrence procedure is no longer needed, since multiple occurrences of a word do not appear in the **WordTypes** array, and it therefore should not be included in this program; (2) the Distribute procedure should be modified to deal with the new scheme for organizing the data—specifically, the routine will now traverse the linked list of items in the **Tokens** array associated with a word to get the linear position numbers for that word, and compute the segment number as usual; and (3) because it does not deal with the arrays in which the words and information related to the words is stored, the Histogram routine will remain as it was in the previous program.

4. Modify the program in the chapter (or the program for exercise 1 or 2) so that it prints out the following statistics for the text, just after the text has been loaded and before prompting the user for a word: the type/token ratio for the text (the number of distinct words divided by the total number of words in the text), the number of word types in the text, the number of tokens in the text, the number of sentences in the text, the number of chapters in the text, the average number of words per sentence, and the average number of letters per word.

5. One of the most time-consuming parts of this program is in the procedure SetTokenLink, where the linked list of elements in the **Tokens** array is traversed to find the end of the list. This potentially lengthy traversal could be avoided if the location of the *last* item in the linked list of tokens for a given word were stored along with that word in the **WordTypes** array. Currently, only the address of the first item in the linked list is stored with the word in the **WordTypes** array. Modify the program to store the address of the last as well as the first item in its linked list with each word in the **WordTypes** array and use this information to avoid traversing the list in the SetTokenLink procedure.

6. (Slightly more difficult.) The number of the line in which a word appears in the text can be important information for the user as well as chapter, sentence, and word-in-sentence number. Modify the program so that it also stores the line number—the number of the line within the file from which the text is being read—for each word token in the text, as described in the Niceties section of this chapter. When the word index is produced, the line number should appear in each of the sets of location information for the word in question.

7. (More difficult.) Do exercise 9 from Chapter Ten, which asks you to write a spelling check program. Implement the enhancement that enables the user to specify an additional list of words. However, in this case use the Insert procedure to add them to the list in the array that holds the dictionary. Note that you do not need to implement a **WordTypes** and **Tokens** array for the dictionary—a simple array like **Words** will do.

13

Generating a Concordance

In this chapter a program will be developed to generate a *concordance* for any word the user chooses. A concordance is an elaboration of the word index: it provides location information for each of the occurrences of a word, but it also gives the *context* for each occurrence of the word. That is, each set of location information is accompanied by a line or lines of text or perhaps the sentence in which that instance of the word occurs. The amount and kind of context that should be provided for a word in a concordance is an open question, and the tendency recently is to avoid the question entirely by giving the user the ability to specify the amount of context desired. In the program for this chapter, each instance of the word will be printed in the context of the sentence in which it appears for the sake of simplicity; a modification to the program that enables the user to specify the amount of context desired is described in the Exercises.

As before, this program requires no new Pascal language features to implement. The program builds on the new scheme for organizing the data in memory that was developed in the previous chapter. In fact, given that structure, a concordance for any word is very easy to generate with one small addition to the data structure used in the word index program.

Modifications to the Data Structures

The overall process for generating a concordance for a given word is the same as for the word index—that is, the word will be found in the WordTypes array, and then the linked list of sets of location information for the word will be traversed and the location information printed. The difference here is that each time a set of location information is printed, the context for the word will be printed as well.

How can this be accomplished? Quite easily, in fact, as you will see once you recall the organization of the Tokens array. Sets of location information for words are stored in the Tokens array in the order in which the words appear in the text, which means that for any set of location information, the set of location information that is stored in the slot that precedes it in the Tokens array is the location information for the word that precedes it in the text. Similarly, the set of location information stored in the slot that follows it in the Tokens array is the information for the word that follows it in the text. To make this clear, consider the setup shown below for the following single-sentence text. The location information for the word IS, for example, is in slot 3 in the Tokens array. The location information in the slot that precedes it—slot 2—is for the word that precedes it in the text, which is CAT. The location information in slot 4 is for the word IN, which follows IS in the text.

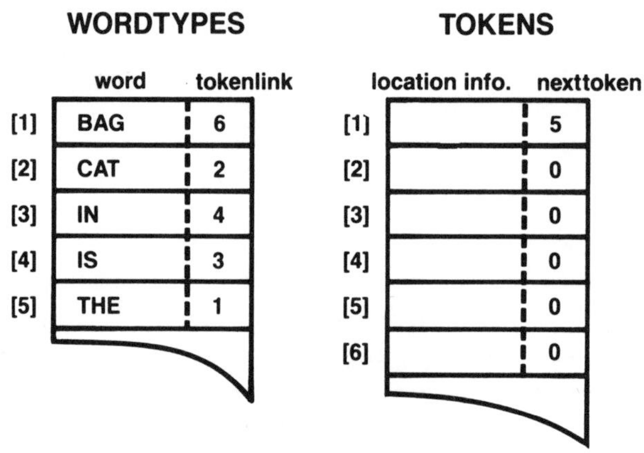

Now suppose that you are generating a concordance for the word IS. You would search the WordTypes array and find IS in slot 4 of that array. To get to the first set of location information for IS, you would follow the Link stored along with the word to get to slot 3 of the Tokens array. At this point you could print the location information for the word. But you must also print all the words in the same sentence as this occurrence of IS in the text. By looking at the setup pictured above, it should be clear that the location information for the first word in the sentence in which this occurrence of the word IS appears is stored in slot 1 in the Tokens array, and that the location information for the last word in the sentence in which this occurrence of IS appears is in slot 6. And it should soon become obvious that if you could back up to slot 1 of the array and then proceed down the Tokens array slot by slot, *printing the word with which the location information in that slot is associated* until you reach slot 6, you will print the sentence in which IS appears.

This whole process can be described algorithmically as follows:

1. Determine the slot number of the token in the **Tokens** array.
2. Find the slot in which the first word in the sentence in which the token appears is stored in the **Tokens** array.
3. Find the slot in which the last word in the sentence in which the token appears is stored in the **Tokens** array.
4. For each successive token in the **Tokens** array, from the first one in the same sentence as the token under consideration to the last, do the following:
   a. Print the word associated with the token.

The concordance program will operate exactly according to this algorithm, but in order to do so, the **Tokens** array must be modified slightly. With this configuration there is no way to implement step 4.a if all you have is the slot number for that set of location information. If you find a word in the **WordTypes** array, you can get to its sets of location information in the **Tokens** array through the **TokenLink** field; but the sets of location information in the **Tokens** array have no similar link back to the words in the **WordTypes** array with which they are associated. In order to enable the concordance program to work, this connection will have to be made.

The connection between each set of location information in the **Tokens** array and the word it applies to can be made by creating yet another link. Here, the slot number in the **WordTypes** array in which the word to which each set of location information applies will be stored with that set of information. This means adding a field to the records in the **Tokens** array to accommodate the link. If these links are established for the example text given above, the resulting structure is as shown in the diagram.

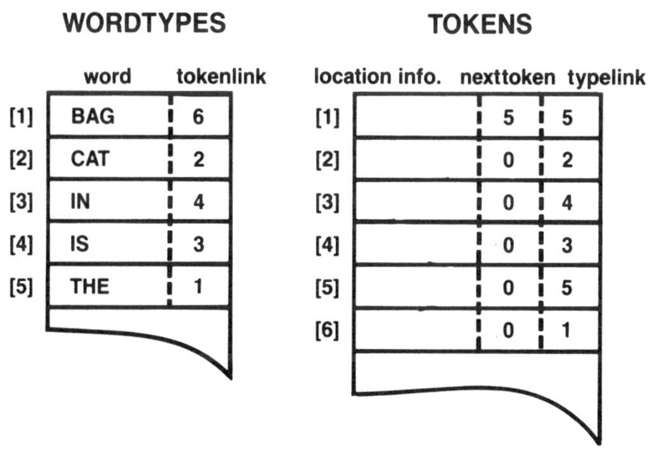

Let us reconsider generating a concordance for the word "is." Having located the set of location information in the **Tokens** array that applies to IS in slot 3, you back up to slot 1 where the location information for the first word in the sentence is stored. You use the contents of the **TypesLink** field of this record to index the **WordTypes** array; here, since the **TypesLink** field contains the value 5, you go to slot 5 in the **WordTypes** array and print the contents of its **Word**

field, which is THE. Then, returning to the **Tokens** array, you simply move down a slot to slot 2. You use the **TypesLink** field of this record—the value 2—to index the **WordTypes** array again, and print the contents of the **Word** field in this record, which is CAT. If you repeat this process for successive slots in the **Tokens** array until you reach the location information for the last word in the sentence, then the entire sentence will be printed.

If the word IS appeared several times in the text above, each of the sentences in which it appeared can be printed by invoking the process above for each set of location information on the linked list for IS. So the loop implementing the steps above will appear within a loop that traverses the linked list of sets of location information for the word in question.

CONSTRUCTING THE PROGRAM

The concordance program requires only very minor changes to the declarations in the main program and the statements within the main program.

Modifying the Tokens Array

The only change required in the Declarations section of the main program is to add a field to the definition of *TokenRecord*. This field will hold the link that will give the position in the **WordTypes** array of the word to which the location information in that record applies. This field will have type *ArrayBounds* because it is the number of a slot in the **WordTypes** array. So the definition of *TokenRecord* in the Type Declarations section of the main program should be changed to

```
TokenRecord = RECORD
                Chapter : INTEGER;
                Sentence : INTEGER;
                WordInSentence : INTEGER;
                NextToken : TokenBounds;
                TypesLink : ArrayBounds;
              END;
```

The new field is named **TypesLink** to indicate that it is a link to the **WordTypes** array.

The Main Program

The statements within the main program will be almost identical to those in the word index program. As before, after the text is read and stored by the Load procedure, the user enters the word he or she is interested in. Search is then called, and if the word is found in the **WordTypes** array, a concordance for the word is generated. So the only change that needs to be made in the statements in the main program is to replace the call to ShowIndex with a call to a procedure that generates a concordance for a given word.

The concordance procedure will need access to the following variables and structures to do its job: the WordTypes array, the Tokens array, NumberOfTokens, and Position, which indicates the location at which the user's word was found in the WordTypes array. Note that unlike ShowIndex, the concordance procedure needs to know the value of NumberOfTokens—this is because the concordance procedure will be moving up and down in the Tokens array, and it must be sure to avoid going beyond the last word in the array. If the procedure is called "Concordance," the call to the procedure will be

```
Concordance(WordTypes,Tokens,NumberOfTokens,Position);
```

Changes to Load

Since Load is the procedure responsible for setting up the WordTypes and Tokens arrays, Load must take care of establishing the new link in each record in the Tokens array that points to the associated word in the WordTypes array.

How should Load go about this? Your first impulse might be to assume that this can be done as the words are read in, just as setting the Link field of the records in the WordTypes array is. This is a very good first impulse, but unfortunately it is the wrong one. It is impossible to set links pointing to records in the WordTypes array until the entire text is read in, because as words are read in they may be inserted into the WordTypes array. And insertion, of course, almost always moves records around in the WordTypes array. Therefore the words in the WordTypes array are not necessarily in their final positions until all of the words in the text have been stored. However Load goes about setting the TypesLink fields in the Tokens array, the statement or statements that do this must appear *after* the WHILE loop in Load, since it is at this point that all of the words have been read from the file and stored in the WordTypes array.

If the text has been read in and stored and the linked lists of tokens have been established, in order to set up the TypesLink field in the Tokens array the following needs to be done:

1. For each word in the WordTypes array, do the following:
   a. For each token on the linked list associated with the word, do the following:
      (1) Set the TypesLink field to point to the record in the WordTypes array containing that word.

Looking at this algorithm, it should be clear that the controlling structure that implements the algorithm will be a loop that enables going through the WordTypes array word by word. Within that loop, statements to implement step 1.a must appear. Step 1.a, of course, involves a traversal of the linked list of tokens for a word, and for this the familiar WHILE loop is used. So the statements above can be implemented with a loop to step through the elements in the WordTypes array, and within that loop, a WHILE loop to traverse the linked list of tokens for an individual word. Inside the WHILE loop a statement to implement step 1.a.1 will appear.

Although the set of statements required to implement the algorithm to set up the TypesLink field is relatively short, it makes sense to set them apart in a separate procedure because this process is really a "sub-task" of Load's overall purpose—to set up the WordTypes and Tokens arrays. The statements in Load take care of keeping track of location information as words are read in and filling in the information in the Tokens array. The business of handling the links in both the WordTypes and Tokens arrays is relegated to sub-procedures, where it can be handled separately and will not clutter up the flow of events within Load itself. So another procedure—call it "SetTypesLinks"—will be established and called from Load, just after the WHILE NOT EOF loop.

What variables and structures will SetTypesLinks need from Load? Obviously, since the procedure will go through the WordTypes array, it needs WordTypes (which has the pseudonym FileTypes within Load), and since it sets the TypesLink field for each record in the Tokens array, it needs Tokens (here, FileTokens) as well. Does the procedure need anything else? Yes—it needs to know the number of words that have been stored in the WordTypes array, because it will go through this array from the first word to the last. Therefore, NumberOfWords(WordsInFile) must be passed as a parameter to the procedure. But note that the procedure does not need to know the value of NumberOfTokens(TokensInFile), since it will access elements of the Tokens array only as members of a linked list.

The call to SetTypesLinks within Load will be

```
SetTypesLinks(FileTypes,FileTokens,WordsInFile);
```

and this statement will appear just after the END on the WHILE loop that reads the words from the file. The addition of this statement is the only change to the Load procedure.

The SetTypesLinks Procedure

Given the call from Load above, the heading on SetTypesLinks will be

```
PROCEDURE SetTypesLinks(SetTypes : WordArray;
          VAR SetTokens : Token Array; EndOfTypes : ArrayBounds);
```

Notice that only the Tokens array is passed as a VAR parameter. SetTypesLinks will change the contents of the TypesLink field for each record in the Tokens array, and these modifications to the contents of the array are, of course, to be retained after the procedure terminates. On the other hand, the procedure makes no changes to the array WordTypes, nor will it change the value of NumberOfWords. Therefore these variables can be passed as Value parameters.

SetTypesLinks implements the algorithm given earlier in the section on "Changes to Load." Therefore the procedure will include a WHILE loop nested within a loop that steps through the WordTypes array.

Since the number of elements in the WordTypes array is known, a FOR loop can be used to step through the array, element by element, accessing each word that is stored in the array. This loop will need a counter that starts at the value 1, is incremented each time the loop iterates, and stops when the counter's value exceeds NumberOfWords, as in the following loop:

```
FOR Counter := 1 TO EndOfTypes DO BEGIN
                        .
                        .
                        .
END;      { for }
```

The variable Counter should be declared with type *ArrayBounds* within SetTypesLinks.

This loop will enable access to each successive word in the WordTypes array as well as its frequency and the pointer to the linked list of tokens for that word, if within the loop Counter is used as a subscript into the WordTypes array. So within the loop we can concentrate on the statements required to handle the word that is stored in slot-number Counter in the WordTypes array. All of the tokens on the linked list associated with that word must be accessed in order to set their TypesLink fields to point to the word in the WordTypes array, and so the statements

```
Next := SetTypes[Counter].Link;
WHILE Next <> 0 DO BEGIN
                .
                .
                .
  Next := SetTokens[Next].NextToken;
END;      { while }
```

Next is the variable that is used to temporarily hold the address of the next item on the linked list and should be declared locally with type *TokenBounds* within the procedure SetTypesLinks. The ellipses indicate the place where the statement(s) that operate on individual items in the linked list of tokens should be inserted. The operation to be performed is setting the TypesLink field of the token to point to the word with which it is associated. The location of the word with which the token is associated is stored in the variable Counter. So, in order to set the TypesLink field to point to the appropriate word, the statement

```
SetTokens[Next].TypesLink := Counter;
```

is all that is necessary.

Putting all of this together, you have

```
FOR Counter := 1 TO EndOfTypes DO BEGIN
  Next := SetTypes[Counter].Link;
  WHILE Next <> 0 DO BEGIN
    SetTokens[Next].TypesLink := Counter;
    Next := SetTokens[Next].NextToken;
  END;      { while }
END;      { for }
```

This does the trick. Very simply. The entire SetTypesLinks procedure is therefore

```
PROCEDURE SetTypesLinks(SetTypes : WordArray;
          VAR SetTokens : TokenArray; EndOfTypes : ArrayBounds);
VAR Counter : ArrayBounds;
      Next : TokenBounds;
BEGIN     { SetTypesLinks }
  FOR Counter := 1 TO EndOfTypes DO BEGIN
    Next := SetTypes[Counter].Link
    WHILE Next <> 0 DO BEGIN
      SetTokens[Next].TypesLink := Counter;
      Next := SetTokens[Next].NextToken;
    END;     { while }
  END;     { for }
END;     { SetTypesLinks }
```

The Concordance Procedure

The main program passes the WordTypes and Tokens arrays, NumberOfTokens, and a variable named Position, containing the slot number in the WordTypes array where the word to be concorded was found, to Concordance. Concordance does not change the contents of any of these variables, and so all of them are passed as Value parameters. The heading of Concordance will therefore look like this:

```
PROCEDURE Concordance(ContextWords : WordArray; Locations : TokenArray;
          NumberOfLocs : TokenBounds; WordPosition : ArrayBounds);
```

A general algorithm describing how to move up and down through the Tokens array in order to generate the sentence in which a specific instance of a word appears was given earlier in the chapter. Before considering how to implement the algorithm in Pascal, you should be reminded that this process must be repeated for every token that is on the linked list associated with the word for which the user has requested a concordance. This means that the process will be repeated once for each token on the list associated with the word. Obviously, this will require a traversal of the linked list of tokens for that word, and of course, the trusted WHILE loop for linked list traversal will come into play. The statement preceding the WHILE loop will put the address of the first item in the list in a variable which we usually give the name Next; since the word for which the concordance is to be generated is in slot number Position in the WordTypes array, the statement

```
Next := ContextWords[WordPosition].Link;
```

will perform this function, given that WordPosition is the parameter corresponding to Position in the header of procedure Concordance. This will be the first statement within the procedure. This is followed, as usual, by the standard WHILE loop structure for linked list traversal:

```
WHILE Next <> 0 DO BEGIN
          .
          .
          .
  Next := ContextWords[Next].NextToken;
END;
```

As usual, the statements that operate on the individual token in the linked list will be inserted where the ellipses appear. In Concordance the operation involves printing the sentence in which the token appears.

The statements within the WHILE loop in the Concordance procedure will print both the location information for each token and the sentence in which the token appears. To print the location information, you need only print out the Chapter, Sentence, and WordInSentence fields of the record at position Next in the Tokens array as well as the value of Next itself, which is the linear position of the word in the text. The WRITELN statement to do this can be borrowed directly from ShowIndex. The statement will be the first statement within the WHILE loop that traverses the linked list of tokens.

The algorithm to generate the sentence in which a particular token appears was given earlier in this chapter; it is

1. Determine the slot number of the token in the Tokens array.
2. Find the slot in which the first word in the sentence in which the token appears is stored in the Tokens array.
3. Find the slot in which the last word in the sentence in which the token appears is stored in the Tokens array.
4. For each successive token in the Tokens array, from the first one in the same sentence as the token under consideration to the last, do the following:
   a. Print the word associated with the token.

Within the WHILE loop, we are of course dealing with a specific token located at slot number Next in the Tokens array. In order to move through the Tokens array from the first token in the same sentence to the last one in the same sentence, it is necessary to first *find* the first and last tokens that are in the same sentence as the token at slot number Next. This is a preliminary step in the process of generating the concordance, and therefore the Concordance procedure will relegate this task to another procedure that it can call upon before it gets down to the business of printing the sentence in which the token occurs. If this procedure is given the name FindContext, then the statement

```
FindContext(Locations,NumberOfLocs,Next,First,Last);
```

will be the second statement inside the WHILE loop.

Concordance passes the Tokens (Locations) array, NumberOfTokens (NumberOfLocs) (because FindContext will move around in the Tokens array and must be sure not to move beyond the last token), Next, and two variables named First and Last (declared within Concordance) to FindContext. When FindContext is called, First and Last will have no values; it is the procedure's job to put the slot number of the token corresponding to the first word in the sentence in the variable First, and the slot number of the last word in the sentence in the variable Last. Concordance can then use these values to move through the appropriate portion of the Tokens array in order to print the sentence.

Once Concordance has access to the slot number of the location information for the first word in the sentence and the slot number of the location information for the last word in the sentence, printing the sentence is a matter of moving through the Tokens array from slot number First to slot number Last, and printing the word associated with the location information stored in each successive slot along the way. For this a straightforward FOR loop will suffice, with the following heading:

```
FOR Counter := First TO Last DO...
```

Inside the loop, successive elements of the Tokens array can be accessed by using Counter as a subscript into the array. Counter should be declared locally, within the procedure Concordance, since the values it contains are not used by the main program.

Now, since the object is to print the word that is associated with each set of location information stored between slot First and slot Last in the Tokens array, it is actually the information about the token in the WordTypes array (where the words are actually stored) that must be accessed. With the addition of the TypesLink field to the records within the Tokens array, of course, the word associated with each token can be accessed easily. Inside the FOR loop, the location of that word in the WordTypes array can be obtained with the statement:

```
NextType := Locations[Counter].TypesLink;
```

This statement assumes that a variable with type *ArrayBounds* named NextType has been declared within Concordance. The contents of the TypesLink field in the slot numbered Counter in the Tokens (Locations) array is stored in NextType; NextType can now be used as a subscript into the WordTypes array. The Word field of the element of the WordTypes (ContextWords) array at position NextType contains the word associated with the token at position Counter in the Tokens array. To print the word, then, the statement

```
WRITE(ContextWords[NextType].Word);
```

can be used.

The FOR loop and the WRITE statement given above are technically all that is needed to print the sentence in which the token under consideration appears, assuming that after the FOR loop terminates, a WRITELN statement is inserted to issue a line eject. However, it should be obvious that the output will not be especially readable if the simple scheme above is used. This is because the WRITE statement above will write out all twenty characters in ContextWords[NextType].Word, and usually this means that a string of several blanks will follow each word. The way to avoid this is to use the procedure WriteWord given in the Niceties section of Chapter Eight, which prints only the non-blank characters in a word. WriteWord takes the *String*-type variable containing the word to be printed as a parameter, so, if the WRITE statement above is replaced with a call to WriteWord, the statements to write out the sentence will be

```
FOR Counter := First TO Last DO BEGIN
  NextType := Locations[Counter].TypesLink;
  WriteWord(ContextWords[NextType].Word);
  WRITE(' ');
END;     { for }
WRITELN;
```

The statement after the call to WriteWord writes a single blank following the word; if this were not done, all of the words in the sentence would be strung together with no blanks in between them.

This set of statements does the basic job of writing the sentence, and you should be sure to understand how and why it works before continuing on. A few statements must be added to this basic loop, though, in order to take into consideration the possibility that the sentence that is being printed is longer than the output line, in which case either an error will result or the line will be wrapped around when you try to add more characters to the line. The only solution to this problem is simply to keep track of the length of the sentence as it is being generated. When tacking another word on to the end of the sentence as it has been generated so far would cause the line to exceed the output line length, then a WRITELN can be issued and a new line begun.

To do all this you will need another variable, which you can call LineLength, that keeps track of the length of the line so far. Just before issuing the call to WriteWord, which will add the word to the end of the line, you can check to see if adding this word will cause the length of the line you are printing to be greater than the maximum line length (or, as you will see, greater than some line length you decide on). If so, you can issue a WRITELN to generate a line eject, and then go on to call WriteWord, which will add the word to the "end" of a new line.

In order to keep track of the line length, you will have to be able to ascertain the number of characters in the word that is to be printed. This can be accomplished by using the Length function described in Chapter Eight. Length can be called upon to determine the length of the word; this value can be added to the current value of LineLength, and if the resulting value exceeds the allowed line length, appropriate action can be taken. This process can be described algorithmically as follows:

1. Set LineLength to 0.

2. As each word is retrieved from the WordTypes array, do the following:
   - **a.** Ascertain the length of the word.
   - **b.** Add the length of the word, plus 1 to account for the blank that follows the word, to LineLength.
   - **c.** If LineLength exceeds the maximum value, do the following:
     - **(1)** Issue a line eject.
     - **(2)** Set LineLength to be the length of the word about to be printed, plus 1 to account for the blank printed after it.
   - **d.** Write the word.

The statements implementing the steps under step 2 will appear within the FOR loop given above, since they are taken for each word in the sentence. Note that **LineLength** is set to 0 *before* the FOR loop begins executing. Within the loop, if a new line is started (step 2.c), **LineLength** is set to equal the length of the word plus 1, since the length of this new line is the same as the length of the word and the blank that follows it.

The maximum allowable length of the line does not have to correspond to the maximum allowed—for instance, you might want your lines to be only 80 characters long (a reasonable length for display on most terminal screens). If so, then the value that you will use to ensure that **LineLength** does not exceed will be 80. In fact, a good strategy here is to declare a constant that specifies a maximum line length. This will make the maximum line length easily modifiable. Whatever value you decide on for the maximum line length, each time a word is about to be added to the output line within the FOR loop above, you will check that the value of **LineLength** does not exceed the value of the constant.

The statements within the FOR loop will now be something like this:

```
LineLength := 0;
FOR Counter := First TO Last DO BEGIN
  NextType := Locations[Counter].TypesLink;
  WordLength := Length(ContextWords[NextType].Word);
  LineLength := LineLength + (WordLength+1);
  IF Linelength > MaxLine THEN BEGIN
    WRITELN;
    LineLength := WordLength + 1;
  END;
  WriteWord(ContextWords[NextType].Word);
  WRITE(' ');
END;
WRITELN;
```

This set of statements assumes a variable **WordLength** of type *StringBounds*, declared within Concordance, and a constant named **MaxLine** that can also be declared in Concordance. Note also the call to the function Length in the second statement inside the FOR loop.

This set of statements can be modified to produce output that is formatted more elaborately than what will be produced by the loop above. In particular, note that with the statements given, the location information for each occurrence of the word will be printed on one line and the sentence will be printed below it. You might want to try something fancier, perhaps including a header labeling the information. For example, your output could be

```
Concordance for the word OLD

Ch  Sent  WIS  Pos    Context
 1    1    21   21    SIR I LOVE THE ACQUAINTANCE OF YOUNG PEOPLE
                      BECAUSE IN THE FIRST PLACE I DON'T LIKE TO
                      THINK MYSELF GROWING OLD
 1    2    23   44    IN THE NEXT PLACE YOUNG ACQUAINTANCES
                      MUST LAST LONGEST IF THEY DO LAST AND THEN
                      SIR YOUNG MEN HAVE MORE VIRTUE THAN OLD
                      MEN THEY HAVE MORE GENEROUS SENTIMENT IN
                      EVERY RESPECT
```

This is one possible format, and you can be as creative as you like in deciding how you would like your output to look, since output format is up to the discretion of the designer of the concordance program. If you have access to special features for controlling the display on your screen you can even consider fancy enhancements such as highlighting the concorded word in its context.

The overall structure of the Concordance procedure is defined by the skeleton WHILE loop for linked list traversal given earlier. Within this loop the statements to print the location information for a specific token (at position Next), the call to FindContext to get the locations of the First and Last words in the sentence, and the FOR loop given above will appear.

Several local variables must be declared within Concordance: First, Last, Counter, Next, LineLength, WordLength, and NextType. The constant MaxLine should be declared in the Constant Declarations section of Concordance. So Concordance ultimately looks something like this:

```
PROCEDURE Concordance(ContextWords : WordArray;
            Locations : TokenArray; NumberOfLocs : TokenBounds;
            WordPosition : ArrayBounds);
  { Produces a concordance for the word in position }
  { WordPosition of the ContextWords array. }
CONST MaxLine = 80;
VAR Next, First, Last : TokenBounds;
     LineLength : INTEGER; WordLength : StringBounds;
BEGIN      { Concordance }
   Next := ContextWords[WordPosition]TokenLink;
   WHILE Next <> 0 DO BEGIN
                              .
                              .
                              .
     Statements to print chapter, sentence, word in sentence,
     and linear position number
                              .
                              .
                              .
     FindContext(Locations, NumberOfLocs,Next,First,Last);
     LineLength := 0;
     FOR Counter := First TO Last DO BEGIN
        NextType := Locations[Counter].TypesLink;
        WordLength := Length(ContextWords[NextType].Word);
        LineLength := LineLength + (WordLength + 1);
        IF LineLength > MaxLine THEN BEGIN
           WRITELN;
           LineLength := WordLength + 1;
        END;      { then begin }
        WriteWord(ContextWords[NextType].Word);
        WRITE('  ');
     END;      { for }
     WRITELN;
     Next := Locations[Next].NextToken;
  END;      { while }
END;      { Concordance }
```

The FindContext Procedure

The final procedure to be written for the Concordance program is FindContext. FindContext takes as parameters the **Tokens** array, the variable **Next**, which gives it the location of the token under consideration, the variable **NumberOfLocs**, and two variables **First** and **Last** in which it will store the slot numbers of the tokens corresponding to the first and last words in the same sentence as the token at slot **Next**, respectively. Because FindContext modifies the values of only **First** and **Last**, these two are the only variables passed as VAR parameters. The heading to the procedure, then, is

```
PROCEDURE FindContext(ContextTokens : TokenArray;
            EndOfTokens, ThisToken : TokenBounds;
            VAR FirstInSentence, LastInSentence : TokenBounds);
```

Actually, the FindContext procedure has already been written for the most part, because the process of moving backwards and forwards in an array until a particular entity is found is described by the procedure Occurrence that was given in Chapter Ten. That procedure used two loops, one to go backwards in the array until the first occurrence of a given word was found, and one to go forward until the last occurrence was found. Here you need to do exactly the same thing, except that instead of continuing to move up or down in the array while the word is the same as the word in the original position, you will continue while the *sentence number* is the same as that of the token at position **ThisToken**. This algorithm describes the overall process:

1. Set a counter named **FirstInSentence** to be 1 less than the slot number of the token.
2. While the token at position **FirstInSentence** is in the same sentence as the original token, do the following:
   a. Subtract 1 from **FirstInSentence**.
3. Add 1 to **FirstInSentence**.
4. Set a counter named **LastInSentence** to be 1 greater than the slot number of the original token.
5. While the token at position **LastInSentence** is in the same sentence as the original token, do the following:
   a. Add 1 to **LastInSentence**.
6. Subtract 1 from **LastInSentence**.

Occurrence implemented a nearly identical algorithm by using a BOOLEAN variable to signal when a word different from the one under consideration was found in the array. The two loops in that procedure were based on the standard model for moving through an array until some condition arises. Two loops nearly identical to these can be used here:

```
FirstInSentence := ThisToken - 1;
SameContext := TRUE;
WHILE (FirstInSentence > 0) AND (SameContext) DO BEGIN
  IF ContextTokens[ThisToken].Sentence =
            ContextTokens[FirstInSentence].Sentence THEN BEGIN
    FirstInSentence := FirstInSentence - 1;
  END    { then begin }
```

```
    ELSE BEGIN
      SameContext := FALSE;
    END;     { else begin }
  END;     { while }
  FirstInSentence := FirstInSentence + 1;
  LastInSentence := ThisToken + 1;
  SameContext := TRUE;
  WHILE (LastInSentence <= EndOfTokens) AND (SameContext) DO BEGIN
    IF ContextTokens[ThisToken].Sentence =
            ContextTokens[LastInSentence].Sentence THEN BEGIN
      LastInSentence := LastInSentence + 1;
    END     { then begin }
    ELSE BEGIN
      SameContext := FALSE;
    END;     { else begin }
  END;     { while }
  LastInSentence := LastInSentence - 1;
```

This set of statements is all that is needed in FindContext. Note that it assumes a local BOOLEAN variable named SameContext.

The Program as a Whole

This program adds three procedures, SetTypeLinks, FindContext, and Concordance, to the program as it existed in the last chapter. ShowIndex can be eliminated from the program (except where it is needed for programs in the Exercises).

Concordance, of course, is declared in the main program's Procedure Declarations section, because the main program calls Concordance. But FindContext is a specialized procedure that only Concordance calls and so it can be declared inside Concordance. Similarly, SetTypesLinks can be declared in Load. This gives the overall program structure:

```
PROGRAM Concord(INPUT,OUTPUT,TextFile);
  Constant declarations: StringLength, MaxWords, Blank, Blanks,
          MaxTokens
  Type Declarations: String, StringBounds, ArrayBounds, WordRecord,
          WordArray, TokenArray, TokenBounds
  Variable Declarations: Words, NumberOfWords, Tokens, NumberOfTokens
          Position, TextFile
  Procedure Declarations:
  PROCEDURE ReadWord(VAR NextWord : String; VAR InputFile : TEXT);
    Variable Declarations: Letter, Counter
    Procedure Declarations:
    PROCEDURE SkipBlanks (VAR NextChar : CHAR; VAR InFile : TEXT);
      Variable Declarations: none
    BEGIN     { SkipBlanks }
      .
      .
      .
    END;     { SkipBlanks }
```

```
BEGIN     { ReadWord }
   .
   .
   .
END;     { ReadWord }
FUNCTION Length(LengthWord : String) : StringBounds;
  Variable Declarations: LastChar, EndOfWord
BEGIN     { Length }
   .
   .
   .
END;     { Length }
FUNCTION Index(FirstString, SecondString : String) : StringBounds;
  Variable Declarations: First, Last, LengthFirst,
         LengthSecond, Found, Lasted
BEGIN     { Index }
   .
   .
   .
END;     { Index }
PROCEDURE SubString(FromWord : String; Start, Stop : StringBounds;
         VAR ToWord : String);
  Variable Declarations: Counter, ToPos
BEGIN     { SubString }
   .
   .
   .
END;     { SubString }
FUNCTION Capitalize(Lowerletter : CHAR) : CHAR;
  Variable Declarations: none
BEGIN     { Capitalize }
   .
   .
   .
END;     { Capitalize }
PROCEDURE Standardize(VAR StandardWord : String);
  Variable Declarations: Counter, FirstLetter
BEGIN     { Standardize }
   .
   .
   .
END;     { Standardize }
FUNCTION Search(SearchWords : WordArray; Last : ArrayBounds;
         WordToFind : String) : ArrayBounds;
Variable Declarations: First, MidPoint, Found
BEGIN     { Search }
   .
   .
   .
END;     { Search }
PROCEDURE Insert(VAR InWords : WordArray;
         VAR TotalWords : ArrayBounds; NewWord : String;
         VAR NewPosition : ArrayBounds);
Variable Declarations: Counter, Found
```

```
BEGIN     { Insert }
   .
   .
   .
END;     { Insert }
PROCEDURE Load(VAR FileTypes : WordArray; VAR FileTokens : TokenArray;
        VAR WordsInFile : ArrayBounds; VAR TokensInFile : TokenBounds;
        VAR WordFile : TEXT);
  Constant Declarations: Period, QuestionMark, Exclamation
  Variable Declarations: Word, EndOfSentence,
          ChapterNumber, SentenceNumber, WordNumber
  Procedure Declarations:
  PROCEDURE SetTokenLink(VAR TypesList : WordArray;
        VAR TokensList : TokenArray; VAR TypesInList : ArrayBounds;
        TokensInList : TokenBounds; WordJustRead : String);
   Variable Declarations: Position, Next
  BEGIN     { SetTokenLink }
     .
     .
     .
  END;     { SetTokenLink }
  PROCEDURE SetTypesLinks(SetTypes : WordArray;
        VAR SetTokens : TokenArray; EndOfTypes : ArrayBounds);
   Variable Declarations: Counter, Next
  BEGIN     { SetTypesLinks }
     .
     .
     .
  END;     { SetTypesLinks }
BEGIN     { Load }
   .
   .
   .
END;     { Load }
PROCEDURE Concordance(ContextWords : WordArray; Locations : TokenArray;
        NumberOfLocs : TokenBounds; WordPosition : ArrayBounds);
  Constant Declarations: MaxLine
  Variable Declarations: Next, First, Last,
          LineLength, WordLength
  Procedure Declarations:
  PROCEDURE FindContext(ContextTokens : TokenArray;
        EndOfTokens, ThisToken : TokenBounds;
        VAR FirstInSentence, LastInSentence : TokenBounds);
   Variable Declarations: SameContext
  BEGIN     { FindContext }
     .
     .
     .
  END;     { FindContext }
BEGIN     { Concordance }
   .
   .
   .
END;     { Concordance }
```

```
BEGIN     { Concord }
  Load(Words,NumberOfWords,TextFile);
  WRITE('Enter a word for which a  ',
        'concordance will be printed:  ');
  ReadWord(UsersWord,INPUT);
  Standardize(UsersWord);
  Position := Search(WordTypes,NumberOfWords,UsersWord);
  IF Position > 0 THEN BEGIN
    Concordance(WordTypes,Tokens,NumberOfTokens,Position);
  END     { then begin }
  ELSE BEGIN
    WRITELN('The word ',UsersWord,' does not appear in the text.');
  END;    { else begin }
END.     { Concord }
```

SUMMING UP THE PROGRAM

This completes the concordance program in its basic form. The Exercises suggest several interesting enhancements to the program that make it quite flexible and useful. If you have been modifying the program so that the user will have the option of generating a distribution graph, a word index, or a concordance, the program you now have performs a variety of the fundamental tasks of text analysis. More importantly, the program forms a base upon which to build a system that is even more flexible, general, and tailored to your own needs.

NICETIES

Saving and Retrieving the WordTypes and Tokens Arrays

Generating a concordance for various words in a text is something a user might want to do at different times and over the course of days or even months. The program written in this chapter enables the user to re-run the program any time he or she wants to see a concordance for a given word, but this involves loading, structuring, and storing the text each time the program is run. The loading process may actually consume a fair amount of computer time, if not "real time," especially if you are using a microcomputer. The ideal situation would enable the user to save, in a file on disk, the structured version of a text—that is, the contents of the WordTypes and Tokens arrays. Then, when the program is run at a later time and will use the same text, instead of reading the raw text from the file as the program usually does, the program will read in the structured text instead and store it directly in the WordTypes and Tokens arrays. The time needed to read in each word, standardize it, search the WordTypes array to see if it exists, insert in the WordTypes array in some cases, and finally set up the links in the WordTypes and Tokens arrays will be saved, and the program will execute potentially much faster. Pascal provides a very economical way to store and retrieve data structures from disk by using what are called *structured files*.[1]

Structured Files. Pascal's structured files are a variation on the files of type TEXT that you are familiar with already. Files of type TEXT are, from Pascal's perspective, regarded as files consisting of a sequence of individual characters. The "component element" of which the TEXT file is composed is the character—in Pascal's terms, this means that when a READ is issued for a file of type TEXT, a single character is read.[2] Structured files are simply files in which the component element—the smallest element that can be read from or written to the file—is something other than a single character. You, the programmer, are the one who defines the component element of a structured file.

In your program, you will need two structured files—one that holds the information contained in the WordTypes array and one that holds the information contained in the Tokens array. The component element of the file that holds the information in the WordTypes array will be type-*WordRecord*, and the component element of the file that holds the information in the Tokens array type *TokenRecord*. Your program will have the capability to both read from these files (in the event that the structured text has already been stored on a previous run of the program) and write to these files (if the user wants to retain the structured text for later use). When it reads from the file containing the information for the WordTypes array, whole *WordRecords* (word, frequency, and link) will be read at a time, and when the file is written to, whole *WordRecords* will be written at a time. Reading from and writing to the file associated with the Tokens array will involve whole *TokenRecords*. Again, you can think of a component element as the individual entity that is read from or written to a file.

There are one or two things that you need to know about structured files before going on.

A structured file can be created only from within a Pascal program—you cannot create a structured file with a text editor, for example.

---

1. Again, be warned that file manipulation can differ substantially from version to version of Pascal. This is especially true for Turbo Pascal, which does not implement structured files. If you are using Turbo Pascal, the discussion below is irrelevant; if you are using any other version of Pascal, the discussion below will apply, but nonetheless you should re-familiarize yourself with the method of file handling in your version of Pascal before going on.

2. The exception to this in standard Pascal is reading numbers—when a READ is issued for a TEXT file and the variable into which what is read is to be stored in type INTEGER or REAL, then a number which may consist of several digits or "characters" is actually read. (See Chapter Four for a discussion of reading numbers from a file.) The ability to read numbers from a TEXT file in this way violates the notion of the TEXT file as a file consisting of characters, but the designers of Pascal saw that the language would have a serious flaw if you were not able to read numbers as numbers from a text file, since all user-created files are of type TEXT. If only characters could be read from a text file, then numeric data typed by the user and then inputted into a Pascal program would have to be read each digit as a character, and an elaborate set of statements to translate the digits into their numeric equivalents would have to be written. Therefore the exception was allowed.

Once your program stops executing after it has written a structured file out on disk, the file is just like any other file that you may have in your directory of files. However,

You cannot print or display the stored structured file with operating system commands or manipulate it in any other way, except by reading it back into a Pascal program.

The reason for this is that the file is stored in its *internal Pascal representation*—a representation of the data in main memory as a code consisting of 0's and 1's, which may differ from implementation to implementation of Pascal. This internal representation is different from the ASCII or EBCDIC codes discussed earlier in Chapter Five. In fact, in order to display data at a terminal or on a printer, the internal Pascal codes for the data must be translated into either the ASCII or EBCDIC code (whichever your system uses), and then this code interpreted by the terminal or printer in order to display the corresponding character. Data is also translated into ASCII or EBCDIC when it is written to a file of type TEXT. By storing the data in a structured file in its internal Pascal representation, the step of translating it into the ASCII or EBCDIC code is eliminated. Furthermore, when the file is read again by the Pascal program, the ASCII or EBCDIC codes do not need to be translated back into internal Pascal codes. This clearly saves time.

Declaring Structured Files. In the programs you have written so far, in order to read from the file containing your text you had to establish a name within the program by which the file would be known. You did this by first listing the name by which the file would be known in the Program Heading, and second declaring the file in the Declarations section of the program. In order to use a structured file in your program, you will do both of these things. The name by which the file will be known in the program will be put in the Program Heading. And the file will be declared in the Declarations section of the program, but it will not have the type TEXT. Instead, you will have to define a type in the Type Declarations section of the main program that can be assigned to your file; to do this, you use a type definition in the following form:

```
<typename> : FILE OF <component-type>;
```

where <*typename*> is a name of your choosing for the new file type, and <*component-type*> is the type of the component elements of which a file with this type is made up. For example, you will want a file capable of holding *WordRecords*, the elements of which the WordTypes array is composed. You can define a type for a file of *WordRecords* with

```
TypeFile = FILE OF WordRecord;
```

Note that this type definition must appear after the type definition WordRecord in the Type Declarations section. If you name this file StoredTypes, then the declaration of this file in the VAR Declarations section is

```
StoredTypes : TypeFile;
```

A type for a file that holds items of type *TokenRecord* can be defined as

```
TokenFile = FILE OF TokenRecord;
```

and a file to hold *TokenRecords* is then declared in the VAR Declarations section as

```
StoredTokens : TokenFile;
```

assuming the file is named StoredTokens.

If the two file declarations above appear in the VAR Declarations section of the main program, then the Program Heading must be modified to look like this:

```
PROGRAM Concord(INPUT,OUTPUT,TextFile,StoredTypes,StoredTokens);
```

This sample heading assumes that you name your program "Concord."

The declarations above indicate to Pascal that two names—StoredTypes and StoredTokens—will be used in the program to designate files. StoredTypes designates a file from which whole *WordRecords* are read and to which whole *WordRecords* are written. StoredTokens designates a file from which whole *TokenRecords* are read or to which *TokenRecords* are written. Pascal at this point does not know whether the program will read or write to the files. It only knows that the names stand for files and what the types of those files are.

Remember that your system may have additional mechanisms for associating the names by which files are known *within* the Pascal program with actual operating system names. The mechanism will be the same for TEXT files and structured files.

Once the declarations above are made and the Program Heading is modified to include the new file names, all of the preliminary work of using structured files has been done. Structured files require special statements for input and output, as you will see, but again, many of the concepts you will encounter here will be relatively familiar from your understanding of TEXT files.

GET, PUT, and the File Window

As mentioned above, your program will need to both read from and write to the structured files, because the user of your program needs the ability to both store and retrieve the contents of the WordTypes and Tokens arrays. Instead of using READ and WRITE and the variations of these statements to read from and write to a structured file, you will use the Pascal statements GET and PUT. To understand how GET and PUT work, you need to know about the *File Window.*

Each file read or written by a Pascal program consists of a sequence of its component elements—in the case of our StoredTypes given above, the component elements are *WordRecords*, of course. The file window is essentially a halfway house between the computer and the file with which it is working. In it at any given time you will find what is about to be read from a file or what is about to be written to a file.

The name of any file followed by either an up-arrow (↑) or a circumflex (^) can be regarded as a variable name that refers to the contents of the file window for that file.

This can be somewhat confusing at first, so sit back and read on to get the general idea before re-reading to absorb the details.

The GET Statement. When a file is being read with READ or READLN statements, what really happens is that successive elements are brought into the file window and then stored in some variable in main memory for use by the program. However, when dealing with structured files the process is performed explicitly: first, the next component of the file is brought into the file window, and then in a separate Pascal Statement the contents of the file window are assigned to some variable. The Pascal GET statement is the one used to bring the next component of the file into the file window. The GET statement has the form

```
GET(<filename>);
```

where *<filename>* is, of course, the name of the file you are dealing with. Again, this statement will go to the file and get the next component, whether that component is of type CHAR or *WordRecord* or *TokenRecord*, and bring it into the area within main memory known as the file window. The contents of the file window is not yet actually in a *variable* in main memory where it can be manipulated; that requires a second step. This step involves using the file window name given above to access the contents of the file window—in this case, to access the contents in order to assign it to a variable. Now, if your file name is AFile, a statement like this will work here:

```
SomeVariable := AFile^;
```

The reference to AFile^ is a reference to the contents of the file window. This statement assigns the contents of the file window to the variable named SomeVariable. Of course, SomeVariable *must have the same type as the type of the component elements of the file* AFile. After this statement executes, the contents of the file window are the same as before—assigning its contents to a variable does not effectively issue another GET. This has to be done explicitly within the program. So when reading from a structured file you will always have the statement pair

```
SomeVariable := AFile^;
Get(AFile);
```

You are justified if you wonder why the GET statement appears *after* the assignment in this example. The reason is that this is the order in which the statements will always appear in your program. You recall that before any file (except INPUT) is read, you must issue a RESET statement for that file, which puts you back at the beginning of the file and ready to read the first element in it. You are now in a position to understand exactly what RESET does—it goes to the beginning of the file named in parenthesis in the RESET statement and issues a GET for that file, bringing the first element to be read into the file window. Therefore, you will assign that element to a variable first, and then issue a GET to get ready for the next assignment. Your program will typically involve a RESET for a file, followed by a loop which includes the assignment and GET statements above, in the order given. The loop, of course, will execute until the end-of-file is encountered.

Note that a READ from a TEXT file is really a GET for the file (whether that file is named InFile or INPUT or anything else) followed by an assignment of the file window into the variable that appears in the READ statement. You should also note that the functions EOF and EOLN use the file window to examine the element that is about to be read from a file.

The PUT Statement. PUT effectively reverses the process involving GET outlined above. The set of statements used with PUT are

```
AFile^ := SomeVariable;
PUT(AFile);
```

These statements do the following: the first stores the contents of the variable SomeVariable in the file window for the file named AFile. Note again that the file name followed by the circumflex functions like a variable name. The subsequent PUT statement will add the contents of the file window to the end of the file AFile.

When a file is written, of course, the REWRITE statement described in Chapter Three should be issued before the first statement that writes to the file (or manipulates the file window) to ready the file for writing. So, very much in parallel with the sequence of statements that you will use to read a structured file, the statements to write to a structured file will include a REWRITE followed by a loop containing the two statements given above.

Providing for the Options

Given all of the discussion above, you can modify your program to store and retrieve the structured data. The program obviously will only store the data in the WordTypes and Tokens arrays at the user's request, and will only read in the structured data when the user indicates that it exists in a file. Therefore, the program will need to be modified in order to determine whether or not these steps are necessary by prompting the user for information.

Prompting the User. When your program starts executing, it now goes directly to the Load procedure to read and store the user's text from a file on disk. Now, however, your program may not call on Load at all, depending upon whether or not the structured data already exists—if it does, the program will instead read from a file containing the structured data directly into the WordTypes and Tokens arrays. So instead of calling Load without question, you will need to add statements to the main program to prompt the user in order to determine whether the text is already structured or exists in "raw" form in a regular text file, and then take appropriate action accordingly.

You can prompt the user and read the response with a set of statements like this:

```
REPEAT
  WRITE('Please enter a 1 or a 2, indicating one of the following:');
  WRITELN;WRITELN;
  WRITELN('   (1) The text exists in a file in structured form');
  WRITELN;
  WRITELN('   (2) The text exists in its original form in a file');
  WRITELN;WRITELN;
  READLN(Choice);
UNTIL Choice IN ['1','2'];
```

After these statements execute, the variable Choice will contain user's response. The set of statements above can be surrounded by a REPEAT-UNTIL loop whose condition checks the value of Choice for validity, and repeats the statements above if anything but a 1 or 2 is entered by the user. Choice is declared as a CHAR-type variable. Note that declaring Choice with type CHAR rather than INTEGER avoids the possibility that your program will crash in the event that the user enters a non-integer in response to the prompt.

You should precede the loop above with a series of WRITELNs that explain to the user what the two choices above are all about, or add an explanation of the choices to the introductory statement your program now generates.

Once you have ascertained that the user has entered a valid choice, you need to modify the main program so that if the user entered 1 in response to the prompt above, the program goes to the file containing the structured data, reads it, and stores it in the WordTypes and Tokens arrays. If the user entered a 2 in response to the prompt, then Load is called as usual. Now, you can assume that the tasks of reading the structured data will be relegated to a procedure, which will be called GetArrays in this example; if so, then all you need to provide for the option of loading from raw text or reading the structured data is a straightforward IF-THEN-ELSE statement:

```
IF Choice = '1' THEN BEGIN
  GetArrays(WordTypes,Tokens,NumberOfWords,NumberOfTokens,
            StoredTypes,StoredTokens);
END     { then begin }
ELSE BEGIN
  Load(WordTypes,Tokens,NumberOfWords,NumberOfTokens,InFile);
END;     { else begin }
```

What about storing the structured text? Again, this is something you want to ask the user about. You should not automatically store the structured text each time the program is run, because first of all, the structured files may already exist and there is no sense in recreating them. Second, the user may never want to use the structured data again, and it is not a good idea to create files for a user that he or she may not know about or want, especially if file space is limited. So you will need another prompt to get the user's opinion about whether or not the structured data should be saved in files for later use and retrieval. This prompt could conceivably appear anywhere in the main program after the call to Load or GetArrays, but it makes better sense to ask the user whether the structured data is to be saved just before the program is about to terminate. Why? Well, the idea behind saving the structured text is to enable the user to more efficiently use the program later on the same text. But the user may not know that he or she wants to re-use the concordance program until after seeing the results from the current execution. So the most logical place for the prompt is after the statements that generate the concordance and just before the END that terminates the program.

If the user says yes to the offer to save the structured data, then a procedure which you can call PutArrays can be called on to do the job, and otherwise the program can simply terminate. You can modify the set of statements given above and re-use the variable Choice for this purpose:

```
REPEAT
  WRITE('Please enter a 1 or a 2, indicating one of the following:');
  WRITELN;WRITELN;
  WRITELN('   (1) Save the structured data for later use');
  WRITELN;
  WRITELN('   (2) Terminate the program');
  WRITELN;WRITELN;
  WRITE('   Enter a 1 or a 2:   ');
  READLN(Choice);
UNTIL Choice IN ['1','2'];
IF Choice = '1' THEN BEGIN
  PutArrays(WordTypes,Tokens,NumberOfWords,NumberOfTokens,
            StoredTypes,StoredTokens);
END;      { then begin }
```

Again, you should print a message explaining what it means to store the structured text and under what conditions it is a good idea to do so before issuing the prompt above.[3]

The PutArrays Procedure. It is easier to think about reading the data from a structured file if you have considered putting it there first, so we will look at procedure PutArrays before procedure GetArrays. PutArrays takes as parameters the WordTypes and Tokens arrays, since it will write the contents of these

3. If you really want to be fancy, you could enclose the entire set of statements above (including the explanatory WRITELNs) in an IF-THEN statement, the condition of which would check a BOOLEAN variable set within the set of statements given earlier to determine if the input data is raw or structured. This BOOLEAN variable would indicate whether or not the data had been read from a structured file; if so, then it is redundant to store it again, since the file already exists. If the BOOLEAN variable is named "Structured," then you could insert a statement setting Structured to TRUE after the call to GetArrays and a statement setting it to FALSE after the call to Load. The statements above could then be enclosed in an IF-THEN statement whose condition reads, IF NOT Structured THEN... . This way, the user is asked if the data should be saved in structured form only if it has not been saved in structured form already.

arrays to the files, the variables NumberOfWords and NumberOfTokens, because it will write only the filled elements of the arrays to the files (not the entire arrays including empty slots), and the two files to be written—StoredTypes and StoredTokens. Only the two files will be passed as VAR parameters; recall that files *must* be passed as VAR parameters regardless of how they are used in a procedure. The other variables can be passed as Value parameters because their contents are not changed, only accessed in order to be written to the files. PutArrays' heading is therefore

```
PROCEDURE PutArrays(OutputTypes : WordArray; OutputTokens : TokenArray;
        LastOutWord : ArrayBounds; LastOutToken : TokenBounds;
        VAR TypesStorage : TypeFile; VAR TokenStorage : TokenFile);
```

Within PutArrays you need statements that write the filled elements of the WordTypes array to the file StoredTypes (called TypeStorage in the procedure) and the filled elements of the Tokens array to StoredTokens (TokenStorage).

As you think back to the discussion of structured files and the PUT statement, consider what will have to be done to write the contents of the WordTypes array to StoredTypes. A loop is needed that can sequentially access each element of the WordTypes array in order to write each one to the file—obviously, a FOR loop is appropriate here that goes from 1 to NumberOfWords (LastOutWord). *Before* the loop a REWRITE for the file must be issued to ready it for writing, and so that will be the first statement in the program. Within the loop, the statements that (1) assign the appropriate variable to the file window for the file, and (2) add the contents of the file window to the end of the file will appear, since these are the statements that are executed once for each element in the WordTypes array:

```
REWRITE(TypeStorage);
FOR Counter := 1 TO LastOutWord DO BEGIN
  TypeStorage^ := OutputTypes[Counter];
  PUT(TypeStorage);
END;      { for }
```

Since the file StoredTypes holds *WordRecords*, a whole element of the WordTypes array can be written at a time, instead of writing each of its fields individually. The loop to write out the Tokens array is almost identical:

```
REWRITE(TokenStorage);
FOR Counter2 := 1 TO LastOutToken DO BEGIN
  TokenStorage^ := OutputTokens[Counter2];
  PUT(TokenStorage);
END;      { for }
```

Do not forget to declare Counter with type *ArrayBounds*, and Counter2 with type *TokenBounds* in PutArrays.

The GetArrays Procedure. GetArrays takes exactly the same parameters as PutArrays, but all of its parameters must be passed as VAR parameters since

GetArrays modifies the contents of both the WordTypes and Tokens arrays as well as NumberOfWords and NumberOfTokens. Its heading looks like this:

```
PROCEDURE GetArrays(VAR InputTypes : WordArray;
          VAR InputTokens : TokenArray; VAR TypesRead : ArrayBounds;
          VAR TokensRead : TokenBounds; VAR TypesIn : TypeFile;
          VAR TokensIn : TokenFile);
```

Internally, the GetArrays procedure is very similar to the PutArrays procedure—a loop for each file is used to read successive elements into the WordTypes or Tokens array. The only differences are, first, that the number of elements to be read is not known, whereas in PutArrays, the number of elements to be written was stored in either NumberOfWords or NumberOfTokens. Second, GetArrays must assign values to NumberOfWords and NumberOfTokens, since these values can only be determined by the number of items read in from each of the files. Instead of using FOR loops, GetArrays uses WHILE loops that execute until the end-of-file is reached, and the final count of the number of times each executes determines the values assigned to NumberOfWords and NumberOfTokens.

```
RESET(InputTypes);
Counter := 0;
WHILE NOT EOF(InputTypes) DO BEGIN
  Counter := Counter + 1;
  InputTypes[Counter] := InputTypes^;
  GET(InputTypes);
END;     { while }
TypesRead := Counter;
RESET(InputTokens);
Counter2 := 0;
WHILE NOT EOF(InputTokens) DO BEGIN
  Counter2 := Counter2 + 1;
  InputTokens[Counter2] := InputTokens^;
  GET(InputTokens);
END;     { while }
TokensRead := Counter2;
```

Counter and Counter2 are used in the loops as indexes to the next available slot in the WordTypes and Tokens arrays, respectively, and must of course be incremented explicitly within the loops. At the end of each loop the counter's value indicates the number of times the loop has executed and therefore the number of word types or word tokens that were read from the file.

APPLICATIONS AND CONSIDERATIONS

The idea behind a concordance is to provide easy access to all uses of a given word throughout an author's corpus or a particular work. This is obviously useful for the literary scholar, who may want to look at the way a certain image is used in an author's works, where a certain theme appears, where allusions to earlier passages or other works occur, how an author varies his use of a given word over his career, or the syntactic configurations in which a word is involved in a particular text or across an author's entire corpus.

As mentioned earlier, concordance generation was one of the first and is certainly the most common use of the computer for the manipulation of texts. Before computers were available, concordances were generated by hand and often constituted a scholar's life work. As you can now see, a concordance can be generated quite easily by machine. Most early computer-generated concordances were full concordances for a given author and were often published in book form. However, as computing power and authoritative versions of machine-readable texts become more widely and readily available, it is likely that most concordances will be generated interactively and printed on the display screen, as in the program you have just written. Hard-copy concordances may well become a thing of the past in the years to come.

Although concordance-generation seems a mundane task that is well suited to the machine, there are some aspects of concordance generation that often require human judgement to be handled. Homographs are a problem in a concordance, just as they are in a frequency distribution or a word index. And for all of the same reasons given in the previous chapter, lemmatizing the entries in a full concordance is generally preferable to simply outputting words in alphabetic sequence, as the program in this chapter does. With a concordance, other issues arise: for instance, how much context should the concordance provide? This question was given a lot of consideration in the early years of machine-generated concordances, but now interactive environments are making the question a pointless one, since users can quite easily specify the amount of context they want or ask for more if it is needed. Another issue that has plagued concordance-makers is which words to omit from a full concordance, if any. Because of the bulk of a full concordance, very frequent function words (such as "the" and "in") are sometimes omitted. Others omit all words above a certain frequency. Again, this is a problem that is largely solved in interactive environments where users can ask for exactly what they want from a concordance program and quite likely ask for a full concordance only rarely.

A special form of the concordance and one that was very popular in the early days of computer-generated concordances is the *keyword-in-context* (KWIC) index. The KWIC index is a concordance where all of the occurrences of the word being concorded are lined up, usually down the middle of the page, with their context to the right and left of each entry. The KWIC index usually looks something like this:

```
       This is an example of a KWIC index.
Here is another example of a KWIC index format.
                        The KWIC format looks like this.
```

This makes the location of the word in the sentence easily accessible, but for obvious reasons the amount of context that can be displayed on either side of the word is limited to what can fit in a single line. A word index is called a *keyword-out-of-context* (KWOC) index.

Another variation on the concordance is a *reverse concordance,* in which words are listed in alphabetical order by their endings. That is, each word is reversed, and then the reversed words are sorted as usual before the full concordance is produced. Thus words with common endings appear together in the concordance. Reverse concordances are used to study rhyme scheme and in syntactic or morphological studies that are concerned with word endings.

EXERCISES

1. Modify the program to repeat the process of prompting for a word and generating a concordance for that word until the user signals that he or she wants to stop.

2. Modify the program to give the user the option of seeing a concordance for the entire text.

3. Modify the program to give the user three options: a concordance for a single word, a full concordance, or a reverse concordance, as described in the Applications and Considerations section of the chapter. The easiest way to provide for the reversed concordance is to reverse each word as it is read in and store it in both its original and reversed forms. The Niceties section of Chapter Nine describes a procedure that reverses a word.

4. Modify the program to enable the user to store and retrieve the structured data as described in the Niceties section of this chapter.

5. Modify the program to give the user the option of generating a concordance, a word index, or a frequency distribution for a given word. (See exercise 3 at the end of Chapter Twelve to see how to modify the program to generate a frequency distribution.)

6. Modify the program so that the output appears in KWIC format, as described in the Applications and Considerations section of the chapter.

7. Do exercise 2 or 3, enhance the portion of the program that generates the full concordance so that the user can specify that the full concordance should omit words that occur *more than* a certain number of times in the text.

8. Modify the program so that it gives the user the option of (a) seeing each instance of a word in the context of a sentence, as in the program in this chapter, or (b) specifying the number of words on either side of the word that should be printed. If option (b) is chosen, the program should prompt for a number, and if, say, 10 is entered, then each instance of the word is printed in the context of the ten words that precede it and the ten words that follow it in the text.

9. (Slightly more difficult.) Modify the program so that the user can ask for a concordance for any word, when it appears in the same sentence as some other user-specified word. For example, if the user asks for a concordance for the word "lamb," then the user is asked if an additional context is desired. If so, then the user enters a second word, and the sentences in which the first word appear are printed *only* if the second word appears within the sentence as well.

This exercise can be modified to enable the user to specify that he wants to see those sentences in which a given word appears but in which a second word does *not* appear, or to enable the user to ask for sentences in which three words (or more) appear.

10. (Slightly more difficult.) Do exercise 2 or 3; enhance the portion of the program that generates the full concordance so that the user can specify that function words are to be omitted from the concordance. To do this you will have to first decide which words are function words. You can maintain them as a list within your program by storing them in a separate array of *String*-type variables. In the process of generating the full concordance, before the concordance for any word is generated, you can search the list of function words to see if your word is on the list. If so, then don't generate the concordance and go on to the next word.

Note that you cannot use the binary search to search for a word in a list of function words if the array in which the function words are stored is not of type *WordArray,* which, since this array contains only words and not frequencies and links to the **Tokens** array, it likely will not be. However, since your list of function words is probably relatively short—doubtless, under one hundred words—then using the linear search technique outlined in Chapter Seven to search the list of function words is not terribly inefficient.

11. (Still more difficult.) Do exercise 10, but give the user the option of specifying the list of words to be omitted from the full concordance.

12. (Still more difficult.) The concordance program outlined in this chapter reproduces a standardized version of the sentences in the text, translated to upper case and without punctuation. Modify the program so that the concordance program reproduces the sentences in the text as they appear in the input file. One way to do this is to store the unstandardized version of each word along with its location information in the **Tokens** array, and to print this version of the word when the concordance is generated, rather than the standardized form of the word that is stored in the **WordTypes** array. (Note that the standardized version must appear in the **WordTypes** array for the purposes of searching. Note also that because a word may appear in many forms in a text—capitalized or not capitalized and with any of a variety of combinations of punctuation—a single unstandardized version of the word will not suffice if the text is to be reproduced exactly.)

13. (More difficult.) An alternative to the scheme for reproducing the sentences in the text outlined in exercise 11 is to regard *each* punctuation mark that is read in as a word, store it in the **WordTypes** array, and set up a list in the **Tokens** array for its sets of location information, just as if it were a word. As your program goes through the **Tokens** array in order to generate a concordance, occasionally a "word" that is printed will be a punctuation mark, and thus the punctuation in the text will be restored. Your program should capitalize the first word in a sentence and print all other alphabetic characters in lower case—assuming your text is normal prose, this will provide a version that looks very similar to the original, although capital letters within a sentence will be printed in lower case. Note that unless you want spaces around your punctuation marks, you should provide statements to avoid printing a blank space following a "word" if that word is *followed* by a punctuation mark. Of course, this does not apply to punctuation that precedes a word, such as left parentheses, opening quotation marks, and so on—and then you also have the problem of determining whether quotation marks precede or follow a word. In general, you should avoid printing a blank in the following circumstances: (a) *preceding* a period, question mark, exclamation point, comma, right parenthesis, or closing quotation mark; (b) *following* a left parenthesis or opening quotation mark, or any punctuation mark that is followed by another punctuation mark *except* the left parenthesis or opening quotation mark. To determine whether or not a quotation mark is an opening or closing quotation mark, you will have to set a flag when a quotation mark is encountered to indicate whether or not a closing set of quotation marks is expected next. Apostrophes that precede and follow a word cannot be distinguished by this means.

Obviously, restoring punctuation is a very tricky business and requires a lot of extra programming. The only reason for attempting to reproduce the text is that maintaining the original copy of each word, as suggested in exercise 12, requires a great deal of extra storage. If storage is at a premium, but you have ample computing time at your disposal, then you may want to try the method outlined in this exercise. You may be able to think of alternative schemes or variations for reproducing the text—keep in mind the amount of time and storage required for your methods, and adjust the program to fit your situation.

14. (More difficult.) Modify the program so that the user has the option of specifying that instead of producing a concordance for a specific word, a concordance for words containing a specific string is to be produced. For example, if the user enters ANT, then words such as ANTELOPE, MANTLE, and BELLIGERANT will be included. You can use the Index function to implement this exercise.

15. (Still more difficult.) Do exercise 14, but give the user three alternatives under the option that enables specifying a string: (1) to see a concordance for all words beginning with a certain prefix, (2) to see a concordance for all words ending with a certain suffix, and (3) to see all words containing a specific string, as described above.

16. (Very difficult.) Do exercise 14 or 15, but allow the user to also specify complex configurations of characters that are to be present in the words for which the concordance is produced. For example, if the user specifies S*C*R, all words that contain the letters S, C, and R in that order and separated by zero or more characters will be included (SECURE, SCARE, SECRET, and SCRAM would all be included in this case). Similarly, F* gives all words beginning with F, and *W gives all words ending in W. *OU* gives all words that begin, end, or contain OU.

Appendix A

Pascal Keywords

The following is a list of the keywords that are reserved in standard versions of Pascal.

AND	END	MOD	REPEAT
ARRAY	FILE	NIL	SET
BEGIN	FOR	NOT	THEN
CASE	FORWARD	OF	TO
CONST	FUNCTION	OR	TYPE
DIV	GOTO	PACKED	UNTIL
DO	IF	PROCEDURE	VAR
DOWNTO	IN	PROGRAM	WHILE
ELSE	LABEL	RECORD	WITH

Appendix B

Built-in Functions

The list of functions below are built into all versions of Pascal; your implementation may provide additional functions.

Note that in the examples, x is used to stand for any real or integer variable or value, *i* is used to represent an integer variable or value, *r* is used to represent a REAL variable or value, *c* is used to represent a CHAR variable or value, and *f* is used to represent a file name. The character *a* is used to represent any *ordinal* variable or value—that is, an INTEGER, CHAR, or BOOLEAN value, or a value that is part of an enumerated type.

Functions that return a result of type REAL:

ABS(x)	*returns the positive value of* x.
ARCTAN(x)	*returns the arctangent of* x.
COS(x)	*returns the cosine of* x.
EXP(x)	*returns e (the base of the natural log system) raised to the power* x.
LN(x)	*returns the natural log (log to the base e) of* x.
SIN(x)	*returns the sine of* x.
SQRT(x)	*returns the square root of* x.

Functions that return a result with type INTEGER:

ORD(c)	*returns the integer code for character c in the collating sequence.*
ROUND(r)	*returns r rounded to the nearest integer value.*
TRUNC(r)	*returns r as an integer with everything to the right of its decimal point chopped off (no rounding).*

Functions that return a result with type BOOLEAN:

EOLN(f)	*returns TRUE if the next character in file f is a carriage return; returns FALSE otherwise.*
EOF(f)	*returns TRUE if the next character in file f is the end-of-file marker; returns FALSE otherwise.*
ODD(i)	*returns TRUE if i is odd; returns FALSE otherwise.*

Functions that return a result with type CHAR:

CHR(i)	*returns the character with code i in the collating sequence.*

Functions that return a result whose type is the same as that of its parameter:

PRED(a)	*returns the predecessor of a in the ordinal sequence to which it belongs (e.g., the predecessor of "G" is "F", the predecessor of 98 is 97, etc.)*
SQR(x)	*returns the square of x.*
SUCC(a)	*returns the successor of a in the ordinal sequence to which it belongs (see PRED).*

Functions for arithmetic values

SQR	SQRT	ARCTAN
SIN	COS	
EXP	LN	
ABS		
ROUND	TRUNC	
ODD		

Functions for ordered values

CHR	ORD
SUCC	PRED

Functions for files

EOLN	EOF

Appendix C

The ASCII and EBCDIC Codes

Each of the ASCII and EBCDIC codes includes the "printable" characters that are on the keyboard as well as many unprintable control characters. Control characters are used internally by the computer and are not included in the charts below.

ASCII Codes

Code	*Character*	*Code*	*Character*	*Code*	*Character*
32	<*blank*>	64	@	95	_
33	!	65	A	96	‘
34	"	66	B	97	a
35	#	67	C	98	b
36	$	68	D	99	c
37	%	69	E	100	d
38	&	70	F	101	e
39	’	71	G	102	f
40	(	72	H	103	g
41	)	73	I	104	h
42	*	74	J	105	i

43	+	75	K	106	j
44	,	76	L	107	k
45	-	77	M	108	l
46	.	78	N	109	m
47	/	79	O	110	n
48	0	80	P	111	o
49	1	81	Q	112	p
50	2	82	R	113	q
51	3	83	S	114	r
52	4	84	T	115	s
53	5	85	U	116	t
54	6	86	V	117	u
55	7	87	W	118	v
56	8	88	X	119	w
57	9	89	Y	120	x
58	:	90	Z	121	y
59	;	91	[	122	z
60	<	92	\	123	{
61	=	93	]	124	|
62	>	94	^	125	}
63	?				

EBCDIC Codes

Code	*Character*	*Code*	*Character*	*Code*	*Character*
64	*<blank>*	133	e	198	F
74	¢	134	f	199	G
75	.	135	g	200	H
76	<	136	h	201	I
77	(	137	i	209	J
78	+	145	j	210	K
79	|	146	k	211	L
80	&	147	l	212	M
90	!	148	m	213	N
91	$	149	n	214	O
92	*	150	o	215	P
93	)	151	p	216	Q
94	;	152	q	217	R
95	¬	153	r	226	S
96	-	162	s	227	T
97	/	163	t	228	U
106	^	164	u	229	V
107	,	165	v	230	W
108	%	166	w	231	X
109	_	167	x	232	Y
110	>	168	y	233	Z
111	$	169	z	240	0

122	:	177	\	241	1
123	#	178	{	242	2
124	@	179	}	243	3
125	’	180	[	244	4
126	=	181	]	245	5
127	”	193	A	246	6
129	a	194	B	247	7
130	b	195	C	248	8
131	c	196	D	249	9
132	d	197	E		

Appendix D

More About Pascal

Several important Pascal language features are not covered in the body of this text, but are included here because they might be of use or interest to the reader.

ENUMERATED TYPES

When you declare a variable with a given type you are actually indicating a group of values from which the value stored in that variable can be taken. For example, if you declare a variable with type CHAR, you indicate that the variable can hold any one of the characters in the collating sequence. Pascal allows users to define limited kinds of types of their own, for which the user himself specifies explicitly the set of values that any variable with that type can take on. Examples will make this clearer.

You can define a type and a variable with that type as follows:

```
TYPE PartsOfSpeech = (Noun, Adjective, Verb, Adverb, Preposition);
VAR SyntacticCategory : PartsOfSpeech;
```

This accomplishes the following: a new type named *PartsOfSpeech* is established, and in the definition of the type, *the values that variables with this type are specified*. This means that when SyntacticCategory is declared below, it is set up as a slot in memory where one of the values listed in the definition of *PartsOfSpeech* can be stored. So any of the following assignments to SyntacticCategory are valid:

```
SyntacticCategory := Noun;
SyntacticCategory := Adjective;
SyntacticCategory := Verb;
SyntacticCategory := Adverb;
SyntacticCategory := Preposition;
```

Once a value is assigned to SyntacticCategory, it can be compared to values of its type like any variable:

```
IF SyntacticCategory = Verb THEN ...
```

or, if another variable named WordCat also has the type *PartsOfSpeech*,

```
IF SyntacticCategory = WordCat THEN ...
```

Note that the values in the type specification are *ordered* according to their position in the list in the type declaration. This means that you can specify ranges of these values, like this:

```
IF SyntacticCategory IN [Verb..Preposition] THEN ...
```

But note that [Adverb..Noun] is invalid because these values are not sequential in the listing in the type declaration.

You can use enumerated values in the heading of a FOR loop:

```
FOR SyntacticCategory := Noun TO Preposition DO ...
```

The advantage of using enumerated types is the readability they lend to your program. As an example, consider a declaration like the following:

```
CONST  Stringlength = 20;
       MaxWords = 1000;
TYPE   String = PACKED ARRAY[1..StringLength] OF CHAR;
       PartsOfSpeech = (Noun,Adjective,Verb,Adverb,Preposition);
       WordRecord = RECORD
                          Word : String;
                          Frequency : INTEGER;
                          SyntacticCategory : PartsOfSpeech;
                        END;
       ArrayBounds = 0..MaxWords;
       WordArray = ARRAY[1..MaxWords] OF WordRecord;
VAR Words : WordArray;
    NumberOfWords, Counter : ArrayBounds;
    Category : PartsOfSpeech;
```

Without enumerated types, integer codes would probably be used to indicate the syntactic category of a word. But enumerated type names are much more readable than integer codes and show exactly what the values stand for. For example, suppose that the SyntacticCategory field of each filled slot in the Words array is assigned a value based on the word that is stored there. Then statements like these can appear in the program:

```
FOR Category = Noun TO Verb DO BEGIN
  FOR Counter := 1 TO NumberOfWords DO BEGIN
    IF Words.SyntacticCategory = Category
      THEN BEGIN
        WRITELN(Words.Word);
    END;      { then begin }
  END;      { for }
  WRITELN;WRITELN;
END;      { for }
```

This set of statements will write out all of the nouns, then all of the adjectives, etc., in the Words array.

Another example is

```
FOR Counter := 1 TO NumberOfWords DO BEGIN
  CASE Words.SyntacticCategory OF
    Noun        : WRITELN(Words.SyntacticCategory,' is a noun.');
    Adjective   : WRITELN(Words.SyntacticCategory,' is an adjective.');
    Verb        : WRITELN(Words.SyntacticCategory,' is a verb.');
    Adverb      : WRITELN(Words.SyntacticCategory,' is an adverb.');
    Preposition : WRITELN(Words.SyntacticCategory,' is a preposition.');
  END;      { case }
END;      { for }
```

In both of these examples, it is clear to the reader of the program what the values stored in the SyntacticCategory field of the records in the Words array represent. If integer codes were used instead of enumerated value names, it would be difficult to tell what the values stand for unless the programmer provides very good comments.

In standard Pascal, you cannot write out the value of an enumerated type. That is, you cannot say

```
WRITELN(Words.SyntacticCategory);
```

SETS

You have been using Pascal sets implicitly ever since Chapter Four, where the IN operator was introduced. When you use a construct such as

```
Letter IN ['A'..'Z','a'..'z']
```

you are saying something like "Letter is in the *set* of items consisting of the upper and lower case letters of the alphabet." The group of items inside the square brackets specifies a subset of a larger set of items—in this case, the upper and lower case letters are a subset of the set of all characters in the collating sequence.

Pascal allows you to declare variables that will consist of or "contain" a *group* of items that are to be regarded as a subset of some larger set. To do this, you first declare a type to be a SET and indicate the type of the values the set will contain, as follows:

```
TYPE CharacterSet = SET OF CHAR;
```

In this example, the type *CharacterSet* is defined as a set of values of type CHAR.

The maximum number of items that can be included in a set is dependent on the implementation of Pascal you are using. The type CHAR includes 256 values, and so your implementation must allow at least this number of values in a set if you are to use the type declaration above.

A set of type CHAR values is allowed in most implementations, and it will be assumed throughout the remainder of this discussion that a definition like the one given above is valid.

Having defined a SET type, you can then declare a variable with this type in the VAR Declarations section of the program:

```
VAR Alphabet : CharacterSet;
```

Like any variable, Alphabet *has no value* at the time it is declared. The declaration simply indicates the kind of variable it is—that is, the kind of values it can hold. Again, a variable declared as a set is capable of holding several values drawn from the set specified in the declaration of its type.

So Alphabet is a variable that will hold one or more values drawn from the characters in the collating sequence. How are the values assigned to Alphabet? The usual way—with an assignment statement in which the type of the expression on the right of the assignment operator is the same as the variable on the left. As pointed out earlier, you have actually been explicitly enumerating set values in conditions involving the IN operator. That is, a set of values is given explicitly by listing the values between square brackets. So to assign Alphabet a value, you can use a statement like this:

```
Alphabet := ['A'..'Z','a'..'z'];
```

This statement assigns to Alphabet the values drawn from the set of characters in the collating sequence that consist of the upper and lower case letters.

Suppose that in addition to Alphabet, Punctuation and SpecialCharacters are declared in the VAR Declarations section of a program, like this:

```
VAR Alphabet, Punctuation, SpecialCharacters : CharacterSet;
```

Then these assignments are valid:

```
Alphabet := ['A'..'Z','a'..'z'];
Punctuation := ['.',',',';',':','?','!'];
SpecialCharacters := Punctuation;
```

The first set is indicated with two *ranges* of values, the second set is indicated by giving an explicit list, and the third is indicated with another SET variable of the same type as the variable on the left of the assignment operator.

You can even *add* two sets together, like this:

```
SpecialCharacters := SpecialCharacters + Alphabet;
```

If this statement is executed after the set of assignment statements above, it will add the contents of the set of values contained in Alphabet to the current contents of SpecialCharacters, so that SpecialCharacters contains both its original contents and the contents of Alphabet. However, note that if both Alphabet and SpecialCharacters contain the value 'x' among their set values before the statement above is executed, SpecialCharacters will not contain two x's afterwards. *Only one of each value in the domain of the set is included in a set of values at any time.*

Subtraction is valid too:

```
Alphabet := Alphabet - ['a'..'z'];
```

This statement *subtracts* the lower case letters from the current contents of Alphabet. If before this statement executes Alphabet contains both the upper and lower case letters, this leaves Alphabet with only the upper case letters.

A set may contain only one member. All of the following assignments are valid:

```
Alphabet := [Letter];
Punctuation := ['!'];
SpecialCharacters := [CHR(12)];
```

The first statement sets the contents of Alphabet to be the character contained in the variable Letter. The second statement assigns another set with a single member to Punctuation, but the value is specified explicitly. In the final statement, an explicit but unprintable character is specified by using the CHR function. You can also say

```
SpecialCharacters := [Blank];
```

assuming Blank is a constant containing a single blank.[1]

Note that if Alphabet is a SET OF CHAR, the assignment

```
Alphabet := 'Z';
```

is not valid. A *set* of values must appear on the right of the assignment operator, and so if this assignment is to be valid, the statement

1. Note that you could not assign a set including the constant Blanks to a SET OF CHAR variable, because Blanks contains a *string* of characters rather than a single character.

```
Alphabet := ['Z'];
```

must be used instead.

This takes care of giving SET variables values, but how are these variables actually used in a program? Once again, you have been using sets all along, but you specified them explicitly; with a SET variable at your disposal, you can use it in conditions as you would any set of values:

```
IF Letter IN Alphabet THEN ...
```

or

```
WHILE Character IN SpecialCharacters DO ...
```

So you can include appropriate SET declarations in your program and replace the conditions within your program in which sets are explicitly specified with something like the above.

When you use SET type variables do not forget to do the following things:

1. Declare the SET type in the Type Declarations section of the program, indicating the type of values it is to contain.
2. Declare the SET variable in the VAR Declarations section of the program with the type defined in the Type Declarations section.
3. Assign the desired set of values to the SET variable.

After these three steps have been taken, the SET variable can be used in conditions and other assignment statements like those given above.

Here are two short programs that demonstrate special uses of sets.

```
PROGRAM PrintSpecialChars(INPUT,OUTPUT,TextFile);
  { Prints the non-alphabetic characters in a text file }
  TYPE CharacterSet = SET OF CHAR;
  VAR Letter : CHAR;
          AlphabetPlusBlank, SpecialCharacters : CharacterSet;
          TextFile : TEXT;
BEGIN     { main program }
  AlphabetPlusBlank := ['A'..'Z','a'..'z',' '];
  SpecialCharacters := [];      { makes SpecialCharacters an empty set }
  RESET(TextFile);
  WHILE NOT EOF(TextFile) DO BEGIN
    READ(TextFile,Letter);
    SpecialCharacters := SpecialCharacters + [Letter];
  END;     { while }
  SpecialCharacters := SpecialCharacters - AlphabetPlusBlank;
  WRITELN('Non-alphabetic characters in the file are:');
  WRITELN;WRITELN;
  FOR Letter := CHR(0) TO CHR(255) DO BEGIN
    IF Letter IN SpecialCharacters THEN BEGIN
      WRITELN(Letter);
    END;     { then begin }
  END;     { for }
END.     { main program }
```

Since the collating sequence includes characters with codes from 0 to 255, we can include all of them in the final FOR loop by specifying CHR(0) TO CHR(255) in the loop header. Note that attempting to write certain codes may yield unusual results.

```
PROGRAM FileDifference(INPUT,OUTPUT,FirstTextFile,SecondTextFile);
  { Prints the characters in one text file }
  { that do not appear in another file }
  TYPE CharacterSet = SET OF CHAR;
  VAR Letter : CHAR;
      CharsInFile : CharacterSet;
      FirstTextFile, SecondTextFile : TEXT;
BEGIN     { main program }
  CharsInFile := [];     { makes CharsInFile an empty set }
  RESET(FirstTextFile);
  WHILE NOT EOF(FirstTextFile) DO BEGIN
    READ(FirstTextFile,Letter);
    CharsInFile := CharsInFile + [Letter];
        { adds the characters in first file to the set }
  END;     { while }
  RESET(SecondTextFile);
  WHILE NOT EOF(SecondTextFile) DO BEGIN
    READ(SecondTextFile,Letter);
    CharsInFile := CharsInFile - [Letter];
        { removes the characters in second file from the set }
  END;     { while }
  WRITELN('The characters in the second file    ',
          'that do not appear in the first are:');
  WRITELN;WRITELN;
  FOR Letter := CHR(0) TO CHR(255) DO BEGIN
    IF Letter IN CharsInFile THEN BEGIN
      WRITELN(Letter);
    END;     { then begin }
  END;     { for }
END.     { main program }
```

Note that although all of the examples here deal with sets of characters, sets can be of subranges of INTEGERs or enumerated types. For example, you can declare set types like this:

```
TYPE OneToAHundred = 1..100;
  Hundreds = SET OF OneToAHundred;
  PartsOfSpeech = (Noun,Adjective,Verb,Adverb,Preposition);
  SpeechCategories = SET OF PartsOfSpeech;
VAR LowNumbers : Hundreds;
  MajorCategories : SpeechCategories;
```

Given all of this, you can then assign and use the SET variables like this:

```
LowNumbers := [1..30];
MajorCategories := [Noun, Verb];
IF (Word.Frequency IN LowNumbers) AND
  (Word.SyntacticCategory IN MajorCategories) THEN ...
```

This example assumes Word is defined as it was in the example in the section on enumerated types, above.

THE FORWARD STATEMENT

If one procedure calls another, the callee must be declared before the caller in the Procedure Declarations section of a program. However, in some situations this is either inconvenient or impossible (as in the case of *indirect recursion,* mentioned in the section on Recursion in the Niceties of Chapter Ten). There is a way to get around this restriction in Pascal by using what is called a FORWARD declaration.

It works like this: if procedure One calls procedure Two, but procedure Two is declared after procedure One in the program, you can let the computer know that procedure Two exists *before* it actually sees its declaration by giving the procedure's heading earlier than its declaration. Here is the example:

```
PROCEDURE Two(<parameters>); FORWARD;
PROCEDURE One (<parameters>);
  Variable declarations
BEGIN     { One }
  .
  .
  .
  Two(<parameters>);
  .
  .
  .
END;     { One }
PROCEDURE Two;
  Variable declarations
BEGIN     { Two }
  .
  .
  .
END;     { Two }
```

In a forward declaration, the heading of the procedure appears first, followed by the statement

FORWARD;

A shortened heading, without parameters, appears in the actual declaration of the procedure that appears later in the Procedure Declarations section of the program.

The FORWARD declaration in the example above provides all of the information needed about procedure Two (name, parameters and their types) in order to process the call to that procedure in One.

Functions can be declared with the FORWARD declaration as well.

Note that the FORWARD declaration of a procedure or function need not immediately precede the declaration of a procedure that calls it; the FORWARD declaration can appear *anywhere* in the Procedure Declarations section prior to the declaration of a procedure or function that calls it.

GOTO AND LABELS

It has been proven that any computer program can be written without the use of GOTO statements. Modern computer scientists (most of them, at least) eschew the use of the GOTO in computer programs, because it fosters sloppy programming habits and generally violates the tenets of structured, modular programming. Nonetheless, the designers of modern programming languages have not had the courage to eliminate the GOTO from a programming language altogether, because in very special circumstances it is simply easier to use GOTO than to write the program in any other way.

For those who are not familiar with GOTO, this statement causes an unconditional, unequivocal branch to some specified location in a program. Consider this example:

```
PROGRAM GetOut(INPUT,OUTPUT,TextFile);
  LABEL 99;
          .
          .
          .
    other declarations
          .
          .

PROCEDURE ReadFile(VAR TextFile : TEXT);
  BEGIN     { ReadFile }
    WHILE NOT EOF(TextFile) DO BEGIN
              .
              .
              .
      IF Letter IN InValidCharacters THEN BEGIN
        GOTO 99;
              .
              .
              .
      END;     { then begin }
    END;     { while }
  END;     { ReadFile }
BEGIN     { main program }
  .
  .
  .
99:  END.     { main program }
```

The LABEL declaration declares an integer, in this case 99, as a label for a statement—that is, an identifying flag for the location of a certain statement. Within procedure ReadFile, when some bad input is encountered, the GOTO 99 statement causes whatever is going on to stop—including the execution of a loop or the execution of the procedure—and control goes immediately to the statement labeled 99. In this example that statement is the END of the main program, and so this piece of code causes the program to terminate as soon as bad data is encountered.

Note that in the sample set-up above, there are two ways that control can reach the statement labeled 99 (the END of the main program): the GOTO statement can send it there explicitly, or control can reach there through normal means by simply proceding through the statements within the main program until control reaches that point.

This example shows one of those rare instances when using a GOTO is grudgingly accepted by most people. Here a quick exit must be made from a procedure which would be somewhat complicated to do any other way. Furthermore, the branch in this instance is to a very clear location—the end of the program. Had the branch been to some other location in the procedure or in the main program, it would have been far more difficult to follow (by reading the code) the flow of events in the program.

A GOTO cannot go to the middle of a loop or other structured statement such as an IF-THEN or IF-THEN-ELSE. A GOTO can jump out of such a structure, however. In addition, a GOTO cannot go to any location within a procedure that the program or procedure in which it appears cannot call.

Index

Note: For ease of reference, names of programs and procedures appear in italic in this index.